Essentials of Vedic Literature

Essentials of Vedic Literature

Dr. K. B. Archak
P.G. Dept. of Sanskrit
Karnatak University, Dharwad
(Karnataka State)

2012
Kaveri Books
New Delhi-110002

First Published in 2012
ISBN 978-81-7479-135-1

Published by
Kaveri Books
4832/24, Ansari Road
New Delhi - 110 002 (India)
Tel.: 011-2328 8140, 2324 5799,
Fax: 011-2328 8140
E-mail: kaveribooks@vsnl.com,
kaveribooks@gmail.com
Website: www.kaveribooks.com

Laser Typesetting by : Deep Graphics, Delhi

Printed at : Salasar Imaging Systems, Delhi-110 052

PRINTED IN INDIA

Dr. Prof. Nilakantha Pati
M.A. Ph.D., D.Litt.
Vice Chancellor

शुभाशंसनम्

अथेमं समस्तवैदिक वाङ्मयस्य साररूपं "Essentials of Vedic Literature" इत्याख्यं ग्रन्थपुष्पं वेदजिज्ञासुकुशलानां पुरतः उपस्थापयन्तः वेद-वेदान्त-दर्शन-साहित्य-व्याकरणंक्षेत्रेषु कृतभूरिश्रमाः नैक-ग्रन्थप्रणेतारः बहुपदवीलाञ्छनाः कर्नाटक विश्वविद्यालीय-संस्कृतविभागाध्यक्षाः प्राध्यापकाः डा. कृष्णमूर्ति-अर्चक-महाभागाः सरस्वतीभक्ताग्रेसरा इति घोषयितुं मोमुद्यते मे मनः।

समग्रपौर्वात्य-पाश्चिमात्य-संस्कृताध्यायिना-मन्तेवासिनां विदुषां च सौकर्याय द्वादशाध्यायात्मकेऽस्मिन् ग्रन्थे वैदिकसाहित्यान्तरङ्गस्य मूलङ्कषमालोचनं आंग्लगिरैव पल्लवितम्। तथा च भाषासरण्यत्र सरला सुगमावबोधा वैशिष्ट्यपूर्णास्ति। एवं च यावन्तोऽपि पैदिकविषयाः ग्रन्थेऽस्मिन् समासेन विशिष्टवैदुष्येण विशदीकृताः सर्वे च ते तत्तत्प्रमाणो-पपत्तिपूर्वकेण प्रपञ्चिता, अपि च तानि प्रमाणवचनानि तत्तदध्यायान्ते समुपात्तानि वर्तन्ते।

स्थालीपुलाकन्यायेन एतद्ग्रन्थस्य पर्यालोचनेना-वगम्यते यदेषः समस्तवैदिकवाङ्मयपरिचायकग्रन्थः सहृदयमनीषिणां छात्राणां च ज्ञानवृद्धिकरः भवितेति न मे लेशतोऽपि सन्देहः। आशास्येवेदविद्याविपश्चितः अस्य

ग्रन्थसौरभस्य प्रसरं प्रकारं वितेरेयुरिति। प्रस्तुतस्य ग्रन्थस्य सर्वाङ्गीणसाफल्यमहं कामये। अन्ते चाशंस्यते यच्छ्रीमदुचेकेत्युपाह्व-कृष्णमूर्तिरचितो निष्कलङ्कोऽयं ग्रन्थविशेषः श्रीजन्नाथस्य महाप्रभोरनुग्रहेण नितरां विराजतामिति।

1.5.2012
वैशाख शुद्ध दशमी

प्रो. डॉ नीलकण्ठ पतिः
कुलपतिः
श्रीजगन्नाथ-संस्कृतविश्वविद्यालयः
श्रीविहारः पुरी

Preface

Vedic Literature, the candid contribution of ancient Indian scholars of supra-natural wisdom, is a vast and deep ocean of knowledge with multi-dimensional disciplines. The Vedic canon comprises of three main divisions, such as the Saṁhitas, Brāhmaṇas and the Āraṇyakas. Of these three, both Saṁhitas and Brāhmaṇas form the karma-kāṇḍa portion pertaining to the rituals, while the Āraṇyakas dealing with the nature of the Supreme Reality, from the jñāna-kāṇḍa portion of the Vedic Literature.

The historical data of the Ṛgvedic hymns show that the Indo-Aryans were engaged in war with the aborigines. They were moving forward as conquerers as indicated by the Ṛgvedic hymns. Although divided into many tribes, they were conscious of religious and racial unity. Identical references to such historical elements provide a good deal of information about the social conditions of the time. Even so, the finer details of other three Vedic saṁhitas point to the social set up and scientific advancement of the contemporary period.

Having achieved the goals of *Dharma Artha* and *Kāma*, the Vedic people stepped ahead towards *Mokṣa* puruṣārtha by means of studying the Upaniṣads, the portion of *jñānakāṇḍa*. While contemplating on ritual and meditative aspects of the Vedic literature, as aspirant does require to realize the esoteric nature thereof, for which, the study of the Vedaṅgas too is essential. Such realization is possible only when a seeker of the truth should lead the path of righteousness which infact is codified in the Dharmasutras and the Smṛti texts, reckoned as authoritative on par with Vedic texts. A close perusal of entire Vedic literature makes it evident that the knowledge of Vedic texts is verily conducive to the fulfilment of one's life. With a view to unfold this truth of Vedic canon the present work '*Essentials of Vedic Literature*' is placed before the discerning readers.

In the preparation of this work, many a work on Vedic literature have been referred to; hence I owe my indebtedness to the authors thereof. Further, this work would not have seen the light without the blessings of my Guruji, Late Dr. Prof. D.N. Shanbhag, a recipient of Presidential Award, as well as of my parents. Hence, I pay my homage to them. Furthermore, Dr. Prof. Nilakantha Patil, Vice Chancellor, Shri Jagannatha Sanskrit University, Puri (Orissa) has raised the merit of this work by means of his comprehensive शुभाशंसनम्. I therefore, express my heartfelt gratitudes to this great personality. Besides, it is my unstinted duty to place on record, my sincere thanks to the *Kaveri Books* who readily accepted to publish this work, and did their job magnificiently within a short period taking all due care in typesetting and going through the proof meticulously.

I hope this work will certainly be welcomed by the interested readers.

24-4-2012 **Dr. K.B. Archak**

Contents

Abbreviations

A.B.	Aitareya Brāhmaṇa
A.G.S.	Āpastambīya Gṛhyasūtra
A.V.	Atharva Veda
HIP	History of Indian Philosophy
K.S.S.	Kātyāyana Śrauta-sūtra
M.S.	Maitrāyaṇī Saṁhitā
Nir.	Nirukta
R.V.	Ṛgveda
Ś.B.	Śatapatha Brāhmaṇa
S.G.S.	Sāṅkhyāyana Gṛhyasūtra
T.A.	Taittirīya Araṇyaka
T.B.	Taittirīya Brāhmaṇa
T.M.B.	Tāṇḍya Mahā Brāhmaṇa
T.S.	Taittirīya Saṁhitā
V.S.	Vājasaneyī Saṁhitā
Y.V.	Yajur Veda

Chapter - I

Introduction to Vedic Literature

1.1 Vedas : Ancient Indian Literature

At the outset, one should know flawless definition of the Veda. The term 'Veda' which means knowledge is derived from the root '*Vid*' (to know). Also, the term *Veda* denotes the texts containing the most sacred and authoritative knowledge, the texts whose authority can never be questioned, and which are the last tribunal in matters of dispute whether in religion or philosophy or social customs.

The Vedic literature may be divided into three great divisions- the *mantras* or *Saṁhitās*, the *Brāhmaṇas* and the *Sūtras*. The *mantras*[1] and the *Brāhmaṇas* are called *Śruti*, while the *Sūtras* are called *Smṛti*. The *Śruti* is what is heard as opposed to what is composed; it is revealed scripture, and self-authoritative, not composed by any human being. The *Ṛṣis*[2] of the hymns of the Veda are thus called *Mantradṛṣṭāras* 'the seers of the *Mantras*.' They are the medium of communication between gods and men. The *Smṛtis* imbibe the traditional works of human origin, which are solely based on the *Śrutis*. The *Smṛti* applies not only to the *Sūtra* works but also to the metrical codes of Manu, Yājñavalkya, etc.

The Vedic canon, comprises four great sections, viz. the *Ṛgveda*, the *Yajurveda*, the *Sāmaveda* and the *Atharvaveda*. Again, each of these has three main divisions - the *Saṁhitās*, the *Brāhmaṇas* and the *Araṇyakas*. The *Saṁhitās* and *Brāhmaṇas* are loosely designated as '*Karma-kāṇḍa*' the portion pertaining to rituals. The *Araṇyakas* designated as '*Upāsana-kāṇḍa*', the portion relating to meditation, includes the *Upaniṣads* forming '*Jnāna-kāṇḍa*' portion dealing with supreme knowledge.

As far as *Saṁhitā* portion is concerned, there are four principal *Saṁhitāṣ* related to four Vedas : *Ṛgveda Saṁhitā*, *Yajurveda Saṁhitā*, comprising *Taittiriya Saṁhitā* or *Kṛṣṇa Yajurveda* and *Vājasaneyi Saṁhitā* or *Śukla Yajurveda*; *Sāmaveda Saṁhitā* and the *Atharvaveda Saṁhitā*. Besides these, there are three other *Saṁhitās* of lesser importance, viz., the *Kāṭhaka*, the *Kapiṣṭhalakaṭha* and the *Maitrāyaṇī Saṁhitās* of the *Kṛṣṇa Yajurveda*. These are collections of sacred hymns in *mantra* of different metres, and are mostly addressed in prayer to various gods and goddesses. There are, however, four *Saṁhitās*, which are notably different from one another, and each of which has several recensions. These are :

1. The *Ṛgveda Saṁhitā* - A collection of hymns.
2. The *Yajurveda Saṁhitā* - A collection of sacrificial formulas.
3. The *Sāmaveda Saṁhitā* - A collection of songs mostly taken from the *Ṛgveda*.
4. The *Atharveda Saṁhitā* - A collection of spells and charms.

This four-fold division of the *Saṁhitās* evidently speaks of an elaborate development of the sacrificial rites. Since, even the simplest sacrifice requires the four principal priests related to four Vedas - *Hotṛ*, *Udgātṛ*, *Adhvaryu* and *Brahmā*. Originally there were only three Vedas.[3] The *Atharvaveda* has been regarded as later development of Vedic canon. In the *Brāhmaṇas* view, the Vedas and the rituals, enjoined in them, are the correlates of the cosmic system. The *mantras* are the earth, the *Yajus* are the air and the *Sāmans* are the sky. Correspondingly, Agni belongs to the earth, Indra or *Vāyu* to the air and and *Sūrya* to the sky.[4] Hence, by the *mantras*, man conquers the earth, by the *Yajus*, the air, and by the *Sāmans*, the sky,[5] and, in this process, also propitiates Agni, Indra and Sūrya. Hence, by this triad, he conquers the whole cosmos consisting of the three regions of the earth, atmosphere and sky. This is possible through the performance of the *Soma* ritual, since in it, all the three Vedas combine.[6]

The *Brāhmaṇas* are prose works, containing detailed descriptions of the sacrificial rites and the modes of their performance. Not only have all the four Vedas their separate *Brāhmaṇas* but even different schools of the same Veda have different *Brāhmaṇas*. The *Ṛgveda* has two *Brāhmaṇas*. The *Aitareya Brāhmaṇa* relating to the *Śākala* School and the *Kuṣītakī Brāhmaṇa* represents the *Bāṣkala* school. To the *Sāmaveda* belong several *Brāhmaṇas* of which the *Tāṇḍya or Pañcaviṁśa,* and the *Ṣaḍviṁśa* are well-known. To the *Kṛṣṇa Yajurveda* has the *Taittirīya Brāhmaṇa* which is but a continuation of the *Taittirīya Saṁhitā* and the *Śukla Yajurveda* has the *Śatapatha* in two schools. To the *Atharvaveda,* belongs the *Gopatha Brāhmaṇa* which consists of two books. It toto, the *Brāhmaṇas* represent no doubt, a most interesting phase in the history of Indian thought.

The *Araṇyakas* are works to be read in the forest. The *Araṇyakas* and *Upaniṣads* often form the concluding portion of the several *Brāhmaṇas*. The *Upaniṣads* mark an absolutely different path from that of the works that preceded them in the Vedic canon. The *Upaniṣads* like the Vedas, are however regarded as *Śruti* texts. They are popularly called the *Vedānta*. The total number of *Upaniṣads* is very large. Of these, *Aitareya* and *Kauṣītaki* belong to the *Ṛgveda*; the *Kaṭha*, the *Taittirīya,* the

Kaivalya, the *Śvetāśvatara* and the *Nārāyaṇa* to the *Kṛṣṇa Yajurveda*; the *Īṣa*, the *Brahadāraṇyaka* and the *Jābāla* to the *Śukla Yajurveda*; the *Kena* and the *Chāndōgya* to the *Sāmaveda*; and *Praśna*, the *Muṇḍaka*, *Māṇḍukya* and the *Nṛsimhatāpani* to the *Atharveda*.

Thus, it may be seen that these three major classes of Vedic literature, the *Brāhmaṇas*, the *Araṇyakas* and the *Upaniṣads* mark three consecutive stages, not only in the Indian thought in general, but in the life of every individual. The *Brāhmaṇas* advocating the actual observances of the sacrifice are meant for the *Gṛhastha*; the *Araṇyakas* whose subject is the allegorical sacrifice, for the *Vānaprastha* and the *Upaniṣads* purely philosophic for the men of wisdom, *Sanyāsins*. They mark the three distinct paths the *Nihśreyas*, viz., *Karma, Upāsanā* and *Jnāna*.

Further, the last phase of the Vedic literature consists of *Śutra* section. The *Śutra* literature forms a connecting link between the Vedic and post-Vedic literature. The most important works belonging to the *Śutra* literature are the six *Vedāṅgas*. These are, *Śikṣā* (pronunciation), *Chandas* (metre), *Vyākaraṇa* (grammar), *Nirukta* (etymology), *Jyotiṣa* (astronomy), and *Kalpa* (ceremonial). The *Vedāṅgas* have been intended to help the understanding of the Vedic texts. In course of time, distinct schools of thought came into existence for a systematic study of the branches of Vedic knowledge. Those schools evolved special texts of their own, known as the *Sūtras*. The *Kalpasūtras* are the manuals on rituals, and there are four divisions of them. The *Śrautasūtras* deal with the rules relating to great sacrifices. The *Gṛhyasūtras* deal with the rules relating to domestic rights. The *Dharmasūtras* deal with *Dharma* or codes of law. The *Śulbasūtras* deal with the measurement of *Yajṅamaṇṭapas* and *Yajṅavedis*. Following is the chart of entire Vedic literature under specific heads :

Veda	Śakhā	Brāhmaṇa	Āraṇyaka	Upaniṣads
Ṛg	Śākala	Aitareya	Aitareya	Aitareya
	Bāṣkala	Kauṣītakī	Kauṣītakī	Kauṣītakī
Sāma	Jaiminīya	Pañcaviṁṣa	Chāndogya	
Rāṇāyanīya	Ṣaḍviṁṣa	Kena		
Kautuma	Jaiminīya			
	Upaniṣad			
	Chāndogya			
Kṛṣṇa Yajur	Taittirīya	Taittirīya	Taittirīya	Taittirīya
	Maitrāyaṇi			Maitrāyaṇi
	Kāṭhaka			Kaṭha
	Kapiṣṭhala kaṭha			Śvetāśvatara
Śukla Yajur	Kāṇva	Śatapatha	Śatapatha	Bṛhadāraṇyaka
(Vajasaneyi	Mādyandina			Īṣa
Saṁhitā)				
Atharva	Śaunaka	Gopatha		Maṇḍūka
	Paippalāda			Praśna
				Mandūkya

1.2 India : The Original Home of Aryans

The theory of the indigenous origin of the Aryans has been advocated by a number of scholars. Ganganath Jha has tried to prove that the original home was the Brahmarshi-deśa. Another scholar suggests that the original home of the Aryans was in the region of the river Devikā in Multān. Some advocate the claims of Kāshmir and the Himālayan region. The various arguments in favour of this view may be summed up as follows:

a. There is no evidence to show that the Vedic Aryans were foreigners or that they migrated into India within traditional memory. Sufficient literary materials are available to indicate with some degree of certainty, that the Vedic Aryans themselves regarded Sapta-Sindhu as their original home (*devakṛita-yoni* or *devanirmita-deśa*).

Migrating races look back to the land of their origin for centuries. The Parsis in India remember their origin after eight hundred years. The ancient Egyptians had remembered their respective lands of origin, even though they had forgotten their location. The Vedic Aryans, if at all they came from outside, therefore, must have lived in Sapta-Sindhu so many centuries before the Vedic period that they had lost all memory of an original home.

b. The linguistic affinities are not positive proofs of Aryan immigration. The Vedic Sanskrit has the largest number of vocables found in the Aryan languages. These are preserved in the languages of the Sanskrit family in different parts of India even when there has been inter-racial contact for centuries. On the other hand, if the pre-Vedic Aryan language was spoken in different parts of Europe and Asia where the Aryans had settled before coming to India, how is it that only a few vocables are left in the present-day speech of those parts, while the largest number of them is found in the distant places of ultimate settlement and racial admixture in India? On the contrary this disparity can easily be explained if the pre-Vedic was the language of the homeland of Aryans and the other Aryan languages came into existence as a result of the contact between migrating Aryans and non-Aryan elements outside India and Persia.

c. The Vedic literature is the earliest extant record of the Aryan mind. How is it that in the course of their journey to the Sapta-Sindhu the Aryans left no such record elsewhere? This absence of literary records in other countries cannot be explained away by a hypothesis that the Aryans only reached a high stage of cultural evolution in India. But we can satisfactorily explain it if we suppose that the Aryans migrated from India, and the migration being only of the superfluous population of roving tribes without great cultural development, they could not impart the literary and cultural tradition to the countries in which they ultimately settled?

d. The sacrificial rituals had long been established before the compilation of the Saṁhitā. Therefore, the home of Soma, the Mūjavant or Munjavant hills in the north of the Punjab, indicates the locality from which the sacrificial rituals developed.

e. It is often argued that Lithuanian being the most archaic in the Aryan family of languages, Lithuania is likely to be the original home of the Aryans. But a language remains archaic even when the persons using it are unprogressive; or if they remain in a locality, where no fusion is possible with races speaking other languages; or if they develop a highly refined technique for preserving and using archaic forms. The first two conditions are probably responsible for the archaic character of Lithuanian.

f. It is argued that the tiger, a native of the Bengal swamps, is not mentioned in the Ṛgveda, but the place of honour is given to the lion. Similarly the elephant, mentioned as the *mṛigahastin*, shows that it was a novelty. These arguments do not carry much weight in view of the fact that the Harappa civilization of the Indus Valley shows little trace of the lion (supposed to be common in the desert of Rājputāna) but is fully conversant with the worship of the tiger and the elephant as indicated by the seals. If in about 3000 B.C. the elephant and the tiger were so well known in the Punjab, it is absurd to suppose that they disappeared so completely as not to be mentioned in the Ṛgveda in c. 1500 B.C. The word *mṛiga-hastin* is merely a poetic term and does not imply novelty. In the same way the word *parvatagiri*, used for a mountain in the same Ṛgveda, clearly does not mean that mountains were strange to the Vedic peoples. Again it is said that rice is not mentioned in the Ṛgveda. Even so, salt is never mentioned in the Ṛgveda. Can we conclude that the consumption of salt was unknown in the Rigvedic times? Rice seems to have been unknown in the Harappa civilization also. This only proves that *yava* (barley) and wheat were the staple cereals of North-West India.

g. The geographical data of the Ṛgveda, clearly show that the Punjab and the neighbouring regions constituted the home of the people who composed these hymns. There is no good ground for the belief that they or their ancestors lived in any other country.

1.3 Validity of the Vedas

The Veda as a whole, has been traditionally recognised as non-human composition, the eternal store-house of highest knowledge, and as endowed with supernatural efficacy. Inspiration and infallibility are the two chief attributes of the Veda. From the *Atharvaveda* and the *Purāṇas*, a large number of passengers may be quoted bearing on this subject, which all agree in preaching that the Veda had a divine or mystic origin. The Veda deals with something supernatural which cannot be made known by ordinary perception and inference. This is clear from the following extract from the *Vedārtha Prakāśa* of Mādhavācārya on the *Taittirīya Yajurveda* :

इष्टप्राप्त्यनिष्टपरिहारयोरलौकिकमुपायं यो ग्रन्थो वेदिषति स वेदः।
अलौकिकपदेन प्रत्यक्षानुमाने व्यावर्त्येत।

It is here essential to find out what the *Mīmāṁsakas* understood by the term 'Veda'. They regard the Vedas as self-revealed (*apauruṣeya*), that is to say, they have not been written or composed like the *Rāmayaṇa* and the *Mahābhārata* by man. Had they been so written, then the author of the Vedas, like Vālmīki and Veda-Vyāsa, the authors respectively of those two books, would have been remembered by us. The Vedic teachers and disciples have maintained a continuous chain of the study of the Vedas from time immemorial, but nobody ever heard the name of the author of the Vedas. From this, it may be inferred that there was no author of the Vedas, because in that case, some one or other of these people would have heard his name. It is therefore the unanimous conclusion of the exponents of the Mīmāṁsa philosophy that the Vedas must be regarded as self-revealed, since there is no remembrance from time immemorial of any special man as the author of the Vedas. The purport of what Śabara Svāmin says in order to arrive at this conclusion is as follows:

We must not think that someone has connected the Vedic words with their meanings in order to give currency to the Vedic rites and ceremonies. This relation is self-evident. Had there been any man who connected the Vedic words with their meanings and introduced the Vedic rites, then at the time of performing such rites the performer must have remembered the author. This remembrance of the connection between the author and the use of the text is absolutely essential to the fulfilment of the aim and object of such performance. For instance, Pāṇini coined the word *vṛddhi* for certain vowel modifications. If we remember him when we hear this word, then only we know that the word *vṛddhi* denotes such and such, and can use it according to the method invented by him and obtain the appropriate result. But when we do not remember the word as a definition of his, we do not ascribe to it any such meaning, nor use it according to his rules, nor get the result thus obtainable. Similarly, a *ṛṣi* named Piṅgala, who is the author of the science of prosody, takes *ma* to denote any group of three consecutive long syllables. When we remember him, we take *ma* to denote a word containing three such long syllables, e.g., Vaiśālī, and use it in metrical compositions and get the desired result. But when we do not think of it as a technical term used by Piṅgala, it fails to suggest to our minds any such group of syllables, e.g., Vaiṣālī, and we do not use *ma* according to the rules of prosody. It follows therefore that unless a sect becomes extinct we always remember the author and user of the technical terms current in the usages of that sect. This is the general rule.

It is now clear that had the Vedas been created by any man and the rites depending on them been first performed by him, then we should always have remembered the author. As we cannot understood the meaning of Pāṇini's aphorism 'वृद्धिर्यस्याचामादिस्तद्वृद्धम्.....' (I.1.73) and cannot apply it unless we know the meaning of his other aphorism 'वृद्धिरादैच्' (I.1.1.), so we should be unable to follow and apply the Vedas. But our actual experience is quite contrary to this. We do not know of any author or originator of the Vedic rites and ceremonies; yet we have been performing them continually from the beginning. Hence it cannot be established by any direct proof that someone conceived the relationship between the Vedic words and their meanings and introduced the Vedic rites of his own free will, and thus was the creator of the Vedas.

Kumārila Bhaṭṭa, the famous author of *Ślokavārttika,* an explanatory treatise on Śabara Svāmin's commentary, explains the passage quoted above thus: 'The study of the Vedas has always been dependent on previous study; for this study is carried on through words, as the present system of Vedic study will show.'

This conclusion of the Mīmāṁsakas regarding the self-revealed character of the Vedas is not accepted by the Naiyāyikas. According to them, the Vedas were revealed by Almighty God as the source of all happiness and prosperity for the first race of men created in this land. It should not, however, be understood that He composed the Vedas a new as a set of books; but that He only revealed the Vedas which existed in the previous cycle (*kalpa*). This He did in the previous cycle also. Hence there is no author of the Vedas except God.

Ācārya Udayana, the author of *Kusumāñjali,* says on this point: What is "Veda?" Every word cannot be called "Veda", because the words of an impostor are not regarded as "Veda". The words of Maharṣi Manu and others about virtue and vice and other unseen things are not regarded as "Veda". Hence the reply is that those words which cannot be traced to any other source and which are accepted by the wise as authority constitute the Vedas. It cannot be said that the words which have come down to us as the Vedas originated from perception and other proofs. Nor can it be said that they sprang from the error of an ignorant person or the imposition of a cheat; for then they would not have been accepted as authority by the good and the wise. The view of the Mīmāṁsakas that the chain of teachers and students from time immemorial is the source of the Vedas is also not tenable, because at the time of dissolution (*mahāpralaya*) such a chain cannot exist.'

Ācārya Udayana has clearly said that the source of the Vedas cannot be the perception or inference of any human being like ourselves, because the supernatural subject-matter of the Vedas is unintelligible to a man with human reasoning. The argument that someone without understanding it rationally has ascribed his own imaginary meaning to it and has introduced it, for some selfish motive is also not sound; for there is no proof that the results of the actions mentioned in the Vedas are not attainable. And as they have been regarded as authority by the wise (*śiṣṭa*) and sages (*mahājana*), their author cannot be an ignorant person or a cheat.

His criticism of the Mīmāṁsaka view deserves careful consideration. He says, 'Like the words used by us, the Vedas also are composed of words and hence they have been made by someone. The argument of the Mīmāṁsakas that there is no author of the Vedas, since the memory of such an author is not handed down to us, is also not valid, because the scriptures themselves declare the divine origin of the Vedas. Says the Smṛti: "Then the Vedas came out of His mouth. Thus in the beginning of each cycle different Vedas are composed;" and "I have composed the Vedānta and I am the knower of the Vedas." And the Śruti : "From that God have sprung all offerings of oblations as well as the *Sāman, Ṛg* and other Vedas." Such remembrance also is current among the students of the Vedas. It may be urged that these are laudatory words designed to praise the Vedas and not to establish their divine origin. But this does not stand the test of reason. There being no rule laid down in the Vedas that the author must be remembered, the priests did not remember the author while performing the rites, and a time came when the author was totally forgotton; but that does not prove that there was no author at all. If words must be regarded as authorless (*apauruṣeya*) when there is no remembrance of the author, then if the name of Kālidāsa be forgotten, *Kumāra-saṁbhava* also should be regarded as authorless - a view which nobody would accept.'

But the Mīmāṁakas have not accepted the divine origin of the Vedas as believed by the Naiyāyikas. Their reasons for rejecting the Naiyāyika view are briefly given below.

It has already been shown above that, in the opinion of the ancient Mīmāṁsakas like Śabara and Kumārila, there is no reliable evidence to show that someone composed the Vedas in the beginning and introduced the Vedic rites. Moreover it is admitted by the Naiyāyikas also that though the Vedic rites have been current among the learned and the wise at all times throughout the length and breadth of India, yet ther is no evidence to show when and by whom these were introduced first. On these auguments, the Mīmāṁsakas base their belief in the authorlessness of the Vedas.

How man was first created on this earth has been explained in different ways by different learned men, who do not agree among themselves. This was done in the past, this is done at the present time; but there is no explanation which has been accepted by all. Those who seek to postulate the existence of the author of the Vedas on the ground that a sentence (*vākya*) must be the creation of man, should admit that the first creator of the Vedic sentences must have been a man; for it is not possible for any other creature to create them. It is common knowledge that it is beyond the power of any other creature to compose a sentence consisting of words made up of vowels and consonants. It is clear therefore that the first author who composed these sentences was a man. It must also be admitted in this connection that man had the knowledge of the technique of combining words into sentences to convey the desired meaning. If it be so, it may be asked how that first man acquired the knowledge of words and the things they signified. We find that one who frames a sentence learns the words and their meanings and their mode of combination from some one else before one can compose a sentence intelligible to others. Hence the existence of the author clearly indicates the existence of a previous author of the words and their meanings. Otherwise it is impossible to frame a sentence to express one's feelings or ideas. We do not come across any deviation from this rule. If this be an established rule for composition by man, this rule must also be observed in Vedic composition.

No theory or conjecture propounded by scientists and philosophers from time to time about the origin of the first man or the mode of his use of words or formation of society has received universal acceptance; and no sane man can hope to find a consensus of opinion in this respect. On the other hand, we find at the present time among those who perform Vedic rites that the student learns them from his teacher who in his turn learnt them from his own teacher, and so on. This continuous chain has come down to us from time immemorial. No reliable evidence is before us to show that this chain was actually broken at any time in the past. Hence this eternal continuous chain of the teacher and the taught is the bed-rock of the belief in the authorlessness of the Vedas.

Granting that the authorlessness of the Vedas has been accepted, how can the authority (*prāmāṇya*) of the Vedas be established? Take for example, a local rumour regarding the abode of an evil spirit in a particular banyan tree. Nobody knows who first gave currency to this report; the people of the locality, however, have known it for a long time as being handed down from father to son. But is it reasonable to accept it as valid on this ground? There are hundreds of such stories current among us; but should we take them as valid? Similarly, though there has been an unbroken chain of teachers and disciples of the Vedas, yet is it reasonable to accept the Vedas as authority on this ground?

In reply to this, the Mīmāṁsakas say that one should understand clearly the axiomatic nature of authority. Correct knowledge is called truth (*pramā*) and incorrect knowledge is called error (*apramā*). Every item of knowledge is not correct and hence not truth. The question, however, is how one should discover what is truth. Different answers are given to this question by different schools of philosophy. According to the Nyāya and Vaiśeṣika schools, the correctness or incorrectness of knowledge cannot be found out at once. If, after proper investigation, we find that the senses through which the knowledge has come, are in a reliably sound condition, then we infer that the knowledge gained is correct. When, for example, the eye sees an object under normal conditions, we conclude that the knowledge obtained is correct (*pramā*). If such knowledge comes from abnormal causes or is based on insufficient data, we know that it is an error. This is the view of the Naiyāyikas and other philosophers who accept extraneous evidence (*paratah-pramāṇa*) as the source of knowledge.

The Mīmāṁsakas say in reply that the argument above cannot bear scrutiny. For the circumstances under which the vision of an object takes place have been assumed to be true or favourable for correct vision without any proof that they are really so. To prove that they are really favourable, normal, or sound, one must prove that their causes are sound and correct; and this process would continue *ad infinitum*. We are thus landed in the haze of imagination; the practical result of such a process is the impossibility of ascertaining the truth of the knowledge in question. Suppose that a man is sitting somewhere in the thick darkness of a new-moon night. A sudden flash of lightening reveals a tiger infront of him with jaws wide open. As soon as he sees the aninal, he runs away in bewilderment without caring for any proof whether the sight of the tiger is real or only an illusion. Still less does he care for the favourability suitability, or soundness of the causes which led to the terrible ocular experience. He believes in the presence of the beast more firmly than any truth proved by anybody and attempts to escape by running away from it. It is clear from this that the power of judging the correctness of the knowledge acquired is inherent in our nature. That is why, man has always carried on his practical affairs accordingly in all ages, and will do so in future. It must be admitted by all therefore that knowledge does not depend for its validity on the subsidiary knowledge of the soundness of its causes. Knowledge is self-revealed and its correctness (*Pramā*) self-evident, and on this self-evident correctness are based on all the actions of man.

Though the proof of its correctness is inherent in knowledge itself, no one admits that there can be no error at all. Though we naturally and automatically accept the validity of knowledge by intution, yet on occasions we question the validity of knowledge under compulsion, and at times we do oppose, criticize, reject, and declare it to be error. But when are we compelled to do so? We do so when find that the knowledge in question is opposed to or sublated by another piece of knowledge which has already been proved to be true; or when we find that the causes from which the knowledge has sprung are faulty and consequently unable to produce the correct knowledge. In short, we reject a newly acquired piece of knowledge as error for two reasons: first, when it is contradictory to what has already been proved to be true; secondly, when the cause of the knowledge is found faulty.

The faults or defects of the cause of knowledge are briefly shown below.

Knowledge is of two kinds, direct (*pratyakṣa*) and indirect (*parokṣa*). Knowledge acquired through the perception of the senses is called direct knowledge, and knowledge gained from inference or verbal authority (*sabdapramāṇa*) is called indirect knowledge. If the eye is weak or affected by jaundice or any other disease, the knowledge acquired through it cannot be free from error. Thus the degree of error in the knowledge is proportional to the weakness or defect of the sense-organ through which the knowledge is gained.

The means or sources of knowledge are called the *pramāṇas,* and they are six according to the school of Bhaṭṭa, i.e., Kumārila. These are direct perception (*Pratyakṣa*), inference (*anumāna*), verbal authority (*śabda*), analogy (*upamāna*), presumption (*arthāpatti*), and non-perception (*anupalabdhi*). *Pratyakṣa* results from the immediate contact between sense and its object. It is objective, i.e. it is conditioned by the object, and is not subjective, i.e. comprising the knowledge and the knower, for these two are not reflected or revealed therein. Prabhākara omits the sixth. Non-perception, according to him, is negation and is identical with its locus and not a separate category.

In inference, the object of knowledge, being mediate or remote, is inferable. The knowledge and the knower, i.e. the subject, are, however, directly cognized. In the view of Prabhākara, ordinary, i.e. secular, verbal testimony has no independent validity as a source of knowledge. For it is included in inference, being an index to the import of the speaker. Vedic texts like injunctions, however, are valid means of proof. In this view, perception alone has validity as proof. In both veiws, validity as proof consists in communicating knowledge unapprehended before and otherwise not contradicted. Memory, which has as its content what was cognized before, is not an independent source. In all kinds of cognition or forms of knowledge, there is revelation of the proof, the probandum, and the prover. In direct perception, all the three are immediately cognized. In inference and the rest, the object is inferable. The prover and the proof are in them also directly cognized. The operation of inference etc. therefore refers to the object portion only.

The cause of indirect knowledge is *vyāpti-jñāna,* or the knowledge of the invariable concomitance of two things. If it is not correct, the inference drawn from it is sure to be erroneous. Thus even when a word is faultless, the indirect knowledge of its meaning, which is based on the word itself, is regarded as an error, if the man using it is unable to pronounce it correctly or is careless or deceitful.

According to this rule, if the indirect knowledge derived from the Vedic words be regarded as erroneous, then we are compelled to admit that there is some fault in the Vedic words themselves, or there is some knowledge in this word higher than what is derivable from the Vedic words.

In reply to the above, the Mīmāṁsakas say that there is no possibility of the knowledge springing from the Vedic words being tainted with the faults mentioned above. From the Vedic words, we understand that those who want to go to heaven should perform certain sacrifices like *jyotiṣṭoma, darśa-paurṇamāsa, agniṣṭoma,* etc. We do not find any contradictory proof, namely, that eternal happiness in heaven is not derivable from these sacrifices. Heaven cannot be proved by any evidence that can be used by men. Similarly, we have strong reason to think that after death a happy life in heaven is not possible. Therefore, there is no strong contrary reason to prove the knowledge of the duty of performing Vedic sacrifices as erroneous. Next, the doubt that the authority of the Vedas must be rejected owing to faults like error, carelessness, defect in the sense-organ, deception, etc. in the author or the propunder of the Vedas, is also not reasonable; for it has been shown above that so long as this doctrine is not refuted by strong reason and evidence, the knowledge of the supernatural meanings derivable from the Vedic words and the self-evident truth inherent in them cannot be discarded. If the existence of the author of the Vedas be proved, then only the possibility of his faults like error etc. is imaginable. Since the Vedas consist of words which have come down from time immemorial, and since there is no author of the Vedas, their axiomatic authority stands unassailable. This is the sum and substance of the Mīmāṁsaka view regarding the authorlessness and self-evident authority of the Vedas.

The *Vedāntins* too, argue that the Vedas are not of human origin. This *Apauruṣeyatva* is technically explained by them thus: "No. In the first place, connection with a person does not mean being uttered by a person, for even according to the *Pūrvamīmāṁsa* school of the Kumārila Bhaṭṭa. The Vedas would be connected with persons, beings handed down from one teacher to another. Nor does connection with a person mean having an origin due to a person, for that inference about the personal origin of the Vedas, which is approved by the logicians is condemned by our school as providing what is already established. But it is being the object of utterance that is independent of any utterance of the same king. For instance, in the beginning of cosmic projection, the Lord produced Vedas having a sequence of words same to that which had already existed in the Vedas in the previous cosmic projection, and not Vedas of a different type. Hence, the Vedas, not being the object of utterance that independent of any utterance of the same kind, are not connected with a person. The utterance of the *Mahābhārata* etc. however, is not at all dependent on any utterance of the same kind. Hence they are connected with a person. Thus two kinds of verbal testimony have been determined, viz., that which is connected with a person, and that which is not."[7] And, the beginning portion of the Viṣṇutattvanirnaya of Madhva elucidates and establishes the theory of non-human composition of the Vedas, on the basis of the logic and scriptural texts.[8]

Besides the aforesaid authoritativeness of the Vedas, there were many other schools of exegesis, most of which have now faded into oblivion. One such school was that of the *Aitihāsikās* who traced the historical personalities to the Vedic sources and located their activities in the settings of events with spatio-temporal contexts. For instance, *Aitihāsikās* hold that Vṛtra was an Asura, the son of Tvaṣṭṛ.[9] The Aśvins as two pious kings.[10]

1.4 Vedic Ṛṣi - Devatā - Chandas

In his Ṛgbhāṣyabhūmika, Sāyaṇācārya quotes an authority declaring that the Vedic mantras should be imparted by the preceptor, are learnt by the students only after knowing the Ṛṣi-devata and chandas thereof; in otherwise case reciter accrues sin:

अविदित्वा ऋषि श्च्छन्दः दैवतं योगमेव च ।
योऽध्यापयेज्जपेद्वापि पापीयान् जायते तु सः ॥

A preson who visualizes and utters the hymn is known as Ṛṣi like Vasiṣṭha, Madhucchandā etc. In case of dialogue-hymns like that of between Ūrvaṣi-Purūravā, Ūrvaṣi is considered as Ṛṣi, for the mantras uttered by her, and Purūrava, the Ṛṣi for the mantras uttered by him. Such is justification shown in the Bṛhaddevatā.

संवादेष्वाह वाक्यं यः स तु तस्मिन् भवेदृषिः ।
यस्तेनोच्येत वाक्येन देवता तत्र सा भवेत् ॥ (II.88)

The Ṛṣis are seers of the various hymns of the Ṛgveda. For each hymn, the *Sarvānukramāṇi* mentions the name of its Ṛṣi, and there are about four hundred such seers, to whom Vedic mantras are revealed. Therefore, these seers are called *mantra-dṛṣṭārah.* Thus Sāyaṇa states that he is regarded as Ṛṣi who for the first time perceives the Vedic mantras by the grace of Parameśvara :

अतीन्द्रियस्य वेदस्य परमेश्वरानुग्रहेण प्रथमतः दर्शनात् ऋषित्वम्।

(Ṛgveda-bhāṣya 1.i.i.)

The Vedic tradition cannot be confined to mere myths and rituals. Significantly, it is informed of the spirit of humanism that pervades the Vedic literature and culture. It, therefore, includes the ideal of Puruṣārtha, the Varṇāśrama system, the dhārmic state, the spirit of harmony as well as the paths of realization through jnāna, karma and bhakti. 'Vedic tradition' stands for the human, social, ethical, religious and spiritual values and traditions revealed in the Vedic literature and emphatically brought out by successive generations of thinkers and commentators over these long centuries.

It is to be noted that in the context of such an all-embracing tradition that has survived for an inordinately long period and acquired several elements from diverse sources, as well as that of a literary heritage, handed down from generation to generation through oral traditions and during the process has gone through modifications and acquired magnificence and vast dimensions, it is really difficult to distinguish the Vedic from the non-Vedic. Therefore, those who claim affiliation with the Vedic tradition, as well as those who reject it, are bound to be vague or imprecise in their references or refutations. More often, they are unaware of what they claim or reject. Most of those who generally or casually rejected or ridiculed the Veda, were ignorant of it. Indeed, it is possible to show by a systematic reappraisal that these seers were staunch champions of Vedic values.

It is difficult to adequately assess the contribution of the ṛṣis to culture. They are, indeed, the founders of culture in all its myriad facets. They acquired supreme knowledge by tapas, preserved it carefully and passed it on to succeeding generations by skillfully devised methods and techniques. A ṛṣi is described as one who, by his knowledge, can move across the limits of this universe (ऋषति ज्ञानेन संसारपारम्). He is a genius, a seer, a poet (मेधावी कवि: क्रान्तदर्शनो भवति कवतेर्वा). He can see the secrets of the manifold universe (viśvarupāṇi pratimuṅcate kavih). He is a ṛṣi also because he transmits knowledge to his disciple. Seers, scholars, poets, scientists, teachers, all kinds of seekers of knowledge are thus called ṛṣis. They contributed most to the fields of Philosophy and Religion and Society as well as to those of Arts and Sciences. The ancient ṛṣis discovered the Ṛta, the basic principle of Universal Harmony, and in conformity with it, they formulated the world's first laws of Nature, principles of social and political order, the basic tenets of art and literature and the methods by which each individual could achieve the highest goal i.e., complete harmony with all creation. They were the first leaders in explorations, discoveries and inventions. Yet, they remain hidden behind their gifts to mankind. It is natural that any student of Vedic culture is bewildered by the rich variety of contributions of the innumerable ṛṣis, about whom practically nothing is known except their names. We have to satisfy ourselves by whatever little we can glean, by way of names, families etc. from the traditional accounts, which, by no strech of imagination, can be taken as 'historical'.

Of the ṛṣis who contributed most to the realm of thought and culture in general, foremost are the seven of the traditional usage, Saptarṣi. They are mentioned in two lists : (1) Kaśyapa, Atri, Bharadvāja, Viśvāmita, Gautama, Jamadagni, Vasiṣtha (*Mbh.* Śalya. 49), and (2) Marīci, Atri, Āngirasa, Pulastya, Pulaha, Kratu, Vasiṣṭha (*Mbh.* Śānti. 343). The names in the first list are more commonly cited. However, all these ṛṣis have made significant contributions.

Kaśyapa, son of Marīci and Kalā, is one of the Ṛgvedic poets. He is described as the progenitor of numerous tribes of men such as daityas, devas, gandharvas, mānavas, yakṣas, as also of animals, birds and plants. Perhaps he maintained a huge zoological and botanical establishment for observation and study. He is described as only second to Brahma in creation.

Of Kaśyapa's descendants, Avatsāra, Nidhruva, Rebha, Devada, Asita, Bhūtāmsa, and Vivṛha are among the seers of the Ṛgveda. This Kaśyapa may be distinguished from another Kaśyapa, the expert in the art of treating the cases of snake-bites, mentioned in the Mahābhārata. The first Kaśyapa was perhaps the inventor of medicine and treatment for snake-bite and therefore, his name seems to have been adopted by later practitioner of that art.

Atri, another Ṛgvedic seer and progenitor, is said to be a mānasaputra of Brahma; in other words, his parentage is forgotten. The whole of the fifth maṇḍala of the Ṛgveda is ascribed to Atri and his family. Of the seers of this family were two women, Viśvavārā and Apālā. Atri and Anasuyā are counted among the ideal couples; Śri Dattātrēya, the famous yogi was born in this gotra.

Bhāradvāja and his family are the seers of the sixth maṇḍala of the Ṛgveda. He was the son of Bṛhaspati and Mamatā, wife of Ucathya, an elder brother of Bṛhaspati. Many Brāhmaṇa and Kṣatriya families are traced to Bharadvāja. Kaṇva and Medhātithi - the seers, kind Duṣyanta, Droṇa, the teacher of the Kuru princes in archery, are some famous members of the family of Bharadvāja.

Dirghatamas, son of Ucathya and uterine brother of Bharadvāja is the seer of the famous Asya Vāmasya hymn (RV. I. 164). It has defied all attempts of scholars to interpret it, and has given rise to several philosophical and astronomical theories.

Much is not known about Kaṇva. The whole of the eighth maṇḍala of the Ṛgveda is ascribed to Kaṇva and his family. This Kaṇva is perhaps different from two other Kaṇvas, one of whom was the disciple of Yājnavalkya (the rsi of the Śukla Yajurveda) and another who was the foster-father of Śakuntala, the daughter of Viśvāmitra, and the queen of Duṣyanta.

Viśvāmitra and his family is ascribed the entire third mandala of the Ṛgveda, which contains the most sacred Savitṛ mantra, more popularly known as Gāyatri mantra. Dēvarāta, Bala, Madhucchanda, Aghamarṣana, Aṣtaka, Lōhita, Devaśrava, Mambudhi, Śiśira, Śālankāyana, Dhananjaya and Reṇu are some of the seers of the Ṛgveda who belong to this family. Viśvāmitra is described as Gāthin and perhaps was one of the first to establish the tradition of the gāthā. Of the seers of this family, Dēvarāta was the adopted son of Viśvāmitra. There is a legend about him. He was a Brāhmaṇa boy, Śunhśepa by name. His father told him to be sacrificed; but Viśvāmitra saved and adopted him as his son.

Viśvāmitra too was a progenitor of a large number of families of the Brāhmaṇas, Kṣatriyas, Vaiśyas and Śūdras. Many powerful ascetics of the subsequent periods have adopted the name of this Vedic seer, and this has created a good deal of confusion in reconstructing the ancient history of India. It is necessary, therefore, to distinguish this Viśvāmitra from others associated with Triśanku, Hariścandra, Śakuntalā, Śri Rāmcandra and others.

Jamadagni belongs to the famous family of Bhṛgu, born of Brahma in the first manvantara. Viśvamitra was his maternal uncle. He was a seer of some mantras of the Ṛgveda and also a progenitor.

It is difficult to say whether this Vedic Jamadagni was the same Jamadagni who married Reṇukā (believed to be an aspect of Śakti) and begot from her, a son, Paraśurāma who is known an avatāra of Viṣṇu.

Marīci is the originator of the family of Kaśyapa, one of the seven sages. Strangely, he is placed in the manvantaras of both Svāyambhuva and Vaivasvata Manus. Some sūktas of the Ṛgveda are ascribed to him.

Vasiṣṭha was perhaps the greatest of the Vedic ṛṣis; to him are ascribed the seventh maṇḍala and several sūktas of the other maṇḍalas of the Ṛgveda. He is at one place described as a son of Brahmā and at another palce, as the son of Mitrāvaruṇa. Arundhati was his wife. Vasiṣṭha and Arundhati are regarded as the ideal, inseparable and the most auspicious couple. He propagated the view that penance and learning were decidedly superior to birth, and that sages, though born of women of lower orders, are to be respected for their valuable achievements. The popular, to a certain extent the purāṇic, tradition of a keen rivalry between Vasiṣṭha and Viśvamitra has some basis in the Ṛgveda. These two ṛṣis are placed in several successive eras and perhaps there existed several ṛṣis by these names in different periods. Vasiṣṭha is also the progenitor of several families. Prominent among his descendants are some seers of the Vedic mantras maharṣi Parāśara, his illustrious son Kṛṣṇa Dvaipāyana Veda Vyāsa and the latter's son Śukamuni.

Āngirasa is the originator of the family to which belonged Bṛhaspati, Dirghatāmas, Bharadvāja and others. He was an ancient seer of the hymns. Along with Atharvan, he is credited with the authorship of the entire Atharvaveda. Later on, the members of the composite family of Bhṛgu and Āngīrasa have done a good deal in establishing the historical tradition that found its full expression in the epics and the purāṇas. Some scholars believe that fire and the cult of fire were discovered by Āngirasa.

The family of Pulaha seems to have become extinct soon while that of Pulastya continued for long. Rāvaṇa, the rākṣasa ruler of Lankā belonged to this family. It may be mentioned that Rāvaṇa was a great yogi and an equally great devotee of Śiva. He is described as a great Brāhmaṇa. Kratu died childless and his name was given to a descendant of Agastya.

Agastya, brother of Vasiṣṭha, was a great ṛṣi and progenitor. He and his family are composers of some hymns of the Ṛgveda.

As in the case of Viśvāmitra, the name of Agastya also seems to have been adopted by many rsis of the subsequent ages. A number of achievements and miracles are attributed to Agastya. He is credited, for example, with the miracles of drinking the whole sea and letting it out, and of subduing the Vindhyas. He has the credit of being the first explorer of the Deccan forests and the first to establish āśramas in the south, the most famous one being on the banks of the Kāveri. He is also believed to be the author of the original Tamil grammar. In any case, there is no doubt that the Vedic Agastya was a great ṛṣi who inspired several of his disciples to spread the Vedic culture in different unexplored regions. Lopamudra, his wife, was also a seer of the hymns.

Of the remaining numerous Ṛgvedic ṛṣis, Gṛtsamada, the composer of the entire second maṇḍala and Vāmadēva, the author of the fourth maṇḍala are important. Unfortunately, no information about them is available. Yama, Manu, Virūpa, Uśana, Kutsa are some of those who have contributed to the development of Vedic philosophy. Rulers like Yayāti, Māndhata are also counted among the seers of the hymns, Samvanana of the Āngīras family is the author of the great Song of Harmony which is given the significant honour of being the concluding mantra of the Ṛgveda. C. Kunhan Raja points out :

"The poem enunciates the philosophy of the nation's emotional integration. Indian history can be a correct history of India, a true presentation of the genius and achievements, intellectual and material, of the Indian nation only if it is a natural continuation of the last poem in the Ṛgveda collection."

Of these poet-philosophers, Atharvan-Āngiras is credited with the discovery of fire, Dirghatāmas with that of Eras, Gārgya, with the first enumeration of constellations, Bharadvāja with the organization of the symposium on medicinal plants, Ātreya Punarvasu with the establishment of the first academy of Medicine, and Medhātithi with the first extension of the numbers of billions.

The four ṛṣis of the first manvantara - Paila, Vaiśampāyana, Jaimini and Sumanta, who were entrusted with the task of preserving the Ṛgveda, the Yajurveda, the Sāmaveda and the Atharvaveda respectively, deserve a place in the cultural history of India. They should not however be confused with the sages of the same names of later ages.

And these seers are of course not responsible for the contents of the mantras. They are only mediums communicating between gods and men. Yāska says that *Dharma* (duty) revealed itself to the seers who handed it down by oral instruction to that descendants :

साक्षात्कृतधर्माणः ऋषयो बभूवुः । तेऽवरेभ्योऽसाक्षात्कृत-
धर्मभ्य उपदेशेन मन्त्रान् सम्प्रादुः । (*Nirukta* I.20)

The deity to whom a particular hymn is addressed, himself should be regarded as *devatā* of that particular hymn. In this way, deities like Agni, Varuṇa, Yama, Soma etc. have been regarded as devatās of respective hymns. Some hymns or mantras are not evident in addressing the names of particular deities. In such case, one should know the nature of the rituals or sacrifices wherein such mantras are uttered. Such method of identifying the Vedic deities and respective hymns has been discussed in detail by Yāska in the *Daivatakāṇḍa* of the *Nirukta*.

In addition, *Chandas* of particular hymn should also be known. The fourteen Vedic metres such as Gāyatri, Anuṣṭub, Bṛhati, Triṣṭub, Jagati Uṣhni, Pankti, Atijagati, Śhakvari, Atiśakvari, Aṣ hti, Atyaṣhti, Dhriti and Atidhriti - are regarded as important ones. The vedic commentator, Katyayana in his *Anukramaṇi,* states these essentials:

यस्य वाक्यं स ऋषिः । या तेनोच्यते सा देवता ।
यदक्षरपरिमाणं तच्छन्दः । अथेप्सवः ऋषयः
देवताः छन्दोभिः उपादावन् ।। (ऋग्वेद-सर्वानुक्रमाणि)

It is thus, the Vedic studies pre-requisites the knowledge of *ṛṣi, devatā* and *chandas* which should be acquired by Vedic student in the beginning itself.

References

1. मन्त्रा मननात् । Yāska, *Nirukta,* VII.13, Motilal Banarasidass, Delhi, 1967, p.138
2. साक्षात्कृ तधर्माण ऋषयो बभूवुः । Yāska, *Nirukta,* I-20
3. त्रयी वै विद्या । ऋचोय्यजूँषि सामानीयमेवर्च्चोऽस्यांह्यर्चन्ति र्योऽर्च्चति स वागेवर्च्चो व्वाचा ह्यर्च्चति सोऽन्तरिक्षमेव यजूँषि ध्यौः सामानि । *Śatapatha Brāhmaṇa*, IV-6-7-1

   The Research Institute of Ancient Scientific Studies, Delhi, Vols-I-III, 1969
4. अग्निः प्रथिवीस्थानः । वायुर्वेन्द्रो वान्तरिक्षस्थानः । सर्यो द्युस्थानः । Yāska, *Nirukta,* VII-5
5. इममेव लोकमृतचा जयति । अन्तरिक्षंय्यजुषा । दिवमेव साम्ना । *Śatapatha Brāhmaṇa*, IV-6-7-2
6. सैषा त्रयी विद्या सौम्येऽध्वरे प्रयुज्यते । *Śatapatha Brāhmaṇa*, IV-6-7-1
7. न हि तावत् पुरुषेण उच्चार्यमाणत्वं पौरुषेयत्वम्, गुरुमतेऽप्यध्यापक परम्परया पौरुषेयत्वापत्तेः । नापि पुरुषाधीनोत्पत्तिकत्वं पौरुषेयत्वम्, नैयायिकभिमतपौरुषेयत्वानुमानेऽस्मदादिना सिद्धसाधनापत्तेः । किन्तु सजातीयोच्चारणानपेक्ष्योच्चारणविषयत्वम् । तथा च सर्गाद्यकाले परमेश्वरः पूर्वसर्गसिद्धिवेदानुपूर्वीसमानानुपूविकं वेदं विरचितवान्, न तु तद्विजातीयं वेदमिति सजातीयोचारणनपेक्षोच्चारणाविषयत्वं पौरुषेयत्वं वेदस्य । भारतादीनान्तु सजातियोच्चारणमनपेक्ष्यैवोच्चारणमिति तेषां पौरुषेयत्वम् । एवं पौरुषेयापोरुषेयभेदेन द्विविध आगमो निरूपितः । Dharmarāja Adhvarīndara, *Vedānta Paribhāṣa,*

   Ed. Swami Mādhavandanda, Advaita Ashrama, Calcutta, 1989 pp-14-15.

8. Madhva, *Viṣṇutattvanirṇaya,* ed. Prof. K. T. Pandurangi, Bangalore, 1992, pp-2-6.
9. तत्को वृत्रः । त्वष्ट्रोऽसुर इत्यैतिहासिकाः । Yāska, *Nirukta,* I 116
10. तत्काविश्विनौ । राजानौ पुण्यकृतावित्यैतिहासिकाः । Yāska, *Nirukta,* XII-1

Chapter - II

Structure of the Ṛgveda

2.1 Arrangement of the Ṛgveda Saṁhitā

The *Ṛgveda Saṁhitā* is rather a group of *mantras* visualised by several seers of that age. The form on which the *Saṁhitā* of the *Ṛgveda* has come down to us clearly shows that the different *Sūktas* were brought together and systematically arranged long before. The different portions of the *Saṁhitā* represent various indications of language, vocabulary, style, grammar, metre and ideas.

The *Ṛgveda Saṁhitā* is a collection of 1,028 *Sūktas* (hymns) divided into ten *Maṇḍalas* (books). These 1,028 *Sūktas* include eleven *Vālakhilya Sūktas*. The number of *mantras* iṇ a *Sūktas* varies from just one (I-99) to 58 (IX-97). The total number of *mantras* is 10,462; thus the average number of *mantras* per hymn is ten. These hymns are seen by various seers.

There are two ways of dividing the contents of the *Ṛgveda*, one into *Aṣṭakas*, *Adhyāyas* and *Vargas*, and the other into *Maṇḍalas, Anuvākas* and *Sūktas*. Of these, the former is popular among traditionalists because of the convenience of study. The *Ṛgveda Saṁhitā* is divided into eight *Aṣṭakas,* each *Aṣṭaka* consists of eight *Adhyāyas* and each *Adhyāya* consists of several *Vargas*. A *Varga* being usually made up of five *mantras,* sometimes more and sometimes less. This is the division popular with the *Vaidikas* with whom a *Varga* is the measure of a lesson. This division is purely mechanical.

The second type of division, however, though no doubt also mechanical in character, has some scientific historical principles to support it. There are ten *Maṇḍalas* divided into several *Anuvākas*. The *Maṇḍala* contains twenty four; the second four; the third and fourth five each; the fifth, sixth and seventh six each; the eighth ten; the ninth seven; and the tenth *Maṇḍala* contains twelve *Anuvākas*. Each *Anuvāka* consists of a number of *Sūktas*, and each *Sūkta* contains different number of *mantras*.

The *Ṛgveda* consisting of three portions follows from the fact that the *Ṛṣis* where divided broadly into three divisions :

1. *Śatārcinah* - the *Ṛṣis* of the first *maṇḍala* each of whom, seems to have contributed nearly hundred *mantras*.
2. *Madhyamāh* - the *Ṛṣis* of two to seven *maṇḍalas*, and
3. *Kṣudrasūktāh and Mahāsūktah* - the *Ṛṣis* of shorter and longer hymn.[1]

In the *Ṛgveda*, two to seven *maṇḍalas* are homogeneous in character as they present a collection of hymns belonging to a particular family. These *maṇḍalas* are known as *Kulamaṇḍalas*, and are attributed to the *Ṛṣis* - Gṛtsamada, Viśvāmitra, Vāmadeva, Atri, Bhāradvāja and Vasiṣṭha respectively. Of these families, only that of Viśvāmitra and Vasiṣṭha appear to have been closely associated with each other for priesthood of the king Sudās. Each family - *maṇḍala* appears to have family - hymn or hymns describing some extraordinary exploit of the illustrious ancestors or the founders of the family.

For example, III-53; V-40; VII-33 etc. these family - *maṇḍalas* exhibit their learning towards some particular deities, besides

Agni and Indra. For example, in the *Gṛtsamada Maṇḍala* the hymns are found addressed to Bṛhaspati, Rudra and Apāmnapāt; in the Viśvāmitra *maṇḍala,* to Mitra; in the Vāmadeva *maṇḍala*, to the Rubhus; in the Atri *maṇḍala* to the Maruts, and Mitra-Vāruṇa; in the Bhāradvāja *maṇḍala* to Pūṣan and in the Vasiṣṭha *maṇḍala* to Mitra-Vāruṇa, Aśvins, Uṣas and Varuṇa. Uncommon hymn or hymns like the *Śakunta-sūkta* (II-42, 43), the *Saṅgrāma-sūkta* (VI-75) and the *Maṇḍūka-sūkta* (VII-103) are found in each of these family - *maṇḍalas*.

The eighth *maṇḍala* is associated with the family of *Kaṇvas*; but its arrangement of hymns is different from that of the other family - *maṇḍalas*.

The ninth *maṇḍala* has a peculiarity of its own as far as the arrangement is concerned. All the sūktas in the *maṇḍala* are, (without exception, IX-67) addressed to the Soma - Pavamāna by the different *Ṛṣis*. They are called Pāvamānyāh. Thus, it is probable that all the Soma hymns of the seers of *maṇḍalas* two to seven were taken out and collected together in one separate *maṇḍala*, and at the same time arranged with regard to the metre. The hymns 1 to 67 are in *Gāyatri*, 68 to 86 in *Jagatī,* 87 to 97 in *Triṣṭub* and the 98 to 144 in miscellaneous.

Maṇḍalas one and ten from the latest portions of the *Ṛgveda*. Of these, first *maṇḍala* contains 14 groups, each referred to one common seer and having hymns arranged according to the deities, on the same principles as in *maṇḍala* two to seven. For example, the first group of first *maṇḍala* consists of eleven hymns and are related to Viśvāmitra Madhuchandas, of which, hymn first is addressed to Agni, second to Vāyu, third to Aśvins and Indra, and the rest to Indra. The language and the contents of the hymns attributed to different seers in the tenth *maṇḍala* point out that it contains a good number of hymns of later origin. The only principle which connects the different hymns of the *maṇḍala* is numerical.

In this tenth *maṇḍala*, a series of collections is arranged in the descending order of the number of hymns in each and extending from hymn 1 to 84. From hymn 85 to 191 single hymns are arranged in the descending order.

Further, hymns of the *Ṛgveda Saṁhitā* may be divided into two classes : religious and secular. The great majority of hymns are mainly the invocations to gods like Agni and Indra requesting them to accept the oblations, and favour the worshippers with generous gifts. The seers glorify the heroic deeds of the deities and munificence of their patrons. The Soma hymns describe the crushing of the Soma-plant, the extraction of the Some-juice, the preparation of Soma-drink by mixing ingredients like milk and honey and its exhilarating effects enabling the deities to perform their valiant deeds.

Among the secular hymns, there are famous *Akṣa-Sūkta* (X-34) recalling the ruin brought by dice; the *Bhikṣu-Sūkta* (X-117) glorifying the gift of food; the *Bhoja-Sūkta* (X-11) singing the glory of prosperity of the donor etc. The hymns comprising dialogues between the River and Viśvāmitra (III-33), Sarama and Paṇis (X-108), Indra and Apāla (VIII-91), Yama and Yamī (X-10), Ūrvaśi and Purūravas (X-95) etc. are interesting even from a literary view-point. Hymns like Svāpana (VIII-55) are supposed to be endowed with miraculous power. The *Sūrya Vivāha-Sūkta* throws light on the contemporary customs and the *Pitṛ-Sūkta* reveals the details of contemporary funeral rites. Hymns like the *Puruṣa-Sūkta* (X-90) and *Nāsadīya-Sūkta* (X-29) help us to trace the Vedic cosmological and philosophical ideas. The Panegyrics like I-126 are semi-historical as they give the genealogical details of the donors and the names of the Vedic tribes. A couple of hymns (I-164 and VII-29) consists of riddles, largely connected with gods. The *Jñāna-Sūkta* (IX-71) declares the supreme importance of knowledge. Besides the religious and mythological details, those hymns reveal various facts of the life of the Vedic people. Thus, the contents of the *Ṛgveda* are richly varied, revealing the contemporary life and thought which form the basis of evolution of Indian thought and culture through the ages.

Vālakhilya Sūktas

A group of eleven hymns is known by the name of *Vālakhilya*, which stands by itself and which is generally put at the end of the eighth *maṇḍala*. They are not recognised by older writers, nor commented on by Sāyaṇa, though mentioned in Kātyāyana's *Sarvānukramaṇī*. That these do not naturally belong to the place where they are found is quite clear. The earliest interpretations of the name *Vālakhilya* are found in *Taittirīya Āraṇyaka*: [2]

स तपोऽतप्यत । स तपस्तप्त्वा शरीरमधूनुत ।
तस्य यन्मांसमासीत्ततोऽरुणाः केतवो वतरशना ऋषयः उदतिष्ठन्।
ये नसस्ते वैसानसाः ये बालास्ते बालस्ल्याः ।

The fact that these Vālakhilya hymns disturb the regularity of both the *maṇḍala* and *Aṣṭaka* divisions, shows that they were later additions.

Aprī - Sūktas

The *Aprī Sūktas* are peculiar in character. They resemble the hymns which are found in the *Sāma* and the *Yajurveda*, being evidently meant for sacrificial purpose. These are ten in number, which are scattered here and there in the ten *maṇḍalas*.

The *Aprī* hymns generally contain eleven *mantras* each, addressed to eleven separate deities in the following order; **First** *mantra* to Agni, **Second** to Tanūnapat or Nārāśaṁsa (to other aspects of Agni), **third** to Iḷā a (gift), **fourth** to Barhih (sacrificial pile of grass), **fifth** to Devi or Dvarah, **sixth** to Uṣasanakau, **seventh** to Devyau Hotārau, (Agni and Āditya etc.), **eighth** to Sarasvatī, Iḷā and Bhāratī, **ninth** to Tvaṣṭah (the creator), **tenth**

Maṇḍala	Sūkta	Ṛṣi
1	13	Medhātithi (Kaṇva clan)
1	142	Dīrghatamas
1	188	Agastya
2	3	Gṛtsamada
3	4	Viśvāmitra
5	5	Vasuśruta
7	2	Vasiṣṭha
9	5	Asita or Devala
10	70	Sumitra
10	110	Rāma-Jamadagni

to Vanaspati, (the tree of the sacrifice), **eleventh** to Svāhākrti. The position of these hymns necessarily presupposes a deliberate arrangement on the part of the collectors.

2.2 Interpretation of the Ṛgveda

The 'word-interpretations' means to bring out clearly the intended meaning of the words employed by a speaker in particular context. Difficulty in understanding the meaning of the Ṛgvedic *mantras*, arises mainly from the fact that the Vedic text contain number of rare obsolate and obscure words which are not met in a later language. The language of the Vedas and specially that of the *Ṛgveda* is highly technical, polished and often figurative. In this connection, the following observation of M. Bloomfield is noteworthy; "the entire Vedic tradition, the *Ṛgveda* not accepted, present rather the conclusion than the bringing of the long period of literary activity. Conventionality of subject matter, style, form (metre) etc. betray themselves at every step."[3] The seers have carefully and purposely selected each word of their hymns after a thorough consideration of the subtleties and shades of the meaning of appropriate words. The seers are very fond of employing figurative speech, and the use of metaphor is quite common in the Vedic language. This particularly of the Vedic style has been noticed in the *Brāhmaṇas* which observe that "the gods love recondite speech and abhor direct statements."[4]

It is mainly due to the figurative use of the Vedic idioms that even, when there is no doubt about the literal meanings of the words employed in the Vedic *mantras,* their real importance remains vague. In this connection Max Muller has remarked: "the Vedic hymns on the contrary, even when we understand every word of them, remain very obscure in their structure or construction."[5] It is obvious that if the Vedic *mantras* are literally translated in accordance with the usage of classical Sanskrit, it creates confusion, and results in sheer absurdity.

The problem of Vedic interpretation is not of recent origin. When Yāska composed his *Nirukta*, the problem of Vedic interpretation was as intricate as it is today. Even prior to Yāska, the meaning of numerous Vedic words and passages has become so much obscure that some persons began to doubt seriously whether the Vedic *mantras* convey any sense at all. Yāska in this connection refers to the view point of Kautsa who boldly declares that the Vedic *mantras* convey no sense.[6] Yāska first reproduces the arguments advanced by Kautsa, then refutes them one by one, and finally proves his own view point ridiculing Kautsa's gross ignorance about the Vedic lore.

Since very early times, scholars have sought to interpret the Vedas in different ways. No uninterrupted reliable tradition of Vedic interpretation was handed down along with the Vedic *mantras*. The inheritors of these texts began to advance their own conjectures with regard to an authentic tradition of Vedic interpretation. The tendency to make surmises and read preconceived notion into the Vedas, led to the emergence of different schools of Vedic interpretation. Already, at the time of Yāska at least the following five schools of Vedic interpretation, had come into existence, namely, those of the *Yājñikas,*[7] *Nairuktas,*[8] the *Aitihāsikas,*[9] the *Parivrājakas,*[10] and the *Naidānas.*[11]

Yājñika School

The Yājñika school of Vedic exegesis which puts ritualistic interpretations on the Vedas, is the most ancient and predominant among all the existing schools of Vedic interpretations. It has a very long uninterrupted tradition. The earliest attempt to put ritualistic interpretations on the Vedic *mantras* is discernible in the compilation of the *Yajurveda* in which a considerable number of *mantras* from the *Ṛgveda* had been adapted from sacrificial purpose. In this connection, Shri Ram Gopal has concluded: "It is imperative to determine the propriety of ritual application of a Vedic *mantra* before passing a judgement on its ritualistic interpretations attempted by ancient Indian commentators. There is no doubt that the tradition of ritual application of Vedic *mantras* has proved both a boon and a bone of Vedic studies. On the one hand, it has contributed a good deal to the preservation of the Vedic texts. But on the other, it has, to a certain extent, proved a hindrance in the correct unbiased interpretation of the Vedas."[12]

Nirukta School

The first systematic attempt to interpret the Vedas was made by the *Nairuktas,* the proponents of the science of etymology. *Nairuktas,* sought to interpret Vedic words on the basis of their derivative connection. It may be termed as *Nairukta* method of Vedic interpretation. The origin of this method may be traced to the *Brāhmaṇas*, which attempt the derivation of a number of Vedic words. The development of *Nairukta* method of Vedic interpretation is closely connected with the progress of grammatical and lexico-graphical studies in India. Therefore, Yāska in his *Nirukta* declares the science of etymology to be complementary to grammar.[13] Yāska's *Nairukta* is the last and best representative of the *Nairukta* school. Yāska refers by name, to about a dozen authorities on *Nairukta*, viz. Aupamanyava, Śākapūṇi, Gālava, Maudgalya, Agrāyaṇa, Kaṭṭhakya, Kraustuki, Aurṇāvabha, Audumbarāyaṇa, Gārgya and Śākaṭāyaṇa.

In fact, *Nairukta* is an independent and isolated branch of study but was only one of the several branches of the linguistic study of the Vedas. The *Padapāṭha* and *Prātiśākhyas* were the other two important branches of the Vedic linguistic study which, being anterior to the *Nirukta*, are explicitly mentioned by Yāska in his work, and which undoubtedly contributed to the development of the science of etymology. The *Prātiśākhyas* are referred to by Yāska as *Paraṣadani*,[14] while *Śākalya*, the author of *Padapāṭha* of the *Ṛgveda* is mentioned by name and his analysis of the Vedic text is questioned in the *Nirukta*.[15]

Mainly, the Yāska's *Nirukta* is explained into two categories, namely, the *Nighaṇṭu* and the *Nirukta*. The term *Nighaṇṭu* signifies a collection of important Vedic words. The *Nighaṇṭu*, or *Samāmnāya* as it is called in the beginning of the *Nirukta*, is divided into five chapters and is therefore also called *Pañcādhyāyī*. The first three chapters containing Vedic synonyms, are regarded to constitute the *Nighaṇṭuka Kāṇḍa*, the fourth chapter which is styled as *Naigama Kāṇḍa* contains a list of such Vedic words whose meaning is not easy to understand and needs to be explained. The fifth chapter called *Daivata Kāṇḍa* is a glossary of the names of Vedic deities.

The word *Nirukta* literally means 'explanation' or etymological interpretation of word. So Yāska's work is entitled as *Nirukta* which is an explanation of the Vedic words listed in the *Nighaṇṭu*. Since it is the holy work of its kind available at present, the title *Nirukta* now means the Vedic commentary composed by Yāska. The *Nirukta* which consists of twelve chapters and an appendix, is the earliest systematic commentary on selected words, the *mantras* and the deities of the *Ṛgveda*.

Aitihāsika School

The followers of the *Aitihāsika* school of Vedic *mantras* to be related to an Itihāsa i.e., a traditional account of ancient events, and interpret the concerned hymn or *mantras* accordingly. The earliest specimens of the *Aitihāsika* interpretation of the Vedic *mantras* are seen in the *Brāhamaṇas*. Several legends concerning the legendary interpretation of Vedic *mantras* are found in the *Brāhamaṇa* portions of the *Kṛṣṇa Yajurveda, Taittiriya Brāhmaṇa, Śatapatha Brāhmaṇa, Aitareya Brāhmaṇa, Jaiminiya Brāhmaṇa* and *Pañcaviṁśa Brāhmaṇa*. The Vedic and post-Vedic literature having nearly fifty legends, forms the basis of the *Aitihāsika* interpretation of certain hymns of the *Ṛgveda*. Amomg them, the legends relating to Indravṛtra, Agastya-Lopāmudrā, Viśvāmitra-Śakti, Yama-Yamī, Saramā-Paṇi, Urvaśi-Purūravas, Nahuṣa-Sarasvatī, Devāpi-Śantanu, Prajāpati-Duhitṛ, Sudās paijvana and Apālā are prominent and well known.

Parivrājaka School

The Parivrājaka school of Vedic interpretations referred to by Yāska,[16] which provides a mystic interpretation of the Vedas. According to this school of exegesis, not only those Vedic *mantras* which are considered to be of philosophical importance both by ancient and modern scholars,[17] but also the other Vedic *mantras* can be interpreted to conform to their mystic ideas.

The earliest specimens of *Parivrājaka* interpretation of the Vedas are seen in the *Brāhmaṇas* as well as in the *Araṇyakas* and *Upaniṣads* too. The followers of *Parivrājaka* school of Vedic exegesis give the mystic interpretation of Vedic deities and sacrifices also. For instance, Mitra and Varuṇa are interpreted as *Prāṇa* (inhalation) and *Apāna* (exhalation) respectively in the prose portion of the *Taittirīya Saṁhita* and many *Brāhmaṇas*.[18] But such mystic explanations offered in the *Brāhmaṇas* suffer from inconsistency, as one and the same Vedic *mantra* has been variously interpreted. For instance, the god Indra has been interpreted in the *Brāhmaṇas* as *Vacas*[19] (speech), *Prāṇa*,[20] *Manah*[21] (mind), the Sun,[22] Vāyu[23] etc. Yāska refers to this tendency of *Brāhamaṇa*[24].

Naidāna School

Yāska refers to the view of the Naidānas with regard to the etymologies of the word Śyāla (VI-9), and Sāman (VII-12). In his commentary on the *Nirukta* VI-9, *Durgācārya* explains *Naidānah* as *Nidānavidah*, i.e., those who are expert in *Nidāna*. Elsewhere in his commentary *Durgācārya* employs the term *Nidāna* in the sense of primary cause of Vedic *mantras* to explain *Itihāsa* and thus makes *Nidāna* as the basis of *Itihāsa*.[25] But Yāska mentions that *Naidānah* and *Aitihāsikah* are separate and different in their approach. The *Naidāna* system of Vedic interpretation is known in name only, and any definite specimen of this system of interpretation is not found.

Anukramaṇīs

In the field of *Ṛgvedic* studies a class of writing called *Anukramaṇīs* or Vedic indices, occupy a very prominent place. They provide lists of the hymns, their seers, metres and the deities in the order in which they appear in the *Ṛgveda Saṁhitā*. These *Anukramaṇīs* were prepared with a veiw to preserving the original text of the *Ṛgveda*.

Śaunaka and *Kātyāyana* are authors of separate works of *Anukramaṇīs*. Seven *Anukramaṇīs* are attributed *Śaunaka*. The *Ārṣānukramaṇī* gives a list of the *Ṛṣis* of the *Ṛgveda*. The *Chandonukramaṇī* enumerates the metres in which the hymns of the *Ṛgveda* are. It also mentions the number in each *Maṇḍala* of *mantras* in each metres as well as the aggregate in all metres. The *Anuvākānukramaṇī* gives the initial words of each of the eighty-five *Anuvākas*, into which the *Ṛgveda Saṁhitā* is divided and the number of hymns contained in these *Anuvākas*. It also states that the *Ṛgveda* contains 1017 *sūktas*, 10,580 *Ṛks*, 153826 words and 432000 syllables. The *Pādānukramaṇī* gives an index of lines of the *Ṛgveda*. The *Sūktānumramaṇī*, which is not available, probably consisted only of the initial words (*Pratikas*) of the hymns. The *Devatānukramaṇī*, of which only ten quotations are preserved in Sadguruśiṣya's commentary on the *Sarvānukramaṇī*, probably consisted of an index of gods.

The *Sarvānukramaṇī* attributed to *Kātyāyana*, deals with all the data contained in the *Anukramaṇīṣ* within a compass of a single work. It gives the initial words of every hymn in the *Ṛgveda*, a number of its *mantras*, the seers, the deities, and the metres even of single *mantra*. Another work namely, *Ṛgvidhāna* attributed to *Śaunaka*, deals with the magical effects, produced by the recitation of suktas or single *mantra* of *Ṛgveda*.

2.3 Age of the Ṛgveda

The age of the *Ṛgveda* is of utmost consequence for the literary history of India and even beyond. It can be safely said that the hymns of the *Ṛgveda* and some hymns of the Atharvaveda from 'the oldest stratum of Indian literature.' Thus the date of *Ṛgveda* is the upper limit of the whole of Vedic literature and any conclusion about the date of the rest of the Vedic literature depends upon the fixing of the date of *Ṛgveda*. Unfortunately the date of *Ṛgveda* is the most vexed problem in the history of Indian literature. Some theories on this problem are, however, advanced by different scholars, western and Indian. A brief account of those theories is given here.

The theories on the date of *Ṛgveda* mainly fall into two categories as : (i) Theories based on literary or linguistic considerations and (ii) Theories based on astronomical calculations. Among the theories based on literary or linguistic considerations, the most famous is that advanced by Max Muller in 1859. He divides the whole of ancient literature into four periods as : (1) Chanda, (2) Mantra, (3) Brāhmaṇa and (4) Sūtra, assuming that each succeeding period pre-supposes each preceding phase. Two writers of the Anukramaṇis Śaunaka and Kātyāyana, are prominent in the last period, i.e., the Sūtra period.

Sadguruśiṣya, in his commentary on Kātyāyani's Anukramaṇi, refers to four generations of teachers in order as: (i) Śaunaka, (ii) Āśvalāyana, (iii) Kātyāyana and (iv) Patañjali. Kātyāyana is identified with Vararuci, who is spoken by Somadeva in his Kathāsaritsāgara as having become a minister under Nanda at Pātalīputra. Nanda was dethroned by Chandragupta Maurya, whose rule was between 321 and 297 B.C. Thus Kātyāyana's date is about 355 B.C. On this basis it can be decided that Āśvilāyana belonged to 359 B.C. and Śaunaka to 490 B.C. Hence Sūtra period extended backwards from 200 B.C. to 600 B.C. This conclusion can be further confirmed by the considerations of language and style. Sūtras presuppose the Brāhmaṇas. The period of Brāhmaṇas extended backwards from 600 B.C. to 800 B.C. This was preceded by the age of collecting classifying and imitating. This was the Mantra period extending from 800 B.C. to 1000 B.C. backwards. This was preceded by the Chandas period, the age of the Ṛṣis, characterised by spontaneity and originality. The Chandas period extended backwards from 1000 B.C. to 1200 B.C. The Ṛgveda belonged to the beginning of this period, i.e., to 1200 B.C.

Max Muller's theory has many weak-points. Firstly, it is based upon some assumptions which have yet to be conclusively proved. For instance, the identity of Vedic Kātyāyana with the grammarian Kātyāyana and historicity of Somedeva's statement have yet to be conclusively decided. Secondly, there is not sufficient reason why 200 years in particular should be assigned to each of the periods. 500 or 1000 years could as well be assigned. Assigning 200 years to each of these periods. Max Muller does not seem to have taken into account the inadequacy of that time for the evolution of language between one period and the other. It is somewhat abitrary to prescribe to a language the rate at which it may change or must have changed. Hence, this theory has now been rejected by most of the scholars.[26] Whitney proceeding more or less on the same lines on the basis of the evolution of language, assigns the Ṛgveda to 2000-1500 B.C. Since the very attempt to measure the language of the Veda by a standard approximating to that of modern living languages is basically defective, theories based on linguistic considerations can be rejected forthwith.

Among the theories based on astronomical calculations, three are very important. First theory of this category is that of Haug. On the ground of the passage in the Vedaṅga Jyotiṣa referring to the position of the solstitial (aynānta) points, Haug determines the age of the Saṁhitā as 2000-1400 B.C. the oldest hymns being fixed between 2400-2000 B.c.

Balagangadhar Tilak has proved even a greater antiquity for the hymns of the Ṛgveda. He has tried to show that "the traditions recorded in the Ṛgveda unmistakably point to a period not later than 4000 B.C., when the Vernal equinox (Mahāviṣuva or Meāṣarāṣi) was in Orion Mṛgaśirṣa constellation or in other words, when the Dog-star (Kukkurasaṁjñā tārā yasyāmuditāyām atyuṣṇakālo bhavati) or Dog as we have it in the Ṛgveda, commenced the equinotical (viṣuvīya) year. Thus during Ṛgveda period the spring equino coincided with Mṛgaśiras (Orion). Later at the time of the Brāhmaṇas, the Kṛttikās (Pleiades), which then were at the beginning of the Nakṣatras, coincided with the spring equinox. This change in the occurrence of the equinox (from the Kṛttikās to the Mṛgaśiras) requires a period of about 2000 years. At about 2500 B.C. the equinox coincided with the Kṛttikās. Hence the occurrence of the equinox in the Mṛgaśiras must have been by about 4500 B.C. This was the period of the Ṛgveda, which could have extended, according to Tilak, as far back as 6000 B.C.

Jacobi's is the third theory based on astronomical calculations. His astronmical calculations are connected with the change in the beginning of seasons which has taken place since the time of the Ṛgveda. The period according to his calculations goes back to 4500 B.C. This was the age of the Ṛgveda.[27]

These theories on the date of the Ṛgveda have their merit in showing the complexity of the problem and the perseverence of the scholars to unravel the mystery about the problem. The theories based on astronomical calculations are commendable for their exactness based on the available data and the interpretation of the basic material of their enquiry. Taking the substance of all the theories together, it may be observed that the lower chronological limit of Vedic literature cannot be lower than 800 B.C. and that the upper limit, which should coincide with the period of the Ṛgveda, can be as unsettled as it was before the attempts were made by the scholars to settle it. This upper limit cannot, however, be pushed lower than 1200 B.C. This is more probably to be sought in the direction shown by the astronomical theories of Tilak and Jacobi.

2.4 Contents of the Ṛgveda

The majority of the hymns of Ṛgveda are concerned with the worship of gods or deified objects. Some hymns contain secular matter such as marriage and funeral customs, literary pursuits and past-time of the ancient people. A few hymns contain cosmogonic and philosophical content. Thus the entire bulk of the contents of the Ṛgveda can be broadly classified into three main groups as - (i) Religious hymns, (ii) Secular hymns and (iii) Cosmogonic and Philosophical hymns.

i) The religious hymns form the majority. They are concerned with the worship of gods. These hymns are invocations to gods and are intended to accompany the oblation of Soma juice or ghee. Almost all of these are connected with some sacrificial rite or the other, as noted by the Anukramaṇis giving their 'viniygoa'. All of them have one characteristic common to them in as much as they end with a prayer to gods to grant wealth in the form of cows, material prosperity heroic sons and full life of hundred years. The fact that various gods are invoked and worshipped shows a polytheistic basis of Ṛgvedic religion. Yet some of the hymns with monotheistic content are apt to prove that the Ṛgvedic Aryans had faith in one Supreme God and that they worshipped the various gods not in their individual capacity, but as the different aspects of the powers of that Supreme God.

ii) The term secular hymns is applied to a small number of hymns (about thirty to thirty-five) dealing with secular matters such as marriage and funeral practices, literary pursuits, sports and past-time of the ancient people. The most famous wedding hymn, the long Sūryasūkta (X.85), reveals the marriage ceremonial in loosely strung groups of stanzas. There are in all five funeral hymns (X.14-18), four of which are addressed to deities concerned with future life, while the last gives information about the funeral customs of ancient times. They reveal that burial as well as cremation were then practised and that widow-marriage was in vogue. There are some dialogue hymns[28] such as Purūravās and Ūrvaśi (X-95), Yama and Yami (X.10), Viśvāmitra and Rivers (III.33). This group of hymns has a special literary interest as the pre-cursors of Sanskrit drama on the one hand and epic poetry on the other. Besides some hymns are of a didactic character. One of these is the famous Akṣasukta (X.34) which presents the monologue of a gambler lamenting the misery he has brought on himself and his family on account of his attraction for dice. The hymn IX.112 describes the various ways in which men seen gain. X.71 praises wise speech and X.117 praises the value of good deeds. These fore-shadow the sentenious poetry in Classical Sanskrit Two of the hymns contain riddles. One of these (VIII.29) portrays the gods without mentioning their names. The famous Asyavāmīyasūkta (I.164), which is a lengthy (52 stanzas) philosophical hymn, contains a number of enigmas. There are panegyrics of liberal patrons yielding geneological information about poets, patrons names and habitat of Vedic tribes. These have semi-historical significance.

iii) Comsogonic and Philosophical hymns are about half a dozen in the Ṛgveda. Two principal topics of these hymns are: (a) speculations about the origin of the world and (b) pantheistic idea of universal soul. The sepculations are mixed up with mythological and theological ideas. The beginning of philosophical thinking can be traced to the doubts about the existence and power of gods expressed in some hymns addressed to different deities. Quite early, for instance, were doubts expressed about Indra's existence.[29] Same scruples are expressed as regards the plurality of gods.[30] The philosophical ideas are found in those hymns which are also cosmogonic in content. Most of the cosmogonic hymns express the older view that gods, various individual deities generated the world Heaven and Earth (Dyāvā-Pṛthivī) are spoken as the parents of gods and paradoxically Indra is said to have begotten his parents from his own body.[31] This is an idea of 'reciprocal generation.' Further speculation led the seers to the conception of a creator apart from any of the principal deities. Thus the creator is called Puruṣa, Viśvakarman, Hiraṇyagarbha or Prajāpati. The Puruṣasūkta (X.90) gives a conception of principal Puruṣa who was offered as oblation in the sacrifice and the different objects and being originated from the different parts of his body.[32] There is a pantheistic idea that puruṣa is all this (universe), what was before and what would follow.[33] In the two hymns addressed to Viśvakarman (X.81-82), some interesting questions are asked about what existed before creation and what was the matter out of which the world was fashionded.[34] In the sukta X.121, Prajāpati is praised as the creator and preserver. The conception of Hiraṇyagarbha (the Golden Egg) is found in the first stanza of this hymn.[35] X.72 presents a view that 'sat' was born from 'asat' (the manifest from the unmanifest).[36] The famous Nāsadīyasūkta (X.129) which is truly philosophical in spirit, commences with the statement that neither 'asat' nor 'sat' existed before creation.[37] It speaks of 'One' which was breathing without wind. Kāma (desire to create) arose in the 'One' as the first seed of his mind.[38] Then there was creation. This conception of 'Ekam' has close affinity with the Upaniṣadic Brahman. The general tone of faith in one Supreme Being is expressed in the famous Asyāvāmīyasūkta that 'sat'is one and the wise call it by different names.[39]

2.5 Commentators on the Ṛgveda

Skandaswāmi

The oldest commentary on the Rgveda is of Skandaswāmin. In the colophon at the end of *Ṛgvedabhāśya* of each *Adhyāya*, he informs that his native place was Vallabhī and the son of Bhartrdhruva.[40] Most of scholars identify Vallabhī as a town in North Gujarat. Hariswāmi, in his commentary on *Śatapatha Brāhmaṇa* states that Skandaswāmi was a his teacher.[41] Most of the scholars opine that Hariswāmi's date to be 639 A.D. So, Skandaswāmi may be said to have lived in the beginning of the seventh century A.D.

According to Skandaswāmi, the knowledge of *Ṛṣi* and *Devatā* is very necessary for the understanding of *mantras*. He does not take the metre as necessary in understanding the meaning of a *mantra*. In the beginning of each hymn, he mentions the *Ṛṣi* and *Devatā* thereof, and substantiates by quoting the statements. In his commentary, he has followed the *Yājñikas method* of interpretation. Hence his commentary may be called *Adhiyajñaparāka*. He has also followed the path of the *Nairuktas* in the interpretation of certain *mantras*. Hence his commentary at times, has become *Adhidaivataparāka*. Skandaswāmi has frequently quoted the passages from the *Brahmaṇas* and the *Āraṇyakas* in support of his interpretation. But unfortunately his commentary is not available in its entirety. Only some portions dealing with *Ṛgveda* I-1-1 to I-56-1; I-62-1 to I-121-15 and V-57-1 to VI-75-6 are available.

Nārāyaṇa and Udgītha

Nārāyaṇa and Udgīta were contemporaries of Skandaswāmi. Nārāyaṇa had commented on the sixth and seventh *Aṣṭaka*, while Udgītha on the remaining eighth *Aṣṭaka*. But Nārāyaṇa's commentary is not available. Only some portions of Udgītha's commentary on *Ṛgveda* X-5-4 to X-12-5, X-13-2 to X-52-3 and X-62-9 to X-83-6 are available. The available portions of the Udgītha's commentary are similar in the treatment of subject matter to that of Skandaswāmi.

Mādhava Bhaṭṭa

The personality of Mādhava Bhaṭṭa is much controversial. Some identify him with Veṅkaṭa Mādhava, from the fact that Veṅkaṭa Mādhava mentions Mādhava Bhaṭṭa as a commentator and places him before Skandaswāmi; so it may be presumed that he preceded Skandaswāmi, though the latter has not mentioned the name of former. From the colophons of his commentary, ग्रामे जातो गोमति व्याचषर ।[42] it is evident that he was an inhabitant of the village Gomān on the south bank of the river Kāveri in the Choḷa country in Dakṣinapatha. His commentary is very brief and therein passages from the *Nighanṭu*, the *Nirukta* and the *Brāhmaṇas* are quoted. His commentary is not available in its entirety. Only some portions of it have been published.

Veṅkaṭa Mādhava

The first writer who has given a complete commentary on the *Ṛgveda*, is Veṅkaṭa Madhava. He lived during tenth century A.D. In the colophons of his commentary, he has given enough information about himself. His father is Veṅkaṭārya and mother Sundarī. His grand-father is Mādhava. He belongs to the gotra *Kauśika*. He claims his commentary to be very brief and concise. In his commentary he has followed *Aṣṭaka* division. According to him, the meanings of the *mantras* is not clear, and they can only be explained the Brāhmaic lore. He, who is well-versed in the *Nirukta* and *Vyākaraṇa*, knows only one-fourth of the *Ṛgveda*. Besides his commentary too, may be regarded as Adhiyajṅaparāka.

Ānanda Tīrtha

Ānanda Tīrtha alias Mādhvācarya, who flourished during 12th cent. A.D. and founder of the *Dvaita* school of *Vedānta*, has interpreted first forty hymns of the *Ṛgveda*. According to him, the main god whom the *mantras* vividly describe, is Nārāyaṇa. Thus his commentary may be called *Nārāyaṇaparāka* or *Bhagavatparāka*.

Ātmānanda

He has interpreted only one *sūkta,* viz., *Asyavāmīya sūkta*. Due to his being a follower of Śaṅkara, his commentary is greatly influended by *Advaita* philosophy. He claims his commentary be called *Ādhyatmaparāka*. His commentary refers to some commentators of the *Ṛgveda*, whose commentaries are not available.

Sāyaṇa

Sāyaṇācārya occupies a unique place in the history of Sanskrit literature. Sāyaṇā's works that have come down to us, are the most important repositories of Vedic lore. This great scholar of academic affairs was simultaneously a great man of letters, a very rare combination even among the ancients.

Sāyaṇā was born in a learned South Indian Brāhmaṇa family. His father was Māyaṇa and his mother Srīmatī. His '*Gōtra*' was '*Bhāradvāja*' *Sūtra Baudhāyana*. He belonged to the *Taittirīya Śākha* of the *Kṛṣṇa Yajurveda*.

Sāyaṇa had two brothers, Mādhavācārya and Bhoganātha. Mādhavācārya was the eldest one and Bhoganātha, the youngest.

Mādhavācārya says that his mother was Srīmatī, his father was the famous Māyaṇa and his two uterine brothers were Sāyaṇa and Bhoganātha (who appeared to be) his mind and intelligence.[43]

Mādhavācārya is known as 'Vidyāraṇya' bearing the burden of sovereignty of Vijayanagara kingdom and as one of the greatest commentators also. When Mādhavācārya was the minister of Hrihara-I and Bukka-I to begin with, his younger brother Sāyaṇa held the high post of chief minister of Kampaṇa who ruled over the Telagu region of the Nellore district. Sāyaṇa continued ruling Nellore as late as the year 1364-65 A.D.; for an inscription of his date at the city of Nellore still states that "*Śriman Māhāmaṇḍaleśvara Vīra Śri Sāyaṇṇa Odayalu was ruling the earth.*"[44] During the period of twelve years from 1364 to 1376 A.D. was the highest position of his political life. Sāyaṇa was the minister of four Vijayanagar kings namely Bukka-I, Kampaṇa, Saṅgama II and Harihara-II. This is made evident in the colophons of his works. Thus in some of commentaries on the Vedas, he styles himself the minister of Bukka-I.[45] In his Subhasita-Sudhanidhi he calls himself the minister of Kamparaja.[46] In his *Dhātuvṛtti*[47] and *Alaṅkāra-Sudhānidhi*, he was the minister of Saṅgama II. In his commentaries on the Satapatha, Tattiriya Brahmanas[48] he calls himself the minister of Harihara-II.

Sāyaṇa's *Vedārtha Prakāśa*, a commentary on the *Ṛgveda*, contains a very scholarly introduction. In this commentary, he has explained each and every word of text. He has pointed out all grammatical and accentual pecularities, giving etymologies of difficult and new words. And at the same time he explains liturgical application of each and every *mantra*. At the beginning of each *sūkta,* before commencing to explain the actual text, he mentions the name of the sacrifice, or the offering at which the *sūkta* or its *mantras* are to be recited. He regards the knowledge of deity and metre as necessary appendage to the understanding of the true sense of the *mantras*. He frequently refers to the passages from the *Sarvānukramaṇi* and the *Bṛhaddevatā* in support of his view. Passages from the *Brāhmaṇas* and the *Āraṇyakas* are also found quoted frequently. He explains the Vedic myths in the light of Purāṇic ideas by which he was very much influenced.

References

1. अथ ऋषयः । शतार्चिनो मध्यमा गृतत्समदो विश्वामित्रो वामदेवोऽत्रिर्भरद्वाजा वसिष्ठः प्रगाथाः पावमान्याः क्षुद्रसूक्ता महासूक्ता इति ।। *Aśvalāyana Gṛhyasūtra,* III-3-3, Ed. K.P.Aithal, the Adyar Library, Madras, 1980,
2. *Tattirīya Āraṇyaka*, I-23
3. M. Bloomfield, *Sacred Books of the East,* Motilal Banarasidass, Delhi, 1884, Vol.42, p.xiii.
4. परोक्ष कामा हि देवाः। *Śatapatha Brāhmaṇa*, NI-1-1-2

   परोक्षप्रिया इव हि देवा भवन्ति प्रत्यक्षा दिशः । *Gopatha Brāhmaṇa*, I-2-21
5. Max Muller, *The Vedas,* Calcutta, 1956, p.49

   ज्ञातेष्वपि पदार्थेषु वाक्यार्थपरिकल्पनम्, अशक्यम् ऋक्सु बह्वीषु-नरैरकृतबुद्धिभिः । Yāska XI.3
6. अनर्थका हि मन्त्राः । Yāska, *Nirukta,* I-15
7. तत्रैतद् यज्ञिका वेदयन्ते । Yāska, *Nirukta,* V-11

   अथान्यत्र यज्ञात्प्राजापत्या इति याज्ञिकाः । *Ibid.,* VII-4

   VII-23; XI-29, 31; XIII-9 etc.
8. वर्षकार्मेति नैरुक्ताः । *Ibid.,* II-8

   प्राश्नुत एनं वर्ण इति नौरुक्ताः । *Ibid.,* I-14

   I-12; II-16; III-8,4, etc.
9. त्वष्ट्रोऽसुर इत्यैतिहासिकाः । *Ibid.,* I-16

   राजानौ पुण्यकृतावित्यैतिहासिकाः। *Ibid.,* XII-1

10. बहुप्रजाः कृच्छ्रमापद्यत इति परिव्राजकाः। *Ibid.*, II-9

11. स्याल आसन्नः संयोगेनेति नैदानाः । *Ibid.*, VI-9
ऋचा समं मेन इति नैदानाः । *Ibid.*, VII-12 etc.

12. Ramagopal, *The History and Principles of the Vedic Interpretation.* Concept Publishing Company, New Delhi, 1983, p.37

13. तदिदं विद्यास्थानं व्याकारणस्य कात्स्र्य स्वार्थसाधकां च । Yāska, *Nirukta,* I-15

14. परः सन्निकर्षः संहिता । पदप्रकृतिः संहिता । पदप्रकृतीति सर्वचरणानां पार्षदानि । Yāska, *Nirukta,* I-17

15. वन इव । वायो वेः पुत्रः । चायन्निति वा । कामयमान इति वा । चेति च य इति च चकार शाषल्यः । उदात्तं त्वेवमाख्यातमभविष्यम्। असुसमाप्तश्चार्थः। रथर्यतीति सिद्धस्तत्प्रेप्सुः । रथं कामयत इति वा । एष देवो रथर्यति । इत्यपि निगमो भवति । *Ibid.*, VI-28

16. बहुप्रजाः कृच्छ्रमापद्यत इति परिव्राजकाः । Yāska, *Nirukta,* II-8

17. *Ṛgveda,* X-72;82;90;121;129 etc., I-20
Atharva Veda, XIII and XV etc.
Vājasaneyī Saṁhitā, XXXI; XXXII-1-12; XXXIV-1-6, etc.

18. *Tattirīya Saṁhitā,* V-3-4,2 ; *Tattirīya Brāhmaṇa*, III-3-6-9; *Pañcaviṁśa Brāhmaṇa*, VI-10-5; IX-8-16; *Śatapatha Brāhmaṇa*, VIII-4-2-6, etc.,

19. वाग्वाऽनुष्टुन्वागिन्द्रऽइन्द्रो लोकम्पृणा न साधयन्यसन्नो । Yāska, *Nirukta,* I-20
सर्व तस्मादाहुरिन्द्रो वागिति । Ibid, XI-1-6-18

20. एषऽएवेन्द्रस्थानेष प्रणान्मध्यतऽइन्द्रियेणैन्द्ध यदैन्द्ध तस्मादिन्धऽइन्धौ हवै तमिन्द्रऽइत्याचक्षते परोक्षं परोक्षकामा हिदेवास्तऽइछद्दाः सप्त नाना पुरुषानसृजन्त। *Ibid.*, VII-1-1-2; XII-9-1-14;XIV-4-3-19 etc.

21. मनवेऽएवेन्द्रः । *Ibid.*, XII-9-1-13

22. शुक्रो य एष तपत्येष (सूर्य) ऽउऽएवेन्द्रः पुरुषो। *Śatapatha Brāhmaṇa*, IV-5-5-7

23. यो वै वायुः स इन्द्रो य इन्द्रः स वायुः । *Ibid.*, IV-1-3-19; XIV 2-2-6 etc.

24. अथापि ब्रह्मणं भवति ।

    अग्निर्वा इतो वृष्टिं समीरयति धामच्छदिवा खलु वै भूत्वा वर्षति मरुतः सृष्टां वृष्टिं नयन्ति। यदा (खलुवै) आसवाइदित्योऽग्नि रश्मिभिः पर्यावर्ततेऽथ वर्षति इति ।

    यथो एतद्रोहात् प्रत्यवरोश्चिकीर्षत इत्याम्नायवचनादेतद् भवति । यथो एतदश्वनारीयो द्वादश कपाले भवतीत्यनिर्वचनं कपालानि भवन्ति । अस्ति हि सौर्य एक कपालः पञ्चकपालश्च। यथो एतद् ब्राह्मणे भवतीति बहुभक्तिवादीनि ब्राह्मणानि भवन्ति । पृथिवी वैश्वानरः । संवत्सरो वैश्वानरः। ब्रैह्मणो वैश्वानरः । इति ।। Yāska, *Nirukta,* VII-24

25. Durgacarya explains Itihasa as based on Naidana (a story explaining the primary cause of composition of a Vedic hymn)

    नैदानभूत इति हैवम् आसीदिति य उच्यते स इतिहासः। Durga on *Nirukta*, II-10

    तत्र इमं निदानभूतम् इतिहासम् आचक्षते इति आचार्याः । *Ibid.*, II-24

26. A. A. Macdonell has accepted it; vide his *Vedic Reader*, p. XII

27. For other views, one based on the discovery of the clay tablets at Boghazkoi in Asia Minor and the other expressed by Dr. R. G. Bhandarkar on the basis of Asura-Assyria identification, vide Peterson's 'Hymns from the *Ṛgveda*' (1922) .

28. H. Oldenberg calls them 'Ākhyāna hymns', the oldest form of epic poetry; Max Muller and Sylvan Levi consider them as 'Ritual dramas' John Hertel ans Schroede as 'Speeches of dramatic performance'; Winternitz as 'Ancient ballads', sources of both epic and drama. His. of Ind. Lit.: Winternitz, Vol.I, pp.100-102.

29. II. 12.5 - उतेमाहुर्नैषो अस्तीत्येनम्; also in VIII. 100. 3-4

30. X. 121 - कस्मै देयाय हविषा विधेम ।

31. X. 54.3 - यन्मातरं पितरं च साकमजनयथा तन्व स्वायाः ।

32. X. 90.6,10,12 and 13

33. X. 90.2 - पुरुष एवेदं सर्व यद्भतं यच्च भव्यम् ।

34. X. 81.2,3,4; X. 82.4,7

35. X.121.1 - हिरण्यगर्भः समवर्तताग्रे भूतस्य जातः पतिरेष आसीत् ।

36. X.72.2 - देवानां पूर्व्ये युगेऽसतः सदजायत ।

37. X.129.1 - नासदासीन्नो सदासीत्तदानीम् ।

38. X.129.4 - कामस्तदग्रे समवर्तदाधि .... मनसो रेतः प्रथमं यदासीत् ।

39. I.164.46 - एकं सद् विप्रा बगुधा वदन्ति ।

40. वल्लभीविनिवास्येताम्गर्थागम संगितम् ।
भर्तृ ध्रुवसुतश्चक्रे स्कन्दस्वामी यथास्मृतिः ॥
Skandaswāmi, Colophon at the end of each Adhyāya
Ed.D.Kunhan Raja, University of Madras, 1935.

41. तन्नन्दनो हरिस्वामि प्रस्पुरद्वेदवेदिमान् ।
त्रयीव्याख्यानधौरेयोऽधीततन्त्रो गुरोर्मुसत् ॥
यः साम्राज्ञे कृतवान् सप्तसोमसंस्थास्थतथक्कुतिम् ।
व्याख्यां कृत्वाद्यापयन्मा श्रीस्कन्दस्वाम्यस्ति मे गुरुः ॥
Hariswami, Q. *Treatment of Nature in the Ṛgveda,* Dr. Braj Bihari Chaubey, Vedic Sāhitya Sadan, Hoshiarpur. 1970, p.15

42. Mādhava Bhaṭṭa, *Ṛgvedavyākhyā*, Colophon at the end of the Aṣṭka I, Adhyāya 2, ed.C.Kunhan Raja, Adyar Library, 1937

43. श्रीमती जननी यस्य सुषीतिर्मायणः पिता ।
सायणो भोगनाथश्च मनोबुद्धि सगेदरौ ॥
यस्य बोधायनं सूत्रं शास यस्य च याजुषी ।
भारद्वाजं षुलं जन्म सर्वज्ञः स हि माधवः ॥

Parāśarasmṛti, Vyākyā, Prasthāvana, VV-6-7

Cp. Dr. K. Krishnamurthy, Sāyaṇa's *Subhāṣita-Sudhānidhi,* Karnatak University, Dharwad, 1968. Introduction p.2

44. Translation from Telagu : Hail, on Friday the 5th of the dark fortnight of Mārgaśīra of the year Krodhi Correspondent to the year 1286 of the illustrious Śaka era, while Śriman Mahāmaṇḍaleśvara Vīra Śri Sāyaṇṇa (it may be Sāyaṇa) odayalu was rolling the earth, the people of all countries came to agreement in connection with the Friday market established by Kanchaṇṇagaru un Nellore.

45. इत्थं श्रीबुक्क भूपालसाम्राज्यैक धुरन्धरः ।
विद्यातीर्थ गुरोर्द्दृष्ट्या प्राप्तसार्वज्ञयवैभवः ।।
श्रीमत्सायणमन्त्रीशः सकलागम तत्ववित् ।
दाशतय्यां माधवीयो वेदार्थस्य प्रकाशने ।। *Ṛgveda* with Sāyaṇa's commentary- Vaidika Saṁśodhana Maṇḍala, Poona, 1976, Vol.II, p.718

46. मतिमास्तस्य राज्ञो भूत् मन्त्री मायणसायणः ।
यन्मन्त्रेण न सर्पन्ति नित्यं शत्रुविलेषयाः ।।

Dr. K. Krishnamurty, Introduction to *Subhāṣita-Sudhānidhi*, p.4

47. तेन मायणपुत्रेण सायणेन मनीषिणा ।
आख्यय माधवीयेयं धातुवृत्तिर्विरच्यते ।
इति पूर्वपश्चिम समुद्राधीश्वर कम्पराजसुत संगम महाराज–महामन्त्रिणा मायणसुतेन माधवसहोदरेण सायणाचार्येण विरचितायां माधवीयायां धातुवतत्तौ।।

Beginning and Colophon of *Dhātuvṛtti*, Ed. A. Mahadeva Shastry and K. Rangacārya, Govt. of Oriental library, Series Bibliotheca Saṁskrita, No.23

48. इति श्रीमद्राजाधिराज परमेश्वर वैदिकमार्ग प्रवर्तक श्री वीर हरिहर भूपाल साम्राज्यधुरन्धर सायणाचार्यविरचिते माधवीये वेदार्थप्रषाशे कृष्णयजुर्वेदीय तैत्तीरीय ब्राह्मण भाष्ये तृतीयः काण्डः समाप्तः ।।

Chapter - III

Features of Ṛgvedic Gods

3.1 Introduction

Indefiniteness of outline and lack of individuality characterize the Vedic conception of the gods. This is mainly due to the fact that they are nearer to the physical phenomena which they represent, than the gods of any other Indo-European people. Thus the ancient Vedic interpreter Yāska (Nir.7.4) speaking of the nature of the gods, remarks that what is seen of them is not anthropomorphic at all, as in the case of the Sun, the Earth and others. The natural bases of the Vedic gods have to begin with, but few specific characteristics, while they share some of the attributes of other phenomena belonging to the same domain. Thus Dawn, Sun, Fire have the common features of being luminous, dispelling darkness, appearing in the morning. The absence of distinctiveness must be still greater when several deities have sprung from different aspects of one and the same phenomenon. Hence the character of each Vedic god is made up of only a few essential traits combined with a number of other features common to all the gods, such as brilliance, power, beneficence, and wisdom.

Such common features tend to obscure what is essential, because in hymns of prayer and praise they naturally assume special prominence. Again, gods belonging to different departments, but having prominent functions in common, are apt to be approximated. Thus Agni, primarily the god of terrestrial fire, dispels the demons of darkness with his light, while Indra, the aerial god of the thunderstorm, slays them with his lightning. Into the conception of the fire-god further enters his aspect as lightning in the atmosphere. The assimilation is increased by such gods often being invoked in pairs.

These combinations result in attributes peculiar to the one god attaching theselves to the other, even when the latter appears alone. Thus Agni comes to be called Soma-drinker, Vṛtra-slayer, winner of cows and waters, sun and dawns, attributes all primarily belonging to Indra.

In the older parts of the *Ṛgveda,* individual gods are often invoked as the highest, but this notion is not carried out to its logical conclusion. The fact that the Vedic poets frequently seem to be engrossed in the praise of the particular deity they happens to be invoking, that they exaggerate his attributes to the point of inconsistency, has given rise to the much discussed theory. According to this theory, 'the belief in individual gods alternately regarded as the highest,' the Vedic poets attribute to the god they happen to be addressing all the highest traits of divinity, treating him for the moment as if he were an absolutely independent and supreme deity, alone present to the mind. Against this theory it has been urged that Vedic deities are not represented 'as independent of all the rest,' since no religion brings its gods into more frequent and varied justaposition and combination, and that even the mightiest gods of the Veda are made dependent on others. Thus Varuṇa and Sūrya are subordinate to Indra (1, 101.3), Varuṇa and the Aśvins submit to the power of Viśṇu (1,156.4), and Indra, Mitra-Varuṇa, Aryaman, Rudra cannot resist the ordinances of

Savitṛ (2,38.9). It has been further pointed out that in the frequent hymns addressed to the *viśvedevāh*, or All-gods, all the deities, even the lesser ones, are praised in succession, and that as the great mass of the Vedic hymns was composed for the riutal of the Soma offering, which included the worship of almost the entire pantheon, the technical priest could not but know the exact relative position of each god in that ritual. Even when a god is spoken of as unique or chief (*eka*), as is natural enough in laudations, such statements rose their temporarily monotheistic force through the modifications or collections supplied by the context or even by the same verse. Thus a poet says that 'Agni alone, like Varuṇa, is lord of Wealth.' It should also be remembered that gods are constantly invoked in pairs, triads, and larger groups, even the exalted Varuṇa being mostly addressed in conjuction with one other god or with several other gods.

The Vedic gods, had a beginning in the view of the Vedic poets, since they are described as the offspring of heaven and earth or sometimes of other gods. This is itself implies different generations of gods, but earlier (*pūrve*) gods are also expressly referred to in several passages (7,21.7 &c). An earlier or first age of the gods is also spoken of (10, 72.2.3). The AV (11.8.10) speaks of ten gods as having existed before the rest. The gods, too, were originally mortal. This is expressly stated in the AV (11, 5.19; 4, 11.6) The *Brāhmaṇas* state this both of all the gods (SB.10, 4, 3.3) and of the individual gods Indra (AB.8, 14.4), Agni (AB. 3,4) and Prajāpati (SB.10, 1, 3.2). That they were originally not immortal is implied in the RV. For immortality was bestowed on them by Savitr (4, 54.2 VS. 33,54) or by Agni (6,7.4; AV. 4, 23.6). They are also said to have obtained it by drinking Soma (9, 106.8 cp. 109.2.3), which is called the principle of immortality (SB.9,5,1.8). In another passage of the RV (10. 53.10) they are said to have acquired immortality, but by what means is not clear. According to a later conception Indra is stated to have conquered heaven by *tapas* or austerity (10.167.2). The gods are said to have attained divine rank by the same means (TB. 3, 12, 3.1) or to have overcome death by continence and austerity (AV. 11, 5.19) and to have acquired immortality through Rohita (AV. 13, 1.7). Elsewhere the gods are stated to have overcome death by the performance of a certain ceremony (TS. 7, 4, 2.1). Indra and several other gods are said to be unaging (3, 46.2 & c), but whether the immortality of the gods was regarded by the Vedic poets as absolute, there is no evidence to show. According to the post-Vedic view their immortality was only relative, being limited to a cosmic age.

The physical appearance of the gods is anthropomorphic, though only is a shadowy manner; for it often represent only aspects of their natural bases figuratively described to illustrate their activities. Thus head, face, mouth, cheeks, eyes, hair, shoulders, breast, belly, arms, hands, fingers, feet are attributed to various individual gods. Head, breast, arms and hands are chiefly mentioned in connection with the warlike equipment of Indra and the Maruts. The arms of the sun are simply his rays, and his eye is intended to represent his physical aspect. The tongue and limbs of Agni merely denote his flames. The fingers of Trita are referred to only in order to illustrate his character as a preparer of Soma, and the belly of Indra only to emphasize his powers of drinking Soma. Two or three gods are spoken of as having or assuming all forms (*viśvarūpa*). It is easy to understand that in the case of deities whose outward shape was so vaguely conceived and whose connection with natural phenomena was in many instances still clear, no mention of either images or temples is found in the RV.

Some of the gods are spoken of as wearing garments. Thus Dawn is described as decked in gay attire. Some of the gods are equipped with armour in the shape of coats of mail or helmets. Indra is regularly armed with a bolt (*vajra*), while to others spears, battle-axes, bows and arrows are assigned. The gods in general are described as driving luminous cars, nearly every individual deity being also said to possess one. The car is usually drawn by steeds, but in the case of Pūṣan by goats, of the Maruts perhaps by spotted deer as well as horses, and of Uṣas, by cows as well as horses.

In their cars, the gods are frequently represented as coming to seat themselves on the layer of strewn grass at the sacrifice, which, however, from another point of view, is supposed also to be conveyed to them in heaven by Agni ($ 35). The beverage of the gods is Soma. What they eat is the favourite food of men and is of course represented by what is offered to them at the sacrifice. It consists of milk in its various forms, butter, barley and (though perhaps not in the oldest Vedic period) rice; cattle, goats and sheep, with a preference for the animal which in some way is most closely connected with a deity's peculiar qualities. Thus the bull or the buffalo, to which Indra is so often compared, is offered to him and eaten by him, sometimes in extraordinary numbers. Analogously, Indra's steeds are supposed to eat grain. The 'abode of the gods in variously described as heaven, the third heave, or the highest step of Viṣṇu, where they live a joyous life exhilerated by Soma. The gods on the whole are conceived as dwelling together in harmony and friendship. The only one who ever introduces a note of discord is the warlike and overbearing Indra. He once appears to have fought against the gods in general; he slew his own father and shattered the car of Dawn. He seems also to have threatened to one occasion to slay his faithful companions the Maruts.

The gods representing the chief powers of nature, such as fire, sun, thunderstorm, appeared to the successful and therefore optimistic Vedic Indian as almost exclusively beneficent beings, bestowers of prosperity. The only deity in whom injurious features are at all prominent is Rudra. Evils closely connected with human life, such as disease, proceed from lesser demons, while the greater evils manifested in nature, such as drought and darkness, are produced by powerful demons like Vṛtra. The conquest of these demons brings out the beneficent nature of the gods all the more prominently. The benevolence of the gods resembles that of human beings. They are preeminently the receives of sacrifice, the hymns to them being recited while the Soma is pressed, the offering is cast in the fire, and priests attend to the intricate details of the ritual. They are therefore the friends of the sacrifice, but are angry with and punish the niggard. This is expecially the case with Indra, who at the same time is not altogether free from arbitrariness in the distribution of his favours.

The character of the Vedic gods is also moral. All the gods are 'true' and 'not deceitful,' being throughout the friends and guardians of honesty and righteousness. It is, however, the Ādityas, especially Varuṇa, who are the chief upholders of the moral law. The gods are angry with the evil-doer, but it is Varuṇa's wrath which is most closely connected with the conception of guilt and sin. Agni also is invoked to free from guilt, but this is only one of many prayers addressed to him, not their chief purport as in the case of Varuṇa. Indra too is a punisher of sin, but this trait is only superficially connected with his character. The standard of divine morality of course reflects only an earlier stage of civilization. Thus even the alliance of Varuna with righteousness is not of such a nature as to prevent him from employing craft against the hostile and deceitful man. But towards the good and pious the faithfulness of Varuṇa is unswerving. Indra, however, is occasionally not above practising deceitful wiles even without the justification of a good end.

Moral elevation does not, however, occupy so high a position as power among the attributes of the Vedic gods. Epithets such as 'true' and 'not deceitful' are far less prominent than such as 'great' and 'mighty'. The gods can do whatever they will. On them depends the fulfullment of wishes. They have deminion over all creatures; and no one can thwart their ordinances or live beyond the time the gods appoint.

Following the triple classification of RV I, 139.11Yāska (Nir. 7, 5) divides the different deities or forms of the same deity enumerated in the fifth chapter of the Naighaṅṭuka, into the three orders of *prthivīsthāna,* terrestrial (Nir. 7.14-9.3) *antariks-ṣasthāna, madhyamasthāna,* aerial or intermediate (10, 1-11. 50), and *dyusthāna,* celestial (12, 1-46). He further remarks that in the opinion of his predecessors who expounded the Veda (*nairuktāh*) there are only three deities, Agni on earth, Vāyu or Indra in air, Sūrya in heaven. (This view may be based on such passages as RV 10, 158.1: 'May Sūrya protect us from heaven, Vāta from air, Agni from the earthly regions'). Each of these he continues has various appellations according to differences of function, just as the same person may act in the capacity of *hotṛ, adhvaryu, brahman, udgātṛ.* Yāska himself does not admit that all the various gods are only forms or manifestations of the three representative deities, though he allows that those forming each of the three orders are allied in sphere and functions. The fifth chapter of the Naighaṅṭuka on which Yāska comments, contains in its enumeration of gods a number of minor deities and detified subjects, so that the total far exceeds eleven in each division. It is worthy or note that in this list of gods the names of Tvastṛ and Pṛthivī appear in all the three spheres, those of Agni and Uṣas in both the terrestrial and the aerial, and those of Varuṇa, Yama and Savitṛ in the aerial as well as the celestial.

An attempt might be made to classify the various Vedic gods according to their relative greatness. Such a division is in a general way alluded to in the RV. where they are spoken of as great and small, young and old (1, 27.13). It is probable that this statement represents the settled view of the Vedic poets as to gradation of rank among the gods. It is only a seeming contradiction when in one passage. It is said with reference to the gods, 'none of you is small or young; you are all great'; for a poet addressing the gods directly on this point could hardly have expressed himself differently. It is certain that two gods tower above the rest as leading deities about equal in power, Indra as the mighty warrior and Varuṇa as the supreme moral ruler.

Next to Indra and Varuṇa come the two great ritual deities Agni and Soma. These two along with Indra are, judged by the frequency of the hymns addressed to them, the three most popular deities of the RV. For, roughly speaking, three-fifths of its hymns are dedicated to their praise. The fact that the hymns to Agni and Indra always come first in the family books, while the great majority of the hymns to Soma have a whole book, the ninth, to themselves, confirms this conclusion. Following the number of the hymns dedicated to each of the remaining deities, combined with the frequency with which their names are mentioned in the RV., five classes of gods may be distinguished; 1) Indra, Agni, Soma; 2) Aśvins, Maruts, Varuṇa; 3) Uṣas, Savitṛ, Bṛhaspati, Sūrya, Pūṣan; 4) Vāyu, Dyāvāpṛthivī, Viṣṇu, Rudra; 5) Yama, Parjanya. The statistical standard can of course be only a partial guide. For Varuṇa is celebrated (mostly together with Mitra) in only about thirty hymns, his name being mentioned altogether about 250 times, while the Aśvins can claim over 50 hymns and are named over 400 times. Yet they cannot be said to approach Varuṇa in greatness. Their relative prominence is doubtless owing to their close connection with the sacrifice as deities of morning light. Again, the importance of the Maruts is due to their association with Indra. Similar considerations would have to enter into an estimate of the relative greatness of other deities in the list. Such an estimate involves considerable difficulties and doubts. A classification according to gradations of rank would therefore not afford a satisfactory basis for an account of the Vedic gods.

Another but still less satisfactory classification, might take as its basis the relative age of the mythological conception, according as it dates from the period of separate national Indian existence, from the Indo-Iranian, or the Indo-European epoch. Thus Bṛhaspati, Rudra, Viṣṇu may be considered the creations of purely Indian mythology; at least there is no adequate evidence to show that they go back to an earlier age. It has already been indicated that a number of mythological figures date from the Indo-Iranian period. But as to whether any of the Vedic gods besides Dyaus may be traced back to the Indo-European period, considerable doubt is justified. A classification according to the age of the mythological creation would therefore rest too uncertain a foundation.

The stage of personification which the various deities represent, might furnish a possible basis of classification. But the task of drawing a clear line of demarcation would involve too many difficulties.

On the whole, the classification of the Vedic deities least open to objection, is that founded on the natural bases which they represent. For though in some cases there may be a doubt as to what the physical substrate really is, and a risk is therefore involved of describing a particular deity in the wrong place, this method offers the advantage of bringing together deities of cognate character and thus facilitating comparison. It has therefore been adopted in the following pages. The various phenomena have been grouped according to the triple division suggested by the RV. itself and adhered to by its oldest commentator.

3.2 Terrestrial Gods (*Prithivisthāna-devatās*)

3.2.1 Agni

Agni: The chief terrestrial deity is Agni, being naturally of primary importance as the personification of the sacrificial fire, which is the centre of the ritual poetry of the Veda. Next to Indra he is the most prominent of the Vedic gods. He is celebrated in at least 200 hymns of the RV., and in several besides he is invoked conjointly with other deities.

As his name is also the regular designation of fire, the anthropomorphism of his physical appearance is only rudimentary, his bodily parts having a clear reference to the phenomena of terrestrial fire mainly in its sacrificial aspect. He is butter-backed (5, 4.3 &c), butter-faced (3, 1.18 &c) and beautiful-tongued (1, 14.7). He is butter-haired (8, 49.2), flame-haired (1, 45.6 &c) or tawny-haired (3, 2.13), and has a tawny beard (5, 7.7). He has sharp (8, 49.3 &c) or burning jaws (1, 58.5 &c), golden (1, 58.5 &c) or shining teeth (5, 7.4) and iron grinders (10, 87.2). He is once described as footless and headless (4, 1.11), but elsewhere he is said to have a burning head (7, 3.1) or three heads and seven rays (1, 146.1; 2, 5.3). He faces in all directions (2, 3.1 &c). His tongue is often mentioned (8, 61.18 &c). He is also said to have three tongues (3, 20.2) or seven (VS. 17, 79), his steeds also being seven-tongued (3, 6.2). A name was later given to each of these seven tongues. Butter is Agni's eye (3, 26.7); he is four-eyed (1, 31.13), thousand-eyed (1, 79.12), and thousand-horned (6, 1.8). In his hand he bears many gifts for men (1, 72.1). Like Indra, he has the epither *sahasra-muṣka* (8, 19.32). He is called an archer (4, 4.2) or is compared with an archer (1, 70.11), who sharpens his flame like a blade of iron (6, 3.5).

He is often likened to various animals, in most cases doubtless with a view to indicating his functions rather than representing his personal form. He is frequently called a bull (1, 58.5 &c). He is a strong bull with a mighty neck (5, 2.12). As such he bellows (10, 8.1), abounds in seed (4, 5.3) and is provided with horns (5, 1.8; 6, 16.39), which he sharpens (8, 49.13), which he shakes, and which make him difficult to seize (i, 140.6). He is many times spoken of or alluded to when born as a calf. (*vatsa*). He is also often compared with (1, 58.2 &c) or directly called a steed (1, 149.3; 6, 12.6). The tail which he agitates like a horse (2, 4.4) is doubtless his flame. When purified by sacrificers he is compared with a groomed horse (1, 60.5 &c). Sacrificers lead (3, 2.7), excite and set him in motion like a horse (7, 7.1. &c). He is the horse they seek to tame and direct (2, 5.1; 3, 27.3). He is kindled like a horse that brings the gods (3, 27.14). He is attached to the pole at places of sacrifice (2, 2.1). or to the pole of the rite (1, 143.7). He is yoked in order to waft the sacrifice to the gods (10, 51.7). He is also compared with (3, 26.3) or directly called a neighing steed (1, 36.8). He is further likened to a horse as conquering (8, 91.12) or causing to escape from dangers (4, 2.8). Agni is, moreover, like a bird. He is the eagle of the sky (7, 15.4) and a divine bird (1, 164.52). As dwelling in the waters he resembles the aquatic bird *haṁsa* (1, 65.9). He takes possession of the wood as a bird perches on a tree (1, 66.2; 6, 3.5; 10, 91.2). He is winged (1, 58.5; 2, 2.4), his course is a flight (6, 3.7, 4.6 &c) and he darts with rapid flight to the gods (10, 6.4). He is once described as a raging serpent (1, 79.1).

Agni is besides frequently compared with inanimate objects. Like the sun, he resembles gold (2, 2.4; 7, 3.6). When he stretches out his tongue (6, 3.4) he is like a hatchet, to which he is elsewhere also several times compared (1, 127.3e &c). He resembles (1, 141.8 &c) or is directly called a car (3, 11.5), as bringing riches (1, 58.3; 3, 15.5) or as being formidable in battle (1, 66.6). He seems to be thought of as a car directed by others, for he is conducted to the sacrifice like a laden car (10, 176.3). He is even compared to wealth (1, 58.6. 60.1) or to wealth acquired by inheritance (1, 73.1).

Wood (2, 7.6) or ghee (7, 3.1) is his food, melted butter is his beverage (2, 7.6; 10, 69.2). He is nourished by ghee poured into his mouth (3, 21.1; 5, 11.3 &c) and is an eater of oil (AV. 1, 7.2). He eats and chews the forests with sharp tooth (1, 143.5) or eats and blackens them with his tongue (6, 60.10; 10, 79.2). He is all-devouring (8, 44.26). He is nourished three times a day (4, 12.1, cp. 1, 140.2; 7, 11.3). He is sometimes spoken of as the mouth and the tongue by which the gods eat the sacrifice (2, 1.14.14) and his flames are spoons with which he besprinkles or honours the gods (1, 76.5; 10, 6.4). But he is more frequently asked to eat the offerings himself (3, 21.1-4, 28.1-6). With upright, god-ward form he strives after the ghee that is offered (1, 127.1). Though the regular offering to him is fuel or butter, he is sometimes, and then nearly always with other gods, invited to drink the Soma juice (1, 14.10, 19.9, 21.1.3; 2, 36.4). In one hymn he is called *somagopā,* 'guardian of Soma' (10, 45.5.12). He is invited to come to the sacrifice (10, 98.9) and is often spoken of as sitting down on the sacrificial grass along with the gods (3, 14.2; 5, 11.2, 26.5; 7, 11.2. cp. 43.3).

Agni's brightness is naturally much dwelt upon. He is of brilliant lustre (2, 10.2 &c), brilliant-flamed (6, 10.3), bright-flamed (7. 15.10 &c), clear-flamed (8, 43.31) and bright-coloured (1, 140.1; 5, 2.3). He has a golden form (4, 3.1, 10, 20.9). He shines like the sun (1, 149.3; 7, 3.6). His lusture is like the rays of the dawn and the sun and like the lightnings of the rain-cloud (10, 91.4.5). He shines even at night (5, 7.4). Like the sun he dispels the darkness with his rays (8, 43.32). He is a destroyer of darkness and sees through the gloom of the night (1, 94.5; 7, 9.2). Kindled he opens the gates of darkness (3, 5.1). The earth enveloped in darkness and the sky become visible when Agni is born (10, 88.2). For he is kindled at dawn and is the only individual god who is described as 'waking at dawn', *uṣarbudh* (though the gods collectively sometimes receive this epithet).

On the other hand, Agni's course, path or track, and his fellies are black (1, 141.7; 2, 4.6.7; 6, 6.1; 7, 8.2; 8, 23.10), and his steeds make black furrows (1, 140.4). Driven by the wind he rushes through the wood (1, 58.4.5), invades the forests and shears the hairs of the earth (1, 65.8), shaving the earth as a barber a beard (10, 142.4).

His flames are like the roaring waves of the sea (1.44.12). His sound is like the Wind or the thunder of Heaven (5, 25.8; 7, 3.6). He roars like the thundering Dyaus (910, 45.4), or Parjanya (8, 9.15), or a lion (3, 2.12). He bellows like a bull when he invades the forest trees, and the birds are terrified at the noise when his grass-devouring sparks arise (1, 94.10.11). He cannot be checked any more than the sound of the Maruts, an army let loose, or the bolt of heaven (1, 143.5).

Agni flames upwards (6, 15.2). Driven by the wind his flames shoot into the sky (8, 43.4). His smoke wavers and his flame cannot be seized (8, 23.1). His red smoke rises up to the heaven (7, 3.3, 16.3). His smoke spreads in the sky (6, 2.6). Like the erector of a post (*metṛ*), he supports the sky with his smoke (4, 6.2). He touches the ridge of heaven with his crest and mingles with the rays of the sun (7, 2.1). He encompasses heaven with his tongue (8, 61.18) and goes to the flood of heaven, to the water in the bright space above and below the sun (3, 22.3). The Agni of Divodāsa spread along mother earth towards the gods and stood on the ridge of the sky (8, 92.2). 'Smoke-bannered' (*dhūmaketu*) is a frequent epithet exclusively connected with Agni.

Agni is borne on an lightning car (3, 14.2), on a car that is luminous (1, 140.1), bright (1. 141.12), shining (5, 1.11), brilliant (10.1.5), golden (4, 1.8) or beautiful (4, 2.4). It is drawn by two or more horses, which are butter-backed (1, 14.6), ruddy, tawny and ruddy (7, 42.2), beautiful (4, 2.2), omniform (10, 70.2), active (2, 4.2), wind-impelled (1, 94.10), mind-yoked (1, 14.6). He yokes to summon the gods (1, 14.12; 3, 6.6; 8, 64.1). For he is a charioteer (1, 25.3 &c) of the sacrifice (10, 92.1 &c). With his steeds he brings the gods on his car (3, 6.9). He comes seated on the same car as the gods (3, 4.11; 7, 11.1) or in advance of them (10, 70.2). He brings Varuṇa to the offering, Indra from the sky, the Maruts from the air (10, 70.11).

According to the ordinary view of the Vedic poets, Agni's father is Dyaus, who generated him (10, 45.8). He is the child (*śiśu*) of Dyaus (4, 15.6; 6, 49.2)) and is said to have been born from the belly of the Asura (3, 29.4). He is often called the son of Dyaus and Pṛthivi (3, 2.2. 3.11.25.1; 10, 1.2.27.140.2). He is also spoken of as the offspring of Tvaṣṭr and the Waters, as well as of Heaven and Earth (10, 2.7.46.9), or even simply of Tvaṣṭr (1, 95.2) or of the Waters (10, 91.6; AV. 1, 33.1). It is otherwise incidently said that the Dawns generated Agni as well as the Sun and Sacrifice (7, 78.3) or Indra-Visnu generated Agni besides Sun and Dawn (7, 99.4) or Indra generated Agni between two stones (2, 12.3, cp. 1.1). Agni is also described as the son of Iḷā (3, 29.3) or as the embryo of the rite (6, 48.5). The gods, it is sometimes said, generated him (6, 7.1; 8, 91.17), as a light for the Āryan (1, 59.2), or simply fashioned him for man (10, 46.9) or placed him among men (1, 36.10); 2, 4.3; 6, 16.1; 8, 73.2). At the same time Agni is the father of the gods (1, 69.1, cp.p.12). The different points of view which give rise to these seemingly contradictory statements, are sufficiently clear.

Owing to his slightly developed anthropomorphism, the myths of Agni have little to say about his deeds, being, outside his main activity as sacrificial fire, chiefly concerned with his various births, forms and abodes.

The divergent accounts given of the births of Agni are not inconsistent, because they refer to different places of origin. His daily terrestrial birth by friction from the *two araṇīs* or firesticks is often referred to (3, 29.3.23.2.3; 7, 1.2; 10, 7.9). In this connection they are his parents, the upper being the male and the lower the female (3, 29.3). Or they are his mothers, for he is said to have two mothers (1, 31.2). The two sticks produce him as a newborn infant, who is hard to catch (5, 9.3.4). From the dry (wood) the god is born living (1, 68.2). The child as soon as born devours the parents (10, 79.4). He is born of a mother who cannot suckle him (10, 115.1). With reference to this production by friction, men are said to have generated him, (1, 60.3; 4, 1.1; 7, 1.1) the ten maidens that produce him (1, 95.2) being the ten fingers (cp.3, 23.3) employed in twirling the upright drill, which is the upper *araṇī*. *Pramantha*, the name of this fire-drill, occurring for the first time in a late metrical Smṛti work, the Karmapradīpa (1, 7.5) has, owing to a superficial resemblance, been connected with. The latter word has, however, every appearance of being a purely Greek formation, while the Indian verb *math,* to twirl, is found compounded only with *nis,* never with *pra* to express the act of producing fire by friction.

The powerful friction necessary to produce fire is probably the reason why Agni is frequently called the 'son (*sūnu, putra,* once *yuvan*) of strength' (*sahasah*). This explanation is supported by a passage of the RV. stating that Agni 'rubbed with strength (*sahasā*) is produced (*jāyate*) by men on the surface of the earth' (6, 48.5). According to a later text, the kindling of Agni by friction must not take place before sunrise (MS.1, 6.10). Being produced every morning for the sacrifice Agni approximately receives the very frequent epithet, exclusively connected with him, of 'youngest'. His new births are opposed to his old (3, 1.20). Having grown old he is born again as a youth (2, 4.5). In this sense, he does not grow old (1, 128.2), his new light being like his old (6, 16.22). Like some other gods, Agni is also spoken of simply as 'young'. At the same time he is old. There is no sacrificer older than Agni (5, 3.5), for the conducted the first sacrifice (3, 15.4). He shone forth after former dawns (1, 44.10), and the part played by Agni in the sacrifices of ancestors is often referred to (8, 43.13c). He is thus sometimes in the same passage paradoxically called both 'ancient' and 'very young' (10, 4.1.2).

More generally Agni is spoken of as born in wood (6, 3.3; 10, 79.7), as the embryo of plants (2, 1.14; 3, 1.13) or as distributed in plants (10, 1.2). He is also said to have entered into all plants or to strive after them (8, 43.9). When he is called the embryo of trees or of trees (1, 70.4) as well as plants (2, 1.1), there may be a side-glance at the fire produced in forests by the friction of the boughs of trees.

The terrestrial existence of Agni is further indicated by his being called the 'navel of the earth' (1, 59.2). This expression appears, in the many passages in which it occurs, to allude to the receptacle of the sacrificial Agni on the excavated altar or *vedi*. In the Vedic ritual *nābhi* or 'navel' is the technical term designating the hollow in the *uttarā vedi,* in which Agni is deposited. The earlier use of the term probably suggested the figure, that the gods made Agni the 'navel' or centre of immortality (3, 17.4). The only two occurrences in the RV. of the attribute *vediṣad,* 'sitting on the altar' refer to Agni.

Agni's origin in the aerial waters is often referred to. The 'Son of waters' has, as has been shown ($ 24), become a distinct deity. Agni is also the 'embryo' of the waters (3, 1.12.13); he is kindled in the waters (10, 45.1; AV. 13, 1.50); he is a bull who has grown in the lap of the waters (10, 8.1); he is ocean-girt (8, 91.5). He is also said to descend from the *dhanu* or cloud-island (1, 144.5; 10, 4.5) and to be the shining thunder dwelling in the bright space (6, 6.2). In such passages the ligtning form of Agni must be meant. Some of the later hymns of the RV (10, 51-3. 124) tell a legend of a Agni hiding in the waters and plants and being found by the gods. This legend is also often related in the Brāhmaṇas. In the AV the Agnis in the water are distinguished from those that go on the path of lightning or from the celestial Agni with the lightning (AV. 3, 21.1.7; 8, 1.11) and are said to have dwelt on earth (AV. 12, 1.37). In one passage of the RV. also it is stated that Agni rests in all streams (8, 39.8, cp. Ap.

SS. 5, 2.1) and in the later ritual texts Agni in the waters is invoked in connection with ponds and water-vessels. Thus even in the oldest Vedic period, the waters in which Agni is latent, though not those from which he is produced, may in various passages have been regarded as terrestrial. Oldenberg thinks that the terrestrial waters are chiefly meant in this connection and doubts whether the lightning Agni is intended even in the first hymn of the third book. In any case, the notion of Agni in the waters is prominent throughout the Vedas. Water is Agni's home, as heaven is that of the sun (5, 85.2: AV. 13, 1.50; 19, 33.1). The waters are also often mentioned along with the plants or wood as his abode (2, 1.1 &c).

Agni's origin in heaven is moreover frequently spoken of. He is born in the highest heavens (1, 143.2; 6, 8.2). He existed potentially though not actually in the highest heavens (10, 5.7) and was brought from heaven, from afar by Mātariśvan ($ 25). In such passages Agni doubtless represents lightning; for lightning is regarded as coming from heaven as well as from the waters (AV. 3, 21.1.7; 8, 1.11) and in a Brāhmaṇa passage (AB.7, 7.2) it is spoken of as both celestial *(divya)* and aqueous *(apsumat)*. When lightning is mentioned by its proper name *vidyut* (which occurs hardly 30 times in the RV) along with Agni, it is commonly compared with and thereby distinguished from him, doubtless as a concrete phenomenon in contrast with the god. The myth, too, of the descent of fire from heaven to earth, due undoubtedly to the actual observation of conflagrations caused by the stroke of lightning implies the identity of the celestial Agni and lightning. The heavenly origin of Agni is further implied in the fact that the acquisition of fire by man is regarded as a gift of the gods as well as a production of Mātariśvan; and Agni's frequent epithet of 'guest *(atithi)* of men' may allude to the same notion (5,1.9 &c).

In other passages, again, Agni is to be identified with the sun; for the conception of the sun as a form of Agni, in an undoubted Vedic belief. Thus Agni is the light of heaven in the bright sky, waking at dawn, the head of heaven (3, 2.14). He was born on the other side of the air and sees all things (10, 187.4.5). He is born as the sun rising in the morning (10, 88.6). The AB (8, 28.7.13) remarks that the sun when setting enters into Agni and is produced from him. The same identification is probably alluded to in passages stating that Agni unites with the light or the rays of the sun (5, 37.1; 7, 2.1), that when men light Agni on earth, the celestials light him (6, 2.3), or that Agni shines in heaven (3, 27.12; 8, 44.29). Sometimes, however, it is difficult to decide whether lightning or the sun is intended. The solar aspect of Agni's nature is not often mentioned, the sun being too individual a phenomenon to be generally conceived as a form of fire. Agni is usually thought of in his terrestrial form, being compared rather than identified with the sun. Thus the poet says that the minds of the godly are turned to Agni as eyes towards the sun (5, 1.4). At the same time there is frequently a side-glance at Agni's other forms, it being therefore in many cases doubtful which of his aspects is intended.

Owing to the diverse births above described, Agni is often regarded as having a triple character, which in many passages is expressly referred to with some form of the numeral 'three'. This earliest Indian trinity is important, for on it is based much of the mystical speculation of the Vedic age. Agni's births are three or threefold (1, 95.3; 4, 1.7). The gods made him threefold (10, 88.10). He is threefold light (3, 26.7), has three heads (3, 26.7), three tongues, three bodies, three stations (3, 20.2). The epithet *triṣadhastha,* 'having three stations', is predominantly connected with Agni, and the only passage in which the word *tripastya*, 'having three dwellings', occurs (8, 39.8), it is an attribute of Agni. The triad is not always understood in exactly the same way or mentioned in the same order. Thus one poet says: 'From heaven first Agni was born, the second time from us (=men), thirdly in the waters' (10, 45.1, vv.2.3). The order of Agni's abodes is also heaven, earth, waters in other passages (8, 44.16; 10, 2.7.46.9), while one verse (1, 95.3) has the variation: ocean, heaven, waters. Sometimes the terrestrial Agni comes first. He was first born in houses, at the base of great heaven, in the womb of this atmosphere'(4, 1.11); 'the immortals kindled three flames of Agni: of these they placed one with man for use, and two went to the sister-world' (3, 2.9). A Sūtra passage (Ap. SS. 5, 16.4) distinguishes a terrestrial Agni in animals, an aerial one in the waters, and a celestial one in the sun. Occasionally the terrestrial Agni comes third. He is one of three brothers of whom 'the middlemost brother is lightning (*aśnah*) and the third is butter-backed'(1, 164.1, 141.2). 'Agni glows from the sky, to god Agni belongs the broad air, men kindle Agni, bearer of oblations, lover of ghee'(AV. 12, 1.20, cp. 13.3.21; 18, 4.11).

The third form of Agni is once spoken of as the highest (10, 1.3; 5, 3.3; 1, 72.2.4). Yāska (Nir. 7, 28) mentions that his predecessor Śākapūṇi regarded the threefold existence of Agni referred to in 10, 88.10 as being in earth, air and heaven, a certain Brāhmaṇa considering Agni's third manifestation, which is in heaven, to be the sun (Nir. 12, 19). This threefold nature of Agni, so clearly recognised in the RV., was probably the prototype not only of the posterior traid of Sun, Wind, Fire, (8, 18.19), which is spoken of as distributed in the three worlds (10, 158.1; AV. 4, 390.2) and is implied in another verse (1, 164.44), but also of the triad of Sun, Indra, Fire which though not Rigvedic is still ancient. Here Vāta or Vāyu and Indra have taken the place of Agni Vaidyuta, the lightning Agni, as the Brāhmaṇas and commentators call him. This substitution is perhaps partly due to the transient nature of lightning and partly to the lack of any name other than Agni for the personified lightning, which could therefore be expressed only by epithets or allusions. The triad of Agnis may have suggested and would explain the division of the sacrificial fire into the three sacrificial fires which in the Vedic ritual are kept distinct from the domestic fire and which form an essential feature of the cult in the Brāhmaṇas. The ritual may have then reacted on the myth. At any rate, later Hindu literature took the three fires as representative of the three form of Agni known to the RV. The three sacrificial fires may go back to the time of the RV., possibly even to an anterior period. Thus Agni is besought to bring the gods and to seat himself in the three receptacles (*yoniṣu*: 2, 36.4, 5, 11.2; 10, 105.9).

The triple nature of Agni gave rise to the notion of three brothers (1, 164.1); while the multiplicity of sacrificial fires may have suggested the idea of Agni's elder brothers who are spoken of in the plural (10, 51.6). The number of these is later stated to be three (TS. 2, 6, 6.1). The same are probably meant by the four Hotṛs of the gods, of whom the first three died (Kaṭh.25, 7). Varuṇa is once spoken of as Agni's brother (4, 1.2). Elsewhere Indra is said to be his twin brother (6, 59.2). Indra indeed more associated with Agni than with any other god and is, with two slight exceptions, the only god with whom Agni forms a dual divinity. It is doubtless owing to this association that Agni is described as bursting the rock with heat (8, 46.16) and vanquishing the unbelieving Paṇis (7, 6.3). In one entire hymn (1, 93) Agni is also coupled with Soma.

Agni is occasionally identified with other gods, especially with Varuṇa and Mitra (2, 1.4; 3, 5.4; 7, 12.3). He is Varuṇa when he goes to the sacrifice (10, 8.5). He is Varuṇa when he is born and Mitra when he is kindled (5, 3.1). Agni in the evening becomes Varuṇa, rising in the morning he becomes Mitra; becoming Savitṛ he traverses the air, becoming Indra he illumines the sky in the midst (AV. 13, 3.13). In one passage of the RV. (2, 1.3.7) he is successively identified with about a dozen gods besides five goddesses. He assumes various divine forms (3, 38.7) and has many names (3, 20.3). In him are comprehended all the gods (5, 3.1), whom he surrounds as a felly the spokes (5, 13.6).

What is probably the oldest function of fire in regard to its cult, that of burning and dispelling evil spirits and hostile magic, still survives in the Veda. Agni drives away the goblins with his light (3, 15.1 &c) and receives the epithet *rakṣohan*, 'gobin-slayer' (10, 87.1). When kindled he consumes with iron teeth and scorches with heat the sorcerers as well as the goblins (10, 87.2.5.14), protecting the sacrifice with keen glance (ib. 9). He knows the races of the sorcerers and destroys them (AV. 1, 8.4). Though this function of dispelling terrestrial demons is shared with Agni by Indra (as well as by Bṛhaspati, the Aśvins and especially Soma), it must primarily have belonged to Agni alone, just as, conversely, that of slaying Asuras or aerial demons is transferred to Agni though properly peculiar to Indra. This is borne out by the fact that Agni is undoubtedly more prominent as a goblin-slayer than Indra, both in the hymns and in the ritual.

Agni is more closely connected with human life than any other god. His association with the dwellings of men is peculiarly intimate. He is the only god to whom the frequent eithet *gṛhapati,* 'lord of the house' is applied. He dwells in every abode (7, 15.2), never leaving his home (8, 49.19). The attribute 'domestic' (*ďamūnas*) is generally connected with him (1, 60.4 &c). This household deity probably represents an old order of ideas; for in the later elaborate ritual of the three sacrificial fires, the one from which the other ṭwo (the *āhavanīya* or eastern and the *dakṣina* or southern) were taken, is called the *gārhapatya* or that which belongs to *gṛhapati.* In this connection it is interesting to observe that even as early as Rigvedic times there are traces of the sacrificial fire having been ttansported. For Agni is led round (4, 9.3. 15.1), strides round the offerings (4, 15.3) or goes round the sacrifice three times (4, 6.4.5. 15.2); and as soon as he is released from his parents, he is led to the east and again to the west (1, 31.4).

He is further constantly designated a 'guest' (*atithi*) in human abodes. He is an immortal (a term much more commonly applied to Agni than to any other god), who has taken up his abode among mortals (8, 60.1). He has been established or settled among human habitations (3, 5.3; 4, 6.2). It is the domestic Agni who caused mortals to settle (3, 1.17). He is a leader (3, 2.5) and a protector of settlers (1, 96.4), and the epithet *viśpati,* 'lord of settlers' is mainly connected with him.

Agni is further brought into close relation with the daily life of man in the sacrifice. He is, however, not merely a passive receiver of the offering, but is an intermediary between heaven and earth. He transmits the oblation to the gods, who do not get exhilarated without him (7, 11.1). On the other hand, he brings the gods (3, 14.2) to the sacrifice as well as takes it to them (7, 11.5). He seats them on the strewn grass (1, 31.17; 8, 44.3), to eat the offering (5, 1.11 &c). He goes on the paths leading both to the gods (10, 98.11) and to earth (8, 7.2), knowing these paths (6, 16.3). He is therefore constantly and characteristically called a messenger (*dūta*), who knows the paths and the conveys the sacrifice (1, 72.7) or visits all abodes (4, 1.8); who flies swiftly (10, 6.4), moving between heaven and earth (4, 7.8. 8.4; 10, 4.2), or the two races, gods and men; who has been appointed by the gods (5, 8.6 &c) and by men, to be an oblation-bearer (*havya-vah* or *vāhana,* terms always connected with Agni) and to announce the hymn of the worshipper (1, 27.4) or to bring the gods to the place of sacrifice (4, 8.2). He is the messenger of the gods (6, 15.9) and of Vivasvat (p. 42); but as knowing the innermost recesses of heaven, as conveying the sacrifice, and bringing the gods (4, 7.8.8.1) he is mainly to be considered the messenger of men. A later text states that Agni is the messenger of the gods, and Kāvya Uśanas or Daivya that of the Asuras (TS 2, 5, 8.5.11.8).

Another describes Agni not as the messenger of, but as the path leading to, the gods, by which the summit of heaven may be reached (TB. 2, 4, 1.6).

Agni is a seer (*ṛṣi*) as well as a priest (9, 66.20); he is kindled as an eminent seer (3, 21.3); he is the most gracious seer (6, 14.2); he is the first seer Aṅgiras (1, 31.1). He is the divine one (*asura*) among the sages (3, 3.4). Agni knows the sacrifice exactly (10, 110.11) and knows all rites (10, 122.2). Knowing the proper seasons he reflects the mistakes which men commit through ignorance of the sacrificial ordinances of the gods (10, 2.4.5). He knows the recesses of heaven (4, 8.2.4). He knows everything (10, 11.1) by his wisdom (10, 91.3). He has all wisdom (3,17; 10, 21.5), which he embraces as the felly the wheel (2, 5.3) and which he acquired as soon as born (1, 96.1). He is 'all-knowing' (*viśvavid*); and the epithets 'possessed of all knowledge' (*viśvavedas*), 'sage' (*kavi*), and 'possessing the intelligence of a sage' (*kavikratu*) are predominantly applicable to him. He exclusively bears the epithet *jātavedas,* which occurs upwards of 120 times in the RV. and is there (6, 15.13) explained as meaning 'he who knows all generations' (*viśvā veda janimā*). He knows the divine ordinances and the generations of men (1, 70.1.3). He knows and sees all creatures (3, 55.10; 10, 187.4) and hears the invocations addressed to him (8, 43.23). Agni is also producer of wisdom (8, 91.8). Wisdom and prayers arise from him (4, 11.3). He is an inspirer (10, 46.5), an inventor of brilliant speech (2, 9.4), the first inventor of prayer (6, 1.1). He is also said to be eloquent (6, 4.4) and a singer (*jaritṛ*).

Agni is a great benefactor of his worshippers. He protects them with a hundred iron walls (7, 3.7. 16.10, cp. 6, 48.8; 1, 189.2). He preserves them from calamities or takes them across calamities as in a ship over the sea (3, 20.4; 5, 4.9; 7, 12.2). He is a deliverer (8, 49.5) and a friend of the man who entertains him as a guest (4, 4.10). He grants protection to the worshipper who sweats to bring him fuel (4,2.6). He watches with a thousand eyes the man who brings him food and nourishes him with oblations (10, 79.5). He consumes his worshippers' enemies like dry bushes (4, 4.4) and strikes down the malevolent as a tree is destroyed by lightning (6, 8.5, AV. 3, 2.1C). He is therefore invoked in battle (8, 43.21), in which he leads the van. (8, 73.8) The man whom he protects and inspires in battle wins abundant food and can never be overcome (1, 27.7). All blessings issue from him as branches from a tree (6, 13.1). He gives riches, which he abundantly commands (1, 1.3.31.10.36.4). All treasures are collected in him (10.6.6) and he opens the door of riches (1, 68.10). He commands all riches in heaven and earth (4, 5.11) or in earth, heaven and ocean (7, 6.7; 10, 91.3). He gives rain from heaven (2, 6.5) and is like a water-trough in the desert (10, 4.1). He is therefore constantly besought to bestow every kind of boon: riches deliverance from poverty, childlessness, enemies and demons. The boons which Agni bestows are rather domestic welfare, offspring, and prosperity, while Indra for the most part gives power, victory and glory. Agni also forgives sin committed through folly, makes guildless before Aditi (4, 12.4; 7, 93.7.) and averts Varuṇa's wrath (4, 1.4). He even frees from guilt committed by a man's father and mother (AV. 5,30.4; TB. 3, 7, 12.3.4).

Although Agni is the son of Heaven and Earth he is nevertheless called the generator of the two worlds (1, 96.4, cp. 7, 5.7), his ordinance, which does not perish (2, 8.3), being followed by heaven and earth (7, 5.4). He stretched them out (3, 6.5; 7, 5.4) or spread them out like two skins (6, 8.3). With his flame or his smoke he supported the vault of heaven (3, 5.10; 4, 6.2). He kept as under the two worlds (6, 8.3). He supported earth and heaven with true hymns (1, 67.3). He stands at the head of the world or is the head of the earth at night (10, 88.5.6), but he is also the head and summit (*kakud*) of the sky (1, 59.2; 6,

7.1; 8, 44.16). He measured out the air and touched the vault of heaven with his greatness (6, 8.2). He measured out the aerial spaces and the bright realms of heaven (6, 7.7). He caused the sun to ascend the sky (10, 156.4). The notion that the kindling of Agni exercised a magical influence on the sunrise seems not to be entirely absent in the RV. Such appears to be the meaning of the poet when he exclaims: 'Let us light Agni, that thy wondrous brand may shine in heaven' (5, 6.4). This notion is clearly stated in a Brāhmaṇa passage: 'By sacrificing before sunrise he produces him (the sun), else he would not rise' (SB. 2, 3, 1.5, cp. TS. 4, 7, 13.3). Otherwise the kingling of Agni and the sunrise are represented merely as simultaneous in the RV.: 'The sun became visible when Agni was born' (4, 3.11). This trait of the Agni myth resembles the winning of the sun in the Indra myth, but the original point of view in the two cases is clearly different. Agni is further said to have adorned the sky with stars (1, 68.5). He created all that flies, walks, stands or moves (10, 88.4). He placed the germ in these beings (3, 2.10), in plants, in all beings, and engendered offspring in the earth and in women (10, 183.3). Agni is once spoken of as having generated these children of men (1, 96.2); but this is a mere incidental extension of the notion expressed in the same stanza, that he created heaven, earth and the waters, and cannot be interpreted as a general belief in Agni as father of the human race. Finally, Agni is the guardian (7, 7.4) and lord (7, 4.6) of immortality, which he confers on mortal men (1, 31.7).

Besides epithets of celestial fire which, like Apām napāt, have become separate names, some epithets of Agni exhibit a semi-independent character. The epithet Vaiśvānara, occurring about sixty times in the RV and with two exceptions restricted to Agni, is, apart from some five detached verses, to be found in fourteen hymns of the RV., in nearly all of which, according to the native tradition of the Anukramaṇī, Agni Vaiśvānara is the deity addressed. The attribute is never in the RV unaccompanied by the name of Agni. It means 'belonging to all men' and seems to designate 'Universal Agni', fire in all its aspects, celestial as well as terrestrial. Thus the hymns addressed to this form of Agni sometimes refer to the myth of Mātarśvan and the Bhṛgus, which is connected with the descent of celestial fire to earth (3, 2.4; 6, 8.4), and Agni Vaiśvānara is once even directly styled Mātariśvan (3, 26.2). In the Naighaṅṭuka (5, 1) Vaiśvānara is given as one of the names of Agni. Yāska in commenting on the epithet states (Nir. 7, 23) that ancient ritualists (*yājnikāh*) took Agni Vaiśvānara to be the sun, while Śākapūṇi considered him to be this Agni. Later on (Nir. 7., 31) he states as his own opinion that the Agni Vaiśvānara who receives praise and sacrifice is this (i.e. terrestrial) Agni, while the two higher (*uttare*) lights (i.e. the aerial and the celestial) only occasionally share this designation. In the ritual texts Vaiśvānara is distinguished as a special form of Agni (ASS. 1, 3.23; KSS. 23, 3.1; PB. 21, 10.11; SB. 1, 5, 1.16).

The epithet Tanūnapāt, generally unaccompanied by the name of Agni, occurs eight times in the RV. and, with two exceptions (3, 29.11; 10, 92.2) always in the second verse of the Āprī hymns, which are liturgical invitations introducing the animal sacrifice and in which fire under various names and forms is invoked. The word occurs as an independent name in the Naighaṅṭuka (5, 2). The explanations given by Yāska (Nir. 8,5) are artificial and improbable. It seems to mean 'son of himself', as spontaneously generated in wood and cloud. According to BERGAIGNE'S interpretation, it signifies 'the bodily (i.e. own) son' of the divine father. Tanūnapāt as contrasted with Mātariśvan and Narāśaṁsa is said to be 'the divine (*āsura*) embryo' (3, 29.11). The dawns are said to kiss Agni 'the domestic priest, the Tanūnapāt of the ruddy one' (10, 92.2., cp. 5, 58.6). Tanūnapāt is beautiful-tongued (10, 110.2). He is besought to take the sacrifice to the gods (1,

13.2; 10, 110.2); he distributes the sacrifice rich in ghee and mead (1, 142.2, cp. 188.2). The gods honour him three times a day, Varuṇa, Mitra, Agni, everyday (3, 4.2). HILLEGRANDT (comparing 9, 5.2) identifies Agni Tanūnapāt with Agni Somagōpa or the lunar Fire, which he assumes to be a special form of Agni.

The somewhat more frequent epithet Narāśaṁsa which is given as an independent appellation in the Nighaṅṭuka (5, 3) and is unaccompanied by the name of Agni in the RV., is not restricted to Agni, being twice connected with Pūṣan (1, 106.4; 10, 64.3). It has the third verse as its fixed place in the Āpri hymns and the second in those which are technically called Āpra. Narāśaṁsa is 'four-limbed' (10, 92.11) and is the 'lord of a celestial wife' (*gnspati*: 2, 38.10). With honey on his tongue and in his hand, he performs the sacrifice (1, 13.3; 5, 5.2). Three times a day he besprinkles the sacrifice with honey (1, 142.3). He anoints the three heavens and the gods (2, 3.2). He comes at the head of the gods and makes the sacrifice pleasant for them (10, 70.2). Through his sacrifices worshippers praise the greatness of the gods (7, 2.2). Soma is said to go between Narāśaṁsa and the celestial (*daivya*) one (9, 86.42), which seems to mean, between the terrestrial and the celestial Agni. As contrasted with Tanūnapāt and Mātariśvan, Agni is Narāśaṁsa when he is born (3, 29.11). In one hymn to Bṛhaspati (10. 182.2) Narāśaṁsa is invoked for protection, and in another he is spoken of as the sacrificer of the seat of heaven (1, 1.89). He thus seems in these two passages to be identified with Bṛhaspati. The word *nārā-śāṣsa* is apparently an improper compound (in which the *m* of the genitive plural has disappeared), having a double accent and having its parts separated by particles in two passages (9, 86.42; 10, 64.3). As the expressions *narāṁ śaṁsa* and *devānām śaṁsa* occur (2, 34.6; 1, 141.11) and a poet once calls Agni *śaṁsa āyoh*, 'Praise of Āyu' (4, 6.11), Narāśaṁsa appears to mean 'Praise of men' in the sense of 'he who is the object of men's praise'. BERGAIGNE expresses the opinion that the exact aspect of Agni represented by Narāśaṁsa, is that of a good of human prayer, like a second Bṛhaspati.

3.2.2 Prithivi

The Earth, Pṛthivi, being, generally celebrated conjointly with Dyaus, is lauded alone in only one short hymn of three stanzas in the RV. (5, 84) and in a long and beautiful one in the AV. (12, 1). The personification is but slight, the attributes of the goddess being chiefly those of the physical earth. According to the RV. she abounds in heights, bears the burden of the mountains, and supports the trees of the forest in the ground (*kṣmā*). She quickens the soil, for she scatters rain, and the showers of heaven are shed from the lightning of her cloud. She is great (*mahī*), firm (*dṛḷhā*) and shining (*arjunī*).

The meaning of Pṛthivi is 'the broad one'; and a poet of the RV. (2, 15.2) alludes to the etymology when he says that Indra upheld the earth (*pṛthivī*) and spread it out (*paprathat*). The TS. (7, 1, 5) and TB. (1, 1, 3.5) in describing the origin of the earth, expressly derive the name of Pṛthivī from the root *prath*, to extend, beçause she is extended.

Pṛthivī is spoken of as 'kindly Mother Earth', to whom the dead man in a funeral hymn (10, 18.10), is exhorted to go. When mentioned with Dyaus, Pṛthivī frequently receives the epithet of 'mother'.

3.2.3 Nadi-hymns

Beside the divine Waters, defied rivers occupy a not unimportant position in the RV. The whole of one hymn (10, 75) celebrates the Sindhu or Indus with the exception of the fifth verse, in which several of its tributaries are invoked besides other streams, while in the sixth verse a number of other rivers are mentioned as affluents of the Indus. Another entire hymn (3, 33) is devoted to the invocation and praise of the sister streams Vipāś amd Śutudrī.

The Sarasvati is, however, more greatly celebrated than any river. But though the personification in this case goes much further than in the others, the connection of the goddess with the river is in the RV. always present to the minds of the poets. Sarasvati is lauded in three hymns of the RV. and in numerous detached verses. Sarasvati, Sarayu and Sidhu are invoked as great streams (10, 64.9) and elsewhere (10, 75.5) Gaṅgā, Yamunā, Sarasvati, Sutudri, Paruṣṇī and others known and unknown, altogether twenty-one, are addressed. Kings and peoples living on the banks of the Sarasvatī are referred to (7, 96.2; 8, 21.18). Sarasvatī, an iron fort, flows with fertile flood, a stream (*sindhu*) surpassing all other waters in greatness; she alone of rivers appeared pure, flowing from the mountains, from the (celestial) ocean (7, 95.2; cp. 5, 43.11). She tears away with her mighty waves the peaks of mountains, and her immense and impetuous flood moves roaring (6, 61.2.8). She is distinguished by greatness among the great, she is the most active of the active, and is implored not to withhold her milk (6, 61.13). The poet says that she may not be removed from fields which are strange (6, 61.14). She has seven sisters and is sevenfold (6, 61.10.12). She is one of seven, a mother of streams (7, 36.6). She is the best of mothers, of rivers and of goddesses (2, 41.16). She is called *pāvīravī,* an epithet (applied also to *tanyatu,* 'thunder', in 10, 65.13) probably meaning 'daughter of lightning', and is said (6, 49.7) to be the wife of a hero (probably, Sarasvat). She fills the terrestrial regions and the wide atmosphere space and occupies three abodes (6, 61.11.12). She is invoked to descend from the sky, from the great mountain, to the sacrifice (5, 43.11). The last three passages (cp. also 7, 95.2) seem to allude to the notion of a celestial origin, like that of Gaṅgā in post-Vedic mythology. She is once called *asuryā* or divine (7, 96.1). The goddess comes to the sacrifice on the same chariot as the Fathers and seats herself on the sacrificial grass (10,1 17.8.9). Even here she must be conceived as the river goddess, for in the following two verses the waters are invoked to cleanse from defilement.

She herself is a purifier (1, 3.10). She is besought to come 'swelling with streams' (6, 52.6) and, along with the waters, the bestowers of wealth, progeny and immortality, to grant vitality (10, 30.12). She bestows vitality and offspring (2, 41.17) and is associated with deities who assist procreation (10, 184.2). She is also said to have given a son named Divodāsa to Vadhryaśva (6, 61.1). Her unfailing breat (AB. 4, 1) yields riches of every king (1, 164.49). She is often said to bestow wealth, plenty, and nourishment (7, 95.2; 8, 21.17; 9, 67.32; 10, 17.8.9), and several times receives the epithet *subhaga,* 'bountiful' (1, 89.3; 7, 95.4.6; 8, 21.17). As a mother (*ambā*) she grants reputation to the unrenowned (2, 41.16). She stimulates, directs, and prospers the devotions of her worshippers (1, 3.10.11; 2, 3.8; 6, 61.4). She is invoked along with the goddesses of prayer (7, 37.11; 10, 65.13). She destroys the revilers of the gods, is terrible, and a Vṛtra-slayer (6, 61.3.7). But to her worshippers she affords protection and conquers their enemies (7, 95.4.5; 2, 30.8; 6, 49.7).

Sarasvati is often invoked with other deities. Besides Pūṣan and Indra, she is particularly associated with the Maruts (3, 54.13; 7, 9.5 39.5. 40.3) and is said to be accompanied by them (2, 30.8) or to have them as her friends (7, 96.2). She is also once in the RV. connected with the Aśvins. With the later aided Indra, Sarasvati is said to have refreshed him (10, 131.5). With reference to the same myth the VS. (19, 12) states that when the gods celebrated a healing sacrifice, the Aśvins as physicians and Sarasvati through speech (*vācā*) communicated vigour to Indra. The VS. even speaks of Sarasvati as the wife of the Asvins (19, 94). Sarasvati is several times associated in the eighth and ninth verses of the *āprī* and *āpra* hymns with the sacrificial goddesses

Iḍā and Bhāratī (with whom she forms s triad), and sometimes also with Mahī and Hotrā. This association may have been due to the sacred character of the river. Allusion is made to Agni being kindled for sacrifice on the banks of the Sarasvati and Dṛṣadvatī (3, 23.4); and the AB (2, 19) refers to a sacrifice performed by Ṛṣis on the Sarasvatī. Hence on the banks of the Sarasvatī there were perhaps places of worship of the Bharatas; in that case, Bhāratī, the personified offering of the Bharatas, would naturally find a fixed place along with Sarasvatī in the Āprī litany which accompanied the animal sacrifice?

Though there is nothing to show distinctly (cp. 7, 35.11) that Sarasvatī is ever anything more in the RV. than a river goddess, we find her identified in the Brāhmaṇas (SB. 3, 9, 1.7' AB. 3, 1.10), with Vāc, Speech, and in post-Vedic mythology she has become goddess of eloquence and wisdom, invoked as a muse and regarded as the wife of Brahmā. The transition from the older to the later conception is perhaps to be found in passages like VS. 19, 12 quoted above.

Sarasvati has a male correlative named Sarasvat, who after the praises of the river goddess have been sung in three verses of one hymn (7, 96), is invoked in the next three by worshippers desiring wives and offspring, protection and plenty. Here his fertilizing waters and even his exuberant breast are referred to. In another passage (1, 164.52), Sarasvati, here apparently a name of the bird Agni, is spoken of as refreshing with rain. Roth regards him as a guardian of the celestial waters who bestows fertility.

3.2.4 Bṛhaspati

Bṛhaspati - occupies a position of considerable prominence in the RV., eleven hymns being dedicated to is praise. He also forms a pair with Indra in two hymns (4, 49; 7, 97). His name occurs about 120 times and in the form of Brāhmaṇaspati about 50 times besides. The two forms of the name alternate in different verses of the same hymn (e.g. in 2, 23). The physical features of Bṛhaspati are few. He is seven-mouthed and seven-rayed (4, 50.4), beautiful-tongued (1, 190.1; 4, 50.1) sharp-horned (10, 155.2), blue-backed (5, 43.12), and hundred-winged (7, 97.7). He is golden-coloured and ruddy (5, 43.12), bright (3, 62.7; 7, 97.7), pure (7, 97.7) and clear-voiced (7, 97.5). He has a bow, the string of which is the rite (*ṛta*), and good arrows (2, 24.8; cp. AV. 5, 18.8.9). He also wields a golden hatchet (7, 97.7) and is armed with an iron axe, which Tvaṣṭṛ sharpens (10, 53.9). He has a car (10, 103.4) and stands on the car of the rite, which slays the gobins, bursts the cowstalls, and wins the light (2, 23.3). He is drawn by ruddy steeds (7, 97.6)

Bṛhaspati was first born from great light in the highest heaven and with thunder (*raveṇa*) drove away darkness (4, 50.4; cp. 10, 68.12). He is the offspring of the two worlds (7, 97.8), but is also said to have been generated by Tvaṣṭṛ (2, 23.17). On the other hand, he is called the father of the gods (2, 26.3), being said to have blown forth the births of the gods like a black-smith (10, 72.2).

Bṛhaspati is a domestic priest (2, 24.9; VS. 20, 11; TS. 6, 4, 10; AB. 8, 26.4), a term almost peculiar to Agni (p. 96). The ancient seers placed him at their head (*puro-dhā*) (4, 50.1). He is Soma's *purohita* (SB. 1, 2.4). He is also a *Brahman* or praying priest (2, 1.3; 4, 50.8), once probably in the technical sense (10, 141.3). In later Vedic texts Bṛhaspati is the *brahman* priest (in the technical sense) of the gods. He is even called the prayer or devotion (*brahma*) of the gods (TS. 2, 2, 9.1 &c). Bṛhaspati promotes the yoking of devotion, and without him sacrifice does not succeed (1, 18.7). As a pathmaker he makes good the access to the feast of the gods (2, 23.6.7). From him even the gods obtained their share of sacrifice (2, 23.1). He awakens the gods with sacrifice (AV. 19, 63.1). He himself pronounces the hymn in which Indra, Varuṇa, Mitra, Aryama, the gods take pleasure

(1, 40.5). He sings chants (10, 36.5). His song (*śloka*) goes to heaven (1, 190.4) and metre (*chandas*) belongs to him (MS. 1, 9.2). He is associated with singers (7, 10.4); 10, 14.3). He sings with his 'friends that cry like Haṁsas' (10, 67.3), by whom the Aṅgirases (54) mentioned in the preceding verse (10. 67.2) seem to be meant. He is also said to be accompanied by a singing (*ṛkvat*) host (*gaṇa*: 4, 50.5). This is doubtless the reason why he is called *ganapati,* 'lord of a host' (2, 23.1), a term once applied to Indra also (10, 11.29).

As the name Brāhmaṇaspati shows, the god is a 'lord of prayer'. He is also described as the supreme king of prayers, the most famous sage of sages (2, 23.1). Mounting the car of the rite he conquers the enemies of prayer and of the gods (2, 23.3.8). He is the generator of all prayers (1, 190.2). He utters prayer (1, 40.5) and communicates prayers to the human priest (10, 98.27). Thus he comes later to be called a 'lord of speech', *vācaspati* (MS. 2, 6.6, SB. 14, 4, 1.23), a term specially applied to Bṛhaspati as god of eloquence and wisdom in post-Vedic literature.

There are several passages in which Bṛhaspati appears identified with Agni. Thus 'the lord of prayer, Agni, handsome like Mitra' is invoked (1, 38.13). In another passage (2, 1.3) Agni, though identified with other gods as well, is clearly more intimately connected with Brahmaṇaspati, as only these two names are in the vocative. In one verse (3, 26.2) both Mātariśvan and 'Bṛhaspati the wise priest, the guest, the swiftly-moving' seem to be epithets of Agni, while in another (1, 190.2) Mātariśvan seems to be an epithet of Bṛhaspati. Again, by Bṛhaspati, who is blue-backed, takes up his abode in the house, shines brightly, is golden-coloured and ruddy (5, 43.12). Agni must be meant. In two other verses (1, 18.19; 10, 182.2) Bṛhaspati seems to be the same as Narāśaṁsa, a form of Agni (p. 100). Like Agni, Bṛhaspati is a priest, is called 'Son of strength' (1, 40.2) and Aṅgiras (2, 23.18) as well (the epithet *āṇgirasa* belonging to him exclusively), and burns the goblins (2, 23.14) or slays them (10, 103.4). Bṛhaspati is also spoken of as ascending to heaven, to the upper abodes (10, 67.10). Like Agni, Bṛhaspati has three abodes (4, 50.1); he is the adorable one of houses (7, 97.5) and 'lord of the dwelling' *sadasas pati* (1, 18.6; Indra-Agni are once called *sadaspati,* 1, 21.5). On the other hand, Agni is called *brahmaṇas kavi*, 'sage of prayer'(6, 16.30) (*brahmaṇā*). But Bṛhaspati is much more commonly distinguished from Agni (2, 25.3; 7, 10.4; 10, 68.9), chiefly by being invoked or named along with him in enumerations (3, 20.5 &c).

Like Agni, Bṛhaspati has been drawn into and has obtained a firm footing in the Indra myth of the release of the cows. The mountain yielded to his splendour, when Bṛhaspati, the Aṅgiras, opened the cowstall and with Indra as his companion let loose the flood of water enveloped by darkness (2, 23.18, cp. 1,56.5., 89.9). Accompanied by his singing host (cp. 54) he with a roar rent Vala; shouting he drove out the lowing cows (4, 50.5). He won treasures and the great stalls full of cows; desiring waters and light, the irresistible Bṛhaspati slays his foe with flames (6, 73.3). What was firm was loosened, what was strong yield to him; he drove out the cows, he cleft Vala with prayer; he covered up the darkness and made heaven with might, that the celestials drank, while they poured out together abundantly the watery fountain (2, 24.3.4). When Bṛhaspati with fiery gleams rent the defences of Vala, he revealed the treasures of the cows; as if splitting open eggs, he drove out the cows of the mountain; he beheld the honey enclosed by the stone; he brought it out, having cloven (Vala) with his roar; he smote forth as it were the marrow of Vala (10, 68.4.9). He drove out the cows and distributed them in heaven (2, 24.14). Bṛhaspati fetched the cows out of the rock; seizing the cows of Vala, he took possession of them(10, 68.5). His conquest of Vala is so characteristic that it became proverbial (AV. 9,3.2). Being in the clouds (*abhriya*) he shouts aloud after the many cows (10, 68.12, cp. 67.3). These cows may represent the waters, which are expressly mentioned (2, 23.18; 6, 73.3) or possibly the rays of dawn (cp. 10, 67.5., 68.9)

In releasing the cows Bṛhaspati seeks light in darkness and finds the light; he found the Dawn, and Agni, and dispelled the darkness (10, 68.4.9). In shattering the fort, he found the Dawn, the Sun, the Cow (10, 67.5). He hid or dispelled the darkness and made visible the light (2, 24.3; 4, 50.4). Bṛhaspati thus comes to acquire more general warlike traits. He penetrated the mountain full of riches and split open the strongholds of Sambara (2, 24.2). Bṛhaspati Aṅgirasa, the first-born holy one, cleaver of rocks, roars as a bull at the two worlds, slays Vṛtras (*vṛtrāṇi*), shatters forts, overcomes foes (6, 73.1.2). He disperses foes and wins victory (10, 103.4). No one can overcome him in great fight or small (1, 40.8). He vanquishes the enemy in battle (2, 23.11). He is to be invoked in combats (2, 23.13) and is a priest much praised in conflict (2, 24.9).

Being the companion and ally of Indra (2, 23.18, 24.2; 8, 85.15), he is often invoked with that deity (4, 50.10.11 &c). With Indra he is a soma-drinker (4, 49.3, 50.16) and like him, is styled *maghavan,* 'bountiful' (2, 24.12). Indra, too, is the only god with whom he forms a pair (2, 24.12; 4, 49.1.6). Thus he comes to be styled *vajrin,* 'wielder of the bolt' (1, 40.8) and to be described as hurling the bolt, the Asura-slaying missile (AV. 11, 10.13). He is also invoked with the Maruts at the same time as Indra (1, 40.1) and is once besought to come accompanied by the Maruts, whether he be Mitra, Varuṇa or Pūṣan (10, 98.2). In one passage he is said to have heard the prayer of Trita buried in a well and to have delivered him (1, 105.17).

Bṛhaspati favours the man who offers prayer (2, 25.1) but scourges the hater of prayer (2, 23.4). He protects the pious man from all dangers and calamities, from curse and malignity, and blesses him with wealth and prosperity (1, 18.3, 2, 23.4.10)/ Possessed of all desirable things (7, 10.4.97.4), he is opulent, a procurer of wealth, and an increaser of prosperity (1, 18.2). He is a prolonger of life and a remover of disease (1, 18.2). Having such benevolent traits he is called a father (4, 50.6; 6, 73.1)

He is *asurya,* 'divine' (2, 23.2), belongs to all the gods (3, 62.4; 4, 50.6), and is the most god-like of the gods (2, 24.3). As a god he widely extended to the gods and embraces all things (2, 24.11, cp. 8, 61.18). Mightily he holds as under the ends of the earth with his roar (4, 50.1). It is his inimitable deed that sun and moon rise alternately (10, 68.10). He is also spoken of as stimulating the growth of plants (10, 97.15.19). Later Bṛhaspati is brought into connection with certain stars. Thus in the TS. (4, 4, 10.2) he is stated to be the deity of the constellation Tiṣya, and in post-Vedic literature he is regarded as the regent of the planet Jupiter.

Bṛhaspati is a purely Indian deity. Both forms of the name occur throughout the older as well as the later books of the RV. But since appellations formed with *pati* (like *vācas pati, vāstoṣ pati kṣetrasya pati*) to designate deities presiding over a particular domain, must be comparatively recent as products of reflexion, this mythological creation can hardly go much further back that the beginning of the Rigvedic period. The accentuation of the word *bṛhaspati* shows it to be an improper compound. The prior member might possibly be a neuter noun in *-as*, but the contemporaneous form *brahmaṇaspati*, which is a kind of explanation, indicates that the poets of the RV. regarded it as the genitive of a noun *bṛh*, from the same root as *brahman*.

3.2.5 Soma

Since the Soma sacrifice forms the main feature of the ritual of the RV., the god Soma is naturally one of the most important deities of that Veda. All the 114 hymns of the ninth besides 6 in other books, are dedicated to his praise. He is also celebrated in portions of four or five other hymns, and as a dual divinity with Indra, Agni, Pūṣan or Rudra, in about six more. The name of Soma, in its simple form and in compounds, occurs hundreds of times in the RV. judged by the standard of frequency, Soma therefore comes third in order of importance among the Vedic gods. Soma is much less anthropomorphic than Indra or Varuṇa, the constant presence of the plant and its juice setting limits to the imagination of the poets who describe its personification. Consequently little is said of his human form or action. The marvellous and heroic deed attributed to him are either colourless, because common to almost all the greater gods, or else only secondarily belong to him. Like other gods, he is, under the name of Indu as well as Soma, invoked to come to the sacrifice and receive the offerings on the strewn grass. The ninth book mainly consists of incarnations sung over the tangible Soma while it is pressed by the stones, flows through the woolen strainer into the wooden vats, in which it is finally offered on a litter of grass to the gods as a beverage, someitmes in fire (1, 94.14' 5, 5.1; 8, 43.11) or drunk by the priests. The processes to which it is subjected are overlaid with the most varied and chaotic imagery and with mystical fancies often incapable of certain interpretation.

In order to make intelligible the mythology of Soma, the basis of which are the concrete terrestrial plant and the intoxicating juice extracted therefrom, it is necessary briefly to describe these as well as the treatment they undergo. The part of the Soma plant which is pressed is called *aṁśu,* 'shoot or stalk' (9, 67.28). The shoots swelling give milk like cows with their udders (8, 9.19). As distinguished from the stalk, the whole Soma plant seems to be intended by *andhas* (8, 32.28; 10, 94.8 &c), which is said to have come from heaven (9, 61.10) and to have been brought by the eagle (5, 45.9; 9. 68.6; 10, 144.5). The same term is applied to the juice also and is distinguished from Indu the god (9, 51.3;

10, 115.3). The juice is also designated by *soma* (which means the plant as well) and generally by *rasa* fluid. In one hymn (1, 1.87) the juice is called *pitu*, the 'beverage'; and it is often styled *mada,* 'intoxicating draught'. Some is occasionally also referred to with *anna* 'food' (7, 98.2; 8, 4.12; SB. 1, 6, 4.5). The term *madhu* which in connection with the Aśvins means 'honey' or 'mead', comes to be applied, in the general sense of 'sweet draught', not only to milk (*payas*) and ghee (*ghṛta*), but especially to the Soma juice (4, 27.5; 8, 69.6). Mythologically *madhu* is the equivalent of Soma when the latter means the celestial ambrosia (*amṛta*). Conversely, *amṛta* is frequently used as an equivalent of ordinary Soma (5, 2.3; 6, 37.3 &c; VS. 6. 34; SB. 9, 5, 1.8). King Soma when pressed is *amṛta* (VS. 19, 72). Another expression is *somyam madhu,* 'Soma mead' (4, 26.5; 6, 20.3). Figuratively the Soma juice is called *piyūṣa* (3, 48.2 &c), milk (9, 107.12), the wave of the stalk (9, 96.8) or the juice of honey (5, 43.4). The most frequent figurative name applied to Soma is *indu*, the 'bright drop', another term of similar meaning, *drapsa,* 'drop', being much less common.

The extraction of the juice is generally described by the root *su,* 'to press' (9, 62.4 &c), but often also by *duh* 'to milk' (3, 36.6.7 &c). The juice is intoxicating (1, 125.3; 6, 17.11. 20.6) and 'honied' *madhumat* (9, 97.14). The latter expression simply means 'sweet', but as applied to Soma originally seems to have meant 'sweetened with honey', some passages pointing to this admixture (9, 17.8, 86.48. 97.11. 109.20). As flowing from the press, Soma is compared with the wave of a stream (9, 80.5) and directly called a wave (9, 64.11 &c) or a wave of honey (3, 47.1). With reference to the juice collected in the vat, Soma is spoken of as a sea (*arṇava*: 10, 115.3) and frequently as an ocean (*samudra*: 5, 47.3; 9, 64.8 &c). The heavenly Soma is also called a well (*utsa*), which is in the highest place of the cows (5, 45.8), which is placed in the cows and guided with ten reins (i.e. fingers:

6, 44.24), or a well of honey in the highest step of Viṣṇu (i, 154.5)

The colour of the plant and juice, as well as of the god, is described as brown (*babhru*) or ruddy (*aruṇa*), but most frequently as tawny (*hari*). The Soma is the branch of a ruddy tree (10, 94.3); it is a ruddy milked shoot (7, 98.1); the tawny shoot is pressed into the strainer (9, 92.1). The colour of the Soma plant or its substitute prescribed in the Brāhmaṇas is ruddy (SB. 4, 5, 10); and in the ritual the cow which is the price paid in purchase of Soma, must be brown or ruddy because that is Soma's colour (TS. 6, 1, 6.7; SB. 3, 3, 1.14).

Soma is described as purified with the hands (9, 86.34), by the ten fingers (9, 8.4. 15.8 &c), or, figuratively, by the ten maidens who are sisters (9, 1.7. 6.5), or by the daughters (*saptī*) of Vivasvat (9, 14.5). Similarly, the maidens of Trita are said to urge on the tawny one with stones as a drop for Indra to drink (9, 32.2. 38.2) Soma is also spoken of as purified or brought by the daughter of the sun (9, 1.6. 72.3. 113.3). Sometimes it is said to be purified by prayer (9, 96.13. 113.5). The priests who press Soma are Adhvaryus (8, 4.11).

The shoot is crushed with a stone (9, 67.19) or pressed with stones (9, 107.10); the plant is pounded to produce the Soma draught (10, 85.3). The stones tear its skin (TB. 3, 7, 13.1). The stones lie on a skin; for they 'chew him on the hide of the cow' (9, 79.4). They are placed on the *vedi* or altar (5, 31.12): practice differing from that of the late ritual. They are held with hands or arms (7, 22.1; 9, 79.4; AV. 11, 1.10). The two arms and ten fingers yoke the stone (5, 43.4). Hence the stones are said to be guided by ten reins (10, 94.8). Being spoken of as yoked, they are compared with horses (10, 94.6). The usual name for the pressing stones is *adri* (generally used with the verb *su,* to press) or *grāvan* (generally connected with *vad*, to speak, or verbs of cognate meaning, and hence showing a greater tendency to personification than *adri*). 'Both terms nearly always occur either in the singular or the plural, and not in the dual. The stones are also once respectively called *aśna* (8, 2.2), *bharitra* (3, 36.7), *parvata* (3, 35.8) and *parvatā adrayah* (10, 94.1). The pressing of Soma by means of stones was the usual method in the period of the RV. But the extraction of the juice by mortar and pestle, which is also sanctioned by the ritual texts, was already known to the RV. (1, 28.1.4); and as this method is in use among the Parsis, it may go back to the Indo-Iranian age.

The pressed drops are poured upon (9, 63.10 &c) and pass over the strainer of sheep's wool (9, 69.9). For it removes Soma's impurity, so that he goes cleansed to the feast of the gods (9, 78.1). this strainer, which is very frequently mentioned, passes under various names. It is called a skin (*tvac*), hair (*roman*), wool (*vāra*), filter (*pavitra*), or ridge (*sānu*, as the top of the contrivance). All these terms are used with or without an adjective formed from *avi,* sheep. The word *avi* itself is sometimes figuratively employed in this sense. As passing through the strainer Soma is usually called *pavamāna* or *punāna*, 'flowing clear' (from *pū*). The more general term *mṛj*, 'to cleanse', is not only applied to the purification of Soma with the strainer, but also to the addition of water and milk (9, 86.11 91.2). The purified (unmixed) Soma juice is sometimes called *śudddha*, 'pure', but much oftener *śukra* or *śuci,* 'bright' (8, 2.10; 9, 33.2; 1, 5.5, 30.2). This unmixed Soma is offered almost exclusively to Vāyu and Indra, the epithet *śucipā,* 'drinking clear (Soma)' being distinctive of Vāyu (p. 82). This agrees with the later ritual, where, in the Grahas or draughts for dual divinities, clear Soma is offered to Vāyu and Indra-Vāyu, but is mixed with milk for Mitra-Varuṇa and with honey for the Aśvins.

After passing the filter, Soma flows into jars (*kalaśa,* 9, 60.3 &c) or vats (*droṇa*). The streams of Soma rush to the forest of the vats like buffaloes (9, 53.1. 92.6); the god flies like a bird to settle in the vats (9, 3.2); like a bird sitting on a tree, the tawny one settles in the bowls (*camū*: 9, 72.3). Soma is mixed with water in the vat. United with the wave, the stalk roars (9, 74.5). Like a bull on the herd, he rushes on the vat, into the lap of the waters, a roaring bull; clothing himself in waters, Indu rushes around the vat, impelled by the singers (9, 76.5. 107.26). The wise milk him into the waters with their hands (9, 79.4). Having passed over the wool and playing in the wood, he is cleansed by the ten maidens (9, 6.5). Several other passages refer to the admixture of water with Soma (9, 30.5. 53.4. 86.8.25). The Soma drops are said to spread brightness in the streams (9, 76.2). Besides the verb *mṛj,* 'to cleanse', which is commonly used to express the admixture of water (e.g.9, 63.17), *ā-dhāv,* 'to wash', is also employed (8. 1.17). In the preparation of Soma, the pressing (*su*) comes first, then the mixing with water (7, 32.6; 8, 1.17; AV. 6, 2.1), just as in the later ritual the *savana*, 'pressure', precedes the *ādhāvana,* 'washing'. In the bowls Soma is mixed with milk (9, 8.6 &c), which is said to sweeten it (8, 2.3). In several passages the addition of both water and milk is mentioned. Thus it is said that Soma clothes himself in waters, that streams of water flow after him, when he desires to clothe himself in cows (i.e. milk; 9, 2.3.4). They press him with stones, they wash him in water, clothing him as it were in cow-garments, men milk him out of the stalks (8, 1.17; cp. 2, 36.1; 6, 40.2; 9, 86.4.5. 96.19).

Soma is recognised in the RV as having three kinds of admixture (*tryāśir*: 5, 27.5), with milk (*gavāśir*), sour milk (*dadhyāśir*), and barley (*yavāśir*). The admixture is figuratively called a garment (*vastra, vāsas, atka*) or a shining robe (*nirṇij*: 9, 14.5) the latter term being applied to the strainer also (9, 70.7). Hence Soma is spoken of as decked with beauty (9, 34.4 &c) and as richly adorned (9, 81.1). Mention is also made, though rarely, or mixture with ghee (9, 82.2); but neither this addition nor that of water, is a regular *āśir*.

In the ritual there is a ceremony called *āpyāyana* or causing the half-pressed Soma stalks to swell by moistening them with water afresh. The beginnings of it are found in the MS. (4, 5.5). The verb *ā-pyā*, 'to swell', occurs in the RV. in connection with Soma (1, 91.16.8; 10, 85.5) but here it seems to refer to Soma as identified with the moon. In one other passage, however, (9, 31.4) it may have a ritual application. Soma is also said in the RV. to swell (*pi, pinv*), like a sea or river (9, 64.8. 107.12).

Soma is described in the RV. as pressed three times in the day. Thus the Ṛbhus are invited to the evening pressing (4, 33.11 &c), Indra to the midday pressing (3, 332.1; 8, 37.1), which is his along (4, 36.7), while the morning libation in his first drink (10, 112.1).

The abode (*sadhastha*) of Soma is often referred to; once, however, mention is made of three, which he occupies when purified (9, 103.2), the epithet *triṣadhastha,* 'having three abodes', being also applied to him in another passage (8, 83.5). These three abodes may already designate the three tubs used at the Soma sacrifice of the later ritual (TS. 3, 2, 1.2; KSS. 9, 5.17. 7.4; cp. RV. 8, 2.8); but BERGAIGNE (BRV. 1, 179) regards them as purely mythological. A similar remark applies to the three lakes of Soma which Indra drinks (5, 29.7.8; 6, 17.11; 8, 7.10). The epithet *tripṭstha*, 'three-backed', is peculiar to Soma. Being applied to the juice at least once (7, 37.1) it probably refers (as Sāyaṇa thinks) to the three admixtures, much as the Agni's epithet *ghṛtapṛṣtha* alludes to ghee being thrown on the fire.

The sound made by the Soma juice as it is being purified and rushes into the vats or bowls, is often referred to. It is compared with that of rain (9, 41.3). But the language is generally hyperbolical. Thus the sweet drop is said to flow over the filter like the din of combatants (9, 69.2). The noise is constantly designated by various verbs meaning to roar or bellow (*krand, nad, mā, ru, vās*: 9, 91.3. 5.4 &c). Even the verb *stan*, 'to thunder', is used (9, 86.9) and the wise are described as 'milking the thundering unfailing stalk' (9, 72.6). Lightning also is in some verses connected with the purification of Soma (9, 41.3. 80.1. 84.3. 87.8); this in all probability alludes to the purification of the celestial Soma and may have referred to the phenomena of the thunderstorm.

When Soma is said to roar he is commonly compared with or directly called a bull. 'As a bull he bellows in the wood' (9, 7.3); 'the tawny bull bellows and shines with the Sun' (9, 2.6). As the waters, added with or without milk, are figuratively called cows, the relation of Soma to them is usually that of a bull to cows. He is a bull among the cows (9, 16.6. 69.4. 96.7) or is lord of the cows (9, 72.4). He bellows like a bull traversing the cows (9, 71.9) or like a bull towards the cows (9, 71.7), the cows also bellowing towards him (9, 80.2 &c). He is the bull of heaven as well as of the earth and the streams (6, 44.21). The impetuosity of Soma is also several times illustrated by comparison with a buffalo (*mahiṣa*). Thus he even comes to be called an animal (*pasu*: 9, 86.43). Being a bull among the cow-waters, Soma is the fertilizer of the waters (10, 36.8, cp. 9, 19.5). He is also (9, 86.39) an impregnator (*retodhā*), an epithet especially applied to the moon in the YV. (e.g. MS. 1, 6.9). Hence he is a bestower of fertility (9, 60.4. 74.5). Soma being so frequently called a bull (*ukṣan, vṛṣan, vṛṣabha*) is sharp-horned (*tigmaṣṛṅga*), an epithet which in five of its six occurrences in the RV is accompanied by a word meaning 'bull'. Thus the brewed drink (*mantha*) of Indra is like a sharp-horned bull (10, 86.15). Soma is also said (like Agni) to sharpen his horns (9, 15.4. 70.7)

Soma is swift (1, 4.7) and, in illustration of the speed with which the pressed juice flows, is very often compared with or designated a steed. Thus the ten maidens are said to cleanse him like a swift steed (9, 6.5). The drop which intoxicates Indra is a tawny steed (9, 63.17). Soma flowing into the vats is sometimes also compared with a bird flying to the wood (9, 72.5 &c).

Owing to the yellow colour of the juice, the physical quality of Soma mainly dwelt on by the poets, is his brilliance. His rays are often referred to and he is frequently assimilated to the sun. He shines like or with the sun or clothes himself in its rays (9, 76.4. 86.32; cp. 71.9). He ascends the car of the sun and stands above all beings like the sun. He fills heaven and earth with rays like the sun (9, 41.5). When born a bright son, he caused his parents to shine (9, 9.3). The daughter of the sun purifies him (9, 1.6). Thus it comes to be said of him that he combats the darkness (9, 9.7), wards it off with light (9, 86.22), or creates bright light, dispelling the darkness (9, 66.24, 100.8. 1.8.12 &c).

Its mysteriously exhilerating and invigorating action, surpassing that of ordinary food or drink and prompting to deeds beyond the natural powers, led to Soma being regarded as a divine drink which bestows immortal life. Hence it is mythologically called *amṛta*, the bestower of immortality. It is an immortal stimulant (1, 84.4), which the gods love (9, 85.2) and of which, when pressed by men and mixed with milk, all the gods drink (9, 109.15); for Soma is immortal (1, 43.9; 8, 48.12; 9, 3.1 &c); and the gods drank him for immortality (9, 106.8). He confers immortality on the gods (1, 91.6; 9, 108.3) and on men (1, 91.1; 8, 48.3). He places his worshipper in the everlasing and imperishable world where there is eternal light and glory, and makes him immortal where king Vaivasvata lives (9, 113.7.8).

Thus Soma naturally has medicinal power also. It is medicine for a sick man (8, 61.17). Hence the god Soma heals whatever is sick, making the blind to see and the lame to walk (8, 68.2; 10, 25.11). He is the guardian of men's bodies and occupies their every limb (8, 48.9), bestowing length of life in this world (1, 91.6; 8, 48.4.7; 9, 4.6.91.6). The Soma draught is even said to dispel sin from the heart, to destroy falsehood and to promote truth.

When imbibed Soma stimulates the voice (6, 47.3; 9, 84.4. 95.5. 97.32), which he impels as the rower his boat (9, 95.2). This is doubtless the reason why Soma is called 'lord of speech' *vācas pati* (9, 26.4.101.5) or leader of speech, *vaco agriya* or *agre* (9, 7.3. 62.25-6. 86.12. 106.10). He is also said to raise his voice from heaven (9, 68.8). In the Brāhmaṇas *vac,* 'speech', is described as the price paid by the gods for Soma. Soma also awakens eager thought (6, 47.3). So his worshippers exclaim : 'We have drunk Soma, we have become immortal, we have entered into light, we have known the gods' (8, 48.3). Thus he is also spoken of as a lord of thought and a father, leader, or generator of hymns. He is a leader of poets, a seer among priests (9, 96.6). He has the mind of seers, is a maker of seers (9, 96.18) and a protector or prayer (6, 52.3). He is the 'soul of sacrifice' (9, 2.10.6.8), a priest (*brahmā*) among the gods (9, 96.6), and apportions to them their share of sacrifice (10, 85.19). Soma's wisdom thus comes to be predominantly dwelt upon. He is a wise seer (8, 68.1). He knows the races of the gods (9, 81.2. 95.2. 97.7. 108.3). He is a wise man-seeing wave (9, 78.2). Soma with intelligence surveys creatures (9, 71.9). Hence he is many-eyed (9, 26.5) and thousand-eyed (9, 60.1)

Soma stimulated the Fathers to activities (9, 96.11); through him the Fathers found the light (9, 97.39). Soma is also said to be united with the fathers (8, 48.13) or to be accompanied by them (AV. 18, 4.12; SB. 2, 6, 1.4, &c), the Fathers, conversely, being called Soma-loving (*somya*: 10, 14.6; AV. 2, 12.5).

The exhilerating effect of the draught on man was naturally transferred to the gods, to whom the Soma was offered. The main applications of its intoxicating power is its stimulating effect on Indra in his conflict with the hostile powers of the air. That Soma strengthens Indra for the fight with Vṛtra, is mentioned in innumerable passages of the RV. (8, 81.17 &c). In the intoxication of Soma Indra slays all foes (9, 1.10) and no one can resist him in battle when he has drunk it (6, 47.1). Soma is the soul of Indra (9, 85.3), the auspicious friend of Indra (10, 25.9), whose vigour he stimulates (9, 76.2) and whom he aids in slaying Vṛtra (9, 61.22). With Soma as a companion Indra made the waters to flow for man and slew the dragon (4, 28.1). Thus Soma is sometimes even called the bolt (*vajra*) of Indra (9. 72.7. 77.1. 111.3). Soma Indra's juice, becomes a thousand-winning bolt (9, 47.3). It is the intoxicating draught which destroys a hundred forts (9, 48.2) and is a Vṛtra-slaying intoxicating stalk (6, 17.11). Thus the god Soma is said to be 'like Indra a slayer of Vṛtras and a fort-destroyer' (9, 88.4), and comes to receive half of a dozen times the epithet *vrtrahan*, 'Vṛtra-slaying' which primarily belongs to Indra.

When drunk by Indra Soma caused the sun to rise in heaven (9, 86.22). So this cosmic action comes to be attributed to Soma independently. He caused the sun to shine (9, 28.5. 37.4), caused the lights of the sky to shine (9, 85.9), and produced the sun in the waters (9, 42.1). He caused the sun to rise, impelled it, obtained and bestowed it, and caused the dawns to shine. He makes his worshippers participate in the sun (9, 4.5) and finds light for them (9, 35.1). He found the light (9, 59.4) and wins light and heaven (9, 3.2). Just as even the sacrificial butter is spoken of as the 'navel of immortality', on which rests the whole world (4, 58.1.11), the conception of Soma comes to be extended to that of a being of universal dominion (9, 86.28.29), who is 'lord of the quarters' (9, 113.2), who performs the great cosmic actions of generating the two worlds (9, 90.1), of creating or establishing heaven and earth, of supporting heaven, and of placing light in the sun (6, 44.23-4. 47.3.4).

Being so intimately connected with Indra in the conflict with Vṛtra, Soma comes to be spoken of independently as a great fighter. He is a victor, unconquered in fight, born for battle (1, 91.21). He is the most heroic of heroes, very terrible, and ever victorious (9, 66.16-7). He conquers for his worshippers cows, chariots, horses, gold, heaven, water, a thousand boons (9, 78.4), and everything (8, 68.1). Without reference to his warlike character, he is constantly said to bestow all the wealth of heaven and earth, food, cattle, horses, and so forth (9, 45.3. 49.4. 52.1 &c). Soma himself is occasionally called a treasure (*rayi*: 9, 48.3) or the wealth of the gods (SB. 1, 6, 4.5). Soma can also afford protection from foes (10, 25.7). He drives away goblins (9, 49.5) and, like some other deities but more frequently, receives the epithet of goblin-slayer (*rakṣohan*). Soma is the only god who is called a slayer of the wicked (9, 28.6 &c). In the later Vedic literature the statement occurs that Brāhmans who drunk Soma are able to slay at a glance (MS. 4, 8.2).

Being a warrior, Soma ia said to have weapons (9, 96.16), which like a hero he grasps in his hand (9, 76.2) and which are terrible and sharp (9, 61.30. 90.3). In one passage he is said to have obtained his weapons by robbing his malignant father of them (6, 44.22). He is described as armed with a thousand-pointed shaft (9, 83.5. 86.40) and his bow is swift (9, 90.3)

Soma rides in the same chariot as Indra (9, 87.9, 96.2. 103.5). He is charioteer to the car-fighter Indra (AV. 8, 8.23). He drives in a car (9, 3.5), which is heavenly (9, 111.3). He has light (9, 86.45) or a filter for his car (9, 83.5). He is the best of charioteers (9, 66.26). He has well-winged mares of his own (9, 86.37) and a team like Vāyu (9, 88.3).

Soma is naturally sometimes connected with Indra's intimate associates, the Maruts. They are said to milk the bull of heaven (9,.108.11, cp. 54.1) and to adorn the child when born (9, 96.17). Like Indra, Soma is attended by the Maruts (6, 47.5) or the troop of the Maruts (9, 66.22). The winds, too, are said to be gladdening to Soma (9, 31.3) and Vāyu is his guardian (10, 85.5). Soma forms a pair with Agni, Pūṣan and Rudra respectively (p. 128-9). A few times he is mystically identified with Varuṇa (9, 77.5. 95.4; cp. 73.3-9; 8, 41.8).

Though Soma is a terrestial plant, it is also celestial (10, 116.3); in fact its true origin and abode are regarded as in heaven. Thus it is said that the birth of the plant is on high; being in heaven it has been received by earth (9, 61.10). The 'intoxicating juice' is the 'child of heaven' (9, 38.5), an epithet frequently applied to Soma. In one passage, however, he is called the offspring (*jāh*) of the sun (9, 93.1) and in another Parjanya is spoken of as the father of the mighty bird (9, 82.3 cp. 113.3). In the AV. the origin of *amṛta* is also traced to the seed of Parjanya (AV. 8, 7.21). When Soma is called a child (*śiśu*) simply (9, 96.17) or a youth (*yuvan*), this is doubtless in allusion to the fact that, like Agni, he is continually produced a new. Soma is the milk (*piyūṣa*) of heaven (9, 51.2 &c), is purified in heaven (9, 83.2. 86.22 &c). He flows with his stream to the dear places of heaven (9, 12.8). He runs through heaven across the spaces with his stream (9, 3.7). He occupies heaven (9, 85.9), is in heaven (SB. 3, 4, 3.13), or is the lord of heaven (9, 86.11.33). As bird of heaven he looks down on earth and regards all beings (9, 71.9). He stands above all worlds like god Sūrya (9, 54.3). The drops being purified have been poured from heaven, from the air, on the surface of the earth (9, 63.27); for he is a traverser of space (*rajastur*: 4, 48.4, 108.7). Fingers rub him surrounded with milk 'on the third ridge, in the bright realm of heaven' (9, 86.27). His place is in the highest heaven (3, 32,10; 4, 26.6; 9, 86.15) or in the third heaven (TS. 3, 5, 7.1 &c). 'Heaven', however also seems to be frequently a mystical name of the striner of sheep's wool. This seems to be the case when Soma is spoken of as being 'on the naval of heaven, on the sheep-filter' (9, 12.4), as traversing the lights of heaven, the sheep-filter (9, 37.3), as running with Sūrya in heaven, on the filter (9, 27.5); or when it is said that 'the full has occupied heaven, the king goes soaring over the strainer' (9, 85.9. cp. 86.8). The term *śanu*, 'summit', so frequently applied to the filter, is suggestive of *divah sānu,* 'the summit of heaven'. Such terms would naturally come to be connected with the terrestrial Soma, because heaven is the abode of the celestial Soma or *amṛta* (6, 44.23) at the Some offering is called an eagle (10, 99). 'Eagle of heaven' is an epithet applied to Agni (7, 15.4; otherwise twice said of the Maruts), the term eagle is connected with Agni Vaidyuta or lightning (TB. 3, 10, 5.1 cp. 12, 1.2), and Agni is often called a bird in the RV. (p. 89). On this evidence Bloomfield, who subjects his predecessors' interpretations of RV. 4, 27 to a searching criticism, with much plausibility, explains the carrying off of Soma by the eagle as a mythological account of the simple phenomenon of the descent of lightning, darting from the cloud (i.e. the iron castle) and causing the fall of the ambrosial fluid Soma (i.e. the water of the cloud). At the same time he refers to a passage of the RV. (1, 93.6) in which the descent of fire and of Soma are mentioned together. A detail of the myth (probably a mere embellishment added by the individual poet) is the trait that as the eagle carried away Soma, the archer Kṛśānu shot at him knocking out a feather (4, 27.3.4; cp. AB. 3, 25). This trait is related with greater detail in the Brāhmaṇas. Either a feather or a claw is here stated to have been shot off. Falling to the ground, it became a *parṇa* (*palāśa*) or a *śalyaka* tree. The tree hereby acquired a specially sacred character in connection with the ritual.

Being the most important of herbs Soma is said to have been born as the lord of plants (9, 114.3), which are also said to have Soma as their king (9, 97.18-9). He receives the epithet *vanaspati*, 'lord of the wood' (1, 91.6; 9, 12.7) and is said to have generated all plants (1, 91.22). In the Brāhmaṇas plants are connected with Soma, being styled *saumya* (SB. 12, 1, 1.2). Irrespectively of his being lord of plants, Soma is often, like other leading gods, called a king. He is also a king of rivers (9, 89,2), a king of the whole earth (9, 97.58), a king or father of the gods (9, 86.10. 87.2. 109.4) a king of gods and mortals (9, 97.24), and a king of Brāhmans (VS. 9, 40; TS. 1, 8.10; MS. 2, 6.9). He is of course often called a god; but in one passage he is described as 'a god pressed for the gods' (9, 3.6.7).

In the post-Vedic literature Soma is a regular name of the moon, which is regarded as being drunk up by the gods and so waning, till it is filled up again by the sun. In the Chāndogya Upaniṣad (5, 10.1) the statement is found that the moon is king Soma, the food of the gods, and is drunk up by them. Even in the Brāhmaṇas the identification of Soma with the moon is already a common-place. Thus the AB. (7,11) remarks that the moon is the Soma of the gods; the SB. (1, 6, 4.5), that king Soma, the food of the gods, is the moon; and in the Kauṣītaki Br. (7, 10; 4, 4) the sacrificial plant of juice is symbolical of the moon-god. The mythology of the Brāhmaṇas already explains the phases of the moon as due to the gods and Fathers eating its substance, which consists of ambrosia. Soma, as the moon, is the YV. also conceived as having the lunar asterisms, the daughters of Prajāpati, for his wives. In the AV., moreover, Soma several times means the moon (7, 81.3.4; 11, 67, &c). A large number of scholars agree that even in a few of the latest hymns of the RV. (in the first and tenth books) Soma is already identified with the moon. Most of them, however, hold that Soma as a god is celebrated in the Vedic hymns only as a personification of the beverage, regarding his identification with the moon as merely a secondary mythological growth. The most important of the passages in which the identification is generally admitted, is that which describes the wedding of Soma and the sun-maiden Sūryā (10, 85). Here Soma is spoken of as 'in the lap of the stars', (v.2), and it is said that no one eats of that Soma which the priests know and which is contrasted with that which they crush (v.3). The Soma nature of the moon being referred to as a secret known to Brāhmans only, shows that it cannot yet have been a popular notion. The process by which the celestial Soma gradually coalesced with the moon is not difficult to understand. Soma is, on the one hand, continually thought of as celestial and bright, sometimes as dispelling darkness and swelling in the waters; on the other hand, it is very often called a 'drop', *indu* (6, 44,21). Comparison with the moon would therefore easily suggest itself. Thus Soma in the bowls is said in one passage to appear like the moon in the waters (8, 71.8; cp. 1, 105.1); and in another, Soma beind described as the drop (*drapsa*) which goes to the ocean, looking with the eye of a vulture (10, 123.8), is generally admitted to allude to the moon.

Chapter - IV

Atmospheric Gods

(Antarikṣasthāna-devatās)

4.1 Indra

Indra is the favourite national god of the Vedic Indians. His importance is indicated by the fact that about 250 hymns celebrate his greatness, more than those devoted to any other god and very nearly one-fourth of the total number of hymns in the Ṛgveda. If the hymns in parts of which he is praised or in which he is associated with other gods, are taken into account, the aggregate is brought up to at least 300. As the name, which dates from the Indo-Iranian period and is of uncertain meaning, does not designate any phenomenon of nature, the figure of Indra has become very anthropomorphic and much surrounded by mythological imagery, more so indeed than that of any other god in the Veda. The significance of his character is, however, sufficiently clear. He is primarily the thunder-god, the conquest of the demons of drought or darkness and the consequent liberation of the waters or the winning of light forming his mythological essence. Secondarily Indra is the god of battle, who aids the victorious Aryan in the conquest of the aboriginal inhabitants of India.

He is the dominant deity of the middle region. He pervades the air (1, 51.2). He occurs among the gods of the air alone in the Naighantuka (5, 4), and is the representative of the air in the triad Agni, Indra (or Vāyu), Sūrya.

Many of Indra's physical features are mentioned. He has a body, a head, arms and hands (2, 16.2; 8, 85.3). His belly is often spoken of in connection with his powers of drinking Soma (2, 16.2 &c). It is compared when full of Soma to a lake (3, 36.5). His lips (the probable meaning of *śiprā*) are often referred to, the frequent attributes *suśipra* or *śiprin,* 'fair-lipped', being almost peculiar to him. He agitates his jaws after drinking Soma (8, 65.10). His beard is violently agitated when he is exhilerated or puts himself in motion (2, 11.17; 10, 23.1). He is tawny-haired (10, 96.5.8) and tawny-bearded (10, 23.4). His whole appearance is tawny, the changes being rung on that word (*hari*) in every verse of an entire hymn (10, 96) with reference to Indra. He is a few times described as golden (1, 7.2; 8, 55.3), an attribute distinctive of Savitṛ, as golden-armed (7, 34.4), and as iron-like (1, 56.3; 10, 96.4.8). His arms as wielding the thunderbolt are mentioned particularly often. They are long, far-extended, great (6, 19.3; 8, 32.10. 70.1), strong and well-shaped (SV. 2, 1219). Indra assumes the most beautiful forms and the ruddy brightness of the sun (10, 1123) and takes many different forms at will (3, 48.4. 53.8; 6, 47.18).

The thunderbolt (*vajra*) is the weapon exclusively appropriate to Indra. It is the regular mythological name of the lightning stroke. It is generally described as fashioned for him by Tvaṣṭr (1, 32.2 &c), but Kāvya Uśanā is also said to have made it and given to him (1, 121.12; 5, 34.2). In the AB. (4, 1) it is the gods who are said to have provided Indra with his bolt. It lies in the ocean enveloped in water (8, 89.9). Its place is below that of the sun (10, 27.12). It is generally described as *āyasa* or metalic (1, 52.8 &c), but sometimes as golden (1, 57.2 &c), tawny (3, 44.4;

10, 96.3) or bright (3, 44.5). It is four-angled (4, 22.2), hundred-angled (4, 17.10), hundred-jointed (8, 6.6 &c), and thousand-pointed (1, 80.12 &c). It is sharp (7, 18.18 &c). Indra whets it like a knife or as a bull his horns (1, 130.4. 55.1). It is spoken of as a stone (*aśman*) or rock (*parvata*:7, 104.19). The bolt in Indra's hand is compared with the sun in the sky (8, 59.2). Epithets derived from or conpounded with *vajra*, some of which are very frequent, are almost entirely limited to India. *Vajrabhṛt*, 'bearing the bolt', *vajrivat,* 'armed with the bolt' and *vajradakṣina,* 'holding the bolt in his right hand' are applied to him exclusively, while *vajrabāhu* or *hasta,* 'holding the bolt in his arm or hand' and the commonest derivative *vajrin*, 'armed with the bolt', otherwise occur as attributes of Rudra, the Maruts, and Manyu only once each respectively.

Indra is sometimes said to be armed with a bow and arrows (8, 45.4. 66.6.11; 10, 103.2.3). The latter are golden, hundred-pointed, and winged with a thousand feathers (8, 66.7.11). He also carries a hook (*aṅkuśa*) with which he bestows wealth (8, 17.10; AV. 6, 82.3) or which he uses as a weapon (10, 44.9). A net with which he overwhelms all his foes is also attributed to him (AV. 8, 8.5-8).

Indra is borne on a car which is golden (6, 29.2 &c) and is swifter than thought (10,112.2). The epithet 'car-fighter' (*ratheṣ ṭhā*) is exclusively appropriated to Indra. His car is drawn by two tawny steeds (*harī*), a term very frequently used and in the great majority of instances referring to Indra's horses. In a few passages a greater number than two, up to a hundred and even a thousand or eleven hundred are mentioned (2, 18.4-7; 4.46.3; 6,47.18; 8,1.9.24). These steeds are sun-eyed (1, 16.1.2). They snort and neigh (1, 30.16). They have flowing manes (1, 10.3 &c) or golden manes (8, 32.29.82.24). Their hair is like peacock's feathers or tails (3, 45.1; 8, 1.25). They swiftly traverse vast distances and Indra is transported by them as an eagle is borne by its wings

(2, 16.3; 8, 34.9). They are yoked by prayer (2, 18.3 &c), which doubtless means that invocations bring Indra to the sacrifice. Indra is a few times said to be drawn by the horses of Sūrya (10, 49.7) or by those of Vata (10, 22.4-6), and Vāyu has Indra for his charioteer (4, 46.2. 48.2) or his car-companion (7, 91.6). Indra's car and his steeds were fashioned by the Ṛbhus (1, 111.1; 5, 31.4). Indra is once said to be provided with a golden goad (*kaśā*: 8, 33.11).

Though the gods in general are fond of Soma (8, 2.18. 58.11), Indra is preeminently addicted to it (1, 104.9 &c). He even stole it in order to drink it (3, 48.4; 8, 4.4). He is the one Some-drinker among gods and men (8, 2.4), only Vāyu, his companion, coming near him in this respect. It is his favourite nutriment (8, 4.12). The frequent epithet 'Soma-drinker' (*soma-pā, pavan*) is characteristic of him, being otherwise only applied a few times to Agni and Brhaspati when associated with Indra, and once besides to Vāyu alone.

Soma is sometimes said to stimulate Indra to perform great cosmic actions such as supporting earth and sky or spreading out the earth (2, 15.2). But is characteristically exhilerates him to carry out his warlike deeds, the slaughter of the dragon or Vṛta (2, 15.1; 19.2; 6, 47.1.2) or the conquest of foes (6, 27; 7, 22.2; 8, 81.6). So essential is Soma to Indra that his mother gave it to him or he drank it on the very day of his birth (3, 48.2.3 32.9.10; 6, 40.2; 7, 98.3). For the slaughter of Vṛtra he drank three lakes of Soma (5, 29.7. cp. 6, 17.11), and he is even said to have drunk at a single draught thirty lakes of the beverage (8, 66.4). One entire hymn (10.119) consists of a monologue in which Indra describes his sensations after a draught of Soma. But just as too much Soma is said to produce disease in men, so Indra himself is described as suffering from excessive indulgence in it and having to be cured by the gods with the Sautrāmaṇī ceremony. Indra also drinks milk mixed with honey (8, 4.8).

He at the same time eats the flesh of bulls (10, 28.3), of one (10, 27.2), of twenty (10, 86.14), or of a hundred buffaloes (6, 17.11; 8, 66.10), or 300 buffaloes roasted by Agni (5, 29). At the sacrifice he also eats an offering of cake (3, 52.7.8), as well as of grain (3, 35.3.43.4; 1, 16.2), and the latter his steeds are supposed to eat as well (3, 35.7. 52.7).

Indra is often spoken of as having been born. Two whole hymns (3, 48; 4, 18) deal with the subject of his birth. Once (4, 18.1.2) he is represented as wishing to be born in an unnatural way through the side of his mother. This trait may possibly be derived from the notion of lightning breaking from the side of the storm-cloud. On being born he illuminates the sky (3, 44.4). Scarcely born he set the wheel of the sun in motion (1, 130.0). He was a warrior as soon as born (3, 51.8; 5, 30.5; 8, 45.4.66.1; 10, 113.4) and was irresistible from birth (1, 102.8; 10, 133.2). Through fear of him when he is born, the firm mountains, heaven and earth are agitated (1, 61.14). At his birth heaven and earth trembled through fear of his wrath (4, 17.2) and all the gods feared him (5, 30.5). His mother is often mentioned (3, 48.2.3 &c). She is once (4, 18.10) spoken of as a cow (*gṛṣṭi*), he being her calf; and he is spoken (10, 111.2) of as a bull, the offspring of a cow (*gārṣṭeya*). He is once (10, 101.12) called the son of Niṣṭigrī, whom Sāyaṇa regards as synonymous with Aditi. According to the AV. (3, 10.12.13) Indra's (and Agni's) mother is Ekāṣṭakā, daughter of Prajāpati. Indra has the same father as Agni (6, 59.2), who is the son of Dyaus and Pṛthivī (35). According to one interpretation of a verse in a hymn (4, 17.4) in which his father is twice mentioned, the latter is Dyaus. A similar inference may be drawn from a verse in an Indra hymn (10, 120.1) where it is said that 'among the worlds that was the highest from which this fierce (god) was born, and from a few other passages (cp. 6, 30.5; 8, 36.4 with 10, 54.3 and 10, 138.5 with 1, 164.11). His father is said to have made his thunderbolt (2, 17.6), which is elsewhere generally described as fashioned by Tvaṣṭṛ. Indra drank Soma in the house of his father, where it was given to him by his mother (3, 48.2). He drank Soma in the house of Tvaṣṭṛ (4, 18.3) and having stolen the Soma, drank it in the cups (3, 48.4). Indra seizing his father by the foot crushed him, and he is asked in the same verse who made his mother a widow (4, 18.12). From these passages it is clearly to be inferred that Indra's father whom he slays in order to obtain the Soma, is Tvaṣṭṛ (cp. 1, 80.14). The hostility of the gods, who in one passage (4, 30.3) are said to have fought against him, is perhaps connected with the notion of his trying to obtain Soma forcibly.

A few different accounts are given of the origin of Indra. He is said to have been generated by the gods as a destroyer of foes (3, 49.1), but the verb *jan* is here no doubt only used in the figurative sense of 'to constitute' (cp. 2, 13.5; 3, 51.8). Soma is once spoken of as the generator of Indra and some other gods (9, 96.5). In the Puruṣa hymn Indra and Agni are said to have sprung from the mouth of the world-giant (10, 90.13). According to the Śatapatha Brāhmaṇa. (11, 1, 6.14) Indra, as well as Agni, Soma and Parameṣṭhin, is said to have been created from Prajāpati. The Tandya Brāhmaṇa. (2, 2, 10.1) states that Prajāpati created Indra last of the gods.

Agni is Indra's twin brother (6, 55.5). The sons of Indra's brother are once mentioned (10, 55.1), but who are meant by them is uncertain.

Indra's wise is several times referred to (1, 82.5.6; 3, 53.4.6; 10, 86.9.10). Her name is Indrāṇī in a hymn in which she is represented as conversing with Indra (10, 86.11.12) and occurs in a few other passages which contain enumerations of goddesses (1, 22.12; 2, 32.8; 5, 46.8). The SB. expressly states Indrāṇi to be Indra's wife (14, 2, 1.8). The AB. (3, 22.7), however, mentions Prāsahā and Senā as Indra's wives? These two are identified with Indrāṇi (TB. 2, 4, 2.7.8; MS. 3, 8.4; 4, 12.1). PISCHEL (VS.

2, 52) thinks that Saci is the proper name of Indra's wife in the RV. as well as in post-Vedic literature. The AV. (7, 38.2) refers to an Asura female who drew Indra down from among the gods; and the Kāṭhaka (IS. 3, 479) states that Indra enamoured of a Dānavī named Vilistengā, went to live among the Asuras, assuming the form of a female among females and of a male among males.

Indra is associated with various other gods. His chief friends and allies are the Maruts, who in innumerable passages are described as assisting him in his warlike exploits (20). His connection with these deities is so close that the epithet *marutvat*, 'accompanied by the Maruts', though sometimes applied to other gods, is characteristic of Indra, this epithet, as well as *marudgaṇa* 'attended by the Marut host', being sufficient di designate him (5, 42.6; 9, 65.10). With Agni Indra is more frequently coupled as a dual divinity than with any other god (44). This is natural, as lightning is a form of fire. Indra is also said to have produced Agni between two stones (2, 12.3) or to have found Agni hidden in the waters (10, 32.6). Indra is further often coupled with Varuṇa and Vāyu, less frequently with Soma, Bṛhaspati, Pūṣan, and Viṣ ṇu (44). The latter is a faithful friend of Indra and sometimes attends him in his conflict with the demons (17.44).

Indra is in three or four passages more or less distinctly identified with Sūrya. Speaking in the first person (4, 26.1) Indra asserts that he was once Manu and Sūrya. He is once directly called Sūrya (10, 89.2); and Sūrya and Indra are both invoked in another verse (8, 82.4) as if they were the same person. In one passage Indra receives the epithet Savitṛ (2, 30.1). The Śatapatha Brāhmaṇa (1, 6, 4.18), too, once identifies Indra with the sun, Vṛtra being the moon.

The gigatic size of Indra is dwelt upon in many passages. When Indra grasped the two boundless worlds, they were but a handful to him (3, 30.5). He surpasses the greatness heaven, earth and air (3, 46.3). The two worlds are but equal to the half of him (6, 30.1; 10, 119.7). Heaven and earth do not suffice for his girdle (1, 173.6). If the earth were ten times as large, Indra would be equal to it (1, 52.11). If Indra had a hundred heaven and a hundred earths, a thousand suns would not equal him nor both worlds (8, 59.5).

His greatness and power are lauded in the most unstinted terms. He has no parallel among those born or to be born (4, 18.4). No one, celestial or terrestrial, has been born or shall be born, like to him (7, 32.23). No one, god or man, either surpasses or equals him (6, 30.4). Neither gods nor men nor waters have attained to the limit of his might (1, 100.15). No one like him is known among the gods; no one born, past or present, can rival him (1, 165.9). He surpasses the gods (3, 46.3). All the gods yield to him in might and strength (8, 51.7). Even the former gods subordinated their powers to his divine glory and kingly dignity (7, 21.7). All the gods are unable to frustrate his deeds and counsels (2, 32.4). Even Varuṇa and Sūrya are subject to his command (1, 101.3 cp. 2, 38.9 p. 16). He is besought to destroy the foes of Mitra, Aryaman and Varuṇa (10, 89.8.9) and is said to have acquired by battle ample space for the gods (7, 98.3). Indra alone is king of the whole world (3, 46.2). He is the lord of all that moves and breathes (1, 101.5). He is the king of things moving and of men (5, 30.5); he is the eye of all that moves and sees (10, 102.12). He is the leader of human races and divine (3, 34.2). He is several times called a universal monarch (4, 19.2 &c) and still oftener a self-dependent sovereign (3, 46.1 &c; cp. p. 24). He is also said to rule alone (*eka*) by his might as an ancient seer (8, 6.41). A few times receives the epithet *asura* (1, 174.1; 8, 79.6). Indra bears several characteristic attributes expressive of power. *Śakra* 'mighty' applies to Indra about 40 times and only about five times to other gods. *Śacīvat,* 'possessed of might' describes Indra some fifteen times and other deities only twice. The epithet *śacīpati* 'lord of might' occurring eleven times in the

Ṛgveda belongs to Indra with only one exception (7, 67.5), when the Aśvins as 'lords of might' are besought to strengthen their worshippers with might (*śacībhih*). In one of these passages (10, 24.2) Indra is pleonastically invoked as 'mighty lord of might' (*śacīpate śacīnām*). This epithet survives in post-Vedic literature as a designation of Indrain the sense of 'husband of Śaci'. The very frequent attribute *śatakratu,* 'having a hundred powers', occurring some 60 times in the Ṛgveda is with two exceptions entirely limited to Indra. In the great majority of instances *satpati,* 'strong lord', is appropriated to Indra. Indra's strength and valour are also described with various other epithets. He is strong (*tavas*), nimble (*nṛtu*), victorious (*tura*), heroic (*śūra*), of unbounded force (1, 11.4. 102.6), of irresistible might (1, 84.2). He is clothed in might like the elephant and bears weapons like the terrible lion (4, 16.14). He is also young (1, 11.4 &c) and unaging (*ajara*), as well as ancient (*pūriya*).

It is however rather as mountains (*parvata, giri*: p. 10) that they appear in the Indra myth. They are the mountains (1, 32.1) on which the demons dwell (1, 32.2; 2, 12, 11), or from which he casts them down (1, 130.7; 4, 30.14; 6, 26.5). Indra shoots forth his well-aimed arrow from these mountains (8, 66.6). He cleft wide the mountain to release the cows (8, 45.30). Or the cloud is a rock (*adri*) which encompasses the cows and which Indra moves from its place (6, 17.5). He loosened the rock and made the cows easy to obtain (10, 112.8). He released the cows which were fast within the stone (6, 43.3. cp. 5, 30.4). The cloud rocks or mountains would seem to represent the stationary rainless clouds seen during drought, while the cloud cows would rather be the moving and roaring rain-cloud. Oldenberg thinks that to the poets of the Ṛgveda the mountains as well as the rivers in the Vṛtra-myth are terrestrial, though he admits that they were originally aerial and at a later period also were understood as such.

In the mythical imagery of the thunderstorm the clouds also very frequently become the fortresses (*purah*) of the aerial demons. They are spoken of as ninety, ninety-nine, or a hundred in number (2, 14.6. 19.6; 8, 17.14. 87.6). These fortresses are 'moving' (8, 1.28), antumnal (1, 130.7. 174.2; 6, 20.10), made of metal, (2, 20.8) or stone (4, 30.20). Indra shatters them (1, 51.1 &c), and so the epithet 'fort-shatterer' (*pūrbhid*) is peculiar to him. In one verse (10, 111.10) he is spoken of as a fort-shatterer and lover of waters at the same time. In another the various features of the myth are mentioned together; he slew Vṛtra, broke the castles, made a channel for the rivers, pierced the mountain and made over the cows to his friends (10, 89.7).

Owing to the importance of the Vṛtra-myth the chief and specific epithet of Indra is *Vṛtrahan,* 'Vrtra-slayer'. It is applied about 70 times to him in the Ṛgveda The only other deity who receives honour along with him is Agni; but this is due to Agni's frequent association with Indra as a dual divinity. The few applications of the epithet to Soma are clearly secondary. Though Indra is sometimes expressly stated to have slain Vṛtra by his own might alone (1, 165.8; 7, 21.6; 10, 138.6) other deities are very often associated with him in the conflict. The gods in general are said to have placed him in the van for action or battle (1, 55.3; 6, 17.8) or the slaughter of Vṛtra (8, 12.22). They are also said to have increased his vigour for the fray with Vṛtra (10, 113.8), or to have infused might or valour into him (1, 80.15; 6, 20.2; 10, 48.3. 120.3), or to have placed the bolt in his hands (2, 20.8). But most frequently he is urged on and fortified by the Maruts (3, 32.4; 10, 73.1.2. &c 29). Even when the other gods terrified by Vṛtra fled away (8, 85.7 cp. 4, 18.11; AB. 3, 20), they stood by him; but the maruts themselves are in one passage said to have deserted him (8, 7.31). Agni, Soma, and Viṣṇu are often also allied with Indra in the fight with Vṛtra. Even priests on earth sometimes associate themselves with Indra in his combats

(5, 30.8; 8, 51.11; 10, 44.9). The worshipper (*jaritā*) is said to have placed the bolt in Indra's hands (1, 63.2), and the sacrifice is spoken of as having assisted the bolt at the slaughter of the dragon (3, 32.12). Hymns, prayers and worship, as well as Soma, are also often described as increasing (*Vṛdh*) the vigour of Indra.

Besides Vṛtra, Indra engages in conflict with many minor demons also one of these, Uraṇa, mentioned only once (2, 14.4) is described as having 99 arms, while another, Viśvarupa, is three-headed and six-eyed (10, 99.6). He does not always slay them with his bolt. Thus one of them, Arbuda, he crushes with his foot or pierces with ice (1, 51.6; 8, 32.26). Sometimes Indra is described as destroying demons in general. Thus he is said to sweep away the Asuras with his wheel (8, 85.9), to consume the Rākṣasas with his thunder bolt as fire in a dry forest (6, 18.10) and to overcome the *druhali* or malignant spirits (4, 23.7. 28.2).

With the liberation of the waters is connected the winning of light, sun and dawn. Indra who light and the divine waters (3, 34.8). The god is invoked to slay Vṛtra and win the light (8, 78.4). When Indra had slain the dragon Vṛtra with his metalic bolt, releasing the waters for man, he placed the sun visibly in the heavens (1, 51.4. 52.8). Indra, the dragon-slayer, set in motion the fold of waters to the sea, generated the sun, and found the cows (2, 19.3). He gained the sun and the waters after slaying the demons (3, 34.8..9). When Indra slew the chief of the dragons and released the waters from the mountain, he generated the sun, the sky and the dawn (1, 32.4; 6, 30.5). The sun shone forth when Indra blew the dragon from the air (8, 3.20). Though the sun is usually the prize of the conflict, it also appears as Indra's weapon, for he burns the demon with the rays of the sun (8, 12.9). Without any reference to the Vṛtra fight, Indra is said to find the light (3, 34.4; 8, 15.5; 10, 43.4) in the darkness (1, 108.8; 4, 16.4). Indra is the generator of the sun (3, 49.4). He placed the sun, the brilliant light, in the sky (8, 12.30). He made the sun to shine (8, 3.6. 87.2), and made it mount in the sky (1, 7.3). He gained the sun (1, 100.6.18; 3, 34.9) or found it in the darkness in which it abode (3, 39.5) and made a path for it (10, 111.3).

Indra's activity in the thunderstorm is sometimes more directly expressed. Thus he is said to have created the lightnings of heaven (2, 13.7) and to have directed the action of the waters downwards (2, 17.5).

With the Vṛtra that of Soma. When Indra drove the dragon from the air, fires, the sun, and Soma, Indra's juice, shone forth (8, 3.20). After his victory over the demon, he chose Soma for his drink (3, 36.8). After he conquered the demons, Soma became his own property (7, 98.5); he became the king of the Soma mead (6, 20.3), Indra disclosed the juice pressed with stones and drove out the cows (3, 44.5). He won Soma at the same time as the cows honey accumulated in the ruddy cow (*usriyāyām*: 3, 39.6). The raw cow goes with ripe milk, in the ruddy cow is accumulated all sweetness, which Indra placed there for enjoyment (3, 30.14). Indra places ripe milk of the cows (8, 32.25), which are raw (8, 78.7) black or red (1, 62.9), and for which he opens the gates (6, 17.6). These passages seem to have primarily at least a mythological reference to rainclouds, as the context in most cases describes the great cosmological actions of Indra.

Indra is said to have settled the quaking mountains and plains (2, 12.2; 10, 44.8). In a later text Indra is said to have cut off the wings of the mountains, which originally alighted wherever they pleased and thus made the earth unsteady. The wings became the thunder clouds (MS. 1, 10.13). This is a favourite myth in post-Vedic literature. Pischel (VS. 1, 174) traces its origin to a mantra of the RV. (4, 54.5).

Indra, the wielder of the thunderbolt, who destroys the aerial demons in battle, is constantly invoked by warriors (4, 24.3 &c).

As the great god of battle he is more frequently called upon than any other deity as the helper of the Aryans in their conflicts with earthly enemies. He protects the Aryan colour and subjects the black skin (3, 34.9; 1, 130.8). He dispersed 50000 of the black race and rent their citadels (4, 16.13). He subjected the Dasyus to the Aryan (6, 18.3) and gave land to the Aryan (4, 26.2). He turns away from the Ārya the weapon of the Dasyu in the land of the seven rivers (8, 24.27). Other deities are only occasionally referred to as protectors of the Āryas, (1, 117.21), Agni (8, 92.1), or the gods in general.

Though the main myth concerning Indra is his combat with Vṛtra, various other stories attached themselves to him as the performer of heroic deeds. Some passages describe Indra as coming into conflict with Uṣas. He struck down the wain (*anas*) of Dawn (10, 73.6). He shattered the wain of Uṣas with his bolt and rent her slow (steeds) with his swift (mares: 2, 15.6). Terrified at the bolt of Indra, Uṣas abandoned her wain (10, 138.5). Indra performed the heroic manly exploit of striking and crushing the female meditating evil, Uṣas, the daughter of the sky; her wain lay shattered in the river Vipāś and Uṣas fled away in terror (4, 30.8-11). The obscuration of the dawn by a thunderstorm is usually regarded as the basis of this myth. Aganist such an interpretation Bergaigne urges that it is not Indra who obscures the sky but a demon, and that the application of the bolt, Indra's characteristic weapon, need not be restricted to the Vṛtra-fight. He concludes that the sunrise overcoming the delaying dawn (cp. 2, 15.6; 5, 79.9) is here conceived as a victory of Indra bringing the sun.

Indra comes in conflict with the sun in the obscure myth about a race run between the swift steed Etaśa, who draws a car, and the sun drawn by his yellow steeds. The sun being ahead is hindered by Indra. His car loses a wheel, a loss which is some way seems to have been caused by Indra. With this myth probably connected the statement that Indra stopped the tawny steeds of the sun (10, 92.8). Indra is also associated with the myth of the rape of Soma. For it is to him that the eagle brings the draught of immortality. Another myth which is not often mentioned and the details of which chiefly occur in a single hymn (10, 108) is that of the capture by Indra of the cows of the Paṇis. These demons, who here seem to be the mythical representatives of the niggards who withhold cows from the pious sacrificer, possess herds of cows which they keep hidden in a cave far away beyond the Rasā, a mythical river. Saramā, Indra's messenger, tracks the cows and asks for them in Indra's name, but is mocked by the Paṇis. In another passage (6, 39.2) Indra desiring the cows around the rock is said to have pierced Vala's unbroken ridge and to have overcome the Paṇis. Elsewhere the cows are spoken of as confined by the demon Vala without reference to the Paṇis, and driven out by Indra (2, 12.3; 3, 30.10). In various passages the Aṅgirases are associated with Indra in piercing Vala, shattering his strongholds, and releasing the cows.

Fragmentary references, often in enumerations, are frequently made to the victory of Indra over Dāsas or Dasyus. These are primarily human foes whose skin is black (1, 130.8 cp. 2, 20.7), who are noseless (5, 29.10) are godless and do not sacrifice. Though mythological elements are no doubt largely mingled in the account of his victory over individual Dāsas, the foundation of these myths seems to be terrestrial and human. For while Vṛtra is slain for the good of man in general, individual human beings are mentioned for whom or with whom Indra overcame the Dāsa or Dāsas. These *protīgīs* of Indra are not as a rule ancestors of priests but are princes or warriors who seem to have been historical. Thus Divodāsa Atithigva is the father of the famous king Sudās, his Dāsa foe being Sambara, the son of Kulitara. But when the term *dāsa* is applied to the dragon (*ahi*), from whom Indra wrests the waters (2, 11.2) or to the three-headed six-eyed monster whom Trita combats (10, 99.6) or to Vyaṁsa who struck off Indra's jaws (4, 18.9), it unmistakably designates regular demons. An account of Namuci and other Dāsas vanquished by Indra will be found in the chapter on demons.

Among stories preserving historical traits is that of Indra having safely brought Turvaśa and Yadu across the rivers (1, 174.9 &c). They are the eponymous heroes of two closely connected Aryan tribes, which are, however, sometimes mentioned by the poets in a hostile sense. This varying attitude is a tolerably sure indication of historical matter. Here the national warrior god appears as the patron of Aryan migrations. In another passage Indra is said with Suśravas to have crushed twenty chiefs and their 60099 warriors with fatal chariot wheel. The accounts of the conflicts of king Sudās have all the appearance of a historical character. Thus Indra is said to have helped him in the battle of the ten kings (7, 33.3), to have aided him in answer to the prayers of his priests the Tṛtsus (among whom Vasiṣṭha is prominent), and to have drowned his foes in the river Paruṣṇī (7, 18.9.13).

Finally the hymn of the RV. (8, 80) relates how a maiden named Apālā having found Soma beside a river and having pressed it with her teeth, dedicates it to Indra who approaches and from whom she receives as a reward the fulfilment of certain desires.

Regarded as a whole the attributes of Indra are chiefly those of physical superiority and of dominion over the physical world. Energetic action is characteristic of him, while passive sway is distinctive of Varuṇa. Indra is a universal monarch, not as the applier of the eternal laws of the universe nor as a moral ruler, but as an irresistible warrior whose mighty arm wins victory, whose inexhaustible liberality bestows the highest goods on mankind, and who delighting in the exhileration of magnificent Soma sacrifices, confers rich rewards on the hosts of priests officiating in his worship. The numerous hymns which celebrate him dwell on these features in more or less stereo typed terms and are seldom free from references to the Soma offering. He is not usually described as possessing the moral elevation and grandeur of Varuṇa. There are, however, several passages which ascribe to Indra actions characteristic of Varuṇa. There are also a few, mostly in the later books, in which an ethical character is attributed to him and faith in him is confessed or enjoined as against the disbelief of sceptics (2, 12.4 &.). Once he is said in a late passage of the Ṛgveda to have attained heaven by austere fervour (10, 167.1 cp. 159.4).

To the more intense anthropomorphism of Indra's nature are doubtless due certain sensual and immortal traits which are at variance with the moral perfection elsewhere attributed to him and essential to the character of the Vedic gods. This incongruity cannot be accounted for by different passages representing chronologically different stages in the development of his character, for it is apparent in the words of the same poet, sometimes even in the same verse. It is chiefly connected with his excessive fondness for Soma. In one passage (8, 67.5.6) he is said to hear and see everything, viewing the zeal of mortals, and in the next verse his belly is described as full of the vigorous draught. One entire hymn (10, 119) consists of a monologue in which Indra is intoxicated with Soma, boasting of his greatness and capricious power. It is even indicated that he once suffer from the effects of excessive drinking. His love of Soma is even represented as having driven him to parricide (4, 18.12). In judging morally of Indra's immoderate indulgence in Soma, it must be borne in mind that the exhilaration of Soma partook of a religious character in the eyes of the Vedic poets and that the intoxicating influence of Soma itself led to its being regarded as the drink of immortality. It is probably from the latter point of view that Indra is conceived as having performed his grandest cosmical feats, such as fixing heaven and earth, under the influence of Soma (2, 15.2). And the evident sympathy of the poets with the effect of Soma on the god but reflects the moral standard to the age. Amorous adventures, on the other hand, are entirely absent from the exploits of Indra in the Ṛgveda and there is hardly a trace of such even in the Brāhmaṇas, except that he is spoken of as the paramour of Ahalyā the wife of Gautama. It is only natural that the poetry of the Soma offering should have dwelt on the thirsty aspect of his nature.

The name of Indra occurs only twice in the Avesta. Beyond the fact of his being no god, but only a demon, his character there is uncertain. Indra's distinctive Vedic epithet *vṛtrahan* also occurs in the Avesta in the form of *verethraghna,* which is, however, unconnected with Indra or the thunderstorm myth, designating merely the God of Victory. Thus it is probable that the Indo-Iranian period possessed a god approaching to the Vedic form of the Vṛtra-slaying Indra. It is even possible that beside the thundering god of heaven, the Indo-European period may have known as a distinct conception a thundergod gigantic in size, a mighty eater and drinker, who slays the dragon with his lightning bolt. The etymology of Indra is doubtful, but that the root is connected with that in *indu,* drop, seems likely.

4.2 Vāyu-vāta

Each of the two names of wind Vāyu and Vāta is used to express both the physical phenomenon and its divine personification. But Vāyu is chiefly the god and Vāta the element. Vāyu is celebrated alone in one whole hymn besides parts of others, and in about half a dozen others conjointly with Indra. Vāta is invoked only in two short hymns (168 and 186) at the end of tenth book of the RV. The names of both sometimes occur in the same verse (6, 50.12; 10, 92.13). The difference between the two is illustrated by the fact that Vāyu alone is as a god associated with Indra, the two deities being then often invoked as Indravāyū. This couple was regarded as so closely connected by the ancient native interpreters, that either of them might represent the deities of the atmospheric region in the Vedic triad (Nir. 7, 5). Vāta on the other hand, being less fully personified, is only associated with parjanya, whose connection with the thunderstorm is much more vivid than that of Indra. Different sets of epithets are applied to the two wind-gods, those belonging to Vāta being chiefly expressive of the physical attributes of swiftness and voilence.

Few references are made to Vāyu's origin. The two worlds are said to have generated him for wealth (7, 90.3). He is once spoken of as the son-in-law of Tvaṣṭṛ (8, 26,21-2),.though his wife's name is not mentioned (cp. 38). In the Puruṣa hymn he is said to have sprung from the breath of the world-gaint (10, 90.13). Vāyu is rarely connected with the Maruts. He is, however, once said to have generated them from the wombs of heaven (1, 134.4) and to be accompanied by them (1, 142.12) as well as by Pūṣan and the Viśvedevas. His personal attributes are rather indefinite. He is beautiful (1, 2.1) and with Indra is spoken of as touching the sky, swift as thought, and thousand-eyed (1, 23.2.3). He is once said to have roaring velocity (10, 100.2). Vāyu has a shining car drawn by a team or by a pair of red (*rohita*) or ruddy (*aruṇa*) steeds. His team consists of 99 (4, 48.4), 100 or even 1000 (4, 46.3) horses yoked by his will. The attribute *niyutvat,* 'drawn by a team', often occurs with reference to Vāyu or his car, being otherwise used only once or twice in each case with reference to Indra, Agni, Pūṣan or the Maruts. Vāyu's car, in which Indra is his companion (4, 46.2. 48.2; 7, 91.5), has a golden seat and touches the sky (4, 46.4). Like the other gods, Vāyu is fond of Soma, to which he is often invited to come with his teams and the first draught of which he obtains as his share (also in company with Indra : 1, 135.4), for he is the swifted of the gods (SB. 13, 1, 27 &c). The Aitareya Brāhmaṇa (2, 25) tells a story of how in a race which the gods ran for the first draught of Soma, Vāyu reached the goal first and Indra second. He is in the Ṛgveda also called a protector of Soma (10, 85.5) and has the characteristic epithet *śucipā,* 'drinking the clear (Soma)', an epithet which Indra once shares with him. He is also once connected with the 'nectar-yielding' (*sabardughā*) cow (1, 134.4). Vāyu grants fame, offspring, wealth in steeds, oxen, and gold (7, 90.2.6). He disperses foes (4, 48.2) and is invoked for protection by the weak (1, 134.5).

Vāta, as the ordinary name of wind, is celebrated in a more concrete manner. His name is frequently connected with the root *vā*, to blow, from which it is derived. One of the hymns devoted to his praise (10, 168) describes him as follows. Shattering everything and thundering, he goes along whirling up the dust of the earth; he wanders in the air on his paths; he does not rest even a day. Firstborn, he is a friend of the waters; but the place of his birth is unknown. This deity wanders where he lists; one hears his roaring, but his form one does not see (cp. 1, 164.44). He is the breath of the gods (cp. 7, 87.2; 10, 92.13) and is worshipped with oblations.

Vāta, like Rudra, also wafts healing and prolongs life, for he has the treasure of immortality in his house (10, 186). This healing power of wind doubtless represents its purifying character (cp. p. 77). The activity of wind is chiefly mentioned in connection with the thunderstorm (4, 17.12; 5, 83.4; 10, 168.1.2). Blasts of wind being coincident with the appearance of lightnings and preceding the reappearance of the sun, Vāta is spoken of as producing ruddy lights (10, 168.1) and of making the dawns to shine (1, 134.3). The swiftness of wind often supplies a comparison for the speed of the gods (4, 17.12; 5, 41.3; 9, 97.52) or of mythical steeds (1, 163.11; 4, 38.3). Its noise is also frequently mentioned (4, 22.4; 8, 91.3; 10, 168.1.4). The name of Vāta has been identified with that of the Germanic god of storm and battle, Odhin or Wodan, which is explained as formed with a derivative suffix from the cognate base. But this identification seems to be very doubtful.

4.3 Parjanya

This god plays a very subordinate part among the deities of the Ṛgveda, being celebrated in only three hymns, while the name is mentioned less than thirty times. His praises are also sung in one hymn of the Atharva Veda., (4, 15), which, however, chiefly consists of verses from the Ṛgveda. In the following passages the word *parjanya* can only have the appellative sense of 'rain-cloud'. 'This same water rises and descends day by day; the rain-clouds (*parjanyah*) quicken the earth, the fires quicken heaven' (1, 164.51). Tha Maruts 'even during the day cause darkness by the water-carrying rain-cloud, when they inundate the earth' (1, 38.9); 'they poured out the pail of heaven, they discharge the raincloud through the two worlds, the rain pervades, the dry places' (5, 53.6). Bṛhaspati is besought to cause the cloud to rain and to send the rain-charged (*vṛṣṭimantam*) cloud (10, 98.1.8). Soma flows 'like the rain-charged cloud' (9, 2.9) and the drops of Soma speed 'like the rains of the cloud' (9, 22.2). In the AV. the rain-shedding cow Vaśā is thus addressed: 'The rain-cloud is thy udder, excellent goddess, the lightnings are thy teats, O Vaśā' (AV. 10, 10.7). In all such passages the native commentators explaining *parjanya* by *megha,* 'cloud'. On the other hand, *parjanya* is used to explain *dysus* in Vajasaneyi Saṁhita 12,6 and *stanayitnu,* 'thunder' in Śatapatha Brāhmaṇa (5.10). In some cases it is hard to say whether we have the appellative or the personified meaning. Thus the might of Agni is said to resound like *parjanya* (8, 91.5); and the frogs are spoken of as uttering their voices when roused by *parjanya* (7, 103.1). In most passages, however, the word clearly represents the personification which presides over the rain-cloud, while generally retaining the attributes belonging to the phenomenon. The latter then becomes an udder, a pail (*kośa*) or water-skin (*dṛti*: 5, 83.8.9; 7, 101.4). The pesonification is to a considerable extent theriomorphic, Parjanya being often spoken of as a bull, though with a certain confusion of gender (probably because clouds are otherwise cows). He is a roaring bull with swift-flowing drops, who places his seed in the plants as a germ (5, 83.1, cp. 7.9; AV. 4, 15.1). The clouds (*abhrāṇi*) impelled by the wind come together, and the roaring waters of the great bellowing aqueous (*nabhasvatah*) bull delight the earth (AV. 4, 15.1). Sometimes Parjanya is like a barren cow, sometimes he is productive, disposing of his body according to his wish (7, 101.3).

The shedding of rain is his most prominent characteristic. He flies around with a watery car and loosens and draws downwards the water-skin (5, 83.7). Like a charioteer urging on his horses, he displays his rainy messengers; when he sheds rain water, the roar of the lion resounds from afar; with thunder he comes shedding rain-water as our divine (*asura*) father (5, 83.3.6). He is besought for rains (7, 101.5) and is implored to withhold rain after shedding it (5, 83.10). It is, however, implied that the action of Parjanya, as well as of the Maruts, in shedding rain is subordinate to that of Mitra and Varuna (5, 63.3-6). He is several times said to thunder (5, 83). Thundering he strikes down trees, demons, evil-doers; the whole world is terrified at his mighty weapon (5, 83.2). He and Vāta are the wielders of mighty thunder (10, 66.10). Parjanya is also associated with lightnings fall, when Parjanya quickens the earth with his seed (5, 83.4). Parjanya thunders with lightning in the (aerial) ocean (AV. 19, 30.4). He also appears to be meant, in a hymn of the RV. to the Viśvedevas, by the god who thunders and roars, rich in clouds and water, who with lightning excites the two worlds, besprinkling them (5, 42.14).

As the shedder of rain Parjanya is naturally in a special degree the producer and nourisher of vegetation. When he quickens the earth with his seed, the plants spring up; in his activity are plants of every form; he has produced plants for nourishment (5, 83.4.5.10, cp. 6, 52.6; AV. 4, 15.2.3.15; 8, 7,21). He is the fructifier and increaser of plants; protected by the god they bear good fruit (7, 101.1.5). Reeds and grass are produced by his action (7, 102.1, cp. 5, 75.15; AV. 1. 2.1 3.1; 19, 30.5). Parjanya places the germ not only in plants but in cows, mares and women (7, 102.2), and is invoked to bestow fertility (5, 83.7 cp. 6, 52.16). He is the bull that impregnates everything: in him is the soul of what moves and stands (7, 101.6; cp. 1, 115.1). He is even described as a self-dependent sovereign, who rules over the whole world, in whom all beings and the three heavens are established, and in whom the threefold waters flow (7, 101.2.4.5). Owing to his generative activity parjanya several times receives the epithet of 'father' (7, 101.3; 9, 82.3; AV. 4, 15.12; 12, 1.12). He is once called 'our divine (*asura*) father' (5, 83.6); and in another passage 'the occult power of the Asura' (5, 63.3.7) perhaps refers to him.

His wife is by implication the Earth (5, 83.4; 7, 101.3). The Atharva Veda (12, 1.12) states that Earth is the mother, Parjanya the father, but elsewhere explicity calls Vāsa his wife (10, 10.6). In these respects as well as the theriomorphic conception of him as a bull, his relation to thunder, lightning, and rain, he approximates to the character of Dyaus (cp. 10, 45.4; 2, 4.6.27.15) whose son he is once called (7, 102.2). Parjanya himself is said to produce a calf (*vatsam*), the germ of plants (7, 101.2, cp. v.3; 5, 83.2), who perhaps represents lightning. Soma may, however, be meant, for his father is once (9, 82.3) said to be Parjanya, and he is spoken of as 'increased by Parjanya' (9, 113,3).

Parjanya is associated with various other deities. His connection is closest with Vāta, who, with the single exception of Agni in one passage, is the only god forming a dual divinity with him (44). The Maruts are also a few times invoked with Parjanya (5, 63.6. 83.5) and are called upon to sing his praises (AV. 4, 15.4). Agni is celebrated with him in two verses of one hymn (6, 52.6.16;). Indra has much in common with the 'rainy' Parjanya, being compared with him in this respect (8, 6.1). The two gods have in fact much the same natural basis, connection with which is, however, much clearer in the case of Parjanya.

4.4 Āpah

The Waters, Āpah, are lauded in four hymns of the R.V. (7, 47. 49; 10, 9.30), as well as in a few scattered verses. They are also invoked in many detached verses along with other deities. The personification is only incipient, hardly extending beyond the notion of their being mothers, young wives, and goddesses who bestow boons and came to the sacrifice. They are goddesses who follow the path of the gods (7, 47.3). Indra armed with the bolt dug out a channel for them (7, 47.4 49.1) and they never infringe his ordinances (7, 47.3). They are also said to be under the commands of Savitṛ (p. 32). They are celestial, as well as flowing in channels, and have the sea for their goal (7, 49.2). It is implied that they abide where the gods are and the seat of Mitra and Varuṇa is (10, 30.1). They are beside the sun and the sun is with them (1, 23.17). King Varuṇa moves in their midst, looking down on the truth and falsehood of men (7, 49.3). In such passages at least, the rain-waters must be meant. But the naighaṅṭuka (5, 3) enumerates the waters among the terrestrial deities only (cp. YN. 9, 26).

Agni is often described as dwelling in the waters (p. 92). He is said to have entered into them (7, 49.4). As mothers, they produce Agni (10, 91.6, cp. 27; AV. 1, 33.1), one of whose forms is called 'Son of Waters'(24). The waters are mothers (10, 30.10). They are besought to give their auspicious fluid like loving mothers (10, 9.2). They are most motherly, the producers of all that is fixed and moves (6, 50.7).

The waters cleanse and purify; these goddesses bear away defilement; the worshipper comes up out of them pure and cleansed (10, 17.10). They are even invoked to cleanse from moral guilt, the sins of voilence, cursing, and lying (1, 23.22 = 10, 9.8). They are remedial (6, 50.7), bestowing remedies and long life, for all remedies, immortality and healing are contained in them (10, 9. 5-7; 1, 23.19-21). They watch over man's health in the house (HGS. 2, 4.5). They dispose of boons and wealth and bestow excellent strength and immortality (10, 9.5, 30.12). Their blessing and aid is often implored (7, 47.4 49.1-4; 10, 9.30.11), and they are invited to seat themselves along with the Son of waters on the sacrificial grass at the offering of the Soma-priest (10, 30.14.15).

The waters are several times associated with honey. As mothers they mix their milk with honey (1, 23.16). The wave of the waters is rich in honey; dripping with ghee it became the drink of Indra, whom it exhilerated (7, 47.1.2). Apāṁ napāt is besought to give waters rich in honey, by which Indra grew to heroic strength (10, 30.4). The waters are invoked to pour the wave, rich in honey and gladdening the gods, for Indra who released them from confinement; the wave which intoxicates, the draught of Indra, which is produced in the sky (10, 30. 7-9). These passages appear to show that sometimes at least the celestial waters were regarded as containing or identical with the heavenly Soma, the beverage of Indra. In other passages the waters used in preparing the terrestrial Soma seem to be meant. When they appear bearing ghee, milk and honey, they are accordant with the priests, bearing well-pressed Soma for Indra (10, 30.13). Soma delights in them as a young man in lovely maidens; he approaches them as a lover; they are maidens who bow down before the youth (10, 30.5-6).

4.5 Apām-napāt

The deity called Apāṁ napāt is celebrated in one whole hymn (2,35), is invoked in two verses of a hymn to the waters (10, 30.3.4), and is mentioned by name nearly thirty times altogether in the RV. The waters stood around the brilliant Son of waters; the youthful waters go around him the youthful; three divine females desire to give food to him the divine; he sucks the milk of the first mothers (2, 35.3-5). He, the bull, engendered the embryo in them; he the child, sucks and they kiss him (v. 13); the

Son of waters growing strong within the waters, shines forth (v.7). He shines without fuel in the waters (v.4; 10, 30.4). Clothed in lightning the Son of waters has mounted upright the lap of the slanting (waters); carrying him the swift (waters) golden in colour go around him (v.9; cp. Agni in 1, 95.4.5). The Son of waters is golden in form, appearance and colour; coming from a golden womb he sits down and gives food to his worshipper (v.10). Standing in the highest place he always shines with undimmed (splendour); the swift waters carrying ghee as food to their son, fly around with their garments (v. 14). The face of the Son waters, whom the maidens kindle, whose colour is golden, and whose food is ghee, increases in secret (v.11). He has a cow which in his own house gives good milk (v.7). Steeds (*vṛṣaṇah*) swift as thought carry the son of waters (1, 186.5). The son of waters is connected with rivers (*nādya*: v.1). The son of waters has engendered all beings, who are merely branches of him (v.2.8). In the last stanza of the Āpām napāt hymn, the deity is invoked as Agni and must be identified with him. Conversely Agni is in some hymns addressed to him, spoken of as āpām napāt (cp. VS. 8, 24). Agni is the Son of waters (3, 9.1). He is the Son of waters who sat down on earth as a dear priest (1, 143.1). But they are also distinguished Agni, accordant with the Son of waters, confers victory over Vṛtra (6, 13.3). The Son of waters unites here with the body of another as it were (2, 35.13). The epithet *āśuheman,* 'swiftly speeding', applied three times to Āpāṁ napāt, is in its only other occurrence used of Agni.

Apāṁ napāt is mentioned in various enumerations, especially with Aja ekapād (2, 31.6; 7, 35.13), Ahi budhnya (1, 186.5; 2, 31.6; 7, 35.13), and Savitṛ (2, 31.6; 6, 50.13). The epithet is directly applied to Savitṛ at least once (p. 33), perhaps because Savitṛ represents another fertilizing form of Agni.

Apāṁ napāt, who is golden, is clothed in lightning, dwells in the highest place, grows in concealment, shines forth, is the offspring of the waters, comes down to earth, and is identified with Agni, appears to represent the lightning form of Agni which is concealed in the cloud. For Agni, besides being directly called Apāṁ napāt, is also termed the embryo (*garbha*) of the waters (7, 9.3; 1, 70.3). As such he has been deposited in human dwellings (3, 5.3), his abode is in the waters (8, 43.9) and the two fire-sticks engender Agni who is the embryo both of plants and of waters (3, 1.13). Agni is also called the the 'son of the rock' (10, 20.7 cp. 6, 48.5), which can hardly refer to anything but the lightning which issues from the cloud mountain. As contrasted with his celestial and terrestrial forms, the third form of Agni is described as kindled in the waters, the ocean, the udder of heaven, the lap of the waters (10, 45.1-3). In fact the abode of the celestial Agni in the waters is one of the best established points in Vedic mythology. The term āptya applied to Trita appears to bear a similar interpretation (23).

Apāṁ napāt is not a creation of Indian mythology, but goes back to the Indo-Iranian period. In the Avesta Apāṁ napāt is a spirit of the waters, who lives in their depths, is surrounded by females and is often invoked with them, drives with swift steeds, and is said to have seized the brightness in the depth of the ocean. Spiegel thinks this deity shows indications of an igneous nature in the Avesta, and Darmesteter considers him to be the fire-god as born from the cloud in lightning. L.V. Schroeder agrees with this view; some scholars, however, dissent from it. Oldenberg is of opinion that Apāṁ napāt was originally a water genius pure and simple, who became confused with the water-born Agni, a totally different being. His grounds are, that one of the two hymns in which he is celebrated (10, 30), is connected in the ritual with ceremonies exclusively concerned with water, while even in 2, 25 his aqueous nature predominates. Hillebrandt, on the other hand, followed by Hardy, thinks Apāṁ napāt is the moon, and Max Muller that he is the sun or lightning.

4.6 Rudra

This god occupies a subordinate position in the RV., being celebrated in only three entire hymns, in part of anther, and in one conjointly with Soma, while his name occurs about 75 times.

His physical features in the Ṛgveda are the following. He has a hand (2, 33.7 &c), arms (2, 33.3; VS. 16.1), and firm limbs (2, 33.11). He has beautiful lips (2, 33.5) and (like Pūṣan) wears braided hair (1, 114.1.5). His colour is brown (*babhru*: 2, 33.5 &c). His shape is dazzling (1, 114.5), and he is multiform (2, 33.9). He shines like the brilliant sun, like gold (1, 43.5). He is arrayed with golden ornaments (2, 33.9) and wears a glorious multiform necklace (*niska*: 2, 33.10). He sits on a car-seat (2, 33.4). The later Saṁhitās (especially VS. 16) add a number of other traits. He is thousand-eyed (AV. 11, 2.2.7, VS. 16, 7). He has a belly, a mouth, a tongue, and teeth (AV. 11, 2.6). His belly is black and his back red (AV. 15, 1.7.8). He is blue-necked (VS. 16, 7) and blue-tufted (AV. 2, 27.6). He is copper-coloured and red (VS. 16, 7). He is clothed in a skin (VS. 3, 61; 16, 51) and dwells in mountains (VS. 16.2-4).

The Ṛgveda often mentions Rudra's weapons of offence. He is once said to hold the thunderbolt in his arm (2, 33.3). His lightning shaft (*didyut*) discharged from the sky traverses the earth (7, 46.3). He is usually said to be armed with a bow and arrows (2, 33.10.11; 5, 42.11; 10, 125.6), which are strong and swift (7, 46.1). He is invoked with Kṛśānu (48) and the archers (10, 64.8); and seems to be intended when Indra is compared with the archer on the car-seat (6, 20.9, cp. 2, 33.11). In the AV. he is also called an archer (1, 28.1; 6, 93.1; 15, 5.1-7). In that and other later Vedic texts his bow, arrow, weapon, bolt or club are frequently referred to (AV. 1, 28.5 &c.; SB. 9, 1, 1.6).

One of the points most frequently mentioned about Rudra is his relationship to the Maruts. He is their father (1, 114.6.9; 2,

33.1); or they are more frequently spoken of as his sons and are also several times called Rudras or Rudriyas. He is said to have generated them from the shining udder of Pṛśni (2, 34.2). But Rudra is never associated, as Indra is, with the warlike exploits of the Maruts, for he does not engage in conflict with the demons. *Tryambaka,* a common epithet of Śiva in, post-Vedic literature, is already applied to Rudra in Vedic texts (VS. 3, 58; SB. 2, 6, 2.9) and seems to refer to him once even in the RV. (7, 59.12). The meaning appears to be 'he who has three mothers' (cp. 3, 56.5) in allusion to the threefold division of the universe (cp. GRV. 1, 555). Ambikā, a post-Vedic name of Śiva's wife is mentioned for the first time in Vajasaneyi Saṁhitā 3, 5, appearing here, however, with Agni. He is also identified with Agni in the AV. (7, 87.1), in the Taittiriya Saṁhitā (5, 4, 3.1; 5, 5, 7.4), and the SB. (6, 1, 3,10, cp. 9, 1, 1.1). The word *rudra* often occurs as an adjective, in several cases as an attribute of Agni though rather often as an attribute of the Aśvins. Śarva and Bhava are, among several others, two new names assigned to Rudra in VS. (16, 18. 28). These two also occur in the AV. where their destructive arrows and lightnings are referred to (2, 27.6; 6, 93.1; 10, 1.23; 11, 2.1.12); but they seem here to have been regarded as deities distinct from one another and from Rudra. Bhava and Śarva are in a Sūtra passage, spoken of as sons of Rudra and are compared with wolves eager for prey (SSS. 4, 20.1). In VS. 39, 8 Agni, Aśani, Paśupati, Bhava, Sarva, Iśāna, Mahādeva, Ugradeva, and others are enumerated as gods or forms of one god. Rudra, Śarva, Paśupati, Ugra, Aśani, Bhava, Mahān Devāh are names given to represent eight different forms of Agni (SB. 6, 1, 3.7; cp. Śāṅkh. Br. 6, 1 &c), and Śarva, Bhava, Paśupati and Rudra are said to be all names of Agni (SB. 1, 7, 3.8). Aśani, one of the above names assigned to Agni Kumāra in the SB. (6, 1, 3.10), is there explained to mean lightning (*vidyut*) but in the Śāṅkh. Br. it is interpreted as Indra. The epithet *Paśuapati*, 'lord of beasts' which Rudra often receives in the Vajasaneyi Saṁhitā, Atharva Veda, and later, is doubtless assigned to him because unhoused cattle are peculiarly exposed to his attacks and are therefore especially consigned to his care.

Rudra is described in the Ṛgveda as fierce (2, 33.9.11; 10, 126.5) and destructive like a terrible beast (2, 33.11). He is the ruddy (*aruṣa*) boar of heaven (1,114.5). He is a bull (2, 33.7.8.15). He is exalted (7, 10.4), strong (1, 43.1; 114.1), strongest of the strong (2, 33.3), unassailable (7, 46.1), unsurpassed in might (2, 33.10), rapid (10, 92.5), and swift (1, 114.4). He is young (2, 33.1; 5, 60.5) and unaging (6, 49.10). He is called *asura* (5, 42.11) or the great *asura* of heaven (2, 1.6). He is self-glorious (1, 129.3; 10, 92.9), rules heroes (1, 114.1.2 &c), and is a lord (*īśāna*) of this vast world (2, 33.9) and father of the world (6, 49.10). He is an ordiner (6, 46.1), and by his rule and universal dominion he is aware of the doings of men and gods (7, 46.2). He makes the stream flow over the earth and roaring, moistens everything (10, 92.5). He is intelligent (1, 43.1), wise (1, 114.4), and beneficient (2, 33.7; 6, 49.10). He is several times called 'bountiful', *midhvas* (1, 114.3), and in the later Vedas the comparative and superlative of this word have only been found in connexion with Rudra. He is easily invoked (2, 33.6) and is auspicious, *Śiva* (10, 92.9), an epithet which is not even in the AV. as yet peculiar to any particular deity.

Malevolence is frequently attributed to Rudra in the Ṛgveda; for the hymns addressed to him chiefly express fear of his terrible shafts and depreciation of his wrath. He is implored not to slay or injure, in his anger, his worshippers, their parents, children, men, cattle or horses (1, 114.7.8), but to spare their horses (2, 33.1), to avert his great malevolence and his bolt from his worshippers, and to prostrate others with them (2, 33.11.14). He is besought to avert his bolt when he is incensed and not to injure his adorers, their children, (6, 28.7. 46.2-4), and to keep from them his cow-slaying, man-slaying missile (2, 33.1). His ill-will and anger are depreciated (2, 33.4-6.15), and he is besought to be merciful to the walking food (10, 169.1). His worshippers pray that they may be unharmed and obtain his favour (2.33.1.6) descend elsewhere (AV.11, 2.25; 10, 1.23). He is even said to assail with fever, cough, and poison (AV. 11, 2.21; 6, 90 cp. 93). Rudra's wide-mouthed, howling dogs, who swallow their prey unchewed, are also spoken of (AV. 10, 1.30, cp. VS. 16, 28). Even the gods were afraid of the strung bow and the arrows of Rudra, lest he should destroy them (SB. 9, 1, 1.1.6). Under the name of Mahādeva he is said to slay cattle (TMB. 6, 9.7). In another Brāhmaṇa passage he is said to have been formed of a compound of all the most terrible substances (AB. 3, 33.1). It is probably owing to his formidable characteristics that in the Brāhmaṇas and Sūtras Rudra is regarded as isolated from the other gods. When the gods attained heaven, Rudra remained behind (SB. 1, 7, 3.1). In the Vedic ritual after offerings to other gods, a remainder is not uncommonly assigned to Rudra (Gobh. GS. 1, 8.28; āp. Dh. S. 2, 4.23). His hosts, which attack man and beast with disease and death, receive the bloody entrails of the victim (SSS. 4, 19.8), just as blood is poured out to demons as their peculiar share of the sacrifice (AB. 2, 7.1). The abode of Rudra in these later texts is commonly regarded as in the north, while that of the other gods is in the east. It is perhaps due to his formidable nature that in the RV. Rudra only appears once associated with another deity (Soma: 44) as a dual divinity in one short hymn of four stanzas.

In the Vajasaneyi Saṁhitā, besides many other epithets too numerous to repeat, several disgraceful attributes of Rudra are mentioned. Thus he is called a 'robber, cheat, deceiver, lord of pilferers and robbers' (16, 20.1). In fact, his character as shown by the various epithets occurring here, approximates to the fierce, terrific, impure and repulsive nature of the post-Vedic Śiva.

Rudra is, however, not purely maleficent like a demon. He is also supplicated in the Ṛgveda to avert the anger or the evil that comes from the gods (1, 114.4; 2, 33.7). He is besought not only to preserve from calamity (5, 51.13), but to bestow blessings (1, 114.1.2; 2, 33.6), and produce welfare for man and beast (1, 43.6). His healing powers are mentioned with especial frequency. He grants remedies (2, 33.12), he commands every remedy (5, 42.11), and has a thousand remedies (7, 46.3). He carries in his hand choice remedies (1, 114.5), and his hand is restorative and healing (2, 33.7). He raises up heroes by his remedies, for he is the greatest physician of physicians (2, 33.4), and by his auspicious remedies his worshipper hopes to live a hundred winters (2, 33.2). He is besought to remove sickness from his worshippers' offspring (7, 46.2) and to be favourable to man and beast, that all in the village may be well-fed and free from disease (1, 114.1). In this connection Rudra has two epithets which are peculiar to him, *jalāṣa,* (perhaps) 'healing' and *jalāṣa-bheṣaja,* 'possessing healing remedies (1, 43.4; AV. 2, 27.6). These medicines against sickness are probably rains (cp. 5, 53.14; 10, 59.9). That this attribute was essential to his nature, appears from a verse of a hymn in which various deities are characterized without being named (8, 29.5): 'One bright, fierce, possessing healing remedies, holds a sharp weapon in his hand'. Rudra's lightning and his remedies are also mentioned together in another verse (7, 46.3). The healing Rudra with the Rudras is invoked to be favourable (7.35.6). The Maruts are also in another verse associated with Rudra as possessing pure and beneficient remedies (2, 33.13). The healing power of Rudra is sometimes referred to in the other Saṁhitās (VS. 3, 59; 16, 5.49; AV. 2, 27.6); but much less frequently than his destructive activity. In the Sūtras, sacrifices to him are prescribed for removing or preventing disease in cattle (AG. 4, 8.40; Kauś. S. 51, 7 &c).

The evidence of the RV. does not distinctly show with what physical basis Rudra is connected. He is generally regarded as a storm-god. But his missile is maleficent, unlike that of Indra, which is directed only against the enemies of his worshippers. Rudra appears therefore to have originally represented not the storm pure and simple, but rather its baleful side in the destructive agency of lightning. This would account for his deadly shafts and for his being the father or chief of the Maruts or Storm-gods, who are armed with lightning and who are said to have been born 'from the laughter of lightning' (1, 23.12). His beneficent and healing powers would be based partly on the fertilizing and purifying action of the thunderstorm and partly on the indirect action of sparing those whom he might say. Thus the depreciations of his wrath gave rise to the euphemistic epithet 'auspicious' (*śiva*), which became the regular name of Rudra's historical successor in post-Vedic mythology. This explanation would also account for Rudra's close connection with Agni in the Ṛgveda.

4.7 Marut-devatās

The Maruts: These are prominent deities in the RV., thirty-three hymns being dedicated to them alone, seven at least to them conjointly with Indra, and one each to them with Agni and Pūṣan. They form a troop, *gaṇa* (a word generally used in connection with them) or *śardhas* (1, 37.1.5 &c), of deities mentioned only in the plural. Their number is thrice sixty (8, 85.8) or thrice seven (1, 133.6; AV. 13, 1.13). Their birth is often referred to (5, 57.5 &c). They are the sons of Rudra (p. 74), being also often called Rudras (1, 39.4.7 &c). and sometimes Rudriyas (1, 38.7; 2. 34.10 &c), and of Pṛśni (2, 34.2; 5, 52.16. 60.5; 6, 66.3), often receiving the epithet *pṛśnimātarah,* 'having Pṛśni for their mother' (1, 23.10 &c; AV. 5, 21.11). The cow Pṛśni (5, 52.16), or simply a cow is their mother (8, 83.1) and they bear the epithet *gomātarah*, 'having a cow for their mother' (1, 85.3, cp. 8, 20.8). This cow presumably represents the mottled strom-cloud (43.61B); and the flaming cows having distended udders with whom they some (2, 34.5), can hardly refer to anything but the clouds charged with rain and lightning. When born from Pṛśni the Maruts are compared with fires (6, 66.1-3). They are also said to have fashioned or begotten them (6, 3.8; 1, 71.8). Vāyu is once said to have engendered them in the wombs of heaven (1, 134.4), and once they are called the sons of heaven (10, 77.2), being also referred to as the heroes (*vīrāh*) of heaven (1, 64.4, 122.1; 5, 54.10) or as the males (*maryāh*) of heaven (3, 54.13; 5, 59.6). Once they are said to have the ocean for their mother, *Sindhumātarah* (10, 78.6 cp.p. 5.1). Elsewhere they are said to be self-born (1, 168.2; 5, 87.2).

They are brothers among whom none is eldest or youngest (5, 59.6, 60.5), for they are equal in age (1, 165.1). They have grown together (5, 56.5); 7, 58.1) and are of one mind (8, 20.1.21). They have the same birthplace (5, 53.3) and the same abode (1, 165.1; 7, 56.1). They are spoken of as having grown on earth, in air and heaven (5, 55.7) or as dwelling in the three heavens (5, 66.6). They are also once described as dwelling in the mountains (8, 83.1.2).

They are associated with the goddess Indrani, who is their friend (10, 86.9), and with Sarasvati (7, 96.2, cp. 39.5). Their connection is, however, closest with the goddess Rodasī, who is described as standing with them on their car bringing enjoyments (5, 56.8) or simply as standing beside them (6, 66.6). In all the five passages in which her name occurs, she is mentioned with them (cp. 1, 167.4.5). She therefore appears to have been regarded as their bride (like Sūrya as the bride of the Aśvins). It is probably to this connection that they owe the epithet *bhadrajānayah,* 'having a beautiful wife' (5, 61.4) and their comparison with bridegrooms (5, 60.4) or youthful wooers (10, 78.6).

The brilliance of the Maruts is constantly referred to. They are golden, of sun-like brightness, like blazing fires, of ruddy aspect (6, 66.2; 7, 59.11; 8, 7.7). They shine like tongues of fire (10, 78.3). They have the form or the brilliance of Agni (10,

84.1; 3, 26.5), with whom they are compared in brightness (10, 78.2). They are like fires (2, 34.1) or kindled fires (6, 66.2) and are expressly called fires (3, 26.4). They have the brilliance of serpents (*ahibhānavah*: 1, 172.1). They shine in the mountains (8, 7.1). They are self-luminuous (1, 37.2 &c.), an epithet almost exclusively applied to them. They are frequently spoken of in a more general way as shining and brilliant (1, 165.12 &c).

They are particularly often associated with lightning, *vidyut* (5, 54.2.3.11; 1, 64.5). The lightning smile down on earth when the Maruts shed their ghee (1, 168.8, cp. 5, 52.6). The lightning follows like a cow, as a mother following her calf, when they shed their rain (1, 38.8). They are like lightinings shining with rain (7, 56.13). Lightning is so characteristic of them that all the five compounds of *vidyut* in the Ṛgveda are connected with the Maruts and, excepting a single instance, with them only. They hold lightnings in their hands (8, 7.25; 5, 54.11), they delight in lightnings and cast a stone (5, 54.3). Their lances (*ṛṣṭi*) are often mentioned, and that these represent the lightning is shown by their epithet *ṛṣṭividyut*, 'lightning-speared' (1, 168.5; 5, 52.13). Less frequently they are spoken of as having axes (1, 37.2. 88.3; 5, 33.4. 57.2; 8, 20.4), which are golden (8, 7.32). Once (ibid), they are said to bear the bolt (*vajra*), Indra's peculiar weapon, in their hands. Sometimes they are said to be armed with bows and arrows (5, 53.4. 57.2; 8, 20.4.12), once being termed archers shooting an arrow; but as this trait is rare in the numerous hymns addressed to them, it may be borrowed from their father Rudra. The Maruts are decorated with garlands and other ornaments (5, 53.4). They wear golden mantles (5, 55.6). Like rich wooers they deck their bodies with golden ornaments (5, 60.4). Armlets or anklets (*khādi*) are an ornament peculiar to them. With these they shine like the sky with stars and glitter like showers from the clouds (2, 34.2). One verse describes their appearance more fully than usual. They have spears on their shoulders, anklets on their feet, golden ornaments on their breasts, fiery lightnings in their hands, golden helmets upon their heads (5, 54.11).

The Maruts ride on cars which gleam with lightning (1, 88.1; 3, 54.13), which are golden (5, 57.1), which have golden wheels or fellies (1, 64.11; 88.5), in which are weapons (5, 57.6), and which have buckets standing in them (1, 87.2). The courses which draw their cars are ruddy or tawny (1, 88.2; 5, 57.4), golden-footed (8, 7.27), and swift as thought (1, 85.4). These courses are spotted, as appears from the epithet *pṛṣadaśva,* 'having spotted steeds', which is several times and exclusively connected with the Maruts. More frequently the animals which draw their car are spoken of in the feminine as *pṛṣatīh* (1, 39.6 &c). These are in two passages (5, 55.6. 58.6), mentioned with the masculine *aśvāh.* The Maruts are also described as having yoked the wins as steeds to their pole (5, 58.7).

The Maruts are great as the sky (5, 57.4), they surpass heaven and earth (10, 77.3), are immeasurable in greatness (5, 58.2), and no others can reach the limit of their might (1, 167.9). The Maruts are young (1, 64.2; 165.2; 5, 42.15) and unaging (1, 64.3). They are divine (*asura*), vigorous, impetuous, without soil (1, 64.2.12) and dustless (6, 66.2). They are fierce (1, 19.4), terrible (5, 56.2.3; 7, 58.2), of terrible aspect (5, 56.2), of fearful form (1, 19.5.64.2), and are terrible like wild beasts (2, 34.1; cp.p. 75). They are playful like children or calves (1, 166.2; 7, 56.16; 10,78.6). They are like black-backed swans (7, 59.7). They are iron-tusked boars (1, 88.5); they are like lions (1, 64.8).

The noise which they make is often referred to (1, 169.7 &c) and is expressly called thunder (1, 23.11); but it is also the roaring of the winds (7, 56.3). At their coming heaven as it were roars with fear (8, 7.26). They are often described as causing the mountains to quake as well as making the earth or the two worlds tremble. With the fellies of their cars they rend the mountains or the rock (1, 64.11; 5, 52.9). It is when they come with the winds that they cause the mountains to quake (8, 7.4). They rend trees and like wild elephants devour the forests (1, 39.5. 64.7). The forests bow down before them through fear (5, 60.2). Resistless as mountains they cast down terrestrial and celestial creatures (1, 64.3). All creatures are afraid of them (1, 85.8). They speed like boisterous winds (10, 78.3) and whirl up dust (1, 64.12). They make the winds or the noise of the winds (7, 56.3). They come with the winds (8, 7.3.4.17) and take them as their steeds (5, 58.7).

They rise from the ocean and shed rain (1, 38.9). Milking the unfailing well, they blow through the two worlds with rain (1, 64.6; 8, 7.16). Rain follows them (5,53.10). They bring water and impel rain (5, 58.3). They obscure their brilliance with rain (5, 59.1). They cover the eye of the sun with rain (5, 59.5). They create darkness with the cloud when they shed rain (1, 38.9). They scatter mist when they speed with winds (8, 7.4). They cause the heavenly pail (5, 53.6. 59.8) and the streams of the mountains to pour (5, 59.7). When they hurry on, the waters flow (5, 58.6). A terrestrial river receives its name, Marudvṛddhā, 'swelled by the Maruts' (10, 75.5), from this action. The sweat of the sons of Rudra became rain (5, 58.7). The rain shed by the Maruts is also figuratively referred to as milk (1, 166.3), ghee (1, 85.3; 10, 78.4), milk and ghee (1, 64.6); or they are said to pour out the spring (1, 85.11) or to wet the earth with honey (5, 54.8). They raise waters from sea to sky and discharge them from the sky upon the earth (AV. 4, 27.4). The waters which they shed are often clearly connected with the thunderstorm. Desiring to give water, whirling hail, violent, they rush on with thunder (5, 54.3). They cause winds and lightnings with their might, milk heavenly gifts from the udder, and fill the earth with milk (1, 64.5). The spring which they milk, thunders (1, 64.6). The sky, the ruddy bull, bellows when they shed the waters (5, 58.6).

They cause the stallion to make water (1, 64.6). They bestow the rain of heaven and shed abundantly the streams of the stallion (5, 83.6). They assume a golden colour when they, make water with the steed (2, 34.13). The streams resound with the fellies of the Maruts, when they raise the voice of the cloud (1, 168.8). The waters which Indra sheds are called *marutvatīh*, 'attended by the Maruts' (1, 80.4). In connection with their character as shedders of rain, the Maruts receive the epithets *purudrapsāh* (5, 57.5) or *drapsinah* (1, 64.2) 'abounding in drops' and the frequent *sudānavah,* 'dripping well'. They also avert heat (5, 54.1). But they likewise dispel darkness (7, 56.20), produce light (1, 86.10), and prepare a path for the sun (8, 7.8). They are also said to have measured out the air (5, 55.2), stretched out the terrestrial regions as well as the bright realms of heaven, and held apart the two worlds (8, 83.9.11).

Being identified with the phenomena of the thunderstorm, the Maruts are naturally intimate associate of Indra, appearing as his friends and allies in innumerable passages. They increase his strength and prowess (3, 35.9; 6, 17.11), with their prayers, hymns, and songs (1, 165.11 &c). They generally assist Indra in the Vṛtra fight (8, 65.2.3; 10, 113.3). They help Trita as well as Indra in slaying Vṛtra (8, 7.24). They are besought to sing a Vṛtra-slaying hymn (8, 78.1-3). They helped Indra in the conflict with the dragon and with Śambara (3, 47.3.4). With them Indra gains the light (8, 65.4), found the cows (1,6.5) and supported the sky (7, 47.5). In fact Indra accomplishers all his celestial exploits in their company (1, 100.101..165; 10, 65). Sometimes the Maruts appear more independent in these exploits. Thus they strike Vṛtra, assisted by Indra (1, 23.9) and are even spoken of alone as having rent Vṛtra joint from joint (8, 7.23) or as having disclosed the cows (2, 34.1). They (like the gods in general) have Indra as their chief (1, 23.8 &c) and are accompanied by Indra (10, 128.2). They are like sons to Indra (1, 100.5) and are called his brothers

(1, 170.2). The Maruts are, however two or three times said to have left Indra in the lurch. They involved him alone in the fight with the (dragon) (1, 165.6) and they abandoned him (8, 7.31). One verse even gives evidence of hostility between Indra and the Maruts, when the latter say to him: 'Why dost thou seek to kill us, Indra? Do not kill us in the fray (1,· 170.2 cp. 171.6). A Brāhmaṇa passage (TB. 2, 7, 11.1) also refers to a conflict between the Maruts and Indra.

When not associated with Indra, the Maruts occasionally exhibit male-violent traits. They then to some extent participate in the maleficent nature of their father Rudra. They are implored to ward off the lightning from their worshippers nor to let their ill-will reach them (7, 56.9), and are besought to avert their arrow and the stone which they hurl (1, 172.2), their lightning (7, 57.4), and their cow- and man-slaying bolt (7, 56.17). Evil can come from them (1, 39.8), their anger is depreciated (1, 171.1; 7, 58.5), and they are said to have the wrath of the serpent (1, 64.8.9). But like their father Rudra, the Maruts are supplicated to bring healing remedies, which abide in the Sindhu, the Asikni, the seas, and mountains (8, 20.23-6), and once they are associated with Rudra in the possession of pure, salutary, and beneficent remedies (2, 33.13). The remedies appear to be the waters, for the Maruts bestow medicine by raining (5, 53.14). Like Agni, they are several times also says to be pure or purifying *pāvaka* (7, 56.12 &c).

Chapter - V

Celestial Gods
(Dyu-sthāna-devatās)

5.1 Varuṇa

Varuṇa, as has been shown (p. 20), is by the side of Indra, the greatest of the gods of the RV. The number of hymns dedicated to his praise is not a sufficient criterion of his exalted character. Hardly a dozen hymns celebrate him exculsively. Judged by the statistical standard he would rank only as a third class deity; and even if the two dozen hymns in which he is invoked along with his double Mitra are taken into account, he would only come fifth in order of priority, ranking considerably below the Aśvins and about on an equality with the Maruts. (cp. p. 20).

The Varuṇa's personality is more fully developed on the moral than the physical side. The descriptions of his person and his equipment are scanty, more stress being laid on his activity. He has a face, an eye, arms, hands and feet. He moves his arms, walks, drives, sits, eats and drinks. The poet regards the face (*anīkam*) of Varuṇa as that of Agni (7, 88.2 cp. 87.6). The eye of Mitra and Varuṇa is the sun (1, 115.1; 6, 51.1; 7, 61.1.63.1; 10,

37.1). The fact that this is always mentioned in the first verse of a hymn, suggest that it is one of the first ideas that occur when Mitra and Varuṇa are thought of. The eye with which Varuṇa is said in a hymn to Sūrya (1, 50.6) to observe mankind, is undoubtedly the sun. Together with Aryaman, Mitra and Varuṇa are called sun-eyed (7, 66.10), a term applied to other gods also. Varuṇa is far-sighted (1, 25.5.16; 8, 90.2) and thousand-eyed (7, 34.10). Mitra and Varuṇa stretch out their arms (5, 64.2; 7, 62.5) and they drive with the rays of the sun as with arms (8, 90.2). Like Savitṛ and Tvaṣṭr they are beautiful-handed (*supāṇi*). Mitra and Varuṇa hasten up with their feet (5, 64.7), and Varuṇa treads down wiles with shining foot (8, 41.8). He sits on the strewn grass at the sacrifice (1, 26.4; 5, 72.2), and like other gods he and Mitra drink Soma (4, 41.3 &c). Varuṇa wears a golden mantle (*drāpi*) and puts on a shining robe (1, 25.13). But the shining robe of ghee with which he and Mitra are clothed (5, 62.4; 7, 64.1) is only a figurative allusion to the sacrificial offering of melted butter. The glistening garments which they wear (1, 152.1) probably mean the same thing. In the SB. (13; 3, 6.5) Varuṇa is represented as a fair, bald, yellow-eyed old man. The only part of Varuṇa's equipment which is at all prominent is his car. It is described as shining like the sun (1, 122.15), as having thongs for a pole (ibid), a car-seat and a whip (5, 62.7), and as drawn by well-yoked steeds (5, 62.4). Mitra and Varuṇa mount their car in the highest heaven (5, 63.1). The poet prays that he may see Varuṇa's car on the earth (1, 25.18).

Varuṇa alone, or conjointly with Mitra, is often called a king (*rājā*), like the other leading deities and Yama (1, 24.7.8 &c). He is king of all, both gods and men (10, 132.4; 2, 27.10), of the whole world (5, 85.3), and of all that exists (7, 87.6). Varuṇa is also a self-dependent ruler (2, 28.1), a term generally applied to Indra. Much more frequently Varuṇa, alone or mostly in association with Mitra, is called a universal monarch (*samrāj*).

This term is also applied to Agni a few times and oftener to Indra. Counting the passages in which Varuṇa and Mitra together are so called, it is connected with Varuṇa nearly twice as often as with Indra. Considering that for every eight or ten hymns celebrating Indra only one is dedicated to Varuṇa in the RV., the epithet may be considered peculiarly appropriate to Varuṇa.

The attribute of sovereignty (*kṣatra*) is in a predominant manner appropriated to Varuṇa, generally with Mitra and twice with Aryaman also. Otherwise it is applied only once respectively to Agni, Bṛhaspati and the Aśvins. Similarly the term 'ruler' (*kṣatriya*) in four of its five occurrences refers to Varuṇa or the Ādityas and once only to the gods in general. The epithet *asura* is connected with Varuṇa, alone or accompanied by Mitra, oftener than with Indra and Agni; and, taking account of the proportion of hymns, it may be said to be specially applicable to Varuṇa's. Mitra and Varuṇa are also called the mysterious and noble lords (*asurā aryā*) among the gods (7, 65.2).

The divine dominion of Varuṇa and Mitra is often referred to with the word *māyā*. This term signifies occult power, applicable in a good-sense to gods or in a bad sense to demons. It has an almost exact parallel in the English word 'craft', which in its old significance meant 'occult power, magic', then 'skillfulness, art' on the one hand and 'deceitful skill, while' on the other. The good sense of *māyā*, like that of *asura* (which might be rendered by 'mysterious being') is mainly connected with Varuṇa and Mitra, while its bad sense is reserved for demons. By occult power Varuṇa standing in the air measures out the earth with the sun as with a measure (5, 85.5), Varuṇa and Mitra send the dawns (3, 61.7), make the sun to cross the sky and obscure it with cloud and rain, while the honied drops fall (5, 63.4); the occult power of the Asura (here = Dyaus or Parjanya). And so the epithet *māyin,* 'crafty', is chiefly applied to Varuṇa among the gods (6, 48.14; 7, 28.4; 10, 99.10. 147.5).

In marked contrast with Indra, Varuṇa has no myths related of him, while much is said about him (and Mitra) as upholder of physical and moral order. Varuṇa is a great lord of the laws of nature. He established heaven and earth and dwells in all the worlds (8, 42.1). The three heavens and the three earths are deposited within him (7, 87.5). He and Mitra rule over the whole world (5, 63.7) or encompass the two worlds (7, 61.4). They are the guardians of the whole world (2, 27.4 &c). By the law of Varuṇa heaven and earth are held apart (6, 70.1; 7, 86.1; 8, 41.10). With Mitra he supports earth and heaven (5, 62.3), or heaven, earth and air (5, 69.1.4). He made the golden swing (the sun) to shine in heaven (7, 87.5). He placed fire in the waters, the sun in the sky, Soma on the rock (5, 85.2). He has made a wide path for the sun (1, 24.8; 7, 87.1). Varuṇa, Mitra and Aryaman open paths for the sun (7, 60.4). The order (*ṛta*) of Mitra and Varuṇa is established where the steeds of the sun are loosed (5, 62.1). The wind which resounds through the air is Varuṇa's breath (7, 87.2).

By Varuṇa's ordinances (*vratāni*) the moon shining brightly moves at night, and the stars placed up on high are seen at night but disappear by day (1, 24.10). In another passage (8, 41.3) it is said that Varuṇa has embraced (*pari ṣarvaje*) the nights, and by his occult power has established the mornings or days (*usrah*). This can hardly indicate a closer connection with night than that he regulates or divides night and day (cp. 7, 66.11). In fact it is the sun that is usually mentioned with him, and not the moon or night. Thus in the oldest Veda Varuṇa is the lord of light both by day and by night, while Mitra, as far as can be judged, appears as the god of the celestial light of day only.

Varuṇa is sometimes referred to as regulating the seasons. He knows the twelve months (1, 25.8); and the kings Mitra, Varuṇa and Aryaman are said to have disposed the autumn, the month, day and night (7, 66.11).

Even in the RV. Varuṇa is often spoken of as a regulator of the waters. He caused the rivers to flow; they stream unceasingly accordingly to his ordinance (2, 28.4). By his occult power the rivers swiftly pouring into the ocean do not fill it with water ((5, 85.6). Varuṇa and Mitra are lords of rivers (7, 64.2). Varuṇa is already found connected with the sea in the RV., but very rarely, perhaps owing to its unimportance in that collection. Varuṇa going in the oceanic waters is contrasted with the Maruts in the sky, Agni on earth, and Vāta in air (1, 161.14). The statement that the seven rivers flow into the jaws of Varuṇa as into a surging abyses (8, 58.12), may refer to the ocean. Varuṇa is said to descend into the sea (*sindhum*) like Dyaus (7, 87.6). It is rather the aerial waters that he is ordinarily connected with. Varuṇa ascends to heaven as a hidden ocean (8, 41.8). Beholding the truth and falsehood of men, he moves in the midst of the waters which drop sweetness and are clear (7, 49.3). Varuṇa clothes himself in the waters (9, 90.2 cp. 8, 69.11.12). He and Mitra are among the gods most frequently thought of and prayed to as bestowers of rain. Varuṇa makes the inverted cask (of the cloud) to pour its waters on heaven, earth and air and to moisten the ground, the mountains then being enveloped in cloud (5, 85.3.4). Mitra and Varuṇa have kine yielding refreshment and streams flowing with honey (5, 69.2). They have rainy skies and streaming waters (5.85.5). They bedew the pasturage with ghee (= rain) and the spaces with honey (3, 62.16). They send rain and refreshment from the sky (7, 64.2). Rain abounding in heavenly water comes from them (8, 25.6). Indeed, one entire hymn (5, 63) dwells on their powers of bestowing rain. It is probably owing to his connection with the waters and rain, that in the fifth chapter of the Naighaṅṭuka Varuṇa is enumerated among the deities of the atmospheric as well as those of the celestial world. In the Brāhmaṇas Mitra and Varuṇa are also gods of rain. In the AV. Varuṇa appears divested of his powers as a universal ruler, retaining only the control of the department of waters. He is connected with the waters as Soma with the mountains (AV. 3, 3.3). As a divine father he sheds rain-waters (AV. 4, 15.12). His golden house is in the waters (AV. 7, 83.1). He is the overlord of waters, he and Mitra are lords of rain (AV. 5, 24.4.5). In the YV. he is spoken of as the child (*śiśu*) of waters, making his abode within the most motherly waters (AV. 10, 7). The waters are wives of Varuṇa (TS. 5, 5, 4.1). Mitra and Varuṇa are the leaders of waters (TS. 6, 4, 3.2).

Varuṇa's ordinances are constantly said to be fixed, the epithet *dhṛtavrata* being preeminently applicable to him, sometimes conjointly with Mitra. The gods themselves follow Varuṇa's ordinances (8, 41.7) or those of Varuṇa, Mitra and Savitṛ (10, 36.13). Even the immortal gods cannot obstruct the fixed ordinances of Mitra and Varuṇa (5, 69.4 cp. 5, 63.7). Mitra and Varuṇa are lords of order (*ṛta*) and light, who by means of order are the upholders of order (1, 23.5). The latter epithet is mostly applied either to them and sometimes the Adityas or to the gods in general. They are cherishers of order or right (*ṛtasya gopā*), but this term is also applied to Agni and Soma. The epithet 'observer of order' (*ṛtāvan*), predominantly used of Agni, is also several times connected with Varuṇa and Mitra.

Varuṇa's power is so great that neither the birds as they fly nor the rivers as they flow, can reach the limit of his dominion, his might, and his wrath (1, 24.6). Neither the skies nor the rivers have reached (the limit of) the godhead of Mitra and Varuṇa (1, 151.9). He embraces the All and the abodes of all beings (8, 41.1.7). The three heavens and the three earths are deposited in him (7, 87.5). Varuṇa is omniscient. He knows the flight of birds in the sky, the path of ships in the ocean, the course of the far-travelling wind, and beholds all the secret things that have been or shall be done (1, 25,7.9.11). He witnesses men's truth and falsehood (7, 49.3). No creature can even wink without him (2,

28.60). The winkings of men's eyes are all numbered by Varuṇa, and whatever man does, thinks, or devises, Varuṇa knows (AV. 4, 16.2.5). He perceives all that exist within heaven and earth and all that is beyond: a man could not escape from Varuṇa by fleeing far beyond the sky (AV. 4, 16.4.5). That Varuṇa's omniscience is typical is indicated by the fact that Agni is compared with him in this respect (10, 11.1).

As a moral governor Varuṇa stands for above any other deity. His wrath is roused by sin, the infringement of his ordinances, which he severly punishes (7, 86.3.4). The feetters (*pāśāh*) with which he binds sinners, are often mentioned (1, 24.15..25.21; 6, 74,4; 10, 85.24). They are cast sevenfold and threefold, ensnaring the man who tells lies, passing by him who speaks truth (AV. 4, 16.6). Mitra and Varuṇa are barriers, furnished with many fetters, against falsehood (7, 65.3). Once Varuṇa, coupled with Indra, is said to tie with bonds not formed of rope (7, 84.2). The term *pāśa* is only once used in connection with another god, Agni, who is implored to loosen the fetters of his worshippers (5, 2.7). It is therefore distinctive of Varuṇa. According to Bergaigne the conception of Varuṇa's fetters is based on the tying up of the waters, according to Hillebrandt on the fetters of night. But is seems to be sufficiently accounted for by the figurative application of the fetters of criminals to moral guilt. Together with Mitra, Varuṇa, is said to be a dispeller, hater, and punisher of falsehood (1, 15.21; 7, 60.5. 66.13). They afflict with disease those who neglect their worship (1, 122.9). On the other hand, Varuṇa is gracious to the penitent. He unties like a rope and removes sin (2, 28.5; 5, 85.7.8). He releases not only from the sins which men themselves commit, but from those committed by their fathers (7, 86.5). He spares the suppliant who daily transgresses his laws (1, 25.1) and is gracious to those who have broken his laws by thoughtlessness (7, 89.5). There is in fact no hymn to Varuṇa (and the Ādityas) in which the prayer for forgiveness of guilt does not occur, as in the hymns to other deities the prayer for worldly goods.

Varuṇa has a hundred, a thousand remedies, and drives away death as well as releases from sin (1, 24.9). He can take away or prolong life (1, 24.11. 25.12; 7, 88.4. 89.1). He is a wise guardian of immortality (8, 42.2), and the righteous hope to see in the next world Varuṇa and Yama, the two kings who reign bliss (10, 14.7).

Varuṇa is on a footing of friendship with his worshipper (7, 88.4-6), who communes with him in his celestial abode and sometimes see him with the mental eye (1, 25.18; 7, 88.2).

The phenomena with which the two greatest gods of the RV. were originally connected, largely accounts for the difference in their personality. Varuṇa as concerned with the regularly recurring phenomena of celestial light, is the supreme upholder of law in the moral as well as the physical world. His character as such afforded no scope for the development of myths. Indra as the god fighting in the strife of the elements, was conceived by the militant Vedic Indian as a sovereign of the warrior type. Owing to his close connection with the meteorological phenomena of the thunderstorm, which are so irregular in time and diversifed in feature, the character of Indra on the one hand shows traits of capriciousness, while on the other he becomes the centre of more myths than any other deity of the RV.

5.2 Mitra

The association of Mitra with Varuṇa is so predominant that only one single hymn of the RV. (3, 59) is addressed to him alone. The praise of the god is there rather indefinite, but the first verse at least contains something distinctive about him. Uttering his voice (*bruvānah*) he brings men together (*yātayati*) and watches the tillers with unwinking eye (*animiṣā,* said also of Mitra-Varuṇa in 7, 60.6).

In another passage (7, 36.2) almost the same words are applied to Mitra who 'brings men together, uttering his voice,' in contrast with Varuṇa who is here called 'a mighty, infallible guide'. This seems a tolerably clear reference to Mitra's solar character, if we compare with it another verse (5, 82.9) where it is said that the sun-gold Savitṛ 'causes all creatures to hear him and impels them.' In the fifth verse of the hymn to Mitra the god is spoken of as the great Āditya 'bringing men together'. This epithet (*yātayaj-jana*) is found in only three other passages of the RV. In one of these it is applied to Mitra-Varuṇa in the dual (5, 72.2), in another to Mitra, Varuṇa, and Aryamān (1, 136.3), and in the third (8, 91.12) to Agni, who 'brings men together like Mitra'. The attribute therefore seems to have properly belonged to Mitra. The hymn to Mitra further adds that he supports heaven and earth, that the five tribes of men obey him, and that he sustains all the gods. Savitṛ is once (5, 81.4) identified with Mitra because of his laws, and elsewhere (Vāl. 4.3) Viṣṇu is said to take his three steps by the laws of Mitra. These two passages appear to indicate that Mitra regulates the course of the sun. Agni who goes at the head of the dawns produce Mitra for himself (10, 84); Agni when kindled is Mitra (3, 5.4); Agni when born is Varuṇa, when kindled is Mitra (5, 3.1). In the AV. (13, 3.13) Mitra at sunrise is contrasted with Varuṇa in the evening, and (AV. 9, 3.18) Mitra is asked to uncover in the morning what has been covered up by Varuṇa. These passages point to the beginning of the view prevailing in the Brāhmaṇas, that Mitra is connected with day and Varuṇa with night. That view must have arisen from Mitra having been predominantly conceived as allied to the sun, Varuṇa by antithesis becoming god of night. The same contrast between Mitra as god of day and Varuṇa as god of night is implied in the ritual literature, when it is prescribed that Mitra should receive a white and Varuṇa a dark victim at the sacrificial post (TS. 2, 1, 7.4. 9.1; MS. 2, 5.7). The somewhat scanty evidence of the Veda showing that Mitra is a solar deity, is corroborated by the Avesta and Persian religion in general. Here Mitra is undoubtedly a sun-god or a god of light specially connected with the sun.

The etymology of the name is uncertain. However, as the word also often means 'friend' in the RV. and the kindly nature of the god is often referred to in the Veda, Mitra even appearing as a god of peace (TS. 2, 1, 8.4), while in the Avesta Mithra is on the ethical side of his character the guardian of faithfulness, it must have originally signified 'ally' or 'friend' and have been applied to the sun-god in his aspect of a beneficent power of nature.

5.3 Sūrya

Ten entire hymns of the RV. may be said to be devoted to the celebration of Sūrya specifically. It is impossible to say how often the name of the god occurs, it being in man cases doubtful whether only the natural phenomenon is meant or its personification. Since his name designates the orb of the sun as well, Sūrya is the most concrete of the solar deities, his connection with the luminary never being lost sight of. The adorable light of Sūrya in the sky is as the face (*anīka*) of great Agni (10, 7.3). The eye of Sūrya is mentioned several times (5, 40.8 &c), but he is himself equally often called the eye of Mitra and Varuṇa (p. 23) or of Agni as well (1, 115.1); and once (7, 77.3) Dawn is said to bring the eye of the gọds. The affinity of the eye and the sun is indicated in a passage where the eye of the dead man is conceived as going to Sūrya (10, 16.3 cp. 90.3. 158.3.4). In the AV. he is called the 'lord of eyes' (AV. 5, 24.9) and is said to be the one eye of created beings and to see beyond the sky, the earth, and the waters (AV. 13, 1.45). He is far-seeing (7, 35.8; 10, 37.1), all seeing (1, 50.2), is the spy (*spaś*) of the whole world (4, 13.3), beholds all beings and the good and bad deeds of mortals (1, 50.7; 6, 51.2; 7, 60.2. 61.1. 63.1.4). Aroused by Sūrya men pursue their objects and perform their work (7, 63.4). Common to all men, he rises as their rouser (7, 63.2.3). He is the soul or the guardian of all that moves or is stationary (1, 115.1; 7, 60.2). He has a car which is drawn by one steed, called *etaśa* (7, 63.2), or by an indefinite number of steeds (1, 115.3; 10, 37.3.49.7) or mares (5, 29.5) or by seven horses (5, 45.9) or mares called *haritah* (1, 50.8.9; 7, 60.3) or by seven swift mares (4, 13.3).

Sūrya's path is prepared for him by Varuṇa (1, 24.8; 7, 87.1) or by the Ādityas Mitra, Varuṇa, Aryaman (7, 60.4). Pūṣan is his messenger (6, 58.3). The Dawn or Dawns reveal or produce Sūrya as well as Agni and the sacrifice (7, 80.2. 78.3). He shines forth from the lap of the dawns (7, 63.3). But from another point of view Dawn is Sūrya's wife (7, 75.5).

He also bears the metronymic Āditya, son of Aditi (1, 50.12.191.9; 8, 90.11) or Āditeya (10, 88.11), but he is elsewhere distinguished from the Ādityas (8, 35.13-15). His father is Dyaus (10, 37.1). He is god-gorn (ibid). The gods raised him who had been hidden in the ocean (10, 72.7). As a form of Agni he was placed by the gods in heaven (10, 88.11). According to another order of ideas he is said to have arisen from the eye of the world-gaint Puruṣa (10, 90.3). In the AV. (4, 10.5) the sun (*divākara*) is even described as having sprung from Vṛtra.

Various individual god are said to have produced the sun. Indra generated him (2, 12.4 &c), caused him to shine or raised him to heaven (3, 44.21 8, 78.7). Indra-Viṣṇu generated him (7, 99.4). Indra-Soma brought up Sūrya with light (6, 72.2); Indra-Varuṇa raised him to heaven (7, 82.3). Mitra-Varuṇa raised or placed him in heaven (4, 13.2; 5, 63.4.7). Soma placed light in the Sun (6, 44.23; 9, 97.41), generated Sūrya (9, 96.5.110.5), caused him to shine (9, 63.7), or raised him in heaven (9, 107.7). Agni establishes the brightness of the sun on high (10, 3.2) and caused him to ascend to heaven (10, 156.4). Dhātṛ, the creator, fashioned the sun as well as the moon (10, 190.3). The Aṅgirases by their rites caused him to ascend the sky (10, 62.3). In all these passages referring to the generation of Sūrya the notion of the simple luminary doubtless predominates.

In various passages Sūrya is conceived as a bird traversing space. He is a bird (10, 177.1.2), or a ruddy bird (5, 47.3), is represented as flying (1, 191.9), is compared with a flying eagle (7, 63.5) and seems to be directly called an eagle (5, 43.9). He is in one passage called a bull as well as a bird (5, 47.3) and in another a mottled bull (10, 189.1 cp. 5, 47.3). He is once alluded to as a white and brilliant steed brought by Uṣas (7, 77.3). Sūrya's horses represent his rays (which are seven in number: 8, 61.16), for the latter (*ketavaḥ*), it is said, bring (*vahanṭi*) him. His seven mares are called the daughters of his car (1, 50.9).

Elsewhere Sūrya is occasionally spoken of as an inanimate object. He is a gem of the sky (7, 63.4 cp. 6, 51.1) and is alluded to as the variegated stone placed in the midst of heaven (5, 47.3 cp. SB. 6, 1, 2.3). He is a brilliant weapon (*āyudha*) which Mitra-Varuṇa conceal with cloud and rain (5, 63.4), he is the felly (*pavi*) of Mitra-Varuṇa (5, 62.2), or a brilliant car placed in heaven by Mitra-Varnūa (5, 63.7). The sun is also called a wheel (1, 175.4; 4, 30.4) or the 'wheel of the sun is spoken of (4, 28.2; 5, 29.10).

Sūrya shines for all the world (7, 63.1), for men and gods (1, 50.5). He dispels the darkness with his light (10, 37.4). He rolls up the darkness as a skin (7, 63.1). His rays throw off the darkness as a skin into the waters (4, 13.4). He triumphs over beings of darkness and witches (1, 191.8.9 cp. 7, 104.24). There are only two or three allusions to the sun's burning heat (7, 34.19; 9, 107.20); for in the RV. the sun is not a maleficent power, and for this aspect of the luminary only passages from the AV. and the literature of the Brāhmaṇas can be quoted.

Sūrya measures the days (1, 50.7) and prolongs the days of life (8, 48.7). He drives away sickness, disease, and every evil dream (10; 37.4). To live is to see the Sun rise (4, 25.4; 6, 52.5). All creatures depend on Sūrya (1, 164.14) and the sky is upheld by him (10, 85.1). The epithet 'all-creating' (*viśva-karman*) is also applied to him (10, 170.4; cp). By his greatness he is the divine priest (*asuryah purohitah*) of the gods (8, 90.12). At his rising he is prayed to declare men sinless to Mitra-Varuṇa and other gods (7, 60.4).62.2). He is said, when rising, to go to the Vṛtra-slayer Indra and is even styled a Vṛtra-slayer himself when invoked with Indra (8, 82.1.2.4).

The only myth told about Sūrya is that Indra vanquished him (10, 43.5) and stole his wheel (1, 175.4; 4, 30.4). This may allude to the obscuration of the sun by a thunderstorm.

5.4 Savitṛ

Savitṛ is celebrated in eleven whole hymns of the RV. and in parts of others, his name being mentioned about 170 times. Eight or nine of these are in the family books, while all but three of those to Sūrya are in the first and tenth. Savitṛ is preeminently a golden deity, nearly all his members and his equipment being described by that epithet. He is golden-eyed (1, 35.8), golden-handed (1, 35.9.10), golden-tongued (6, 71.3), all these epithets being peculiar to him. He has golden arms (6, 71.1.5; 7, 45.2), and is broad-handed (2, 38.2) or beautiful-handed (3, 33.6). He is also pleasant-tongued (6, 71.4) or beautiful-tongued (3, 54.11), and is once called iron-jawed (6, 71.4). He is yellow-haired (10, 139.1), an attribute of Agni and Indra also. He puts on a tawny garment (4, 53.2). He has a golden car with a golden pole (5, 81.2). His car is drawn by two radiant steeds or by two or more brown, white-footed horses (1, 35.2.5; 7, 45.1).

Mighty splendour (*amati*) is preeminently attributed to Savir̥, and mighty golden splendour to him only (3, 38.8; 7, 38.1). This splendour he stretches out or diffuses. He illumines the air, heaven and earth, the world, the spaces of the earth, the vault of heaven

(1, 35.7.8; 4, 14.2.53.4; 5, 81.2). He raises aloft his strong golden arms, with which he blesses and arouses all beings and which extend to the ends of the earth (2, 38.2; 4, 53.3.4; 6, 71.1.5; 7, 45.2). The raising of his arms is characteristic, for the action of other gods is compared with it. Agni is said to raise his arms like Savitṛ (1, 95.7); the dawns extend light as Savitṛ his arms (7, 79.2), and Bṛhaspati is implored to raise hymns of praise as Savitṛ his arms (1, 190.3). He moves in his golden car, seeing all creatures, on a downward and an upward path (1, 35.2.3). He implies the car of the Aśvins before dawn (1, 34.10). He shines after the path of the dawn (5, 81.2). He has measured out the earthly spaces, he goes to the three bright realms of heaven and is united with the rays of the sun (5, 81.3.4). The only time the epithet *sūrya-raśmi* is used in the RV. it is applied to Savitṛ: 'Shining with the rays of the sun, yellow-haired, Savitṛ, raises up his light continually from the east' (10, 139.1). He thrice surrounds the air, the three spaces, the three bright realms of heaven (4, 53.5; cp. Viṣṇu). His ancient paths in the air are dustless and easy to traverse, on them he is besought to protect his worshippers (1, 35.11). He is prayed to convey the departed spirit to where the righteous dwell (10, 17.4). He bestows immortality on the gods as well as length of life on man (4, 54.2). He also bestowed immortality on the Ṛbhus, who by the greatness of their deeds went to his house (1, 110.2.3). Like Sūrya, he is implored to remove evil dreams (5, 82.4) and to make men sinless (4, 54.3). He drives away evil spirits and sorcerers (1, 35.10; 7, 38.7).

Like many other gods Savitṛ is called *asura* (4, 53.1). He observes fixed laws (4, 53.4; 10, 34.8.139.3). The waters and the wind are subject to his ordinance (2, 38.2). He leads the waters and by his porpulsion they flow broadly (3, 33.6 cp. Nir. 2, 26). The other gods follow his lead (5, 81.3). No being, not even Indra, Varuṇa, Mitra, Aryaman, Rudra, can resist his will and independent dominion (2, 38.7.9; 5, 82.2). His praises are celebrated by the Vasus, Varuṇa, Mitra and Aryaman (7, 38.3.4). Like Pūṣan and Sūrya, he is lord that which moves and is stationary (4, 53.6). He is lord of all desirable thing and sends blessings from heaven, air, earth (1, 24.3; 2, 38.11). He is twice (1, 123.3; 6, 71.4) even spoken of as 'domestic' (*damūnas*), an epithet other wise almost entirely limited to Agni. Like other gods, he is a support of the sky (4, 53.2; 10, 149.4). He supports the whole world (4, 54.4). fixed the earth with bonds and made firm the sky in the rafterless (10, 149.1).

Savitṛ is at least once (1, 22.6) called 'child of Waters' (*apām napāt*) an epithet otherwise exclusively belonging to Agni. It is probably also applied to him in 10, 149.2.2. Yāska (Nir. 10, 32) commenting on this verse regard Savitṛ here as belonging to the middle region (or atmosphere) because he causes rain, adding that the sun (*āditya,* who is in heaven) is also called Savitṛ. It is probably owing to this epithet and because Savitṛ's paths are once (1, 35.11) said to be in the atmosphere, that this deity occurs among the gods of the middle region as well as among those of heaven in the Naighaṅṭuka. Savitṛ is once called the *prajāpati* of the world (4, 53.2). In the SB. (12, 3, 5.1) people are said to identify Savitṛ with Prajāpati; and in the TB (1, 6, 4.1) it is stated that Prajāpati becoming Savitṛ created living beings. Savitṛ is alone lord of vivifying power and by his movements (*yāmabhih*) becomes Pūṣan (5, 82.5). In his vivifying power Pūṣan marches, beholding all beings as a guardian (10, 139.1). In two consecutive verses (3, 62.9.10) Pūṣan and Savitṛ are thought of as connected. In the first the favour of Pūṣan who sees all beings is invoked, and in the second, Savitṛ is besought to stimulate (cp. Pūṣan, p. 36) the thoughts of worshippers who desire to think of the excellent brilliance of god Savitṛ. The latter verse is the celebrated *Sāvitri,* with which Savitṛ was in later times invoked at the beginning of Vedic study. Savitṛ is also said to become Mitra by reason of his laws (5, 81.4). Savitṛ seems sometimes (5, 82.1.3; 7, 38.1.6) to be identified with Bhaga also, unless the latter word is here only an epithet of Savitṛ. The name of Bhaga (the good god bestowing benefits) is indeed often added to that of Savitṛ so as to form the single expression *Savitā Bhagah* or *Bhagah Savitā*. In other texts, however, Savitṛ is distinguished from Mitra, Pūṣan and Bhaga. In several passages Savitṛ and Sūrya appear to be spoken if indiscriminately to denote the same deity. Thus a poet says: 'God Savitṛ has raised aloft his brilliance, making light for the whole world; Sūrya shining brightly has filled heaven and earth and air with his rays' (4, 14.2). In another hymn (7, 63) Sūrya is (in verses 1.2.4) spoken of in terms (e.g. *prasavitṛ,* vivifier) usually applied to Savitṛ, and in the third verse Savitṛ is apparently mentioned as the same god. In other hymns also (10, 158.1-4; 1, 35.1-11. 124.1) it is hardly possible to keep the two deities apart. In passages such as the following, Savitṛ is, however, distinguished from Sūrya. 'Savitṛ moves between both heaven and earth, drives away disease, impels (*veti*) the sun' (1, 35.9). Savitṛ declares men sinless to the sun (1, 123.3). He combines with the rays of the sun (5, 81.4) or shines with the rays of the sun (10, 139.1 cp. 181.3; 1, 157.1; 7, 35.8.10). With Mitra, Aryaman, Bhaga, Savitṛ is besought to vivify the worshipper when the sun has risen (7, 66.1).

According to Yāska (Nir. 12, 12), the time of Savitṛ's appearance is when darkness has been removed. Sāyaṇa (on RV. 5, 81.4) remarks that before his rising the sun is called Savitṛ, but from his rising to his setting, Sūrya. But Savitṛ is also sometimes spoken of as sending to sleep (4, 53.6; 7, 45.1), and must therefore be connected with evening as well as morning. He is, indeed, extolled as the setting sun in one hymn (2, 38); and there are indications that most of the hymns addressed to him are meant for either a morning or an evening sacrifice. He brings all two-footed and four-footed beings to rest and awakens them (6, 71.2 cp. 4, 53.3; 7, 45.1). He unyokes his steeds, brings the wanderer to rest; at his command nighτ comes; the weaver rolls up her web and the skillful man lays down his unfinished work (2, 38.3.4). Later the west was assigned to him (SB. 3, 2, 3.18), as the east to Agni and the south to Soma.

The name Savitṛ has all the appearance of being a word of purely Indian formation. This is borne out by the fact that the root *sū*, from which it is derived, is continually used along with it in a manner which is unique in the RV. Some other verb would nearly always be used to express the same action in connection with any other god. In the case of Savitṛ not only it is the root itself used, but also several derivatives (such as *prasavitṛ* and *prasava*) constituting a perpetual play on the name. These frequent combinations show clearly that the root has the sense of stimulating, arousing, vivifying. A few examples may here be given in illlustration of this peculiar usage. 'God Savitṛ has aroused (*prāsāvīt*) each moving thing' (1, 157.1). 'Thou alone art the lord of stimulation' (*prasavasya*: 5, 81.5). 'Savitṛ bestowed (*āsuvat*) that immortality on you (1, 110.3). 'God Savitṛ has arisen to arouse (*savāya*) us' (2, 38.1). 'Thrice a day Savitṛ sends down (*soṣavīti*) boons from the sky' (3, 56.6). 'Do thou, o Savitr, constitute (*suvatāt*) us sinless' (4, 54.3). 'May we being sinless towards Aditi through the influence (*save*) of Savitṛ possess all boons' (5, 82.6). 'Send away (*parā sava*) evil dream, send away all calamities, bestow (*āsuva*) what is good (ib. 4.5). 'May Savitṛ remove (*apa sāviṣat*) sickness' (10, 100.8). With this verb Savitṛ is specially often besought to bestow wealth (2, 56.6 &c). This use of *sū* is almost peculiar to Savitṛ; but it is two or three times applied to Sūrya (7, 63.2.4; 10, 37.4). It also occurs with Uṣas (7, 77.1), with Varuṇa (2, 28.9), with the Ādityas (8, 18.1), and with Mitra, Aryaman coupled with Savitṛ as *sarvasya prasavitā*, 'the stimulator of everything'.

The fact that in nearly half its occurrences the name is accompanied by *deva*, god, seems to show that is has not yet lost the nature of an epithet, meaning 'the stimulator god'. At any rate, the word appears to be an epithet of Tvastṛ in two passages (3, 55.19; 10. 10.5), where the juxtaposition of the words *devas tvaṣṭā savitā viśvarūpa* and the collocation with *deva* indicate that Savitṛ is here identical with Tvaṣṭṛ.

We may therefore conclude that Savitṛ was originally an epithet of Indian origin applied to the sun as the great stimulator of life and motion in the world, representing the most important movement which dominates all others in the universe, but that as differentiated from Sūrya he is a more abstract deity. He is in the eyes of the Vedic poets the divine power of the sun pesonified, while Sūrya is the more concrete deity, in the conception of whom the outward form of the sun-body is never absent owing to the identity of his name with that of the orb (cp. 1, 35.9. 124.1).

5.5 Pūṣan

The name of Pūṣan is mentioned about 120 times in the RV. and he is celebrated in eight hymns (five of them occurring in the sixth, two in the first, and one in the tenth book). He is also lauded as a dual divinity in one hymn (6, 57) with Indra and in another with Soma (2, 40). Thus statistically he occupies a somewhat higher position than Viṣṇu. In the later Vedic and the post-Vedic periods his name is mentioned with increasing rareness. His individuality is indistinct and his authropomorphic traits are scanty. His foot is referred to when he is asked to trample on the brand of the wicked. His right hand is also mentioned (6, 54.10). He has (like Rudra) braided hair (6, 55.2) and a beard (10, 26.7). He wields a golden spear (1, 42.6) and carries an awl (6, 54.3) are spoken of and he is called the best charioteer (6, 56.2.3). His car is drawn by goats (*ajāśva*) instead of horses (1, 38.4; 6, 55.3.4). He eats, for his food is gruel (6, 56.1 cp. 3, 52.7). It is probably for this reason that he is said to be toothless in the SB. (1, 7, 4.7).

Pūṣan sees all creatures clearly and at once (3, 62.9), these identical words being applied to Agni also (10, 187.4). He is 'the lord of all things moving and stationary' almost the same words with which Sūrya is described (1, 115.1; 7, 60.2). He is the wooer of his mother (6, 55.5) or the lover of his sister (*ibid*. 4.5), similar expressions being used of Sūrya (1, 115.2) and of Agnin (10, 3.3). The gods are said to have given him, subdued by love, to the sunmaiden Sūryā in marriage (6, 58.4). Probably as the husband of Sūryā, Pūṣan is connected with the marriage ceremonial in the wedding hymn (10, 85), being besought to take the bride's hand and lead her away and to bless her in her conjugal relation (v. 37). In another passage (9, 67.10) he is besought to give his worshippers their share if maidens. With his golden ships which move in the aerial ocean, subdued by love he acts as the messenger of Sūrya (6, 58.3). He moves onward beholding the universe (2, 40.5; 6, 58.2) and makes his abode in heaven (2, 40.4). He is a guardian, who goes at the instigation of Savitṛ, knowing and beholding all creatures. In a hymn devoted to his praise, Pūṣan is said as best of charioteers to have driven downwards the golden wheel of the sun (6, 56.3), but the connection is obscure (cp. Nir. 2, 6). A frequent and exclusive epithet of Pūṣan is 'glowing' (*āghṛṇi*). He is once termed *agohya*, 'not to be concealed', an attribute almost peculiar to Savitṛ.

Pūṣan is born on the far path of paths, on the far path of heaven and of earth; he goes to and returns from both the beloved abodes, knowing them (6, 17.6). Owing to this familarity he conducts the dead on the far path to the Fathers, as Agni and Savitṛ take them to where the righteous have gone and where they and the gods abide, and leads his worshippers thither in safety, showing them the way (10, 17.3-5). The AV. also speaks of Pūṣan as conducting to the world of the righteous, the beautiful world of the gods (AV. 16, 9.2; 18, 2.53). So Pūṣan's goat conducts the sacrificial horse (1, 162.2.3). Perhaps to Pūṣan's familiarity with the (steep) paths is due to the notion that his car is drawn by the sure-footed goat.

As knower of paths, Pūṣan is conceived as a guardian of roads. He is besought to remove dangers, the wolf, the waylayer, from the path (1, 42.1-3). In this connection he is called *vimuco napāt,* 'son of deliverance'. The same epithet is applied to him in another passage (6, 55.1) and he is twice (8, 4.15.16) called *vimicana* 'deliverer'. As *vimuco napāt* he is invoked to deliver from sin' (AV. 6, 112.3). Pūṣan is prayed to disperse foes and make the paths lead to booty (6, 53.4), to remove foes, to make the paths good, and to lead to good pasture (1, 42.7.8). He is invoked to protect from harm on his path (6, 54.9) and to grant an auspicious path (10, 59.7). He is the guardian of every path (6, 49.8) and lord of the road (6, 53.1). He is a guide (*prapathya*) on roads (VS. 22, 20). So in the Sūtras, whoever is starting on a journey makes an offering to Pūṣan, the road-maker, while reciting RV. 6, 53; and whoever loses his way, turns to Pūṣan (AGS. 3, 7.8.9; SSS. 3, 4.9). Moreover, in the morning and evening offerings to all gods and beings, Pūṣan the roadmaker receives his on the threshold of the house (SGS. 2, 14.9).

As knower of ways he can make hidden goods manifest and easy to find (6, 48.15). He is in one passage (1, 23.14.15 cp. TS. 3, 3, 9.1) said to have found the king who was lost and hidden in secret (probably Soma), and asked to bring him like a lost beast. So in the Sūtras, Pūṣan is sacrificed to when anything lost is sought (AGS. 3, 7.9). Similarly, it is characteristic of Pūṣan that he follows and protects cattle (6, 54.5.6.10. 58.2 cp. 10, 26.3). He preserves back the lost (6, 54.7.10). His road directs cattle straight (6, 53.9). Perhaps connected with the idea of guiding straight is the notion that he directs the furrow (4, 57.7). Pūṣan also protects horses (6, 54.5) and weaves and smooths the clothing of sheep (10, 26.6). Hence beasts are said to be sacred to Pūṣan (1, 5.1.2), and he is called the producer of cattle (MS. 4, 3.7;

TB. 1, 7, 2.4). In the Sūtras verses to Pūsan are prescribed to be recited when cows are driven to pasture or stray (SGS. 3, 9).

Pūṣan has various attributes in common with other gods. He is called *asura* (5, 51.11). He is strong (5, 43.9), vigorous (8, 4.15), nimble (6, 54.8), powerful (1, 138.1), resistless (6, 48.15). He transcends mortals and is equal to the gods in glory (6, 48.19). He is ruler of heroes (1, 106.4), an unconquerable protector and defender (1, 89.5), and assists in battle (6, 48.19). He is a protector of the world (10, 17.3 cp. 2, 40.1). He is a seer, a protecting friend of the priest, the unshaken friend born of old, of every suppliant (10, 26.5.8). He is wise (1, 42.5) and liberal (2, 31.4). His bounty is particularly often mentioned. He possesses all wealth (1, 89.6), abounds in wealth (8, 4.15), gives increase of wealth (1, 89.5), is beneficent (1, 138.2), bountiful (6, 58.4; 8, 4.18), and bestows all blessings (1, 42.6). He is the strong friend of abundance, the strong lord and increaser of nourishment (10, 26.7.8). The term *dasra,* 'wonder-working', distinctive of the Aśvins, is a few times (1, 42.5; 6, 56.4) applied to him, as well as *dasma,* 'wondrous' (1, 42.10. 138.4) and *dasma-varcas,* 'of wondrous splendour' (6, 58.4), usually said of Agni and Indra. He is also twice (1, 106.4; 10, 64.3) called Narāśaṁsa 'praised of men', an epithet otherwise exclusively limited to Agni. He is once spoken of as 'all pervading' (2, 40.6). He is termed 'devotion-stimulating' (9, 88.3), is invoked to quicken devotion (2, 40.6), and his awl is spoken of as 'prayer-instigating' (6, 53.8; cp. Savitṛ, p. 33).

The epithets exclusively connected with Pūṣan are *āghṛṇi, ajāśva, vimocana, vimuco napāt,* and once each *puṣṭimbhara,* 'bringing prosperity', *anaṣṭapaśu,* 'losing no cattle', *anaṣṭavedas,* 'losing no goods', *karambhād,* 'eating gruel'. The latter attribute seems to have been a cause for despising Pūṣan by some (cp. 6, 56.1; 1, 138.4). *Karambha,* mentioned three times in the Ṛgveda., is Pūṣan's distinctive food, being contrasted with Soma as Indra's

(6, 57.2). Indra, however, shares it (3, 52.7), and in the only two passages in which the adjective *karambhin* 'mixed with gruel' occurs, it applies to the libation. Indra (3, 52.1; 8, 80.2). Pūṣan is the only god who receives the epithet *paśupā,* 'protector of cattle' (6, 58.2) directly (and not in comparisons).

The only deities with whom Pūṣan is invoked conjointly in the dual a Soma (2, 40) and Indra (6, 57), whose brother he is once called (6, 55) Next to these two, Pūṣan is most frequently addressed with Bhaga (1, 90; 4, 30.24; 5, 41.4; 46.2; 10, 125.2; cp. SB. 11, 4, 3.3; KSS. 5, 13.1) and Visnu (1, 90, 5, 46.3; 6, 21.9; 7, 44.1; 10, 66.5), his name in all these passages of the Ṛgveda being in juxtaposition with theirs. He is occasionally addressed with various other deities also.

The evidence adduced, does not show clearly that Pūṣan represents phenomenon of nature. But a large number of passages quoted at the beginning point to his being closely connected with the sun. Yāska, too (Nir. 7, 9) explains Pūṣan to be 'the sun (*āditya*), the preserver of all beings and in post-Vedic literature Pūṣan occasionally occurs as a name of the sun. The path of the sun which leads from earth to heaven, the abode of the gods and the pious dead, might account for a solar deity being both a conductor of departed souls (like Savitṛ) and a guardian of paths in general. The latter aspect of his character would explain his special bucolic features as guide and protector of cattle, which fom a part of his general nature as a promoter of prosperity. Mithra, the solar deity of the Avesta, has the bucolic traits of increasing cattle and bringing back beasts that have strayed.

Etymologically, the word means 'prosperer' as derived from the root *puṣ*, 'to cause to thrive'. This side of his character is conspicious both in his epithets *viśvavedas, anaṣṭavedas, purūvasu, puṣṭimbhara,* and in the frequent invocations to him to bestow wealth and protection (6, 4.15 &c). He is lord of great wealth, a stream of wealth, a heap of riches (6, 55.2.3). But the prosperity he confers is not, as in the case of Indra, Parjanya, and the Maruts, connected with rain, but with light, which is emphasized by his exclusive epithet 'glowing'. The welfare which he bestows results from the protection he extends to men and cattle on earth, and from his guidance of men to the abodes of bliss in the next world. Thus the conception which seems to underlie the character of Pūṣan, is the beneficent power of the sun manifested chiefly as a pastoral deity.

5.6 Viṣṇu

Viṣṇu, though a deity of capital importance in the mythology of the Brāhmaṇas, occupies but a subordinate position in the RV. His personality is at the same time more important there than would appear from the statistical standard alone. According to that he would be a deity only of the fourth rank, for he is celebrated in not more than five whole hymns and in part of another, while his name occurs only about 100 times altogether in the RV. The only anthropomorphic traits of Viṣṇu are the frequently mentioned strides which he takes, and his being a youth vast in body, who is no longer a child (1, 155.6). The essential feature of his character is that he takes (generally expressed by *vi-kram*) three strides, which are referred to about a dozen times. His epithets *urugāya,* 'wide-going' and *urukrama,* 'wide-striding', which also occur about a dozen times, allude to the same action. With these three steps Viṣṇu is described as traversing the earth or the terrestrial spaces. Two of these steps or spaces are visible to men, but the third or highest step is beyond the flight of birds or mortal ken (1, 155.5; 7, 99.2). The same notion seems to be mystically expressed (1, 155.3) when he is said to bear his third name in the bright realm of heaven. The highest place of Viṣṇu is regarded as identical with the highest place of Agni for Viṣṇu guards the highest, the third place of Agni (10, 1.3) and Agni with the loftiest station of Viṣṇu guards the mysterious cows (probably = clouds:

5, 3.3). The highest step of Viṣṇu is seen by the liberal like an eye fixed in heaven (1, 22.20). It is his dear abode, where pious men rejoice and where there is a well of honey (1, 154.5), and where the gods rejoice (8, 29.7). This highest step shines down brightly and is the dwelling of Indra and Viṣṇu where are the many-horned swiftly moving cows (probably = clouds), and which the singer desires to attain (1, 154.6). Within these three footsteps all beings dwell (1, 154.2), and they are full of honey (1, 154.4), probably because the third and most important is full of it. Viṣṇu guards the highest abode (*pāthas*), which implies his favourite dwelling-place (3, 55.10) and is else-where expressly stated to be so (1, 154.5). In another passage (7, 100.5) Viṣṇu is less definitely said to dwell far from his space. He is once spoken of (1, 156.5) as having three abodes, *triṣadhastha,* an epithet primarily appropriate to Agni.

The opinion that Viṣṇu's three steps refer to the course of the sun is almost unanimous. But what did they originally represent? The purely naturalistic interpretation favoured by most European scholars and by Yāska's predecessor Aurṇavābha (Nir. 12, 19) takes the three steps to mean the rising, culminating and setting of the sun. The alternative view, which prevails throughout the younger Vedas, the Brāhmaṇas, as well as post-Vedic literature, and was supported by Yāska's predecessor Śākapūṇi and is favoured by Bergaigne and the present writer, interprets the three steps as the course of the solar deity through the three divisions of the universe. With the former interpretation is at variance the fact that the third step of Viṣṇu shows no trace of being connected with sunset, but on the contrary is identical with the highest step. The alternative veiw does not conflict with what evidence the RV. itself supplies, and is supported by the practically unvarying tradition in India beginning with the later Vedas.

That the idea of motion is characteristic of Viṣṇu is shown by other expressions besides the three steps. The epithets 'wide-going' and 'wide-striding' are almost entirely limited to Viṣṇu, as well as the verb *vi-kram*. The latter is also employed in allusion to the sun, spoken of as the varietated stone placed in the midst of heaven, which took strides (5, 47.3). Viṣṇu is also swift *eṣa* (otherwise said only once of Bṛhaspati) or 'swift-going' *evayā*, *vayāvan* (otherwise connected only with the Maruts). Coupled with the constant idea of swift and far-extending motion is that of regularity. In taking is three sides Viṣṇu observes laws (1, 22.18). Like other deities typical of regular recurrence (Agni, Soma, Sūrya, Uṣas), Viṣṇu is the 'ancient germ of order', and an ordainer, who (like Agni, Sūrya, Uṣas) is both ancient and...... (1, 156.2-4). In the same words as the sun-god Savitṛ (5, 81.3), he is said (1, 154.1; 6, 49.13) to have measured out the earthly spaces. With this ... also be compared the statement that Varuṇa measured out the spaces .... the sun (p. 11). Viṣṇu is in one passage (1, 155.6 cp. 1, 164.4.48) described as setting in motion like a revolving wheel his 90 steeds (= days) .... their four names (= seasons). This can hardly refer to anything but the solar year of 360 days. In the AV. (5, 26.7) Viṣṇu is besought to bestow heat on the sacrifice. In the Brāhmaṇas Viṣṇu's head when cut off becomes the sun. In post-Vedic literature one of Viṣṇu's weapons is a rolling wheel which is represented like the sun (cp. RV. 5, 63.4), and his vehicle is Garuḍa, chief of birds, who is of brilliant lustre like Agni, and is also called *garutmat* and *suparṇa,* two terms already applied to the sun-bird in the RV. Finally the post-Vedic *kaustubha* or breast-jewel of Viṣṇu has been explained as the sun by Kuhn. Thus though Viṣṇu is no longer clearly connected with a natural phenomenon, the evidence appears to justify the inference that he was originally conceived as the sun, not in his general character, but as the personified swiftly moving luminary, which with vast strides traverses the whole universe. This explanation would be borne out by the derivation from the root *viṣ,* which is used tolerably often in the Ṛgveda. and primarily means 'to be active'. According to this, Viṣṇu would be the 'active one' as representing solar motion. Oldenberg, however, thinks that every definite trace of solar character is lacking in Viṣṇu, that he was from the beginning conceived only as a traverser of wide space, and that no concrete natural conception corresponded to the three steps. The number of the steps he attributes simply to the fondness for triads in mythology.

Viṣṇu's highest step, as has been indicated, is conceived as his distinctive abode. The sun would naturally be thought of as stationary in the meridian rather than anywhere else. So we find the name of the zenith in Yāska to be *viṣṇupada,* the step or place of Viṣṇu. Probably connected with the same range of ideas are the epithets 'mountain-dwelling' (*girikṣit*) and 'mountain-abiding' (*giriṣṭhā*) applied to Viṣṇu in the same hymn (1, 154.2.3); for in the next hymn (1, 155.1) Viṣṇu and Indra are conjointly called 'the two undeceivable ones, who have stood on the summit (*sānuni*) of the mountains, as it were with an unerring steed.' This would allude to the sun looking down from the height of the cloud mountains (cp. 5, 87.4). It is probably owing to such expressions in the Ṛgveda that Viṣṇu is later called 'lord of mountains' (TS. 3, 4, 5.1).

The reason why Viṣṇu took his three steps is secondly trait. He thrice traversed the earthly spaces for man in distress (6, 49.13); he traversed the earth to bestow it on man for a dwelling (7, 100.4); he traversed the earthly spaces for wide-stepping existence (1, 155.4); with Indra he took vast strides and stretched out the worlds for our existence (6, 69.5.6). To this feature in the RV. may ultimately be traced the myth of Viṣṇu's dwarf incarnation which appears in the Epic and the Purāṇas. The intermediate stage is found in the Brahmaṇas (SB. 1, 2, 5.5; TS. 2, 1, 3.1; TB. 1, 6, 1.5), where Viṣṇu already assumes the form of a dwarf, in order by artifice to recover the earth for the gods from the Asuras by taking his three strides.

The most prominent secondary characteristic of Viṣṇu is his friendship for Indra, with whom he is frequently allied in the fight with Vṛtra. This is indicated by the fact that one whole hymn (6, 69) is dedicated to the two deities conjointly and that Indra's name is coupled with that of Viṣṇu in the dual as often as with that of Soma, though the name of the latter occurs vastly oftener in the RV. The closeness of their alliance is also indicated by the fact that in hymns extolling Viṣṇu alone, Indra is the only other deity incidently associated with him either explicitly (7, 99.5.6; 1, 155.2) or implicitly (7, 99.4; 1, 154.6. 155.1; cp. 1, 61.7). Viṣṇu strode his three steps by the energy (*ojasā*) of Indra (8, 12.17), who in the preceding verse is described as slaying Vṛtra, or for Indra (Vāl. 4.3). Indra about to slay Vṛtra says, 'friend Viṣṇu, stride out vastly' (4, 18.11). In company with Viṣṇu, Indra slew Vṛtra (6, 20.2). Viṣṇu and Indra together triumphed over the Dāsa, destroyed Śambara's 99 castles and conquered the hosts of Varcin (7, 99.4.5). Viṣṇu is Indra's inticate friend (1, 22.19). Viṣṇu accompanied by his friend opens the cows' stall (1, 156.4). In the SB. (5, 5, 5.1) Indra is described as shooting the thunderbolt at Vṛtra, while Viṣṇu follows him (cp. TS. 6, 5, 1.1). Viṣṇu is also invoked with Indra in various single verses (4, 2.4. 55.4; 8, 10.2; 10, 66.4). When associated with Indra as a dual divinity, Viṣṇu shares Indra's powers of drinking Soma (6, 69) as well as his victories (7, 99.4-6), Indra convresely participating in Viṣṇu's power of striding (6, 69.5; 7, 99.6). To both conjointly is attributed the action of creating the wide air and of spreadng out the spaces (6, 69.5) and of producing Sūrya, Uṣas and Agni (7, 99.4). Owing to this friendship Indra drinks Soma beside Viṣṇu (8, 3.8. 12.16) and thereby increases his strength (8, 3.8; 10, 113.2). Indra drank the Soma pressed by Viṣṇu in three cups (2, 22.1 cp. 6, 17.11), which recall Viṣṇu's three footsteps filled with honey (1, 154.4). Viṣṇu also cooks for Indra 100 buffaloes (6, 17.11) or 100 buffaloes and a brew of milk

(8, 66.10 cp. 1, 61.7). Along with Mitra, Varuṇa, and the Maruts, Viṣṇu celebrates Indra with songs (8, 15.9).

Indra's constant attendants in the Vṛtra-fight, the Maruts, are also drawn into association with Viṣṇu. When Viṣṇu favoured the exhilerating Soma, the Maruts like birds sat down on their beloved altar (1, 85.7). The Maruts are invoked at the offering of the swift Viṣṇu (2, 34.11 cp. 7, 40.5). They are the bountiful ones of the swift Viṣṇu (8, 20.3). The Maruts supported Indra, while Pūṣan Viṣṇu cooked 100 buffaloes for him (6, 17.11). Viṣṇu is the ordainer associated with the Maruts (*māruts*), whose will Varuṇa and the Aśvins follow (1, 156.4). Throughout one hymn (5, 87 especially verses 4.5) he is associated with the Maruts, with whom, when he starts, he speeds along.

Among stray references to Viṣṇu in the RV. may be mentioned one (7, 100.6) in which different forms of Viṣṇu are spoken of : 'Do not conceal from us this form, since thou didst assume another form in battle'. He is further said to be a protector of embroys (7, 36.9) and is invoked along with other deities to promote conception (10, 184.1). In the third verse of the *Khila* after 10, 184.17, Viṣṇu is, according to one reading, called upon to place in the womb a male child with a most beautiful form, form according to another, a male child with Viṣṇu's most beautiful form is prayed for.

Other traits of Viṣṇu are applicable to the gods in general. He is beneficent (1, 156.5), is innocuous and bountiful (8, 25.12), liberal (7, 40.5), a guardian (3, 55.10), who is indeceivable (1, 22.18), and an innoxious and generous deliverer (1, 155.4). He alone sustains the threefold (world), heaven and earth, and all beings (1, 154.4). He fastened the world all about with pegs (7, 99.3). He is an ordainer (1, 156.4).

In the Brāhmaṇas Viṣṇu is conceived as taking his three steps in earth, air and heaven (SB. 1, 9, 3.9; TB. 3, 1, 2.7). These three strides are imitated by the sacrificer, who takes three Viṣṇu strides beginning with earth and ending with heaven, for that is the goal, the safe refuge, which is the sun (SB. 1, 9, 3.10.15). The three steps of the Amṣaspands taken from earth to the sphere of the sun, are similarly imitated in the ritual of the Avesta. A special feature of the Brāhmaṇas is the constant identification of Viṣṇu with the sacrifice.

Two myths connected with Viṣṇu, the source of which can be traced to the RV., are further developed in the Brāhmaṇas. Viṣṇu in alliance with Indra is in the RV described as vanquishing demons. In the Brāhmaṇans the gods and demons commonly appear as two hostile hosts, the former not, as in the RV, uniformly victorious, but often worsted. They therefore have recourse to artifice, in order to recover the supremacy. In the AB. (6, 15) it is related that Indra and Viṣṇu, engaged in conflict with the Asuras, agreed with the latter that as much as Viṣṇu could stride over in three steps should belong to the two deities. Viṣṇu accordingly strode over these worlds, the Vedas, and speech. The SB. (1, 2, 5) tells how the Asuras having overcome the gods began dividing the earth. The gods placing Viṣṇu, the sacrifice, at their head, came and asked for a share in the earth. The asuras agreed to give up as much as Viṣṇu, who was a dwarf, could lie on. Then the gods by sacrificing with Viṣṇu, who was equal in size to sacrifice, gained the whole earth. The three steps are not mentioned here, but in another passage (SB 1, 9, 3.9), Viṣṇu is said to have acquired for the gods the all-pervading power which they now possess, by striding through the three worlds. It is further stated in TS. 2, 1, 3.1, that Viṣṇu, by assuming the form of a dwarf whom he had seen, conquered the three worlds (cp. TB. 1, 6, 1.5). The introduction of the dwarf as a disguise of Viṣṇu is naturally to be accounted for as a stratagem to avert the suspicion of the Asuras. This Brāhmaṇa story forms the transition to the myth of Viṣṇu's Dwarf Incarnation in post-Vedic literature.

Another myth of the Brāhmaṇas has its origin in two passages of the RV. (1, 61.7; 8, 66.10). Their purport is that Viṣṇu having drunk Soma and being urged by Indra, carried off 100 buffaloes and a brew of milk belonging to the boar (=Vṛtra), while Indra shooting across the (cloud) mountain, slew the fierce (*emuṣam*) boar. This myth is (TS 6, 2, 4.2.3) developed as follows. A boar, the plunder of wealth, kept the goods of the Asuras on the other side of seven hills. Indra plucking up a bunch of *kuśa* grass and piercing through these hills, slew the boar. Viṣṇu, the sacrifice, carried the boar off as a sacrifice for the gods. So the gods obtained the goods of the Asuras. In the corresponding passage of the Kāṭhaka (IS.XI. p. 161) the boar is called Emūṣa. The same story with slight variations is told in the Caraka Brāhmaṇa (quoted by Sāyaṇa on RV 8, 66.10. This boar appears in a cosmogonic character in the SB. (14, 1, 2.11) where under the name of Emūṣa he is stated to have raised up the earth from the waters. In the TS. 7, 1, 5.1 this comsogonic boar, which raised the earth from the primeval waters, is described as a form of Prajāpati. This modification of the myth is further expanded in the TB. (1, 1, 3.5). In the post-Vedic mythology of the Rāmāyaṇa and the Purāṇas, the boar which raises the earth, has become one of the Avatārs of Viṣṇu.

The germs of two other Avatārs of Viṇṣu are to be found in the Brāhmaṇas, but not as yet connected with Viṣṇu. The fish which in the SB. 1, 8, 1.1 delivers Naby from the flood, appears in the Mahābhārata as a form of Prajāpati, becoming in the Purāṇas an incarnation of Viṣṇu. In the SB. (7, 5, 1.5, cp. TA. 1, 123.3) Prajāpati about to create offspring becomes a tortoise moving in the primeval waters. In the Purāṇas this tortoise is an Avatār of Viṣṇu, who assumes this form to recover various objects lost in the deluge.

The SB (14, 1, 1) tells a myth of how Viṣṇu, the sacrifice, by first comprehending the issue of the sacrifice, became the most eminent among the gods, and has his head, by his bow starting as under, was cut off and became the sun (*āditya*). To this story the TA. (5, 1, 1-7) adds the trait that the Aśvins as physicians replaced the head of the sacrifice and that the gods now able to offer it in its complete form conquered heaven (cp. PB. 7, 5.6).

In the AB (1, 1) Viṣṇu as the locally highest of the gods is contrasted with Agni the lowest, all the other deities being placed between them. The same Brāhmaṇa (1, 30) in quoting RV. 1, 156.4, where 'Viṣṇu accompanied by his friend opens the stall, states that Viṣṇu is the doorkeeper of the gods.

5.7 Ādityas

The group of gods called Ādityas is celebrated in six whole hymns and in parts of two others in the RV. It is rather indefinite both as to the names of the gods it includes and as to their number. Not more than six are anywhere enumerated and that only once; Mitra, Aryaman, Baha, Varuṇa, Dakṣa, Aṁṣa (2, 27.1). In the last books of the RV. the number is once (98, 114.3) stated to be seven and once (10, 72.8) eight, Aditi at first presenting only seven to the gods and bringing the eighth, Mārtaṇḍa, afterwards (ibid.9). The names of the Ādityas are not specified in either of these passage. The AV. states that Aditi had eight sons (8, 9.21), and the TB. (1, 1, 9.1) mentions these eight by name as Mitra, Varuṇa, Aryaman, Aṁśa, Bhaga, Dhātr, Indra, Vivasvat (the first five occur in RV. 2, 27.1), and the same list is quoted by Sāyaṇa (on RV. 2, 27.1) as found in another passage of the Taittiriya branch of the Veda. The SB. in one passage speaks of the Ādityas as having become eight by the addition of Mārtāṇḍa, while in two others (6, 1.2.8; 11, 6, 3.8) they are said to be twelve in number and are identified with the twelve months. In post-Vedic literature they are regularly twelve sun-gods, evidently connected with the twelve months, Viṣṇu being one of them and the greatest. In addition to the six Ādityas mentioned in RV. 2, 27.1, Sūrya is a few times termed an Āditya (p. 30) which is a common name for the sun in the Brāhmaṇas and later. Under the name of Āditya, identified with Agni, Sūrya is said to have been placed by the gods in the sky (10, 88.11). Savitṛ is also once mentioned in an enumeration with the four Ādityas Bhaga, Varuṇa, Mitra, Aryaman (8, 18.3). If therefore the number of the Ādityas was regarded by the poets of the RV. to have been definitely seven, the sun must have been the seventh, the eighth Mārtāṇḍa whom Aditi throws away and brings back (10, 72.8.9) probably being the setting sun. In the AV. (13, 2. 9.37) the sun is called the son of Aditi, the sun and moon Ādityas (8, 2.15), and Viṣṇu is invoked in an enumeration containing gods who in the RV. are Ādityas: Varuṇa, Mitra, Viṣṇu, Bhaga, Aṁśa besides Vivasvata (11, 6.2). The mother of the Ādityas is here once (9, 1.4) said to be not Aditi but the golden-hued Madhukaśā, daughter of the Vasus.

Indra is, however, in the RV. once coupled in the dual as an Āditya with Varuṇa the chief of the Ādityas (7, 85.4), and in Vāl. 4.2 he is directly invoked as the fourth Āditya. In MS. 2, 1.12 Indra is a son of Aditi, but in the SB. (11, 6, 3.5) he is distinguished from the 12 Adityas. When one god alone is mentioned as an Āditya, it is generally Varuṇa, their chief; but in the hymn in which Mitra is celebrated alone (3, 59), that deity is called an Āditya, as well as Sūrya. When two are mentioned, they are Varuṇa and Mitra, once Varuṇa and Indra; when three, Varuṇa, Mitra and Aryaman; when five, which is only once the case, the same three together with Savitṛ and Bhaga. Dakṣa occurs only in the enumeration of six mentioned above. The Ādityas are often invoked as a group, the names of Mitra and Varuṇa being generally mentioned at the same time. They also appear frequently along with other groups Vasus, Rudras, Maruts, Aṅgirases, Ṛbhus, Viśvedevas. The term Ādityas seems not infrequently to be used in a wider sense, as an equivalent for the gods generally. Their nature as a class in fact resembles that of the gods in general, not being specifically characterized like that of their two chiefs, Mitra and Varuṇa. In the aggregate sense they are the gods of celestial light, without representing any particular manifestation of that light, such as sun, moon and stars, or dawn. The hypothesis of Oldenberg that the Ādityas originally represented sun, moon, and the five planets, is based on their abstract ature and names (such as Bhaga, Aṁśa, Dakṣa) and the supposition that their characteristic number is seven, which is also the number of the Iranian Ameṣaspentas. It is here to be noted that the two groups have not a single name in common, even Mithra not being an Ameṣaspenta; that the belief in the Ādityas being seven in number is not distinctly characteristic and old; and that though the identity of the Ādityas and Ameṣaspentas has been generally accepted since Roth's essay, it is rejected by some distinguished Avestan scholars.

In some of the hymns of the RV. in which the Ādityas are celebrated (especially in 2, 27), only the three most frequently mentioned together, Mitra, Varuṇa, and Aryaman, seem to be meant. What is distant is near to them; they support all that moves and is stationary, as gods who protect the universe (2, 27.3.4). They see what is good and evil in men's hearts and distinguish the honest man from the deceitful (2, 27.3; 8, 18.15). They are haters of falsehood and punish sin (2, 27.4; 7, 52.6. 60.5. 66.13). They are besought to forgive sin (2, 27.14. 29.5), to avert its consequences or to transfer them to Trita Āptya (5, 52.2; 8, 47.8). They spread fetters for their enemies (2, 27.16), but protect their worshippers as birds spread their wings over their young (8, 47.2). Their servants are protected as with armour, so that no shaft can strike them (ib. 7.8). They ward off sickness and distress (8, 18.10) and bestow various boons such as light, long life, offspring, guidance (2, 27; 8, 18.22. 56.15.20).

The epithets which describe them are : bright (*śuci*), golden (*hiraṇyana*), many-eyed (*bhūryakṣa*), unwinking (*animiṣa*), sleepless (*asvapnaj*), far-observing (*dīrghadhī*). They are kings, mighty (*kṣatriya*), vast (*uru*), deep (*gabhīra*), inviolable (*ariṣṭa*), having fixed oridnances (*dhṛtavrata*), blameless (*anavadya*), sinless (*avṛjina*), pure (*dhārapūta*), holy (*ṛtāvan*).

The name is clearly a metronymic formation from that of their mother Aditi, with whom they are naturally often invoked. This is also one of the three derivations given by Yāska (Nir. 2, 13, cp. TA. 1. 14.1)

The greater gods belonging to the group have already been dealt with separately, but the lesser Ādityas having hardly any individually may best be described here in succession.

Aryaman though mentioned about 100 times in the RV. is so destitute of individual characteristics, that in the Naighaṅṭuka he is passed over in the list of gods. Except in two passages, he is passed over in the list of gods. Except in two passages, he is always mentioned with other deities, in the great majority of cases with Mitra and Varuṇa. In less than a dozen passages the word has only the appellative senses of 'comrade' and 'groomsman', which are occasionally also connected with the god. Thus Agni is once addressed with the words: 'Thou art Aryaman when the (the wooer) of maidens' (5, 3.2). The derivative adjective *aryamya,* 'relating to a comrade', once occurs as a parallel to *mitrya,* 'relating to a friend' (5, 85.7). Thus the conception of Aryaman seems to have differed but little from that of the greater Āditya Mitra, 'the Friend'. The name goes back to the Indo-Iranian period, as it occurs in the Avesta.

One hymn of the RV. (7, 41) is devoted chiefly to the praise of Bhaga, though some other deities are invoked in it as well; and the name of the god occurs over sixty times. The word means 'dispenser, giver' and appears to be used in this sense more than a score of times attributively, in several cases with the name of Savitṛ. The god is also regularly conceived in the Vedic hymns as a distributor of wealth, comparisons with Bhaga being generally intended to express glorification of Indra's and Agni's bounty. The word *bhaga* also occurs about twenty times in the RV. with the sense of 'bounty, wealth, fortune' and the ambiguity is sometimes played upon. Thus in one passage (7, 41.2) where Bhaga is called the distributor (*vidhartā*), it is stated that men say of the god, 'May I share in Bhaga' (*bhagam bhakṣi*). In another verse (5, 46.6) in which he is termed the 'dispenser' (*vibhaktā*, derived from the same root *bhaj*), he is invoked to be full of bounty (*bhagavān*) to his worshippers.

5.8 Uṣas

Uṣas, goddess of Dawn, is celebrated in about 20 hymns of the RV. and mentioned more than 300 times. Owing to the identity of name, the personification is but slight, the physical phenomenon of dawn never being absent from the poet's mind, when the goddess is addressed. Uṣas is the most graceful creation of Vedic poetry and there is no more charming figure in the descriptive religious lyrics of any other literature...... herself in gay attire, like a dancer, she displays her bosom (1, 92.4, cp. 6, 64.2). Like a maiden decked by her mother she shows her form (1, 123.11). Clothed in light the maiden appears in the east, and unveils her charms (1, 124.3.4). Effulgent in peerless beauty she withholds her light from neither small nor great (ib. 6). Rising resplendent as from a bath, showing her charms she comes with light, driving away the darkness (5, 80.5.6). She is young, being born again and again, though ancient; shining with an uniform hue, she wastes away the life of mortals (1, 92.10). As she is shone in former days, so she shines now and will shine in future, never aging, immortal (1, 113.13.15). The maiden coming again awakes before all the world (1, 123.2). Ever shortening the ages of men, she shines forth, the last of the dawns that have always gone, the first of those to come (1, 124.2). Like a wheel she revolves ever anew (3, 61.3). She awakens creatures that have feet and makes the birds to fly up: she is the breath and life of everything (1, 48.5.10. 49.3). She awakens every living being to motion (1, 92.9; 7, 77.1). The Dawns waken the sleeping and urge the living, the two-footed and the four-footed, to motion (4, 51.5). When Uṣas shines forth, the birds fly up from their nests, and men seek nourishment (1, 124.12). She reveals the paths of men, wakening the five tribes (7, 79.1). She manifests all beings and bestows new life (7, 80.1.2). She drives away evil dreams to Trita āptya (8, 47.14.16). She removes that black robe of night (1, 113.14). She dispels the darkness (6, 64.3. 65.2). She wards off evil spirits and the hated darkness (7, 75.1). She discloses the treasures concealed by darkness and distributes them bountifully (1, 123.4.6). She illumines the ends of the sky when she awakens (1, 92.11). She opens the gates of heaven (1, 48.15. 113.4). She opens the doors of darkness as the cows their stall (1, 92.4). Her radiant beams appear like herds of cattle (4, 52.2-4). She is visible afar, spreading out cattle (*paśūn*) at it were (1, 92.12). The ruddy beams fly up, the ruddy cows yoke themselves, the ruddy dawns weave their web (of light) as of old (ib.2). Thuṣ Uṣas comes to be called 'mother of kine' (4, 52.2.3; 7, 77.2).

Day by day appearing at the appointed place, she never infringes the ordinance of order and of the gods (1, 92.12. 123.9. 124.2; 7, 76.5); she goes straight along the path of order, knowing the way she never loses her direction (5, 80.4). She renders good service to the gods by causing all worshippers to awake and the sacrificial fires to be kindled (1, 113.9). She is besought to arouse only the devout and liberal worshipper, leaving the ungodly niggard to sleep on (1, 124.10; 4, 51.3). Worshippers are however sometimes spoken of as wakening her instead of being awakened her with their (4, 52.4 &c), and the Vasiṣṭhas claim to have first wakened her with their hymns (7, 80.1). She is once asked not to delay, that the sun may not scorch her as a thief or an enemy

(5, 79.9). She is besought to bring the gods to drink Soma (1, 48.12). Hence probably, the gods are often described as 'waking with Uṣas' (1, 14.9 &c).

Uṣas is borne on a car which is shining (7, 78.1), brilliant (1, 23.7), bright (3, 61.2), well-adorned (1, 49.2), all-adorning (7, 75.6), massive (1, 48.10 &c), and spontaneously-yoked (7, 78.4). She is also said to arrive on a hundred chariots (1, 48.7). She is drawn by steeds which are ruddy (7, 75.6 &c), easily guided (3, 61.2), regularly-yoked (4, 51.5), or is said to be resplendent with steeds (5, 79.1-10). She is also described as being drawn by ruddy kine or bulls (*go* : 1, 92.2. 124.11; 5, 80.3). Both the horses and the cows.

As is to be expected, Uṣas is closely associated with the sun. She has opened paths for Sūrya to travel (1, 113.16). She brings the eye of the gods and leads on the beautiful white horse (7, 77.3). She shines with the light of the sun (1, 113.9), with the light of her lover (1, 92.11). Savitṛ shines after the path of Uṣas (5, 81.2). Sūrya follows her as a young man a maiden (1, 115.2). She meets the god who desires her (1, 123.10). She is the wife of Sūrya (7, 75.5); the Dawns are the wives of the Sun (4, 5.13). Thus as followed is space by the sun, she is conceived as his wife or mistress. But as preceding the sun in time she is occasionally thought of as his mother (cp. p.35). She has generated Sūrya, sacrifice, Agni (7, 78.3). She has been produced (*prasūtā*) for the production (*savāya*) of Savitṛ and arrives with a bright child (1, 113.1.2). Uṣas is the sister of the Āditya Bhaga (1, 123.5; cp. p. 45) and the kinswoman (*jāmi*) of Varuṇa (1, 123.5). She is also the sister (1, 113.2.3; 10, 127.3) or the elder sister (1, 124.8) of Night; and the names of Dawn and Night are often conjoined as a dual compound (*uṣāsānaktā* or *naktoṣāsā*). Uṣas is born in the sky (7, 75.1); and the place of her birth suggests the relationship most frequently mentioned in the RV. : she is constantly called the daughter of heaven (1, 30.22 &c). She is once also spoken of as the beloved (*priyā*) of heaven (1, 46.1).

The sacrificial fire being regularly kindled at dawn, Agni is naturally often associated with Uṣas in this connection, sometimes not without a sideglance at the sun, the manifestation of Agni which appears simultaneously with the kindling of the sacrificial fire (1, 124.11 &c). Agni appears with or before the Dawn. Uṣas causes Agni to be kindled (1, 113.9). He is thus like the sun sometimes dalled her lover (1, 69.1; 7, 10.1 cp. 10, 3.3). He goes to meet the shining Uṣas as she comes, asking her for fair riches (3, 61.6). Uṣas is naturally also often connected with the twin gods of the early morning, the Aśvins (1, 44.2 &c). They accompany her (1, 183.2) and she is their friend (4, 52.2.3). She is invoked to arouse them (8, 9.17), and her hymn is said to have awakened them (3, 58.1). When the Aśvins' car is yoked, the daughter of the sky is born (10, 39.12). Uṣas is once associated with the moon, which being born ever anew goes before the dawns as harbinger of day (10, 85.19).

Various gods are described as having produced or discovered the dawns. Indra who is characteristically a winner of light, is said to have generated or lighted up Uṣas (2, 12.7 &c). But he is sometimes also hostile to her, being described as shattering her wain. Soma made the dawns bright at their birth (6, 39.3) and constituted them the wives of a good husband (6, 44.23), as Agni does (7, 6.5). Bṛhaspati discovered the Dawn, the sky (*svar*), and Agni, repelling the darkness with light (10, 68.9). The ancient Fathers, companions of the gods, by efficacious hymns discovered the hidden light and generated Uṣas (7, 76.4).

The goddess is often implored to dawn on the worshipper or bring to him wealth and children, to bestow protection and long life (1, 30.22; 48.1 &c), to confer renown and glory on all the liberal benefactors of the poet (5, 79.6, cp. 1, 48.4). Her adorers ask from her riches and desire to be to her as sons to a mother (7, 81.4). The soul of the dead man goes to the sun and to Uṣas (10, 58.8), and by the ruddy ones in whose lap the Fathers are said to be seated, the Dawns are doubtless meant (10, 15.7).

Besides the sixteen enumerated in the Naighaṇṭuka (1, 8) Uṣas has many other epithets. She is resplendent, shining, bright, white, ruddy, golden-hued, of brilliant bounty, born in law, most Indra-like, divine, immortal. She is characteristically bountiful.

5.9 Aśvins

Next to Indra, Agni and Soma, the twin deities named the Aśvins are the most prominent in the RV. judged by the frequently with which they are invoked. They are celebrated in more than fifty entire hymns and in parts of several others, while their name occurs more than 400 times. Though they hold a distinct position among the deities of light and their appellation is Indian, their connection with any definite phenomenon of light is so obscure, that their original nature has been a puzzle to Vedic interpreters from the earliest times. This obscurity makes it probable that the origin of these gods is to be sought in a pre-Vedic period. They are twins (3, 39.3; 10, 17.2) and inseparable. The sole purpose of one hymn (2, 39) is to compare them with different twin objects such as eyes, hands, feet, wings or with animals and birds going in pairs, such as dogs and goats or swans and eagles (cp. 5, 78.1-3; 8, 35.7-9; 10, 106.2-10). There are, however, a few passages which may perhaps point to their originally having been separate. Thus they are spoken of as born separately (*nānā*: 5, 73.4) and as born here and there (*iheha*), one being called a victorious prince, and the other the son of heaven (1, 181.4). Yāska also quotes a passage stating that 'one is called the son of night, the other the son of dawn' (Nir. 12, 2). The RV., moreover, in another passage (4, 3.6) mentions alone 'the encompassing Nāsatya', a frequent epithet otherwise only designating both Aśvins in the dual.

The Aśvins are young (7, 67.10), the TS. (7, 2, 7.2) even describing them as the youngest of the gods. They are at the same time ancient (7, 62.5). They are bright (7, 68.1), lords of lustre (8, 22.14; 10, 93.6), of golden brilliancy (8, 8.2), and honey-hued (8, 26.6). They possess many forms (1, 117.9). They are beautiful (6, 62.5. 63.1) and wear lotus-garlands (10, 184.2; AV. 3, 22.4; SB. 4, 1, 5.16). They are agile (6, 63.5), fleet as thought (8, 22.16), or as an eagle (5, 78.4). They are strong (10, 24.4), very mighty (6, 62.5), and are several times called 'red' (*rudrā*, 5, 75.3 &c). They possess profound wisdom (8, 8.2) and occult power (6, 63.5; 10, 93.7). The two most distinctive and frequent epithets of the Aśvins are *dasra*, 'wondrous', which is almost entirely limited to them, and *nāsatya,* which is generally explained to mean 'not untrue' (*na-asatya*), but other etymologies, such as 'the savers' have been proposed. The latter word occurs as the name of a demon in the Avsta, which, however, sheds no further light on it. These two epithets in later times became the separate proper names of the Aśvins. The attribute *rudravartani* 'having a red path' is peculiar to them, and they are the only gods called 'golden-pathed' (*hiraṇyavartani*), an epithet otherwise only used (twice) of rivers.

Of all the gods, the Aśvins are most closely connected with honey (*madhu*), with which they are mentioned in many passages. They have a skin filled with honey, and the birds which draw them abound in it (4, 45.3.4). They poured out 100 jars of honey (1, 117.6). Their honey-goad (1, 122.3. 157.4) with which they bestrew the sacrifice and the worshipper, is peculiar to them. Only the car of the Aśvins is described as honey-hued (*madhu-varṇa*) or 'honey-bearing' (*madhu-vāhana*). They only are said to be fond of honey (*madhūyu, mādhvī*) or drinkers of it (*madhupā*). The priest to whom they are invited to come is called honey-handed (10, 41.3). They give honey to the bee (1, 112.21 cp. 10, 40.6) and are compared with bees (10, 106.10). They are, however, like other gods, fond of Soma (3, 58.7.9 &c) and are invited to drink it with Uṣas and Sūrya (8, 35.1). Hillebrandt (VM. 1, 241), however, finds traces showing that the Aśvins were at first excluded from the circle of the Soma-worshipped gods.

The car of the Aśvins is sun-like (8, 8.2) or golden (4, 44.4.5), and all its parts, such as wheels, axle, fellies, reins are golden (1, 180.1; 8, 5.29. 22.5). It has a thousand rays (1, 119.1) or ornaments (8, 8.11.14). It is peculiar in construction, being threefold, having three wheels, three fellies, and some other parts triple (1, 118.1.2 &c). It moves lightly (8, 9.8), is swifter than thought (1, 117.2 &c) or than the twinkling of an eye (8, 62.2). It was fashioned by the Ṛbhus (10, 39.12). The Aśvins' car is the only one which is three-wheeled. One of its wheels is said to have been lost when the Aśvins came to the wedding of Sūrya (10, 85.15; cp).

The Aśvins' name implies only the possession of horses, there being no evidence to show that they are so called because they ride on horses. Their car is drawn by horses (1, 117.2 &c), more commonly by birds (*vi,* 6, 63.6 &c) or *patatrin*, 10, 143.5), swans (4, 45.4), eagles (1, 118.4), bird steeds (6, 63.7) or eagle steeds (8, 5.7). It is sometimes described as drawn by a buffalo (*kakuha*) or buffaloes (5, 73.7; 1, 184.3 &c) or by a single ass (*rāsabga*: 1, 34.9. 116.2; 8, 74.7). In the AB. (4, 7-9) the Aśvins are said at the marriage of Soma and Sūrya to have won a race in a car drawn by asses (cp. RV. 1, 116.7 and Sāyaṇa's comm.). Their car touches the ends of heaven and extends over the five countries (7, 63.2.3). It moves round heaven (1, 180.10). It traverses heaven and earth in a single day (3, 58.8), as the car of the sun (1, 115.3) and that of Uṣas (4, 51.5) are also said to do. It goes round the sun in the distance (1, 112.13). Frequent mention is also made of their course (*vartis*), a word which with one exception is applicable to them only. The word *parijman,* 'going round' is several times connected with the Aśvins or their car, as it is also with Vāta, Agni and Sūrya.

The locality of the Aśvins in variously described. They come from afar (8, 5.30), from heaven (8, 8.7), heaven and earth (1, 144.5), from heaven and air (8, 8.4 9.2), from air (8, 8.3), earth, heaven and ocean (8, 10.1), from the air, from far and near (5, 73.1). They abide in the sea of heaven (8, 26.17), in the floods of heaven, plants, houses, the mountain top (7, 70.3). They come from behind, before, below, above (7, 72.5). Sometimes their locality is inquired about as if unknown (5, 74.2.3; 6, 63.1; 8, 62.4). They are once (8, 8.23) said to have three places (*padāni*), possibly because invoked three times a day.

The time of their appearance is often said to be the early dawn, when 'darkness still stands among the ruddy cows' (10, 61.4) and they yoke their car to descend to earth and receive the offerings of worshippers (1, 22.2 &c). Uṣas awakens them (8, 9.17). They follow after Uṣas in their car (8, 5.2). At the yoking of their car Uṣas is born (10, 39.12). Thus their relative time seems to have been between dawn and sunrise. But Savitṛ is once said to set their car in motion before the dawn (1, 34.10). Occasionally the appearance of the Aśvins, the kindling of the sacrificial fire, the break of dawn, and sunrise seem to be spoken of as simultaneous (1, 157.1; 7, 72.4). The Aśvins are invoked to come to the offering not only at their natural time, but also in the evening (8, 22.14) or at morning, noon and sunset (5, 76.3). The appearance of the Aśvins at the three daily sacrifices may have been the starting-point of the continual play on the word 'three' in the whole of a hymn devoted to their praise (1, 34). As deities of the morning, the Aśvins dispel darkness (3, 39.3) and are sometimes said to chase away evil spirits (7, 73.4; 8, 35.16). In the AB. (2, 15), the Aśvins as well as Uṣas and Agni are started to be gods of dawn; and in the Vedic ritual they are connected with sunrise. In the SB. (5, 5, 4.1) the Aśvins are described as red-white in colour and therefore a red-white goat is offered to them.

The Aśvins are children of Heaven (1, 182.1. 184.1; 10, 61.4), one of them alone being once said to be a son of Heaven (1, 184.4). They are once (1, 46.2) said to have the ocean as their mother (*sindumātarā*). Otherwise they are in one passage (10, 17.2) said to be the twin sons of Vivasvat and Tvaṣṭṛ's daughter Saraṇyū (p. 42), who appear to represent the rising sun and dawn. On the other hand the solar deity Pūṣan claims them as his fathers (10, 85.14). By their sister (1, 180.2) Dawn seems to be meant (cp. p. 48). They are, as male deities of morning light, often associated with the Sun conceived as a female called either Sūrya or more commonly the 'daughter of Sūrya'. They are Sūryā's two husbands (4, 43.6 co/ 1, 119.5), whom she chose (7, 69.4). Sūrya (5, 73.5) or the maiden (8, 8.10) ascended their car. The daughter of the sun mounts their car (1, 34.5. 116.17. 118.5; 6, 63.5) or chose it (1, 117.13; 4, 43.2). They possess Sūryā as their own (7, 68.3), and the fact that Sūryā accompanies them on their car is characteristic (8, 20.8). She must be meant by the goddess called Aśvinī and mentioned with others in 5, 46.8. In a late hymn (10, 85.9) it is said that when Savitṛ gave Sūryā to her husband (*patye*). Soma was wooer (*vadhūyu*) while the Aśvins were groomsmen (*varā*). In another passage (6, 58.4) the gods are said to have given Pūṣan to Sūryā. Owing to their connection with Sūryā the Aśvins are invoked to conduct the bride home on their chariot (10, 85.26). They are also besought along with several other deities to bestow fertility on the bride (10, 184.2). They give the wife of the eunuch a child and make the barren cow yield milk (1, 112.3). They give a husband to the old maid (10, 39.3) and bestowed a wife on one of their favourities (1, 116.1 &c). In the AV. (2, 30.2 &c) they are said to bring lovers together.

The Aśvins may originally have been conceived as finding and restoring or rescuing the vanished light of the sun. In the RV. they have come to be typically succouring divinities. They are the speediest helpers and deliverers from distress in general (1, 112.2. 118.3). They are constantly praised for such deeds. In particular, they rescue from the ocean in a ship or ships. They are also invoked to bring treasures from the ocean or from heaven (1, 47.6) and their car approaches from the ocean (4, 43.5); here, however, the celestial ocean appears to be intended. Their rescue from all kinds of destress is a peaceful manifestation of divine grace, not a deliverance from foes in battle, as is generally the case with Indra (with whom, however, they are once associated in fight, even receiving the epithet of Vṛtra-slayers. They are thus also characteristically divine physicians (8, 18.8 &c), who heal diseases with their remedies (8, 22.10 &c), restoring sight (1, 116.16), curing the blind, sick and maimed (10, 39.3). They are the physicians of the gods and guardians of immortality, who ward off death from the worshipper (AV. 7, 53.1; TB. 3, 1, 2.11). Apart from their character as helpers, healers and wonder-workers, their general beneficence is often praised. They bring their worshipper to old age with seeing eye and reward him with riches and abundance of children (1, 116.25; 8, 8.13 &c).

As to the physical basis of the Aśvins, the language of the Ṛṣis is so vague that they themselves do not seem to have understood what phenomenon these deities represented. The other gods of the morning, the night-dispelling Agni, the man-waking Uṣas, and the rising Sūrya are much more vividly addressed. They may be called possessors of horses, because the latter are symbolical of rays of light, especially the sun's. But what they actually represented puzzled even the oldest commentators mentioned by Yāska. That scholar remarks (Nir. 12.1) that some regarded them as Heaven and Earth (as does also the SB. 4, 1,

5.16), others, as Day and Night, others, as sun and moon, while the 'legendary writers' took them to be 'two kings, performers of holy acts'.

The morning star would indeed naturally be thought of in connection with the evening star, but they are eternally separate, while the Aśvins are joined. The latter are, however, in one or two passages of the RV. spoken of separately; and though the morning in Vedic worship is so important, while sunset plays no part (5, 77.2), the Aśvins are nevertheless sometimes (8, 22.14; 10, 39.1 40.4) invoked morning and evening. The Aśvins, sons of Dyaus, who drive across the sky with their steeds and possess a sister, have a parallel in the two famous horsemen of Greek mythology, sons of Zeus, brothers of Helena, and in the two Lettic God's sons who come riding on their steeds to woo the daughter of the sun, either for themselves or the moon.

5.10 Viśve-devāh

So far, it has been dealt with the nature of the deities of terrestrial, celestial and atmospheric planes. Synchronization of prayers to the deities of all these planes is suggested by the phrase *Viśve-devās* here. In the context of explaining the nature of all the deities, Yāska states : एक एव आत्मा बहुधा स्तूयते । The prayers to different deities culminate into the singular principal God. The vedic statement : एकं विप्रा बहुधा वदन्ति - strengthens this point. Therefore, in the hymn of *Viśve-devās*, the seer prays all the deities for prosperity. Thus, the comprehensive group of All-gods is named as *Viśve-devāh*. And, it occupies an important position, for at least forty hymns are addressed to them. It is an artificial group intended to include all the gods, in order that none should be left out in laudations meant for the whole pantheon.

There is one hymn (VIII.28) addressed to *Viśve-devāh*, in which each mantra describes a deity by his characteristic features, leaving his name to be guessed. Such deities in the successive mantras are: 1. Soma, 2. Agni, 3. Tvaṣṭṛ, 4. Indra, 5. Rudra, 6. Pūṣan, 7. Viṣṇu, 8. Aśvins, 9. Mitrā-varuṇa, 10. Angirasas. The first mantra describes that one is brown, varied in form, bountiful young. He adorns himself with golden ornament. These features apply to Soma. "Another deity has, shining, occupied his receptacle the wise among the gods" - this alludes to Agni. The other deity is praised as bearing in his hand an iron axe, strenuous among the gods - this relates to Tvaṣṭṛ. One mantra (8.29.4) explains that he bears a bolt placed in his hand, with it he slays his foe - this speaks of Indra. The other god is described as bright, fierce with cooling remedies, bears in his hand a sharp weapon (8.29.5); - this indicates Rudra. Again, another god is described as making the *paths prosperous* (8.29.6); it implies Pūṣan. Another mantra (8.29.7) describes the deity as making three strides when the gods are exhilerated. So too, Aśvins in 8.29.8, Mitrāvaruṇa in 8.29.9, and Angirasas in 8.29.10 are described. Here, no one is superior or inferior to the other. Various forms of Supreme Atman are invoked here for welfare.

अग्निरिन्द्रो वरुणो मित्रो अर्यमा
वायुः पूषा सरस्वती सजोषसः ।
आदित्या विष्णुर्मरुतः स्वर्बृगत्
सोमो रुद्रो अदितिः ब्रह्मणस्पतिः ।। - RV. X.65.1

In one of the hymns on *Viśve-devāh*, the Viśvedevas are described as the protectors, prosperous, purifiers and victorious:

स्तुष उ वो मह ऋतस्य गोपा-
नदितिं मित्रं वरुणं सुजातान् ।
अर्यमणं भगमदब्धधीती-
नच्छा वोचे स धन्यः पावकान ।। - RV. VI.51.3

The nature of the *Viśve-devāh* is described in the following mantra:

रिशादसः सत्पतीरदब्धान्
मगेराज्ञः सुक्सनस्यदातृन् ।
यूनः सुक्षत्रान् क्षयतो दिवो नृन्
आदित्यान् यामि अदितिं दुवोयुः ॥ – RV. VI.51.4

O divinities, the sons divine, the offsprings of mother infinity, the scatterers of the malevolent, the defender of virtous, the irresistible, the mighty the donours of good dwellings, ever young, very powerful over-wide dominions and leaders of heaven, I seek your refuge with adoration. Here, the nature of *Viśvedevās* and their relation with human beings, are spoken of. The human activities are dependent on God. There should be a scope for a man to get rid of the taint of the sin which he commits due to ignorance. Being repented, he begs pardon of Him, and he becomes free from the chain of sins. The greatness of God may be identified through His favourable attitude towards His devotees. Thus, the mantra declares:

नम इदुग्रं नम आ विवासे
नमो दाधार पतथिवीमुत द्याम् ।
नमो देवेभ्यो नम ईश एषां
कृतं चिदेनो नमसा विवासे ॥ – VI.51.8

"Reverence to the mighty; reverence I adopt. Reverence sustains earth and heaven; Reverence to Nature's bounties: reverence overwhelms them. I offer penance in the form of reverence for sins which may been committed by me."

With such unstinted devotion, the devotee beseeches welfare for his life in this phenomenal world and in the higher world after death. Treading the right path, he aspires for happiness (RV. VI.52.5; 51.16). For the achievement of the goal in the life, a devotee invokes thus:

ये देवानां यज्ञिया यज्ञियानां
मनोर्यजत्रा अमृता ऋतज्ञाः ।

तेनो रासन्तामुरुगायमद्य
यूयं पात स्वस्तिभि: सदान: ॥ – RV. VII.35.15

"May those, who are most adorable among divinely revered, those who have been honoured by all men, those who are immortal, the observers of truth, grant us today widely spoken reputation; and May you lord along with the divine forces ever cherish as with blessings."

In this way, all hymns in praise of Viśvedevāh proclaim the greatness of all ten deities mentioned before, and imply the contribution of these deities for the well-being of all living beings and inanimate objects too.

Chapter - VI

Historical and Secular Hymns in the Ṛgveda

6.1 Introduction

The historical data of the hymns show that the Indo-Aryans were still engaged in war with the aborigines, many victories over these foes being mentioned, that they were still moving forward as conquerors is indicated by references to rivers as obstacles to advance. Though divided into many tribes, they were conscious of religious and racial unity, contrasting the aborigines with themsleves by calling them non-sacrificers and unbelievers, as well as 'black-skins' and the 'Dāsa colour' as opposed to the 'Āryan colour'.

Identical references scattered throughout the hymns supply a good deal of information about the social conditions of the ṭime. Thus it is clear that the family, with the father at its head, was the basis of society, and that women held a freer and more honoured position than in later times. Various crimes are mentioned, robbery, especially of cattle, apparently being the commonest, Debt, chiefly as a result of gambling, was known. Clothing consisted usually of an upper and a lower garment, which were made of sheep's wool. Bracelets anklets, necklaces and earrings were worn as ornaments. Men usually grew beards, but sometimes shaved. Food mainly consisted of milk, clarified butter, grain, vegetables and fruit. Meat was eaten only when animals were sacrificed. The commonest kind appears to have been beef, as bulls were the chief offerings to the gods. Two kinds of spirituous liquor were made: Soma was drunk at religious ceremonies only, while Surā, extracted from some kind of grain, was used on ordinary occasions.

A semi-historical character attaches to one complete hymn (i.126) and to appendages of 3 to 5 stanzas attached to over thirty others, which are called Dānastutis, or 'praises of gifts'. These are panegyrics of liberal patrons on behalf of whom the seers composed their hymns. They yield incidental genealogical information about the poets and their employers, as well as about the names and the habitat of the Vedic tribes. They are late in date, appearing chiefly in the first and tenth, as well as among the supplementary hymns of the eighth book.

Hardly a score of the hymns are secular poems. These are especially valuable as throwing direct light on the earliest thought and civilizations of India. One of the most noteworthy of them is the long wedding hymn (x. 85). There are also five funeral hymns (x. 14-18). Four of these are addressed to deities concerned with the future life; the last, however, is quite secular in tone and gives more information than any of the rest about the funeral customs of early Vedic India.

About half a dozen hymns consist of speculations on the origin of the world through the agency of a Creator (called by various names) as distinct from any of the ordinary gods. One of them (x. 129), which describes the world as due to the development of the existent (sat) from the non-existent (a-sat), is particularly interesting as the starting-point of the evolutional philosophy which in later times assumed shape in the Sāṅkhya system.

6.2 Ṛgvedic Historiography

A few Ṛgvedic hymns and passages from the Atharvaveda, Yajurveda, Brāhmaṇas and Upaniṣads may be mentioned as examples of historical passages. A Ṛgvedic hymn, I.63, alludes to the destruction of Śuṣṇa and Vṛtra as well as to that of the enemies of Purukutsa and Sudās, while another hymn, IV. 30, mentions that Śambara, Varcin, Arṇa and Citraratha were crushed by Indra, that Turvaśa and Yadu were safely carried over a flood, and that the enemies of kings Divōdāsa and Dabhiti were destroyed. The story of Turvayāṇa's delivery from his enemies, Kutsa, Āyu and Atithigva, is found in hymns I. 53 and VI. 18.

The royal sage Trasadasyu, who identifies himself with Indra and Varuṇa, narrates in his hymn (RV. IV. 42) how he was born by the grace of Indra and Varuṇa. When Purukutsa, son of Durgaha was 'in bonds', the seven ṛṣis were the protectors of his kingdom. With their help, the queen of Purukutsa propitiated Indra and Varuṇa who were pleased to bless her with a son, Trasadasyu.

The hymn, RV. IX. 61, addressed to Soma, refers to the over throwing of 99 cities and Divōdāsa's victory over Śambara, Turvasa and Yadu.

The dialogue between Viśvāmitra and the two rivers, Vipāś, and Śutudri recorded in RV. III. 33, is a lively account of how the Bharatas were able to cross these rivers after Viśvāmitra offered his prayers to them.

Victory of king Abhyāvartin Cāyamāna over Vṛcivatsa and Turvaśa is recorded in RV. VI. 27, while hymn 26 of the same maṇḍala refers to the destruction by Indra of Śuṣṇa for Kutsa, of Śambara for Divōdāsa and of Cumuri for Dabhīti.

The famous battle of ten kings of the Ṛgveda is described in hymns 18, 33 and 83 of the seventh maṇḍala. Though the information culled from these hymns is not free from controversy, the details supplied by the poet are interesting. He vividly brings before our eyes the successive stages of the battle - the exultant march of the ten confederates against the Tritsu ruler Sudās, the resulting panic in Sudās's forces, the sudden turn of fortune, probably due to the prayer of the sage, and the final defeat of the enemies of Sudās, who were either drowned in the river or forced to flee leaving their camp for the victors.

Hymns RV. VII. 33 and III. 53 glorifying the achievements of the families of Vasiṣṭha and Viśvāmitra respectively are examples of the sūktas recording the glorious deeds of the ṛṣis.

There are many passages in the Ṛgveda that describe rivers, mountains, seas and deserts.

The following extract from the Atharvaveda (XX. 127) gives an idea of the prosperity of the people under Parikṣit :

"Listen ye to the high praise of the king who rules over all peoples, the god who is above mortals, of Vaisvanara Pariksit. Pariksit has procured for us a secure dwelling, when he, the most excellent one, went to his seat. (Thus) the husband in Kuruland, when he found his household, converses with his wife; 'what may I bring to thee, curds, stirred milk, or liquor?' thus the wife asks her husband in the kingdom of King Pariksit. Like light the ripe barley runs over beyond the mouth (of the vessels). The people thrive merrily in the kingdom of King Pariksit."

In the Yajurveda, the Brāhmaṇas and the Upaniṣads, we come across several passages that contain references to topography, geography, earthquakes, volcanoes, as well as debates, discussions, conferences etc., that are useful for historians. An extract from the Śatapatha Brāhmaṇa (1.4.1.14) is cited by modern scholars to narrate the story of the migration of some Aryans from the mid-Ganga to the Eastern regions.

6.3 The Dāśarājña War

The *Dāśarājna* war is historically most important fact recorded in the Ṛgveda Saṁhitā. The Ṛgveda is a book containing devotional songs in praise of various gods. Yet, the narration of a historical events like *Dāśarājña* in its conspectus is really very remarkable. In ancient Indian history, the *Dāśarājna* war bears very vital and important aspect. U.C. Sharma remarks "The Indo-Aryan settlers have already been established and had already their roots shown in the soil of this country. They were divided in several tribes and peoples. It seems, there was a tough competition among them to gain power and superiority over others. The aid of non-Aryan tribes was being sought in this conflict of overlordship".[1]

The term '*Dāśarājña*' has been mentioned thrice in the Ṛgveda, and once in the Atharvaveda.[2] The most important event of '*Dāśarājña*' is recorded in the Ṛgveda Maṇḍala, III-53 and VII-18, 33 and 83. The third Maṇḍala is the seership of Viśvāmitra and seventh is of Vasiṣṭha. The number '*Daśa*' in the word *Dāśarājna* is only descriptive and not definitive. It does not refer to a definite number ten, but is intended to convey a number, slightly more or less than ten. It is found that the leader of the Bharatās, Sudās Paijavana and of Tṛtsus fought against the allied forces of the Dāśarājna kings. Aryan and non-Aryan tribes allied to the latter, took part in the war. It is to be noted here that Puru, Yadu, Turvaśa, Anu, Druhyu, Alina, Paktha, Bhalāṇas, Śiva, Viśāṇin, Śimyu, Vaikarṇa etc., from the group of *Dāśarājna* kings.

King Sudās Paijavana, with a small army of his followers, the Bharatas, was once attacked by the allies of the *Dāśarājna* kings and were cornered by the latter on the banks of high-flowing Paruṣṇī. Seeing his futility of resistance, king Sudās prayed the god Indra and he won the war with the help thereof. From the description in the hymn, it appears that some of the ten allies tried to pursue Sudās by crossing the river after him. They were however, drowned because, as soon as they entered the river, they were overpowered by an onrushing flood sent down by Indra. Some of them tried to make the waters of the river shallow by digging channels in different directions; but they miserably failed in their endeavour and met with severe disaster. Many were washed off by the powerful flowing currents of the river. Some who succeeded in reaching the other bank but immediately were killed by Sudās and his Bharatas who were waiting to pounce upon them.

The fifteenth mantra in the eighteen hymn of the seventh Maṇḍala tells that Tṛtsus with the inspiration from Indra, ran down like the released waters evidently against what had remained of the combined forces of the *Dāśarājna* kings after the terrible disaster with which they met in the waters of the flooded Paruṣṇī. Here, probably as may be inferred, Sudās's warriors inflicted a decisive defeat upon them. They were put to flight and had to leave all their important and proud possessions to the victor. On this occasion too, they must have tried a retreat across the river, though without success, and it is possible that the description in mantras VII. 18.5, 6, 8, 9-10 refers to the crossing of the enemy on either way. The reference that the two armies, had actually come to grips at some stage, appears to be a fact from two mantras VII. 18. 16 and 17, wherein Indra is said to have laid low on the ground the arrogant enemy, and to have killed a lioness through a lamb etc. As suggested in the mantra VII. 18.18, Bheda and his allies the Ajās, the Śigrus and Yakṣus, who belonged very likely to an earlier phase of the *Dāśarājña* or to another war. They were won on the banks of the Yamunā by Sudās under the spiritual guidance of the Tṛtsus. The killing of Devaka and Sambara, however, mentioned in mantra VII. 18. 20, seem to be a reference to earlier events which took place in reign of Sudās's grand-father Divodāsa, if they are not to be regarded as purely mythical.

6.4 Dānastutis

It is a fact that the Ṛgvedic hymns are generally meant for purpose of sacrifice. Such hymns however, contain the fact of eloquence of seers praising the god to induce him to grant favourable voice and generosity. The Ṛgvedic hymns inherit the description of some definite families who were at the spiritual climax of the sacrificial ceremony. Instruction of such sacrificial ceremonies in course of time became the source of livelihood of such families. In various places (II-2-9, X-64-12 etc.), the composition of the hymns is compared to milch-cow, taking care of the family of the seer. At times, these seers with their sons were moving to many kings where they use to offer their service of chanting the Mantras. At the time of the sacrifice when such sages bring forward newest compositions and king was giving appropriate *Dakṣiṇa*.

The *Dakṣiṇa* itself is glorified in the Ṛgveda X-107. The idea in this hymn is that the *Dakṣiṇa* is to be considered as a definite gift for the gods and as a divine sacrifice-exactly. At the same time, it is learnt from these hymns, as also from others wherein the *Dakṣiṇa* consists of that which the poet longs for. Mostly, the poet expresses his expectation or his thanks only in general. At times, however, he makes exact sketches and clothes his thanks directly with regard to the offering the gift in a definite hymns or a mantra. Such a hymn or such a mantra has the characteristic of a *Dānastuti*.

The expression *Dānastuti* rather occurs for the first time in the *Bṛhaddevatā*, VI-45, where, it is determined, that the concluding pair of verses (38, 39) of the hymn VIII-15 of the *Ṛgveda*, are considered according to the tradition as the *Dānastuti* of king Kaśu.

The constituents '*Stu*' and '*Dāna*' occur side by side in the *Ṛgveda*.[3] Even there are still other technical expressions in the later literature which may be designated as *Dānastuti*. One employs the designation in narrow sense for an almost definite form of saying of thanks. The verses recognised as *Dānastuti* in the *Bṛhaddevatā* and *Anukramaṇī*, form hymns of *Dānastutis*.

Above all, these accounts which the *Anukramaṇī* gives in its introductory chapter is important (II-23). The *Dānastutis* are even dedicated to kings. Indian commentators consider as a definite characteristic, that only a royal donor should have such a *Dānastuti* and this should not find place in the interior of a true hymn.

The constituents *Stu* and *Dāna* is already mentioned in the *Ṛgveda*, V-33-6. Even there are still other technical expression in the later literature called *Raibhīs*, *Nārāśaṁśis*, and even at times *Gāthās*. These three designations already occur together in the *Ṛgveda*.[4]

Raibhīs :

The word Raibhīs derived from *Rebha* (bard). Therefore, *Raibhīs* are verses of the bards. The three mantras of the Atharvaveda XX-127-4, 5, 6, are called *Raibhīs*. They form an introduction to the praise of Parikṣita. *Gāthā* is to be supplemented by *Raibhīs*.

Nārāśaṁsis :

The word *Nārāśaṁsis* consists of two elements *Nara* and *Śaṁsa* and are referred in the Ṛgveda.[5] In the *Nirukta*, Yāska says - येन नराः प्रशस्यन्ते स्म नाराशंसो मन्त्रः ।[6] A mantra in which the lords are praised is called *Nārāśaṁsa*. The *Nārāśaṁsis* are concerned with the living princes and with eulogy of their generosity. The Bṛhaddevata says : "the stanzas in which the deeds of kings and their gifts great, small and middling, are told should be understood to be called 'Laudations of Men' (*Nārāśaṁsi*), as the praise of kings (is expressed) by them in the tenth maṇḍala of the Ṛgveda.[7] According to the Aitareya Brāhmaṇa,[8] Nābhanediṣṭha-sūkta (X-62) in the Ṛgveda is a Nārāśaṁsa-Sūkta. Even the hymns I-161 and IV-37 are according to the Aitareya Brāhmaṇa - अर्भव नाराशंसम्।[9] wherein, the *Ṛbhus* are said to be men (ऋभवो हि नरो मनुष्याः ।). Sāyaṇa's explanation of the word *Nārāśaṁsa* .... नराः शस्यन्ते (कथ्यन्ते) यस्मिन् सूक्ते तन्नाराशंसम् ।[10] "When in a hymn, men are praised then it is a *Nārāśaṁsa.*" Thus, the *Nārāśaṁsis* essentially designate that which is called as *Dānastuti* in later times.

Gāthās:

Gāthā in the *Ṛgveda* usually means only 'song'. The expression '*Gāthās*' in this context is to be comprehended has even the same significance. In the *Aitareya Brāhmaṇa*, the verse 'आसन्दीवती धान्यादम्', is designated as a यज्ञगाथा ।[11] In the *Śatapatha Brāhmaṇa*, it is simply named as *Gāthā.*[12] The *Atharvaveda* refers to the *Gāthās* to be the special mantras of *Indragāthā* and others. For eg. in the sūkta XX-128 (12 to 16) of the *Atharvaveda*, the five mantras are considered to be *Intragāthā,* particularly, the *Gāthās* treat of the *Yajna.*

The *Dānastuti* and *Nārāśaṁsis* are conpared with the post Vedic '*Praśastis*' (song praise). The *Praśastis* can however be seen in the inscriptions. The praise of the princes, their was deeds, their booty and generosity are the content thereof. The *Ṛgvedānukramaṇī* of *Kātyāyana,* states in its introductory chapter: राज्ञां च दानस्तुतयः । Hence, the *Dānastutis* and *Nārāśaṁsis* may be compared with the *Praśastis* of the Gupta kings. For example, Bhitari-pillar inscription of Skandagupta states as follow.[13]

1. सर्व राजोच्छेत्तुः पृथिव्यामप्रतिरथस्य चतुरुदधिसलिला स्वादितयशसो धनदवरुणेन्द्रान्तकसमस्य ।
2. कृतान्तपरशोः न्यायागतानेकगोहिरण्य कोटिप्रदस्य चिरोत्सन्नाश्वमेधाहतुर्मगराज श्रीगुप्तप्रपौत्रस्य ।

The modern Vedic scholars found that the *Dānstutis* show their little or more distinct historical accounts. Winternitz writes: "In the *Dānastutis* however are always mentioned the names of pious donors and they are concerned undoubtedly with historical results or with real events. There, they are also important.[14]

6.5 Ṛgvedic Tribes: Pañca-Janās

The word *Pañca-janāh* generally means five peoples. But, technically the term *Pañca-janāh* in *Ṛgveda* refers to the varieties of people as *Pañch-kṛṣṭayah* and *Pañca-carṣṇīh*,[15] both suggesting the tilling masses. (*kṛṣ* - to till). Aupamanyava, an earlier teacher than Yāska, states that it denotes the four *Varṇas*, and in addition to this, the *Niṣādas* as the fifth caste.[16] But this interpretation appears to be not sound. Because, the four castes have certainly been mentioned clearly but only once in the tenth maṇḍala of the *Ṛgveda* (X-90).[17] Which of course is said by western scholars, to be a later origin. Yāska thinks that the *Pañca-janāh* are the Gandharvas, Pitṛs, Devas, Asuras and Rākṣasas.[18] A passage from the *Aiteraya Brāhmaṇa* says that *Aditis Pañca-janāh;* and another passage therefrom conveys that it means the Devās, Manuṣyas, Gandharvas, Apsarases, Sarpas and the Manes.[19] The Gandharvas and the Apsarases are taken as one category.

The *Ṛgveda* indicates that the five tribes were Aryans, as Agni is closely associated with them.[20] According to the *Śatapatha Brāhmaṇa*, the *Pañca-janāh* is that which could not achieve the glory of Bharata.[21] In the same context, it suggests a difference between the Bharatas on the one hand, and the five or seven tribes on the other. Probably, this is on the back-ground of the *Dāśarājna* war wherein these were arrayed against Sudās-Bharatas. Generally, the Vedic texts suggest that the term *Pañch-janāh* indicates the Āryan tribes themselves; and they are Anu, Druhyu, Yadu, Turvaśa and Puru; all these are mentioned in the Ṛgveda, but not in association with term *Pañca-jannh*. In the *Ṛgveda*,

Yadu and Turvaśa are mentioned together.[22] Besides, the Matsyas and the Bhṛgus are also included in the same context; thus the groups of tribes during Ṛgvedic age would be seven.[23]

The details regarding the Ṛgvedic tribes may be as below:

Anu :

The tribe of Anus is referred to alongwith the Yadus, Druhyaus, Turvaśas and the Purus, in the hymn addressed to Indra and Agni both.[24] Such references are found often in the Ṛgveda.[25] They fought against the Sudās, but were defeated by the latter.[26] They hid themselves in the waters of Paruṣṇi or present Rāvi.[27]

Druhyu :

The Druhyus are said to be one among the famous tirbes of *Pañca-janāh.*[28] In the Sudās victory, as the hymns from the *Ṛgveda* declare, the Druhyus are recorded to have been defeated by king Sudās, and perished in the water.[29] They are associated with the river Paruṣṇī.[30] They seem to be the inhabitants of the north-west India. The *Purāṇas*[31] also refer to Gandhāra dynasty as the descendents of Druhyus.

Turvaśa :

The tribe Turvaśa is frequently mentioned in the *Ṛgveda*. They are closely described with their allies Yadu, Anus, Purus and Druhyus.[32] Moreover, the Turvaśas are generally mentioned with the Yadus, in the *Ṛgveda*.[33] Two passages of the *Ṛgveda*, refer to an attack by Turvaśa and Yadu on Divodāsa.[34] The Turvaśas people took part in the famous *Dāsarājna* war against the Sudās and defeated their allies. One mantra in the *Ṛgveda* refers to the defeat of the Truvaśa at the hands of the Sṛñjayas.[35] The bank of Paruṣṇī is the home of the Turvaśas at the time of their conflict with the Sudās. They crossed the Paruṣṇī, but the direction of their crossing, is not mentioned.[36]

Yadu :

The term Yadu mentioned often in the *Ṛgveda*, denotes, the name of the king and his group of people. They are mentioned as coupled with Turvaśa.[37] They fought against the Sudās with their allies Turvaśa, Anus, Purus and the Druhyus.[38] They were defeated by the Sudās.[39] The Yadu and the Turvaśa kings seem to have escaped, while the Anu and the Druhyu kings perished.

Puru :

It signifies the name of a tribe and their king. The Purus are mentioned in the *Ṛgveda* with the Anus, Druhyus, Turvaśas and the Yadus.[40] They are referred to as the enemies of Sudās in the *Ṛgveda*.[41] As said in the *Ṛgveda*, due to Agni's favour, the Bharatas became celebrated as victorious over the Purus.[42] On the other hand, the victory of the Purus over the Dasyus is mentioned in the several mantras of the *Ṛgveda*.[43] Purukutsa and the Trasadsyu are the great kings of this tribe.[44] Probably the Kurus and Purus are found to be the two families connected with the Ṛgvedic time.[45] The Purus may be said as living on the bank of river Sarasvati.[46]

Bharata :

The Bharatas form an important tribe, designating Aryan tribes during the period of the *Ṛgveda*. In the *Apri* hymns, occurs a goddess Bhāratī - the personified deity, the protective power of the Bharata tribe.[47] Sudās was the ruler of the Bharatas. Viśvāmitra, his contemporary, was also a Bharata.[48] Vasiṣtha, who was the leader of the Tṛtsus, also belonged to the Bharatas as their priest.[49] The Tṛtsus also seem to be a sub-tribe among the Bharatas. The Bharatas fought against the *Dāśarājna* kings, under the leadership of Sudās, and Vasiṣtha also was there with them in defeating *Dāśarājna* by the favour of Indra.[50] They are mentioned mostly in the third and the seventh maṇḍalas as associated with Divōdāsa also.[51] Bharatas had settled on the banks of the rivers Sarasvatī,

Āpayā and Dārṣadvati,[52] which is called middle region of the famous Madhyadesa. The Bharatas became very famous in the later literature. In the *Śatapatha Brāhmaṇa*,[53] the Bharata kings are recorded to have won victories over the Kāṣi and made offerings over the rivers Gaṅgā and Yamunā. Macdonell and Keith writes - 'moreover, in the formula of the kings porclamation for the people, the variants recorded include *Kuravah, Pāñcālāh, Kuru-Pāñcālāh* and *Bharatāh*;[54] the Mahābhārata consistently recognises the royal family of the Kurus as a Bharata family. It is therefore extremely probable that Oldenberg is right in holding that the Bharatas in the times of the Brāhmaṇas were merging in the Kuru-Pāñcāla people.[55] They ruled over a vast tract of this country on any account an important chapter in the social and political history of India for a long time. Perhaps, this is the cause that the name of our country came to be known a *Bharatavarṣa*.

Krivi :

In the *Ṛgveda*[56] the Krivis are said to have settled on the banks of the rivers Sindhu and Asiknī (Cenab). This Krivi tribe in the later literature was the former name of the Pāñcālās. The *Śatapatha Brāhmaṇa* says that- काव्य इति ह पुरा पाञ्चालान आचक्षते ।[57] Here a king is referred to as *Kṛvya-Pāṇcāla*. Macdonell and Keith, consider Krivi to be a variant of Kuru.[58] According to Zimmer,[59] the Krivis and the Kurus formed the later tribe known Vaikarṇas.

Vaikarṇa :

The Vaikarṇas are already mentioned in the Ṛgveda, as having fought against the king Sudās of the Bharata.[60] In this view, U. C. Sharma concludes - 'Actually, the Bharatas, Kurus, Pāñcālās, Krivis etc., belonged to the same stock which in various divided groups, were referred to with different names in the different times.[61]

Kuru :

The *Ṛgveda* mentions the name of Kuruśravaṇa. Kuruśravaṇa is mentioned as a prince with the epithet Trasadasyava,[62] i.e. the descendent of Trasadasyu. But Trasadasyu is well known as a Puru king.[63] The Purus and the Bharatas are spoken of as kindling fire on the Dṛṣadvatī, the Āpayā and the Sarasvatī.[64] The Atharvaveda[65] mentions Pariksit as a king of the Kurus, and praises him. In the Śatapatha Brāhmaṇa[66] Kuru-Pāñcālās are said to be inhabitants of the Madhyadeśa.

Tṛtsu :

The Tṛtsus are referred to in the *Ṛgveda* in several places.[67] They were one of the most important tribes connected with the *Dāśarājna* War. They helped king Sudas in his battle with the *Dāśarājna*.[68] The *Rgveda* speaks of the alliance of the Tṛtsus with the Bharatas under the leadership of Vasiṣṭha, the priest of the Tṛtsus.[69] It is difficult to determine the relationship between the Tṛtsus and the Bharatas. But they seem to be actually the priests of the Bharatas and can be identified with the Vasiṣṭhas. Moreover, they could not be supposed to be a tride distinctly apart from the Bharatas. At one place in the Ṛgveda, the Tṛtsus are described as having braided hair on the right side of the head.[70] In another mantra, they seem to represent the Vasisthas.[71] Hence the identity of the two tribes can be inferred.

Matsya :

The tribe called Matsya is mentioned in the Ṛgveda as the people who fought against Sudās in the *Dāśarājna* war.[72] Later Vedic texts mention this tribe many times. The *Śatapatha Brāhmaṇa*[73] refers to a king of the Matsyas named Dhvaṣan Dvaitavana as he ruled near the lake of Dvaitavana. The *Kauṣītaki Upaniṣad* [74] mentions the Matsyas with the Vaśas, and the Gopatha *Brāhmaṇa*[75] with the Salvas. According to the Manusmrti,[76] it is said that the Matsyas lived in the Madhyadeśa which comes between Himalaya and Vindhya mountain, and it had its extension upon the bank of Sarasvati, which is now disappeared. The Matsyas stayed in the vicinity of the Kurukṣetra, the Pāñcālās and the Śūrasenas. This Madhyadeśa now includes the places of modern Alwar, Bharatpur and Jaipur.

Sṛñjaya :

The Ṛgveda faintly refers to the tribe Sṛnjaya. Their king Daivavāta is said to have defeated the Vṛcīvanta and Turvaśa king.[77] Thus both Sudās of Bharatas and the Sṛñjayas were enemies of Turvaśa.[78] Again, the *Ṛgveda*[79] celebrates Divōdāsa and a Sṛñjaya prince together. Both the references point alliance between the Tṛtsus and Sṛñjayas. But the Sṛñjayas and the Bharatas got assimilated, as both are mentioned in the same '*Dānastutis*'.[80] In the later period, as *Śatapatha Brāhmaṇa*[81] declares, there was friendly relation between Sṛañjayas and Kurus. It said that Devabhāga Śrautarśa was the priest of both the Kurus and the Sṛñjayas. The geographical position of the Sṛñjayas is uncertain. They may have stayed with their allies, the Tṛtsus in the Madhyadeśa.

Pārāvata :

Pārāvata occurs in several mantras of the Rgveda.[82] A mantra invokes Sarasvati and reads the epithet - *Paravatagni* for her. The varied forms and other specialities of the Pārāvatas are referred in the *Ṛgveda*.[83] The *Ṛgveda*,[84] again makes a mention of the fine steads and great riches of the people. The Pañcaviṁśa Brāhmaṇa[85] mentions the Pārāvatas as staying on the bank of Sarasvatī river. The Pārāvatas, as is clear from the epithet of Sarasvatī were most probably associated with the region on the upper courses of the river Sarasvatī.

Bharadvāja :

Bharadvāja is the seer of the sixth maṇḍala of the *Ṛgveda*. The *Ṛgveda*[86] mentions Bṛbu Bṛṣaya and Pārāvata with Bharadvaja. *Sāṅkhāyana Śrauta Sūtra*[87] records Bharadvāja to have gained largest from Prastoka Sṛñjaya and thus points out a connection between the Bharadvājas and the Sṛñjayas. Later works, *Mahābhārata*[88] and *Purāṇas*[89] mentioned the Bharadvājas are a tribe.

Uśīnara :

The *Ṛgveda* indirectly mentioned Uśīnara people. It refers to their queen-Uśīnarāṇi.[90] In the *Ṛgveda*, one mantra of a hymn of credited seer Śibi Auśīnara.[91] Leter Vedic texts, the *Gopatha Brāhmaṇa*[92] regards both Vaśas and the Uśīnaras as northerners. The *Aitareya Brāhmaṇa*[93] places the people in the middle region. In Indian literature, the Uśinaras are said to have associated with the Śibis and the capital town of the Śibipura. It is identified with the modern town of Shorkot in the Jhang district.

Cedi :

The *Ṛgveda* mentions Cedi tribe.[94] Their king Kaśu Caidya was celebrated with the unparalleled generosity of the Cedis as found in the *Dānastuti*. They are referred later to in the epic period with the Matsyas; and they lived in Bandela Khanda.

Ruśama :

The *Ṛgveda* mentions this tribe with their generous king *Ṛṇaṁcaya*.[95] Ruśama is mentioned in the *Ṛgveda* thrice as a protēgē of Indra.[96] The Atharvaveda mentions them with their king Kaurama.[97]

Varaśikha :

It is the name of a leader of a tribe. This tribe is recorded to have been defeated by Abhyāvartin Chāyamāna, in the *Ṛgveda*.[98] Abhyāvartin Chāyamāna has been referred to as Pārthava or the king Pṛthu.

Ajas :

In the *Ṛgveda*, the Ajas are mentioned with the Yakṣus and the Śigrus.[99] They fought against king Sudās on the bank of river Yamuna under the leadership of Bheda. Ajas were defeated by the Tṛtsus in the war of *Dāśarājna*. Pāṇini[100] mentions *Ajada* as a people. Aja is the ordinary name for goat in Sanskrit. Therefore, Ajas were probably shephered people in the *Ṛgvedic* time.

Śigru :

The Sigrus[101] were a tribe in the *Ṛgvedic* time. They fought against the Sudās accompanied by the Ajas, the Yakṣus, and the Bhedas. The Śigrus were defeated by the Tṛtsus who fought under the leadership of Sudās in *Dāśarājna* battle.

Yakṣu :

Yakṣu is mentioned in the *Ṛgveda*, both in singular and plural forms. They are described as taking in the *Dāśarājna* battle. The Yakṣus[102] having friendship with the Ajas, the Śigrus, and under the leadership of the Bheda fought against the Sudās. The Yakṣus may be taken to be a variant of Yakṣa. The *Amarakośa*[103] speaks of Yakṣa as a branch of Devas. Probably Yakṣus may be Aryan tribe.

Bheda :

It is the name of a tribe and their king also.[104] They were enemies of king Sudās. Bheda was defeated by Sudās on the river Yamunā.

Kīkaṭa :

The name of Kīkaṭa people occurs only in one mantra of the Rgveda.[105] They appear as hostile to the singer and as under the leadership of *Pramagandha*. Yāska[106] declares Kīkaṭa to be the name of a non-Aryan country. Vedic Index[107] says that Kīkaṭa is given as a synonym of Magadha. Sudama Misra[108] comments that the Kīkaṭas were primarily associated with the territories of Magadha and later on coalesced with them.

Vaikarṇa :

Vaikarṇa is mentioned only once in the description of the *Dāśarājna*.[109] It is stated here that Sudās overthrew the twenty one tribes of the two Vaikarṇas. Nothing particular is known about the Vaikarṇas.

Mūjavan :

The Ṛgveda[110] says that Soma is described as Mūjavata i.e coming from the Mūjavantas. Yāska[111] says that Mūjavanta as the name of a mountain. The Mūjavants were the residents of the region surrounding the Mūjavan mountain. The Ṛgvedic people used to obtain the Soma plant regularly from this mountain. It is probable that the people were living in the northern at the foot of the Himālayan mountain.

Paktha :

The Ṛgveda says the Paktha as the one of the tribes. They fought against the Tṛtsu-Bharatas in the *Dāśarājna* battle. The Pakthas and their allies were defeated by the king Sudās on the river Paruṣṇī.[112] The Pakthas also fought against the Puru king Trasadasyu.[113] Sudama Mishra's opinion is the Pakthas seem to be the fore-fathers of the modern Pakhtoons in the eastern parts of Afghanisthan.[114]

Bhalānas :

Bhalānas is also one of five tribes the Pakthas, Bhālanas, Alinas, Viṣānins and Śivas.[115] They fought against the Sudās on the battle of *Dāśarājna,* but were defeated by Sudās.

Alina :

The Alinas are also mentioned in the Ṛgveda with their allies. The Alinas were enemies of king Sudās, in the battle of ten kings and suffered defeat.[116]

Śiva :

In the company of the Alinas, Pakthas, Bhalānas and Viṣānins,[117] the Śivas also fought against Sudās in the battle of *Dāśarājna.* They were defeated by the Tṛtsu-Bharata. Dr. Agarwal puts the view that their original association seem to be with modern Baluchistan and they may be identified with the Greek *Siboi.*[118]

Viṣanin :

The Viṣanin occurs once in the Rgveda, as one of the enemies of the Trtsu-Bharatas.[119] This tribe may be supposed as belonging to the north-west of Paruṣṇi. The *Vedic Index*[120] expresses - "the word seems to mean 'having horns,' but in what sense is unknown; perhaps their helmets were horn-shaped or ornamented with horns."

Vṛcīvanta :

The Vṛcīvanta is referred to as being conquered by the Sṛñjaya king Daivavāta who also routed, the Turvasa king.[121] The people may be regarded as the fore-fathers of modern Nuluchis.

Paraśu :

This tribe is mentioned with the Pṛthu in the *Ṛgveda.*[122] Pāṇini also mentions about the Paraśus.[123] It is probable that the Paraśus were associated with the north-eastern sector of Iran.

Pṛthu :

In the *Ṛgveda* the Pṛthus are mentioned with the Paraśus.[124] Again, the *Ṛgveda* mentions the descendents of the Pṛthu, the Pārthavas as generous doners.[125] It is most probable that the Pṛthus were the fore-fathers of the Pārthins.

Gandhāri :

In the *Ṛgveda*, the good wool of the sheep of Gandhāris is referred to.[126] The *Atharvaveda* mentions with the Mūjavants, Aṅgas and the Magadhas.[127] This group of people lived in the north-west of India. Sudhama Mishra concluded that the tribe most probably was associated with the tracts between the Indus and Kābul rivers, as the same later on became the territory of the Gandhāra Janapada.[128]

6.6 Muṇḍūka Hymn (VII.103)

The Maṇḍūka hymn, intended as a spell to produce rain, is a panegyric of frogs, who are compared during the drought to heated kettles, and are described as raising their voices together at the commencement of the rains like Brahmin pupils repeating the lessons of their teacher. The opening mantra runs :

संवत्सरं शशयाना ब्राह्मणा व्रतचारिणः ।
वाचं पर्जन्यजिन्वितां प्र मण्डूका अवादिषुः ॥

It means that the frogs having lain for a year, like Brāhmans practising a vow, have uttered forth their voice roused by Parjanya.

Further it is expressed that when a heavenly waters came upon him lying like a dry leatherbag in a lake, then the sound of the frogs unites like the lowing of cows accompanied by calves (mantra 2).

When he has rained upon them the eager, the thirsty, the rainy season having come, one with a croak of joy approaches the other while he speaks, as a son (approaches) his father (mantra 3).

The fourth mantra reads :

अन्यो अन्यमनु गृभ्णात्येनोर् अपां प्रसर्गे यदमन्दिषाताम् ।
मण्डूको यदभिवृष्टः कनिष्कन् पृश्निः संपृङ्क्ते हरितेन वाचम् ॥

Here it is revealed that one of the two greets the other when they have revelled in the discharge of the waters. When the frog, rained upon, leaps about, the speckled one mingles his voice with (that of) the yellow one.

The seer of the hymn expresses that when one of them repeats the speech of the other, as the learner of his teacher, all that of them is in unison like a lesson that is eloquent to repeat on the waters (mantra 5). Thus, it is conveyed here that the voices of the frogs sounding together like those of pupils reciting a lesson after their teacher.

The sixth mantra declares thus: one lows like a cow, bleats like a goat; one is speckled, one of them is yellow. Bearing a common name, they have different colours. In many ways they adorn thier voice in speaking.

Referring to the *Atirātra*, a part of the Soma sacrifice, the seer of the hymn asserts thus -

ब्राह्मणासो अतिरात्रे न सोमे सरो न पूर्णमभितो वदन्तः ।
संवत्सरस्य तदहः परिष्ठ यन्मण्डूकाः प्रावृषीणां बभूव ॥

"Like Brahmins at the over-night Some sacrifice speaking around as it were a full lake, ye celebrate that day of the year which, O Frogs, has begun the rains".

In continuation, another mantra declares that - "Soma-pressing Brahmins, they have raised their voice, offering their yearly prayer. Adhvaryu priests, heated, sweating, they appear; none of them are hidden (mantra 8).

Here we have a reference to the Pravargya ceremony in which the milk is heated in a pot. The next mantra of this hymn runs thus:

देवहितिं जुगुपुर्द्वादशस्य ऋतुं नरो न प्र मिनन्त्येते ।
संवत्सरे प्रावृष्यगतायां तप्ता धर्मा अश्नुवते विसर्गम् ।।

That is, they have guarded the divine order of the twelve month: these men infringe not the season. In a year, the rain time having come, the heated milk-offerings obtain release.

In the Aitareya Brāhmaṇa the year, saṁvatsara, is called *dvādaśa* consisting twelve months and *caturviṁśa* consisting of twenty-four half-months. The gen, naturally depends on *devāhitim*, as being in the same *Pāda*. Prof. Jacobi understands *dvādaśāsya* as the ordinal twelfth supplying *māsasya* month, and making it depend of *ṛtum* in the next *Pāda*. This interpretation is then used as evidence to show that the beginning of the year was held in the period of the *Ṛgveda* to commence with the rainy season at the time of the summer solstice, and taken in conjunction with another reference in the *Ṛgveda* to the rainy season at the period to furnish an argument for the very early date of the *Ṛgveda*. But there is no trace here of any reference to the end of the year.

At the end of this hymn, the seer declares that "he that lows like a cow has given us riches, he that bleats like a goat has given them, the speckled one has given them, and the yellow one. The frogs giving us hundreds of cows prolong our life in a thousandfold Soma pressing.

6.7 Gambler Hymn (X. 34)

The Akṣa sūkta (X. 34) is one of the most interesting hymns among what are called the secular hymns in the *Ṛgveda*. Both in tone and content it has the appearance of a non-religious poem. M. Winternitz has this remark about it: "The most beautiful amongst the non-religious poems of the *Ṛgveda* collection is the song of the gambler. It is the soliloquy of a penitent sinner, who by means of his irresistible attraction to dice-playing has destroyed the happiness of his life." This aptly sums up the tone and content of this hymn.

The hymn commences with the gambler's reference to the dice as the dangling ones born in a windy place of the nuts of the lofty tree called Vibhidaka. As they roll down, they gladden the gambler. Each die (vibhīkada) is a source of pleasure to him like a dose of the best Soma from the mount Mujavant. This is the fascination which the dice have for a gambler (Ṛk. 1)

The gambler becomes, by experience, aware of the mysterious power of dice to attract, to deceive and to wound. The irresistible attraction of the dice is such as the gambler thinks for himself at one moment that he should not go with the gamblers only to give up his determination and go to the gambling house like a courtezan to her place of assignation. This is the magical influence of the ratting noice of the brown dice (Ṛk. 5)

This reveals the psychology of every gambler. Every gambler goes to the gamblers' assembly with the confidence that he would win, only to be disappointed when the dice run counter to his expectation and shatter his hopes (Ṛk. 6). This is the mysterious trick of the dice to hold forth a hope and withdraw their favour and shatter the hopes. Like boys, they offer first and then take back their gifts. They are crooked and piercing. They, though handless, overcome the gambler with hands. Although cold while rolling on the dice-board, they burn the heart of the gambler (Ṛks. 7, 9).

This is the most striking description of the most crooked cruelty of dice. What a sway these dice have on man once he submits his will to them! No power on earth can conquer them and surpass them in might. They do not fear at the anger of even the most terrible person. Even the king offers salutations to them (Ṛk. 8).

Caught in the deep mire of his own making, the gambler is only to repent but not to escape from his plight. In his plight he helplessly looks back and bewails the domestic happiness which he has irrevocably lost. What an excellent wife he had! How mercilessly under the evil influence of dice had he driven her away! She never scolded him; she was never angry. She was kind to him and to his friends. For the sake of the dice he had driven away a devoted wife (Ṛk. 2). The natural consequence of this was that his mother-in-law began to hate him; his wife herself rejected him (Ṛk. 3). His father, mother, brothers were unwilling to recognise and said that he should be taken away bound. The worst that could happen to a gambler was that other men would ill-treat his wife (Ṛk. 4).

This is the most pathetic description of the gambler's plight, who cannot turn to any body for help. The sight of domestic happiness in the homes of others, pains him to the core. He envies them. It pains the gambler when he sees women, the wives of others and their well-ordered home (Ṛk. 11).

Finally the gambler resolves to give up gambling and implores the dice to set him free in order that he might look after his field and live happily with his family (Ṛk. 14). The lament of the gambler has a message to give and that is the didactic element of the hymn; "Play not with dice; ply your tillage, rejoice in your property, thinking high of it. There are you cattle; there is you wife. This Savitṛ here, the noble god, reveals to me"(Ṛk. 13).

6.8 Funeral Hymn (X. 14)

The Ṛgveda contains a group of five hymns (x. 14-18) concenred with death and the future life. From them we learn that, thought burial was also practised, cremation was the usual method of disposing of the dead and was the main source of the mythology relating to the future life. Agni conveys the corpse to the other world, the Fathers, and the gods. He is besought to preserve the body intact and to burn the goat which is sacrificed as his portion. During the process of cremation Agni and Soma are besought to heal any injury that bird, beast, ant or serpent may have inflicted on the body. The way to the heavenly world is a distant path on which Savitṛ (i. 35) conducts and Pūṣan (vi. 54) protects the dead. Before the pyre is lighted, the wife of the dead man, having lain beside him, arises, and his bow is taken from his hand. This indicates that in earlier times his widow and his weapons were burnt with the body of the husband. Passing along by the path trodden by the Fathers, the spirit of the dead man goes to the realm of light, and meets with the Fathers who revel with Yama in the highest heaven. Here, uniting with a glorious body, he enters upon a life of bliss which is free from imperfection and bodily fratalities, in which all desires are fulfilled and which is passed among the gods, especially in the presence of the two kings Yama and Varuṇa.

In the beginning, the hymn expresses :

परेयिवांसं प्रवतो महीरनु बहुभ्यः पन्थामनुपस्पशानम् ।
वैवस्वतं संगमनं जनानां यमं राजानं हविषा दुवस्य ।।

Him who has passed away along the mighty steeps and has spied out the path for many, him the son of Vivasvant, the assembler of people, Yama the king, do thou present with oblation.

Further it is said that, "Yama has first found out the way for us: this pasture is not to be taken away. Whither our former fathers have passed away, thither those that have been born since (pass away) along their several paths (mantra 2).

मातली कव्वैर्यमो अङ्गिरोभिर बतग्स्पतिर्ऋक्वभिर्वावतधानः ।
यांश्च देवा वावृधुर्ये च देवान स्वाहान्ये स्वधयान्ये मदन्ति ।

Mātalī having grown strong with the Kavyas, Yama with the Aṅgirases, Bṛhaspati with the Ṛkvans, whom the gods have made strong and who (have made strong) the gods, some rejoice in the call Svāhā, others in the offering to the dead.

इमं यम प्रस्तरमा हिसीदाङ्गिरोभिः पितृभिः संविदानः ।
आ त्वा मन्त्राः कविशस्ता वहन्तु एना राजन्हविषा मादयस्व ।।

Upon this strewn grass, O Yama, pray seat thyself, uniting thyself with the Aṅgirases, the fathers. Let the spells recited by the seers bring thee hither. Do thou, O king, rejoice in this oblation.

अङ्गिरोभिरा गहि यज्ञियेभिर् यम वैरूपैहिर मादयस्व ।
विवस्वन्तं हुवे यः पिता ते अस्मिन्यज्ञे बर्हिवा निषद्य ।।

Come hither with the adorable Aṅgirases; O Yama, with the sons of Virūpa do thou here rejoice. I call Vivasvant who is thy father, (let him rejoice), having sat himself down on the strew at this sacrifice.

अङ्गिरसो नः पितरो नवग्वा अथर्वाणो भृगवः सोम्यासः ।
तेषां वयं सुमतौ यज्ञियानाम् अपि भद्रे सौमनसे याम ।।

The Aṅgirases, our fathers, the Navagvas, the Atharvans, the Bhṛgus, the Some-loving: we would abide in the favour, the good graces of them the adorable ones.

प्रेहि प्रेहि पथिभिः पूर्व्येभिर् यत्र नः पूर्वे पितरः परेयुः ।
उभा राजाना स्वधया मदन्ता यमं पश्यासि वरुणं च देवम् ।।

Go forth, go forth by those ancient paths on which our fathers of old have passed away. Thou shalt see both kings rejoicing in the offering to the dead, Yama and Varuṇa the god.

सं गच्छस्व पितृभिः सं यमेनेष्टापूर्तेन परमे व्योमम् ।
हित्वायावद्यं पुनरस्तमेहि सं गच्छस्व तन्वा सुवर्चाः ।।

Unite with the Fathers, unite with Yama, with the reward of thy sacrifices and good works in the highest heaven. Leaving blemish behind go back to thy home; unite with thy body, full of vigour.

अपेत वीत वि च सर्पतातोऽस्मा एतं पितरो लोकमक्रन् ।
अहोभिरद्रिरक्तुभिर्व्यक्तं यमो ददात्यवसानमस्मै ॥

Begone, disperse, slink off from here : for him the Fathers have prepared this place. Yama gives him a resting-place distinguished by days and waters and nights.

अति द्रव सानमेयौ श्वानौ चतुरज्ञौ शबलौ साधुना पथा ।
अथा पितॄन्सुविदत्राँ उपेहि यमेन ये सधमादं मदन्ति ॥

Run by a good path past the two sons of Saramā, the four-eyed, brindled dogs; then approach the bountiful Fathers who rejoice at the same feast as Yama.

यौ ते श्वानौ यम रक्षितारौ चतुरक्षौ पथिरक्षी नृचक्षसौ ।
ताभ्यामेनं परि देहि राजन् स्वस्ति चास्मा अनमीवं च धेहि ॥

Give him over to those two, O King, that are thy dogs, O Yama, the guardians, four-eyed, watchers of the path, observers of men; bestow on him welfare and health.

उरूणासावसुतृपा उदुम्बलौ यमस्य दूतौ चरतो जनाँ अनु ।
तावस्मभ्यं दृशये सर्यायं पुनर्दातामसुमद्येह भद्रम् ॥

Broad-nosed, life-stealing, ... the two as messengers of Yama wander among men; may these two give us back here to-day auspicious life that we may see the sun.

यमाय सोमं सुनुत यमाय जुहुता गविः ।
यमं ह यज्ञो गच्छत्य् अग्निदूतो अरंकृतः ॥

For Yama press the Soma, to Yama offer the oblation; to Yama goes the sacrifice well prepared, with Agni as its messenger.

यमाय धृतवद्हविर् जुगेत प्र च तिष्ठत ।
स नो देवेष्वा यमद् दीर्क्षमायुः प्र जीवसे ॥

To Yama offer the oblation abounding in ghee, and step forth; may he guide us to the gods that we may live a long life.

यमाय मधुमत्तमं राज्ञे ग्व्यं जुहोतन ।
इदं नम ऋषिभ्यः पूर्वजेभ्यः पूर्वेभ्यः पथिकृद्भ्यः ॥

To Yama the king offer the most honied oblation. This obeisance is for the seers born of old, the ancient makers of the path.

त्रिकद्रुकेभिः पतति षळुर्वीरेकमिद्बृहत् ।
त्रिष्टुब्गायत्री छन्दांसि सर्वा ता यम आहिता ॥

It flies through the three Soma vats. The six earths, the one great (world), triṣṭubh, gāyatrī and (the other) metres, all these are placed in Yama.

This and the following four hymns (x. 15-18) are among the latest in the Ṛgveda. The concluding stanza here, as in some hymns addressed to other deities, sums up the greatness of the god by saying that he embraces all things; cf. i. 32, 15 (Indra); v. 13, 6 (Agni).

6.9 Ṛgvedic Religion

The Ṛgveda is a collection of hymns addressed to the different deities that are largely personifications of the powers of nature. These hymns are intended to accompany the ablation of Soma juice and ghee in various sacrificial rites. Thus they are obviously concerned with the worship of various deities such as Agni, Indra, Varuṇa etc. Side by side with the hymns addressed to various deities, which form the majority, there are hymns which present the conception of a Supreme Being called Puruṣa, Sat etc.

From what is obvious it is surmised that the religion of Ṛgveda was essentially polytheistic, only assuming a pantheistic or monotheistic colouring in a few of what are considered to be later hymns. Max Muller has propounded a theory of Henotheism or Kathenotheism consisting in 'the belief in individual gods alternatively regarded as the highest' with reference to Ṛgvedic gods. This stage of Henotheism is regarded as an intermediary phase between polytheism and monotheism. But strictly speaking, it is difficult to pinpoint whether it is exactly this or that about Ṛgvedic religion. What looks like is polytheism. On close scrutiny one finds a certain under-current in this polytheism which considers all the various deities of the pantheon as manifestations of one Supreme Principle. It is this undercurrent of pantheistic monotheism that should be regarded as the essential and fundamental feature of this religion. It is this that links Ṛgvedic religion with the Upaniṣadic philosophy.

This view can be supported by certain grounds. The conception of Ṛta is one such ground. Some deities are said to originate from the Ṛta. Many gods participate in it and nearly all gods are said to work according to it. Ṛta is the concept of sacrificial cosmic and moral orders moulded into one. It is this that governs the functions of all gods. The want of a real, consistent working out of the personalities and functions of the individual deities is another ground. The personalities of too many deities are overlapping and the functions of many gods are common. This is because they are not seriously considered in their individual capacity. Viśvedeva hymns are also cases in point. They present a veiw of collective divinity leading to the same conception of the Supreme Principle. Hence, it is most congenial to the spirit of the Ṛgveda to say that its religion is concerned with the worship of gods not so much in their individual capacity as in their capacity as the different manifestations of the powers of one Supreme Being called variously as Puruṣa, Sat, Viśvakarman, Hiraṇyagarbha, Prajāpati, etc.

Thus Ṛgvedic religion is considerably advanced. It is the religion of a society that was far advanced in civilization and culture. Hence it is not proper to consider with Kaegi that Ṛgveda represented a religion of an aboriginal people.[129] The artistic skill in composing verses in definite metres, the sense of observation and poetic imagination evident in hymns such as those addressed to Uṣas and the philosophical ideas are sound enough proof of the advanced civilization which formed the ground of this religion.

Ṛgvedic religion according to one view[130] is of practical and utilitarian nature. This is true in view of the fact that in all the religions hymns, the ṛṣis offer prayers and promise oblations of Soma or ghee to the gods expecting in return from them rewards such as long life, prosperity cattle heroic sons etc. The object is not so much immortality or heaven as long life for full hundred years, all the pleasures of the earth. Thus there is no trace of the later (Upaniṣadic) idea of renunciation or nivṛtti. This should not lead one to think that the Ṛgvedic people were materialistic in outlook. One should bear in mind the undercurrent of philosophical attitude amidst this dominant tendency.

It is already observed above that Ṛgvedic religion is concerned with the worship of deities that are largely personifications of the powers of nature, without gainsaying the undercurrent of pantheism flowing through it. These gods arise as it were before our eyes, as the seers visualise them and portray them in the hymns. The 'literary and mythological evolution' of these gods is evident in them. In the case of many gods, the physical or mental phenomena they represent are always before the vision of seers, the personifications coming only as further developments of those phenomena. In some cases, the 'abstract conception of some prominent quality' is personified into a god. This is what one can say about those gods who are 'perspicuous in their origin'. Some gods are not so perspicuous in their origin, the outstanding examples being Indra and Varuṇa, the two of the greatest gods of Vedic pantheon. They are far removed from whatever were their original phenomena. Agni, Sūrya, Uṣas etc., on the other hand are the concrete personalities arising from a clear fact of nature underlying them. Savitṛ is an example of the separation of an abstract attribute from the original concrete fact of nature underlying the Sun and further development into an independent deity.

In the light of the above, the classification of gods into prehistoric, transparent, translucent, opaque, and abstract or symbolic gods proposed by Bloomfield,[131] appears to be relevant. This classification is based on the historical and exegetical principle. However, as rightly pointed out by Peterson, "it is not certain which gods have to be relegated to the prehistoric period, and a god may be transparent translucent or opaque, just as the interpretations offered are accepted or rejected."[132] On the historical principle, there is another classification of gods into Indo-European, Indo-Iranian and Indian deities. This classfication cannot be fully relied upon because there is no 'complete information about the date of every god from the Indo-European down to the Indian period.' Hence for want of more sound classification, the traditional classification of gods according to their place recorded in the Nirukta of Yāska,[133] can be accepted for all practical purposes. This classification has a partial support from a passage in the Ṛgveda itself.[134] According to this clsssification gods are terrestrial (Prthivīsthānāh), atmospheric (Antarikṣasthānāh) and celestial (Dyusthānāh). Agni, Soma and Pṛthivī are terrestrial deities, while Indra, Apām Nāpat, Rudra, the Maruts, Vāyu, Parjanya and Āpas are the atmospheric deities and Dyaus, Varuṇa, Mitra, Sūrya, Savitṛ, Pūṣan, the Aśvins, Uṣas and Rātri are celestial deities.

Reference

1. U.C. Sharma, the *Viśvāmitras* and the *Vasiṣṭas,* Viveka Publications, Aligarh, 1975, p. 269
2. *Ṛgveda* VII-33-3,5; 83-8; *Atharvaveda* XX-128-12.

3. स न एनीं वसवानो रयीं दाः प्रार्य स्तुषे तुविमक्षस्य दानम् । *Ṛgveda,* V-33-6
4. रैभ्यासीदुनुदेयी नाराशंसी न्योचनी ।
   सूर्याया भद्रमिद्वासो गाथयैति परिष्कृतान् ।। *Ṛgveda*, X-85-6
5. *Ṛgveda* II-34-6; VI-24-2; III-16-4
6. Yāska, *Nirukta,* IX-9
7. कर्माणि याभि कथितानि राज्ञाम् दानानि चोच्चवचमध्यमानि ।
   नाराशंसीरिति ऋचस्ताः प्रतीयाद् याभिः स्तुतिर्दाशतयिषु राज्ञाम् ।
8. *Aitareya Brāhmaṇa*, VI-27-14
9. *Aitareya Brāhmaṇa*, VI-13-11
10. Sāyaṇa on *Ṛgveda* x-85-6
11. *Aitareya Brāhmaṇa*, VIII-21-21
12. *Śatapatha Brāhmaṇa*, XIII-5-4-25.
13. Raj Bali Pandey, Historical and Literary Inscriptions, Chowkhamba Sanskrit Series, Varanasi, 1962, p.99
14. Winternitz, *Geschichte Der Indischen Literature,* Vol. I, p. 99
15. पञ्चजनाः । - *Ṛgveda* III-37-9; 59-8; VIII-32-22; IX-65-23; X-45-6

    पञ्चकृष्टयः । - *Ṛgveda* II-2-10; III-53-16; IV-38-10; X-60-4; 119-6

    पञ्चचर्षणयः । - *Ṛgveda* V-86-2; VII-15-2; IX-101-9
16. पञ्चजना मम होत्रं जुषध्वम् ।
    चत्वारो वर्णा निषादः पञ्चमः इत्यौपमन्यवः । - Yāska, *Nirukta,* III-8
17. ब्राह्मणोऽस्य मुस्मासीत् बाहू राजन्यः कृतः ।
    ऊरू तदस्य यद्वैश्यः पद्भ्यां शूद्रो अजायत ।। - *Ṛgveda* X-90-12
18. गन्धर्वाः पितरो देवाः असुरा रक्षांसितेषे ।। - Yāska, *Nirukta,* III-8

19. *Aitareya Brāhmaṇa,* III-31
20. ऊर्जाद उत यज्ञियासः पञ्च जना मम होत्रं जुपध्वम् ॥ - *Ṛgveda* X-53-4
21. *Śatapatha Brāhmaṇa*, XIII-5-4-14
22. तुर्वशं यदुम् । - Ṛgveda I-174-9 तुर्वशा यदू । *Ṛgveda* IV-30-17
23. पुरोळा इत्तुर्वशा यक्षुरासीद्रायो मत्स्यासो निशिता अपीव ।
श्रुष्टिं चक्रुर्भगवो दुह्यवश्च सखा सखायमतरद्विषूचोः ॥ - *Ṛgveda* VII-18-6
24. यदिन्द्राग्नी यदुषु तुर्वशेषु यद्दुह्युष्वनुषु पण्रूषस्थः ।
अतः परिवतषणावा ग्यातथा सोमस्य पिबतं सुतस्य ॥ - *Ṛgveda* I-108-8
25. Ṛgveda VII-18-14; VIII-10-5 etc.
26. नि गव्यवोऽनवो दुह्यवश्च षष्टिः शाता सुषुपुः षट् सहस्रा । षष्टिर्वीरासो अधि षड् दुबोयु विश्वेदिन्द्रस्य वीर्या कृतानि ॥-*Ṛgveda* VII-18-14
27. सत्यमित्वा महेनदी परुष्ण्यव देदिशम् ।
नेमापो अश्वदातरः शविष्ठादस्ति मर्त्यः ॥ - *Ṛgveda* VIII-74-15
28. *Ṛgveda* I-108-8
29. *Ṛgveda* VII-18
30. दुराद्यो अदितिं स्रोवयन्तोऽचेतसो वि जग्रभ्रे परुष्णीम् । - *Ṛgveda* VII-18-8
31. *Matsya Purāṇa,* 48-6; *Vāyu Purāṇa,* 99-9
32. *Ṛgveda* I-108-8
33. *Ṛgveda* I-36-18; 54-6; 174-9; VI-20-12; etc.
34. य आनयत्परावतः सुनीती तुर्वशं यदुम् । - *Ṛgveda* VI-45-1
पुरः सद्य इत्थाधिये दिवोदासाय शम्बरम् । अधत्यं तुर्वशम् यदुम् ॥ - IX-61-2
35. यस्य गवापरुषा सूयवस्यू अन्तरुषु चरतो रेरिहाण ।

स सृञ्जयाय तुर्वशं परादादवृचीवतो दैववताय शिक्षन् । - *Ṛgveda* VI-27-7

36. *Ṛgveda* VII-18
37. तुर्वशं यदुम् । *Ṛgveda* I-174-9; तुर्वशा यदू ॥ IV-30-17
38. *Ṛgveda* I-108-8
39. *Ṛgveda* VII-18-14
40. *Ṛgveda* I-108-8
41. *Ṛgveda* VII-18
42. प्रप्रायमग्नीर्भरतस्य शतण्वे वि यत्सर्ण्यो न रोचते बृहद्भाः ।
    अभि यः पुरुं पततनासु तस्थौ द्युतानो दैव्यो अतिथिः शुशोच ॥
    Ṛgveda VII-8-4
43. *Ṛgveda* Maṇḍala, I, IV, VI and VII
44. सनेम तेऽवसा नव्य इन्द्र प्र पूरवः स्तवन्त एना यज्ञैः ।
    सप्ता यत्पुरः शर्म शारदीर्द्दर्दन्दासीः पुरुकुत्साय शिक्षन् - *Ṛgveda* VI-20-10
45. कुरुश्रवणमावृणि राजानं त्रासदस्यवम् – *Ṛgveda* X-33-4
46. *Ṛgveda* VII-96-1, 2
    सरस्वतीमिन्महया सुवृक्तिभिः स्तोमैर्वसिष्ट रोदसी ।
    उभे यत्ते शुभ्रे महिना शुभ्रे अन्धसी अधिक्षियन्ति पूरवः ॥
47. आ भारती भारतीभिः सजोषा इळा देवार्मनुष्येभिरग्निः ।
    सरस्वती सारस्वतेभिरर्वाक तिस्त्रो देविर्बर्हिरेदं सदन्तु ॥ - *Ṛgveda* III-4-8
48. विश्वामित्रस्य रक्षति ब्रह्मेदं भारतं जनम् । Ṛgveda III-53-12
    विश्वामित्रो यदवहत्सुदासमप्रियायत कुशिकेभिरिन्द्रः *Ṛgveda* III-53-9; III-53-24; III-33-11, 12 etc.
49. दण्डाइवोन्द्रो अजनास आसन्परिच्छिन्ना भरता अर्भकासः ।
    अभवच्च पुरएता वसिष्ट आदित्रृत्सूनां विशो अप्रथन्त । *Ṛgveda* VI-33-6

50. *Ṛgveda* III-53; VII-18; 33 and 83
51. त्वमीळे अध द्विता भरतो वाजिभिः शुनम् । ईजे यज्ञेषु यज्ञियम्।। *Ṛgveda* VI-16-4

    त्वमिमा वार्या पुरू दिवोदासाय सुन्वते । भरद्वाजाय दाशुषे ।। *Ṛgveda* VI- 16-5
52. द्रषद्वत्यां मानुष आपयायां सरस्वत्या रेवदग्ने दीदीहि ।।
    - *Ṛgveda* III-23-4
53. *Śatapatha Brahmana*, XIII-54-11-1
54. The Vājasaneyī Saṁhitā in the Kaṇva recention XI-3-3; 6,3 has, Kuravah, Pāṅcālah evidently as a joint people; Āpastambha, XVIII-12-7 gives Bharatah, Kuravah, Pāṅcalah, Kuru-Pāṅcālah and Janatāh, as alternatives, according to the people to whom the king belongs. Macdonell and Keith, *Vedic Index*, Vol.II, p.96
55. Macdonell and Keith, *Vedic Index,* Vol.II, p.96
56. याभिः सिन्धुमवथ याभिस्तूर्वथ याभिर्दशस्यथा क्रिविम् । - Ṛgveda VIII-20-24
57. Śatapatha Brahmana, XIII-5-4-7
58. Macdonell and Keith, *Vedic Index,* Vol.I, p.166
59. *Altindische Leben,* p. 103
60. श्रवस्या वैकर्णायोर्जनात्राजा - Ṛgveda VII-18-11
61. U. C. Sharma. The *Viśvāmitras* and the *Vasiṣṭhas,* p. 284
62. कुरुश्रवणमावृणि राजानं त्रासदस्यवम् । मंहिष्टं वाधतामतषिः ।।
    - Ṛgveda X-33-4
63. उतो हि वां दात्रा सन्ति पूर्वा या पुरुभ्यस्त्रासदस्युनिदोश ।
    - Ṛgveda IV-38-1
64. द्रषद्वत्यां मानुष आपयायां सरस्वत्यो रेवदग्ने दीदीहि ।।
    - Ṛgveda III-23-4

    इकामग्ने पुरुदंसं सनि गोः शश्वत्तमं हवमानाय साध ।
    - Ṛgveda VII-23-5

65. Atharvaveda, XX-127-7
66. *Śatapatha Brāhmaṇa*, XIII-5-4
67. *Ṛgveda* VII-18-7, 13, 15, 19; VII-33-5-6; VII-83-4, 6, 8 etc.
68. *Ṛgveda* VII-18-6, 7
69. अभवच्च पुरएता वसिष्ट आदित्तृत्सूनां विशो अप्रथन्त ॥
    - *Ṛgveda* III-33-6
70. श्वित्यञ्चो मा दक्षिणतस्कपर्दा धियंजिन्वासो अभि हि प्रमन्तुः ।
    - *Ṛgveda* VII-33-1 compare with
71. विश्वत्यञ्चो यत्र नमसा कपर्दिनो धिया धीवन्तो असपन्त तृत्सवः ॥
    - *Ṛgveda* VII-83-8
72. *Ṛgveda* VII-18-6
73. *Śatapatha Brāhmaṇa*, XIII-5-4-9
74. *Kauṣītakī Upaniṣad*, IV-1
75. *Gopatha Brāhmaṇa*, 1-2-9
76. कुरुक्षेत्रञ्च मत्स्याश्च पाञ्चालाः शूरसेनकाः ।
    एष ब्रह्मषिदेशो वै ब्रह्मावर्तादनंतरः ॥ - *Manusmṛti*, II-19
    कुरुक्षेत्रांश्च मत्स्यांश्च पाञ्चालात् शूरसेनजाम् ।
    दीर्घालधूंश्चैव नरानग्रानिकेषु योजयेत् ॥ - Ibid, VII-193
77. *Ṛgveda* VI-27-7
78. *Ṛgveda* VII-18-6
79. प्रस्तोक इन्नु राधसस्त इन्द्र दश कोशयीर्दश वाजिनोऽदात् ।
    दिवोदासादतिथिग्वस्य राधः शाम्बरं वसु प्रत्यग्रभीष्म ॥ *Ṛgveda* VI-47-22
    मही राधो विश्वजन्यं दधानान्भरद्वाजान्त्साज्र्जयो अभ्ययष्ट ॥ *Ṛgveda* VI-47-25
80. *Ṛgveda* VI-47-23, 25
81. *Śatapatha Brāhmaṇa*, II-4-4-5
82. इयं शुष्मेभिर्बिसखाइवारुजत्सानु गिरीणां तविषेभिरूर्मिभिः ।
    पारावताघ्नीमवसे सुवतक्तिभिः सरस्वतीमा विवासेम धीतिभिः ॥
    Ṛgveda VI-61-2

83. अधा पारावता इति चित्रारुपाणि दर्श्या । - *Ṛgveda* V-52-11
84. पारावतस्य रातिषु द्रवच्चकेष्वाशुषु । तिष्ट वनस्य मध्य आ ॥
    Ṛgveda VIII-34-18
    पारावतं यत्पुरुसंभृतं वस्वपावृणोः शरभाय ऋषिबन्धवे ॥ - *Ṛgveda* VIII-100-6
85. *Pañcaviṁṣa Brāhmaṇa,* IX-4-11
86. इयमददाद्रभसमृणच्युतं दिवोदासं व्रध्य्रश्वाय दाशुषे । या शश्वन्तमाचखादवसं पणिं ता ते दात्राणि तविषा सरस्वति ॥
    -*Ṛgveda* VI-61-1; VI-61-2, 3 etc.
87. *Sāṅkhāyana Śrauta Sūtra,* XVI-11-11
88. *Mahābhārata, Bhīṣmaparva,* IX-68
89. *Matsya Purāṇa,* 114-43; *Vāyu Purāṇa,* 45-119 etc.
90. समिन्द्रेरय गामनड्वाहं य आवहदुशीनराण्या अनः । - *Ṛgveda* X-59-10
91. *Ṛgveda* X-179-1
92. शवसोशीनरेषु उदीत्येषु । - *Gopatha Brāhmaṇa,* II-9
93. *Aitareya Brāhmaṇa,* VIII-14
94. यथाचिच्चैद्यः कशुः शतमुष्ट्रानां ददत् सहस्राा दश गोनाम् । - *Ṛgveda* VIII-5-37
    माकिरेना पथा गाध्येनेमे यन्ति चेदयः । अन्यो नेत्सूरिरोहते भूरिदावत्तरो जनः ॥
    - *Ṛgveda* VIII-5-39
95. *Ṛgveda* V-30-12, 15
96. शग्धि यथा रुशमं श्यावकं कृपमिन्द्र प्रावः स्वर्णरम् ।
    - *Ṛgveda* VIII-3-12
    यद्वा रुमे रुशमे श्यावके कप इन्द्र मादयसे सचा ।
    - *Ṛgveda* VIII-4-2
    तिरश्चिदर्ये रुशमे परीरवि तुभ्येत्सो अज्यते रयिः ।
    - *Ṛgveda* VIII-51-9
97. *Atarvaveda,* XX-127-1

98. *Ṛgveda* VI-27-4, 5

99. आवदिन्द्रं यमुना तृत्सवश्च पात्रे भेदं सर्वताता मुषायत् ।
अजासश्च शिग्रवो यक्षवश्च बलि शीर्षाणि जभ्रुरश्व्यानि ।।
- *Ṛgveda* VII-18-19

100. *Pāṇini* IV-1-171

101. *Ṛgveda* VII-18-19

102. *Ṛgveda* VII-18-19

103. विद्याधरोऽप्सरोयक्षरक्षो गन्धर्व किन्नराः ।
पिशाचो गुह्नकः सद्धोभूतोऽमी देवयोनयः ।। - *Amarakośa,* I-1-10
Ed: Lewis Rice, University of Mysore, 1989, p. 5

104. *Ṛgveda* VII-18-18, 19; 33-3; 83-4

105. किं ते कृाणवन्ति कीकञ्ज़ेषु गावो नाशिरं दुह्रे न तपन्ति क्षर्मम् ।
आ नो भर प्रमगन्दस्य वेदो नेचाशाखं मघवन्रन्धया नः ।।
- *Ṛgveda* III-53-14

106. किं ते कुर्वन्ति कीकञ्ज़ेषु गावः। कीकटा नाम देशोऽनार्यनिवासः । कीकटाः किंकृताः । क्रियाभिरिति प्रेप्सा वा । - Yāska, *Nirukta,* VI-32

107. Macdonell and Keith, *Vedic Index,* Vol. I, p. 159

108. Sudhama Misra, *Janapada State in Ancient India,* p. 36

109. एकं च यो विशति च श्रवस्य वैकर्णयोर्जनान्राजा न्यस्तः ।
- *Ṛgveda* VII-18-11

110. प्रावेपा मा बृहतो मादयन्ति प्रवातेजा इरिणे वर्वतानाः ।
सोमस्येव मैजवतस्य भक्षो विभीदको जागृविर्मह्यमच्छन् ।।
- *Ṛgveda* X-34-1

111. मौजवतो मूजवतस्य जातः । मूजवांन्पर्वतो मुञ्जवान् । मुञ्जोविमुच्यत इषीकया । - Yāska, *Nirukta,* IX-8

112. आ पक्थासो भलानसो भनन्तालिनासो विषाणिनः शिवासः ।
आ योऽनयत्सधमा आर्यस्य गव्या तृत्सुभ्यो अजगन्युधा नृन् ।।
Ṛgveda VII-18-7 *Ṛgveda* VII-18-7

113. यथा कण्वे मघवन्त्रसदस्यवि यथा पक्थे दशव्रजे ।
- *Ṛgveda* VIII-49-10
114. Sudama Mishra, *Janapada State in Ancient India,* p. 40
115. *Ṛgveda* VII-18-7
116. *Ibid*
117. *Ibid*
118. Dr. V. S. Agarwala, *India as Knows 'to Pāṇini,* Lucknow University, 1953, p. 53
119. *Ṛgveda* VII-18-7
120. Macdonell and Keith, *Vedic Index,* Vol. II. p. 313
121. स सृञ्जयाय तुर्वशं परादादृचीवतो दैववताय शिक्षन्
- *Ṛgveda* VII-27-7
122. युवां नरा पश्यमानास आप्यं प्राचा गव्यन्तः पृथुपर्शवो ययुः ।
Ṛgveda VII-83-1
123. *Ibid*
124. युवां नरा पश्यमानास आव्यं प्राचा गव्यन्तः पृथुपर्शवो ययुः ।
Ṛgveda VII-83-1
125. द्वयाँ अग्ने रथिनो विशतीं गा वधूमतो मघवा मह्यं सम्राट्
भ्यावर्तीचायमानो ददति दूणाशेयं दक्षिणा बार्थवानाम् ॥
Ṛgveda VI-27-8
126. सर्वाहमस्मी रोमशा गन्धारीणामिवामिषा । - *Ṛgveda* I-126-7
127. *Atharvaveda*, V-22-14
128. Sudama Mishra, *Janapada State in Ancient India,* p. 40
129. Keigi : Der Ṛgveda; "Vedic religion is very primitive, Vedic people being semi-barbarons, child-like and innocent".
130. Bloomfield : Religion of the *Ṛgveda*, p. 184
131. Religion of the Veda, p. 96
132. Hymns from the Ṛgveda (1922, Bombay), p. LXXIV (Appendix IV)

133. VII, 5 - तिस्रा एव देवता इति नैरुक्ताः । अग्निः पृथिवीस्थानः । वायुर्वेन्द्रोऽन्तरिक्षस्थानः । सूर्यो द्युस्थानः ।

134. Ṛgveda I. 139, 11 - ये देवासो दिव्येकादश स्थ पृथिव्यामध्येकादश स्थ। अप्सु क्षितो महिनैकादश स्थ ते देवासो यज्ञमिमं जुषध्वम् ॥

Chapter - VII

Other Three Veda-Saṁhitās

7.1 The Yajurveda Saṁhita

7.1.1 Introduction

The Yajurveda, to which we now turn, is distinguished above the other Vedas by the great number of different schools which belong to it. This is at once a consequence and a proof of the fact that it became pre-eminently the subject of study, inasmuch as it contains the formulas for the entire sacrificial ceremonial, and indeed forms its proper foundation; whilst the Ṛgveda prominently, and the Sāmaveda exclusively, devote themselves to a part of it only, to the Soma sacrifice. The Yajurveda divides itself, in the first place, into two parts, the Black and the White Yajus. These, upon the whole, indeed, have their matter in common; but they differ fundamentally from each other as regards its arrangement. In the Saṁhita of the Black Yajus the sacrificial formulas are for the most part immediately followed by their dogmatic explanation, &c. and by an account of the ceremonial belonging to them; the portion bearing the name of Brāhmaṇa differing only in point of time from this Saṁhita, to which it must be viewed as a supplement. In the White Yajus, on the contrary, the sacrificial formulas, and their explanation and ritual, are entirey separated from one another, the first being assigned to the Saṁhita, and their explanation and ritual to the Brāhmaṇa, as is also the case in the Ṛgveda and the Sāmaveda.

Just as the Sāmaveda-Saṁhita is the textbook of songs for the Udgātar, so also the Yajurveda-Saṁhitās are the prayer-books for the Adhvaryu-priest. The grammarian Patañjali in his introduction to the Mahābhāṣya speaks of "101 schools of the Veda of the Adhvaryu" and it is understandable that there are many schools of just this particular Veda; because with respect to the individual sacrificial acts as the Adhvaryu had to perform them and to accompany them with his prayers, easily differences of opinion and sectarian variations were caused which led to the creation of their own handbooks and prayer-books. The slightest divergence in ceremony or liturgy was enough for the foundation of a new Vedic school. We know till today the following five Saṁhitās and schools of the Yajurveda.

7.1.2 Schools of the Yajurveda

1. The Kāṭhaka, the Yajurveda-Saṁhitā in the recension of the Kaṭha-school, which was known for a long time only as a manuscript in the Berlin library, but is now published by L.von Schroeder.[1]
2. The Kapiṣṭhala-Kaṭha-Saṁhitā which is preserved in only few fragments of manuscripts.[2]
3. The Maitrāyanī-Saṁhitā, the Yajurveda-Saṁhitā in the recension of the Maitrāyaṇiya-school, which L.von Schoreder has edited.[3]
4. The Taittiriya-Saṁhitā, i.e. the Yajurveda-Saṁhitā in the recension of the Tattirīya-school, according to the āpastamba-school, one of the main schools in which this text was taught, also called "Āpastamba-Saṁhitā". Tha same was edited by A. Weber.[4]

These four recensions are closely related to one another and are described as belonging to the "black Yajurveda". Different from these is -

5. The Vājasaneyi-Saṁhitā or the Saṁhitā of the "white Yajurveda" which derives its name from Yājnavalkya Vājasaneya, the principal teacher of this Veda. Of this Vājasaneyi-Saṁhitā there are two recensions, that of the Kāṇva school and that of the Mādhyandina school, which however differ from each other in minor aspects. This Saṁhitā also was edited by A. Weber.[5]

The main difference between the Saṁhitās of the "black" and the "white" Yajurveda lies in this that the Vājasaneyī-Saṁhita contains only the mantras, i.e. the prayers and sacrificial formulas which the Adhvaryu priest has to say, while the Saṁhitās of the black Yajurveda contain, in addition to the Mantras, also a description of the sacrificial rites together with discussion on them. Thus there is, in the Saṁhitās of the black Yajurveda that which is called "Brāhmaṇa" or "theological discussion" and which constitutes the contents of the Brāhmaṇas to be discussed in the next chapter, mixed with the Mantras. It is therefore easy to understand that in the prayerbooks meant for the use of the Adhvaryus the sacrificial performances were also discussed because these priests had to perform especially the individual sacrificial acts, and the murmuring of prayers and formulas in intimate relationship with these acts constituted only a small part of their duties. It can therefore be scarcely doubted that the Saṁhitās of the black Yajurveda are older than the Vājasaneyī Saṁhitā. Only later systematisers among the Yajurveda theologians perhaps felt the need to have analogous to the other Vedas, a Saṁhitā consisting of only Mantras by the side of a Brāhmaṇa devoid of them.[6]

However significant the differences between the individual Saṁhitās of the Yajurveda might be for the priests and theologians of ancient India, for us they are quite insignificant; and even chronologically the various Saṁhitās of the black and white Yajurveda might not be wide apart from each other. If I now give hereunder a short description of the contents of the Vājasaneyī-Saṁhitā, it is entirely sufficient to give to the reader an idea of the content and character of the Saṁhitās of the Yajurveda in general.

7.1.3 The Vājasaneyī Samhita

The Vājasaneyī-Saṁhitā consists of 40 chapters, of which however the last 15 (perhaps even the last 25) chapters are of a later date. The first 25 chapters contain the prayers for the most important big sacrifices. And the first two chapters give the prayers for the New-moon and Fullmoon-sacrifices (Darśapūrṇamāsa) with their connected sacrifices for the manes (piṇḍapitṛyajña). Then follow in the third chapter the prayers for the daily fire-cult, for the inception of fire and for the fire-offerings (Agnihotra) to be made every morning and evening and for the seasonal-sacrifices (Cāturmāsya) performed once every four months. The prayers for the Soma-sacrifice[7] in general including the animal sacrifice connected with it are found in chapters IV to VIII. Among the Soma-sacrifices there are some which last for one day and some which last for many days. Among the one-day sacrifices is the Vājapeya or "contest drink", a sacrifice which was performed originally perhaps only by warriors and kings which was connected with a chariot-race and in the course of which, apart from the Soma, brandy (surā)[8] which was normally forbidden according to brahminical law, was drunk. The sacrifice at a king's coronation or "Rājasūya" a sacrificial festival connected with some sorts of popular customs- with a symbolic battle march, with the play at dice and with all sorts of magic rites. The prayers for these two kinds of Soma sacrifices are found in the chapters IX and X. Then follow in chapters XI to XVIII numerous prayers and sacrificial formulas for the Agnicayana or the "Fire-altar-laying", a ceremony which extends over one whole year and to which a profound mystic symbolic significance is attributed in the Brāhmaṇas. The fire altar is nothing but "Agni" and is considered as identical with the god of fire. It is built with 10800 bricks in the shape of a big bird with its wings stretched out. In the lowest layer of the altar the heads of five sacrificial animals are immured and the bodies of the animals are thrown into the water out of which the mud is taken for making the bricks and the fire-bowl. The shaping and baking of the fire-bowl and of the individual bricks, of which many have special names and their own special significance, takes place with great ceremony and under incessant chanting of charms and prayer-formulas. The chapters XIX and XXI following that give the prayers for the Sautrāmaṇi ceremony, a peculiar sacrificial ceremony during which brandy is used instead of the Soma drink and is offered to the Aśvins and to goddess Sarasvati and to Indra. The ceremony is recommended to one who has drunk too much Soma or who cannot endure it - and this might be the original purpose of it - but also for a Brahmin who desires success, for a banished king who wants to regain his throne, for a warrior who wants to gain victory and a Vaisya who wants to attain great wealth. The texts connected with this sacrifice make many references to the saga of Indra who had qualms of conscience due to excessive enjoyment of Soma and who had to be cured by the Aśvins and Sarasvati. Finally chapters XXII to XXV with which the old part of the Vājasaneyī-Saṁhitā ends, contain the prayers for the great horse sacrifice (Aśvamedha), which only a powerful kings, a mighty conqueror or "world-ruler" was permitted to perform. Old sagas and epic poems give reports of kings of prehistoric times who performed this sacrifice and it is considered as the highest fame for a ruler if it can be said of him: "He has performed the horse-sacrifice". The purpose of this great sacrifice is given out very beautifully in the prayer Vājasaneyī-Saṁhitā XXII, 22: "O Brahman! May in this kingdom the Brahmin be born who shines by holy knowledge! May the warrior who is a hero, an excellent archer, of perfect aim and a great chariot-fighter! Aslo the cow that yields good milk, the ox that pulls well, the swift horse, the honourable housewife! May to this sacrifice a heroic son be born, who is victorious, an excellent chariot-fighter and eloquent in assembly. May Parjanya send us rain as we desire! May our fruit-bearing plants ripen! May we have luck and prosperity!"

That the last 15 chapters are of later origin is not doubtful. The chapters XXVI to XXXV are termed even by Indian traditions as "khilas" i.e. "additions", "supplements". Actually XXVI to XXIX contain only additions to the prayers of the preceding chapters. The XXX chapter proves itself to be a supplement even by the fact that it does not contain any prayers but only an enumeration of people who shall be sacrificed at the Puruṣamedha or human sacrifice to the most diverse divine beings and powers or to those that have been elevated to the status of deities for the moment. Not less than 184 persons should be butchered during this puruṣamedha; and that is - for example: a Brahmin is sacrificed to priestly honour, a warrior to royal honour, a Vaiśya to the Maruts, a Śūdra to an ascetic, a thief to darkness, a murderer to hell, a eunuch to evil, a whore to pleasure, a singer to noise, a bard to dance, an actor to song, a hunter to death, a gambler to the dice, a blindman to sleep, a deafman to injustice, a washerwoman to the sacrifice, a dyer-woman to greed, a barren woman to Yama, a Vīnā-player to the joy of ceremony, a flute-player to shouting, a cripple to the earth, a bald-headed man to the heaven etc. It is certainly not likely that all these kinds of people were brought together and should have been killed. This is perhaps only a symbolic act which represents a sort of "human sacrifice" by which the great horse sacrifice must be surpassed which however existed only as a constituent of the sacrificial-mystic and sacrificial theory, but which in reality hardly ever happened.[9] Moreover it is also true that the XXXI chapters contains a version of the Puruṣasūkta known to us from the Ṛgveda - i.e. of the hymn RV. X 90 in which the birth of the world is explained as by sacrificing the Puruṣa and the identification of the world with the Puruṣa, and thereby Puruṣa, "the main" is at the same time considered as the highest being - and this that chapter which the Brahmana should recite at the Puruṣamedha is also described as Upaniṣad i.e., secret teaching. The XXXII chapter is also, in form and content, nothing but an Upaniṣad: The Creator Prajāpati is equated here with the Puruṣa and the Brahman. The first six verses of the XXXIV chapter are similarly classified as Upaniṣ ads - and are given the title Śivasaṁkalpa-Upaniṣad. The texts of chapters XXXII to XXXIV are to be used during the so-called Sarvamedha or "All-sacrifice". This is the highest sacrifice that exists and it ends with the sacrificer giving away all his movable and immovable property as sacrificial reward to priests and then retiring as a hermit to the forest to spend the rest of his life there. The XXXV chapter contains some verses for funeral ceremonies which are taken from the Ṛgveda. Chapters XXXVI to XXXIX contain the prayers for a ceremony called Pravargya in which a drum is heated to glow on the sacrificial fire to represent the sun symbolically; in this drum milk is then boiled and offered to the Aśvins. The whole ceremony is considered as a great mystery. At the end the sacrificial implements are put up in such a way the they represent a man: The milk pots are the head, on which a bundle of holy grass represents the locks of hair; two milking tubs represent the ears, two small gold leaves the eyes, two shells the ankles, the flour strewn all over the body the marrow, a mixture of milk and honey the blood etc. To the mysterious ceremonies correspond naturally also the prayers and formulas. The XL and the last chapter of the Vājasaneyī Saṁhitā contains once again an Upaniṣad, and indeed one that is found in all collections of Upaniṣ ads, very important Īśa-Upaniṣad, about which we have to speak once again in the chapter on the Upaniṣads.

If it is clear even from the contents of the last chapters that they are of a late origin, it is still further testified by the fact that the prayers cotained in the Saṁhitās of the Black Yajurveda correspond only to those of the first half of the Vājasaneyī-Saṁhita.[10]

As regards the prayers and sacrificial formulas themselves, which form the main content of the Yajurveda-Saṁhitā, they consist partly of verses (ṛc) and partly of prose texts. It is the latter that are termed as "Yajus" and from which the Yajurveda gets its name. The prose of these texts is sometimes also a measured one and is even clevated here and there to a rhythmic swing. The verses that occur here are also found for the most part in the Ṛgveda-Saṁhitā. The divergent readings however, which the Yajurveda often offers, are not in any way older than the text found in the Ṛgveda, but they are mostly changes intensionally made in order to connect the verses more closely with the sacrificial acts. Only rarely have whole hymns of the Ṛgveda been included in the Yajurveda-Saṁhitās; mostly they are simply individual verses, isolated from the context which appeared to be suitable for some sacrificial ceremony and were hence included in the Veda of prayes. Therefore we have less interest in these verses as well. What is characteristic of the Yajurveda are the prose formulas and prayers.[11]

The simplest prayer that we can imagine, is the dedication of an offering with just mentioning the name of the deity to whom it is offered. Formulas of this kind are very numerous in the Yajurveda. "you are Agni", "you for Indra" of "this for Agni" or even simply "Hail Agni" or "Hail Indra" etc. with such words the offerings were placed or thrown in the sacred fire. And we cán hardly imagine a shorter and simpler hymn of praise to god than the words with which every morning and evening the fire-offering (Agnihotra) consisting of milk is offered: "Agni is light, light is Agni, hail! (in the evening) and "Sūrya is light, light is

Sūrya, hail!" (in the morning). In just as short words the purpose of a sacred act is also often hinted at, when for example the sacrificial priest cuts the branch with which the calves are driven from the cows and says then: "you to sap, you to power!" Or the object serving a holy act is shortly named and a wish is added, when for example the wooden splinter with which the sacrificial fire is to be lit, is consecrated with the words: "This, Agni, is your igniter; through this you shall grow and prosper. May we too grow and prosper!" If there is fear of evil or of a harmful spell, then a short text is used for protection against the same. Thus to the halter with which the sacrificial animal is tied to the post the following words are addressed: "Do not become a snake, do not become a viper!" To the razor with which the sacrificer is shaved of his beard when he is consecrated for the sacrifice, the priest says: "O razor, do not wound him!" During the coronation the king looks down to earth and prays : "Mother earth, may you not wound me, nor I you!"[12]

The majority of the sacrificial ceremonies like the Yajus-formulas do not have the object of "venerating" the gods but of influencing them, of forcing them, in order that they may fulfil the desires of the sacrificer. And even the gods love *panem et circenses,* they too do not want merely to be fed but also to be entertained; that however the gods find a peculiar pleasure in what is mysterious, obscure, and only hinted at, is made clear to us very often by the Vedic texts.[13]

In the Yajurveda we also find already a sort of influencing the gods which later on gained the upper hand to a very great extent. This consists in showering on a god as many names and attributes as possible and to show reverence to him under all his names in this way in order to win some favour from him. Thus we find in later literature texts, which enumerate a thousand names of Viṣṇu, of thousand names of Śiva, and whose recitation is considered as a very effective and meritorious act of worship.

The earliest beginning of this kind of prayers are found in the Śatarudrīya, the enumeratin of the hundred names of the god Rudra, in the XVI chapter of the Vājasaneyī Saṁhitā and in the Taittirīya-Saṁhitā IV, 5.

Finally, there is another sort of "prayers" - as we must of course call them - which we come across even in the Yajurveda and with which in later times a lot of mischief was played. These are the individual syllables or words which do not have any sense or whose sense has been lost, which are pronounced in the most ceremonious way at particular occasions of the sacrificial performance and which are held to be extremely holy. There is firstly the sacrificial invocation "svāhā" which we usually translate with "hail", with which every offering for the gods is thrown into the fire whereas the invocation "Svadhā" is used in the case of sacrificial offerings for the manes. Other quite understandable exclamations of this kind are vaṣat, vet, vat and above all the most sacred syllable om. This syllable, originally nothing but a consent,[14] was considered by the Hindus over many thousands of years and is considered even to the present day as extremely holy and full of mystical significance. In the Upaniṣads it is equated with the Brahman the world-soul and recommended to the wise as the highest object of meditation, the Kaṭha-Upaniṣad (II, 16) says about it; "This syllable is indeed the Brahman, this syllable is the highest, for he who knows this syllable, for him, all the desires will be fulfilled." And this syllable om is joined by the three "great words" (mahāvyāhṛti), namely bhūr, bhuvah, svar (explained by the Indians as "earth, air, heaven, which however is doubtful) of which it is said in a text:[15] "This indeed is the Brahman, this the truth, this the law; without this there is no sacrifice!"

Centuries later, in the Tantras, the religious books of later Indian sects, the use of such mystic syllables and words gained the upper hand in such a manner that often for pages at a stretch we find nothing but unarticulated sounds like "um, am, hrīm, um, em, krom, phaṭ, ah etc. It is also characteristic that the word "mantra" which originally meant the verses and prayers (ṛc and yajus) of the vedic saṁhitās, later on had only the meaning of a magic formula". Even in the Yajurveda we can very well follow this transition from prayer to magic formula these were both never strictly separate from each other.

And however tedious, uninteresting and unedifying the Yajurveda-Saṁhitās may be, if one wants to read them as literary works, still they are of very great imporance and indeed of interest for the investigator of religion who studies them as source-books not only for the Indian but also for general theology. Whoever wants to delve deep into the origin, development and theological significance of prayer- and this is one of the most interesting chapters of theology - should in no case fail to get acquainted with the prayers of the Yajurveda.

7.1.4 Taittirīya Saṁhitā (Black Yajus)

In the first place, the name "Black Yajus" belongs only to a later period, and probably arouse in contradiction to that of the White Yajus. While the theologians of the Rik are called Bahvṛichas, and those of the Sāman Chhandogas, the old name for the theologians of the Yajus is Adhvaryus; and, indeed these three names are employed in the Saṁhitā of the Black Yajus and the Brāhmaṇa of the White Yajus. In the later work the designation Adhvaryus is applied to its own adherents. and the Charakādhvaryus are devoted and censured as their adversaries - an enmity which is also apparent in a passage of the Saṁhitā of the White Yajus, where the Charakāchārya, as one of the persons to be dedicated at the Purushamedha, is devoted to Dushkṛita, or "III deed." This is all the more strange, as the term *charaka* is otherwise always used in a good sense, for "travelling scholar" as is also the root *char,* "to wander about for instruction." The explanation probably consists simply in the fact that the name Charakas is also, on the other hand, applied to one of the principal schools of the Black Yajus, whence we have to assume that there was a direct enmity between these and the adherents of the White Yajus who arose in opposition to them - a hostility similarly manifested in other cases of the kind. A second name for the Black Yajus is "Taittirīya," of which no earlier appearance can be traced than that in its own Prātiśākhya-Sūtra, and in the Sāma-Sūtras. Panini[16] connects this name with a Rishi called Tittri, and so does the Anukramaṇi to the Atreya school, which we shall have frequent occasion to mention in the sequel. Later legends, on the contrary, refer it to the transformation of the pupils of Vaiśampāyana into partridges (*tittiti*), in order to pick up the *Yajus* - verses disgorged by one of their companions who was wroth with his teacher. However absurd this legend may be, a certain amount of sense yet lurks beneath its surface. The Black Yajus is, in fact, a motley, undigested jumble of difference pieces; and I am myself more inclined to derive the name Taittirīya from the variegated partridge (*tittiri*) than from the Ṛishi Tittiri; just as another name of one of the principal schools of the Black Yajus, that of the Khāṇḍikīyas, probably owes its formation to this very fact of the Black Yajus being made up of *khaṇḍas,* fragments, although Pāṇini[17] as in the case of Taittirīya, traces it to a Ṛishi of the name of Khaṇḍika, and although we do really meet with a Khaṇḍika (Audbhāri) in the Brāhmaṇa of the White Yajus (xi. 8. 4.1).

Of the many schools which are allotted to the Black Yajus, all probably did not extend to Saṁhitā and Brāhmaṇa; some probably embraced the Sūtras only.[18] Thus far, at least, only three different recensions of the Saṁhitā are directly known to us, two of them in the text itself, the third merely from an Anukramaṇi of the text. The two first are the *Taittirīya-Saṁhitā*, so called, which is ascribed to the school of Āpastamba, a subdivision of the

Khāṇḍikīyas; and the *Kāṭhaka*, which belongs to the school of the Charaks, and that particular subdivision of it when bears the name of Chārāyaṇīyas. The Saṁhitā &c., of the Ātreya school, a subdivision of the Aukhiyas, is only known to us by its Anukramaṇi; it agrees in essentials with that of Āpastamba. This is not the case with the Kāṭhaka, which stands on a more independent footing, and occupies a kind of intermediate position between the Black and the White Yajus, agreeing freequently with the latter as to be the readings, and with the former in the arrangement of the matter. The Kāṭhaka, together with the *Hāridravika* - a lost work, which, however, likewise certainly belonged to the Black Yajus, viz., to the school of the *Hāridravīyas*, a subdivision of the *Maitrāyaṇīyas* - is the only work of the Brāhmaṇa order mentioned by name in Yāska's Nirukta. Pāṇini, too, makes direct reference to it in a rule, and it is further alluded to in the Anupada-Sūtra and Bṛihaddevatā. The name of the Kaṭhas does not appear in other Vedic writings, nor does that of Āpastamba.

The Saṁhitā of the āpastamba school consists of seven books (called *ashṭakas*); these again are divided into 44 *praśṇas,* 651 *anuvākas,* and 2198 *kandikās,* the later being separated from one another on the principle of an equal number of syllables to each. Nothing definite can be ascertained as to the extent of the Atreya recension; it is like-wise divided into *kāṇḍas, praśnas* and *anuvākas,* the first words of which coincide mostly with those of the corresponding sections of the Āpastamba school. The Kāṭ haka is quite differently divided, and consists of five parts, of which the three first are in their turn divided into forty *sthānakas,* and a multitude of small sections (also probably separated according to the number of words); while the fourth merely specifies the *richas* to be sung by the Hotar, and the fifth contains the formulas belonging to the horse-sacrifice. In the colophons to the three first parts, the Charaka-Śākhā is called *Iṭhimikā,*

Madhyamikā and *Orimikā,* respectively: the first and last of these three appellations are still unexplained. The Brāhmaṇa portion in these works is extremely meagre as regards the ritual, and gives but an imperfect picture of it; it is, however, peculiarly rich in legends of a mythological character. The sacrificial formulas themselves are on the whole the same as those contained in the Samhitā of the White Yajus; but the order is different, although the order of the ceremonial to which they belong is pretty much the same. There are also many discrepancies with regard to the words; we may instance, in particular, the expansion of the semi-vowels *v* and *y* after a consonant into *uv* and *iy,* which is peculiar to the Āpastamba school.[19] As to data, geographical or historical, &c. (here, of course, I can only speak of the Āpastamba school and the Kāṭhaka) in consequence of the identity of matter these are essentially the same as those which meet us in the Saṁhitā of the White Yajus. (In the latter, however, they are more numerous, formulas being also found here for ceremonies which are not known in the former - the *purushamedha,* for instance.) Now these data - to which we must add some other scattered allusions[20] in the portions bearing the character fo Brāhmaṇa - carry us back, as we shall see, to the flourishing epoch of the kingdom of the Kuru-Pañchālas,[21] in which district we must therefore recognise the place of origin of both works. Whether this also holds good of their final redaction is another question, the answer to which, as far as the Āpastamba-Saṁhitā is concerned, naturally depends upon the amount of influence in its arrangement to be ascribed to Āpastamba, whose name it bears. The Kāṭhaka, according to what has been stated above, appears to have existed as an entirely finished work even in Yāska's time, since he quotes it; the Anukramaṇi of the Ātreya school, on the contrary, Yāska makes Paiṅgi[22] (as the pupil of Vaiśampāyana) teach of Tittiri, the latter again the instructor of Ukha, and Ukha the preceptor of Ātreya.[23] This at least clearlv exhibits its author's view of the priority of

Yāska to the schools and and redactions of the Black Yajus bearing the names of Tittiri and Ātreya; although the data necessary to prove the correctness of this view are wanting. That, however, some sort of influence in the arrangement of the Saṁhitā of the Black Yajus is certainly to be attributed to Yāska, is evident further from the fact that Bhaṭṭa, Bhāskara, Miśra, in an extant fragment of his commentary on the Āpastamba-Saṁhiṭā,[24] quotes, side by side with the views of Kāśakṛitsna and Ekachūrṇi regarding a division of the text, the opinion of Yāska also.

7.2 The Sāmaveda Saṁhitā

7.2.1 Introduction

The Saṁhitā of the Sāmaveda is an anthology taken from the Ṛik-Saṁhitā, comprising those of its verses which were intended to be chanted at the ceremonies of the Soma sacrifice. Its arrangement would seem to be guided by the order of the Rik-Saṁhitā; but here, as in case of the two Saṁhitās of the Yajus, we must not think to find any continuous connection. Properly speaking, each verse is to be considered as standing by itself: It only receives its real sense when taken in connection with the particular ceremony to which it belongs. So stands the case at least in the first part of the Sāma-Saṁhitā. This is divided into six *prapāṭhakas,* each of which consists of ten *daśats* or decades, of ten verses each, a division which existed as early as the time of the second part of the Śatapatha-Brāhmaṇa, and within which the separate verses are distributed according to the deities to whom they are addressed. The first twelve decades contain invocations of Agni, the last eleven invocations of Soma, while the thirty-six intermediate ones are for the most part addressed to Indra. The second part of the Sāma-Saṁhitā, on the contrary, which is divided into nine *prapāṭhakas,* each of which again is subdivided into two or occasionally three sections, invariably presents several, usually three, verses closely connected with one another, and forming an independent group, the first of them having generally appeared already in the first part. The principle of distribution here is as yet obscure. In the Saṁhitā these verses are still exhibited in their *rich*-form, although with the *sāman*-accents; but in addition to this we have four *gānas*, or song-books in which they appear in their *sāman*-form. For, in singing they were considerably altered by the prolongation and repetition of the syllables, by the insertion of additional syllables, serving as a rest for the chanting, and so forth; and only thus were they transformed into *sāmans*. Two of these song books, the *Grāmageya-gāna* (erroneously called *Veya-gāna*), in seventeen *prapāṭhakas,* and the *Araṇya-gāna*, in six *prapāṭhakas,* follow the order of the *ṛichas* contained in the first part of the Saṁhitā; the former being intended for chanting in the *grāmas,* or inhabited places, the latter for chanting in the forest. Their order is fixed in a comparatively very ancient Anukramaṇi, which even bears the name of Brāhmaṇa, viz., *Ṛishi-Brāhmaṇa*. The other two *gānas*, the *Ūha-gāna*, in twenty-three *prapāṭhakas,* and the *Ūhya-gāna*, in six *prapāṭhakas*, follow the order of the *ṛichas* contained in the second part of the Saṁhitā. Their mutual relation here still requires closer investigation. Each such *sāman* evolved out of a *ṛich* has a special technical name, which probably in most cases originated from the first inventor of the form in question, is often, however, borrowed from other considerations, and is usually placed in the manuscripts before the text itself. As each *ṛich* can be chanted in a great variety of ways, in each of which it bears a particular name, the number of *sāmans,* strictly speaking is quite unlimited, and is of course far greater than that of the *ṛichas* contained in the Saṁhitā. Of these latter there are 1549, of which all but seventy-eight have been traced in the Ṛik-Saṁhitā. Most of them are taken from its eighth and ninth *maṇḍalas*.

Regarding the antiquity of the readings of the Sāma-Saṁhitā as compared with those of the Ṛk-Saṁhitā, is almost with certainty that the *ṛichas,* constituting the former were borrowed from the songs of the latter as a remote period, before their formation into a Ṛik-Saṁhitā had as yet taken place; so that in the interval they suffered a good deal of wearing down in the mouth of the people, which was avoided in the case of the *ṛichas* applied as *sāmans,* and so protected by being used in worship. The fact has also already been stated that no verses have been received into the Sāma-Saṁhitā, from those songs of the Ṛik-Saṁhitā which must considered as the most modern. Thus we find no *sāmans* borrowed from the Purusha-Sūkta, in the ordinary recensions at least, for the school of the Naigeyas has, in fact, incorporated the first five verses of it into the seventh *prapāṭhaka* of the first part - a section which is peculiar to this school. The Sāma-Saṁhitā, being a purely derivative production, gives us no clue towards the determinaiton of its date. It has come down to us in two recensions, on the whole differing but little from each other, one of which belongs to the school of the Rāṇāyanīyas, the other to that of the Kauthumas. Of this latter the school of the Negas, or Naigeyas, alluded to above, is a subdivision, of which two Anukramaṇīs at least, one of the deities and one of the Ṛishis of the several verses, have been preserved to us. Not one of these three names has as yet been traced in Vedic literature; it is only in the Sūtras of the Sāmaveda itself that the first and second at least mentioned, but even here the name of the Negas does not appear.

7.2.2 Form of the Sāmaveda

The Sāmaveda has come to us in three recensions, that of Kauthauma, which is the popular one, that of Rānāyaṇiya, which appears to have been identical with the former, at least as regards the Saṁhitā, and that of Jainimiya or Talavakāra. This last contains larger collections of melodies than the Kauthuma, while the verses are less numerous, differently arranged, and subject to some sound changes. The text of the Sāmaveda was commented on by Sāyaṇa in the 14th century.

Numbering 1,810 the verses are borrowed for the most part from the Ṛgveda, often with variants of a character or due to the necessities of musical transcription. They belong to the group of verses of complex metre (pragatha), those of the VıIIth and IXth maṇḍalas, which from the start were the concern of the udgātri or "singer", and had their special place in the Soma ritual. In the archika the verses are composed of isolated lines, chosen on the principle that to each one there must correspond a determinate "air", a saman or "melody": these verses or *ṛik* are the Hindus say, the matrices or yoni of the melody and are arranged according to the metre or the divinity: it is a collection for use by the schools. The uttararchika on the other hand is a practical manual for the use of officiants at the rituals: it provides in the order of the ceremonial the texts of all the tiercets (tricha) of which the first line has been given in principle in the archika, and which are to serve as the bases of the "chanted complexes", stotra, used in the course of the sacrifice and characterised by the use of tone. It appears that the uttarachika was compiled later than the archika (Oldenberg).

The Sāmaveda proper thus appears as a sort of handbook. Infact in part it is no more than the index to a handbook. The most intereṣting part would have been the melody: unfortunately the melodies of the age of the Saṁhitā have not been preserved. It is only at a relatively late period that there was recorded in the gana the musical notation in terms of syllables, and more often with figures written above the line.

In order to suit the text to the requirements of the melody it was interspersed with stobha, exclamatory syllables or words, or sometimes short phrases, which have a magical or mystical rather than a semantic value.

The first two gana give the melodies which "are to be sung in the village" and those which "are to be sung in the forest (that is to say, too sacred or dangerous to be heard by human communities): they correspond to the "words" of the archika and follow the same order. The last two gana (the uttaragana), which constitute the uttararchika, like it follow the order of the ceremonial.

As referring to the chanted prayer, the word *sāman* occurs already in the Ṛgveda. The true sense appears to be "propitiation". The *sāmans*, of which tradition knows a very large number, bear names drawn in general from those of the Ṛishis such as Gautama, Naudhas,a Shakala. They derive in part from popular songs, and hence carry certain magical qualities which are referred to in the literature and are confirmed by many indications: this magical air has brought the Sāmaveda to a certain extent into disrepute (cf. Manu). The samans are divided into five or seven groups. They are sung on seven notes and three degrees (octaves?), to the accompaniment of movements of the fingers.

7.2.3 Arrangement of the Sāmaveda

The Sāmaveda consists of two divisions Archika and Uttararchika as said above the Pūrvārchika has six Prapathakas (adhyāyas). Each *khanda* forms *dashati* which runs into many ṛks. The term *dashati* does not necessarily mean *ten* ṛks. The ṛks belonging to one particular dashati are in the same chandas and related to one particular deity.

The First *Prapāṭhaka* is a collection of the mantras addressed to Agni; hence this portion is called Āgneya kāṇḍa.

The mantras of the *second, third* and *fourth* prapāṭhakas addressed to Indra; as such they are known as *Aindra-parva*. The mantras of the *fifth prapāthaka* are addressed to Soma; therefore, this portion is called *Pavamana parva*. All the mantras in these five *prapāṭhakas* are called Grāmagāna. Since the sixth *prapāṭhaka* is ordained to be read in the forest, it is named as Āraṇyakaparva. At the end there is an Appendix called

Mahānamni, consisting of ten ṛks. Thus, the Pūrvārchikā in toto has 650 mantras.

The Uttarārchika consists of *nine* prapāṭhakas. The first-four prapāṭhakas of these, have two-two prapathakas, in accordance with Rāṇāyanīya branch.

This is explicit from the table below :

Pūrvārchikā :

Prapāṭhaka	Kāṇḍa	Dashati	No. of Ṛks
I	Agneyakanda	10	96
II	Aindraparva	10	97
III	Aindraparva	10	99
IV	Aindraparva	10	98
V	Pavamana parva	10	96
VI	Āraṇyaka parva	09	99
	Araṇyakāṇḍa	05	55
	Mahanamni	-	10
	Total	**64**	**650**

Uttarārchikā :

Prapāṭhaka	Prapāṭhakardha	Kāṇḍa	No. of Ṛks
I	2	12	135
II	2	12	114
III	2	14	135
IV	2	13	114
V	2	21	129
VI	3	15	147
VII	3	12	153
VIII	3	13	153
IX	3	09	120
	Mahanāmnyarchikā	**121**	**1209**

Purvārchikā - 650 + Uttarārchikā - 1209 = 1859

7.2.4 Features of Sāmagāna

The gāna of Sāma mantras is of four types:

1) Grāmageya gāna which is also called Prakotigāna or Veyagāna.
2) Āraṇyaka-gāna
3) Uha-gāna
4) Uhya gāna or rahasya-gāna

The mantras of beginning five adhyāyas of Pūrvarchika should be sung in the style of Veyagāna. The mantras of Āraṇyakaparva, the 6th Adhyāya of the Sāmaveda are based on Āranyaka-gāna. The mantras of Uttararchikā should be sung in the style of Ūhagāna as well as Ūhyagāna. The number of the gānas of one particular recension differs from the another.

		Veya	Aranya	Uha	Uhya
Kauthumiya-gāna -2722	=	1197	294	1096	205
Jaiminiya-gāna - 3681	=	1232	291	1802	356

The Nārada-śikṣā, text on ancient Indian Music based on the Sāmaveda, gives the details of different disciplines of ancient Music. Here, seven svaras, three gramas, twenty-one mūrchanas, forty-nine tānas are taken note of. The seven svaras are compared with Venu-svaras as shown below :

Sama-svara	Venu-svara	
1. प्रथम	मध्यम	- म
2. द्वितीय	गन्धार	- ग
3. तृतीय	ऋषभ	- रि
4. चतुर्थ	षड्ज	- सा
5. पञ्वम	निषाद	- नि
6. षष्ठ	धैवत	- ध
7. सप्तम	पञ्चम	- प

The numbers of the respective Samasvaras are written above the mantras, to indicate the particular Samaśvaras. It is known that the *Udātta, anudātta* or *svarita* of Ṛgveda mantras in the *Saṁhitā-pṣṭha* will get changed to other in the padapāṭha. So too, the mantras of the Sāmaveda Saṁhitā, when being sung, some word-changes take place. Such modification or change is technically called *Sāma-Vikāra* which is of six types :

1. **विषार** : It is word modification itself. अग्ने is changed to ओग्नायि
2. **विश्लेषण** : Splitting the Sāma-word is called Viśleṣaṇa. The word वीतये is split as वोयि तोया 2 यि
3. **विकर्षण** : Alongated utterance of particular accent, in a different manner

   Ex. ये is uttered as या 23 यि
4. **निदर्शन** : Repetition of the same word.

   Ex. repeated utterance of the word तोयायि ।
5. **विराम** : Stoppage of utterance near another word.

   Eg. when uttering गृणानो हव्यदातये, one should stop at ह, then continue.
6. **स्तोभ** : The group of the words fit for Sāmagāna, like औ, हो वा हा उ etc.

The *Sāmagāna* understood as *gītī* or *gāna* includes many disciplines - like *Rathantara, Bṛhat* etc. The *Udgātṛ*, one among four ṛtviks, should know all these disciplines, since he sings the Sāma mantra.

7.3 The Atharva Veda Saṁhitā

7.3.1 Introduction

The *Atharvaveda*, though the last one in the enumeration of the four Vedas, is of prime importance in delineating the institutional history of the Vedic people. The *Atharvaveda* is therefore, a priceless treasure supplying reliable data of great value to the ethnologist and to the historian of the social institutions of the Vedic people. On the popular side of religion, the Atharvaveda certainly deals with notions of greater antiquity than those of Ṛgveda, though it is generally believed that on the higher philosophical side, the Atharvaveda represents a more advanced stage.

The Atharvaveda is non-canonical in character except for its last kanda (section). It is mostly a collection of spells and incantations, for promoting happiness and preventing evils of all nature. Thus it is predominantly secular in character. This is the reason why it was not recognized as canonical for a longtime. Although the Ṛgveda contains some spells connected with domestic practices, it has no reference to the Atharvaveda. The Puruṣasūkta (X.90) [25] which refers to rks, samans and yajus formulae, does not mention the Atharvan spells. The Taittrīya saṁhitā of the Kṛṣṇayajurveda refers to the spells of Atharvaveda and mentions Aṅgiras seers. Among the Brāhmaṇas, the Ṛgveda Brāhmaṇas, Aitareya and Kauśītaki, do not mention about the Atharvaveda. Taittirīya and Śatapatha (Śuklayajurvediya) Brāhmaṇas refer to the Atharvaveda. All later Vedic literature and the sūtra works are fully aware of this Veda. Although the Dharmasčtras and Smritis consider the practices of the Atharvaveda as impure, the fact has it is connected with the Brahman priest of the sacrificial ceremony and held in esteem by the purāṇas, epics, shows that there was no total antagonism towards this Veda in the Indian tradition. This is because it has a unique place in the ancient Indian Literature, as being a source of inspiration for certain aspects of Indian life.

In the sphere of religion, the Atharvaveda represents the popular aspect as reflecting the popular usages and customs of the ancient times. As its contents reveal, it is more superstitious than the Ṛgveda. It does not represent the more advanced religious beliefs, but preserves more primitive notions about evil spirits such as demons etc, in its popular spells prevalent, among the masses. Hence, it is more important than the Ṛgveda itself from the point of view of the history of civilization.

The Atharvaveda is also indispensable for the history of Indian medicine and astrology. It contains a lot of material connected with the diagnosis of the various diseases and the prescription of herbal medicines together with spells for the cure of those diseases. It is for this reason called Bhaiṣajyaveda. Thus it provides the foundation for the science in India.[26] Some astronomical data in the nineteenth kāṇḍa makes it a source – book of ancient Astrology.

7.3.2 Significance of the Atharvaveda

The *Atharvaveda* is important from two points of view. It is not only a source of the cultural history of ancient India but also a highly interesting anthropological document. The *Atharvaveda* contains heterogenous material consisting of hymns and stanzas for the cure of diseases, prayers for a healthy and long life, charms for the prosperity of home and children, cattle and fields, expiatory mantras designed to free one from sin and guilt; mantras to pray for harmony in the family and charms concerned with Love and Marriage.

The *Atharvaveda* is Veda of practical importance and Utility par excellence. The majority of its mantras have an practical purpose. The philosophical hymns too aim at a practical purpose.[27]

To understand the Atharvan mantras, one must be fully acquainted with its '*Viniyoga*' aspect. The application or use of a mantra plays a very important role in correctly analyzing and understanding that *mantra*.

The *Atharvaveda* has come down to us in two recensions. The Śaunakīya and the paippalada, though it is traditionally believed to have had nine śākhās.[28] Among these, the Śaunakīya recension is more popularly known.

The Pariśiṣṭas of the *Atharvaveda*, which form a voluminous literature throw light on the Atharvanic traditions, beliefs and practices perhaps more fully than any other ancillary work. They may, accordingly be regarded as constituting the most significant aid for the study of the *Atharvaveda*.

It is often said that the Ṛgveda and the Atharvaveda together present a complete picture of the Vedic man. At the outset, it may be said that Ṛgveda deals with the higher strata of Society consisting of poets, priests, and princely class, while the *Atharvaveda* is the "Veda of the masses". It is concerned with the life of the common man. His hopes and aspirations are clearly portrayed in this Veda.

The two Vedas may be said to be complementary to each other. Going step further it can be said that *Atharvaveda* possesses far greater interest from the cultural and historical points of view. The popular way of life and thought about magic, medicine, witchcraft, spirits, etc., fall within the purview of the *Atharvaveda*. This Veda portrays the life of the common man from birth to death.

The *Atharvaveda* contains matters of a varied nature ranging from the beliefs of Primitive man to the philosophic speculations of a high nature. On the one side one finds in it, the dark and demoniac powers which cause disease and misfortune, and on the other side one sees the great mighty gods whom the seer adores, prays and to whom he offers and requests to bestow happiness and prosperity.[29] The *Aatharvaveda* consists not only of spells incantations, magical and expiatory formulas but also sublime prayers as in the case of the hymn addressed to Varuṇa (AV 4.16). The Atharvan practices reflect a different attitude of mind from the one found in the Ṛgveda. The philosophic hymns of the *Atharvaveda* are the fore runners of the sublime philosophy of the Upaniṣads. They clearly depict the Indian mind.

The fourth Veda is known in Hindu literature by an unusually large number of appellations. The various names by which the *Atharvaveda* is known may be said to refer its heterogenous nature. Each of these names indicates some significant aspects of the contents of that Veda.

Quite frequently however, the members of the compound 'Athavāngirasah' are separated so that each is mentioned by itself, but always in more or less conjunction with one another. In other words, the *Aatharvaveda* actually consists of Atharvan and Aṅgiras matter, and the question arises what elements in the make up of this Veda, these terms refer to. The term Atharvan refers to the auspicious practices of the Veda, the bhesajani those parts of the Veda which are recognized by the Atharvan ritual and the Orthodox Brahmanical writings, as 'Śānta' 'holy' and 'pauṣṭika' conferring prosperity. The term 'Angiras' refers to the hostile sorcery practices of the Veda, the 'Yātu' or 'Abhicara' which is terrible (ghora).

In the names 'Atharvāngirasa' and 'Bhṛgvāngirasa' the two fold nature of the *Atharvaveda* becomes clearly evident. It embodies two types of ritual as stated above.

The *Atharvaveda* is also called the Veda of Kshatram Weber[30] has emphasized the marked relation of the Atharvan to the royal caste. The text of the Samhita abounds in 'Rājarkarmāṇi', 'royal practices' and *Weber* thinks that the name of Kauśika, the author of the great Atharvan Sūtra points to a Kṣatriya connection since Kuśika is identical with Viśvamitra and the latter as is well known, stands forth among the ancient heroes as the representative of royalty. None of these points may be regarded as more than possibilities.

The name *Brahmaveda* presupposes several distinct currents of thought. On account of the peculiar unsophisticated and non-hierarcical character of the contents, the *Atharvaveda* was originally not given official recognition by the hierarcical priests. A strong reaction began to develop against this priestly attitude and as the result of it, the sponsors of the *Atharvaveda* went to the other extreme and claimed that the *Atharvaveda* was to be recognized not as just one of the four Vedas but as a Veda which comprehended the other three Vedas and was thus identical with *Sarvavidya*.[31] Moreover the *Atharvaveda* of all the Vedas contains the largest number of cosmogonic or theosophic hymns which deal explicitly or implicitly with the divine Brahman.[32]

Finally when hierarchial recognition came to be conceded to the *Atharvaveda*, some place had to be found in the scheme of Vedic ritual for the priest belonging to that Veda. But the three main functions in the rituals namely, the actual performance of the various rites, the reciting of the relevant-mantras to accompany that performance and the chanting of Vedic melodies had already been assigned to the priest belonging respectively to the Yajurveda, the Ṛgveda and the Sāmaveda. The office of a fourth principal priest was, therefore evolved. He was called Brahma. He was to belong to the Atharvaveda[33] and his main function in the sacrifice was of the nature of general supervision.

The above discussion of the numerous names of the *Atharvaveda* clearly indicates the richness and variety of the contents of that Veda. The hymns of the *Atharvaveda* may be generally classified under the following broad groups :

i. Bhaiṣajyāni - Remedial charms for curing diseases and possession by evil spirits.

ii. Āyuṣyāni - prayers for health and long life.

iii. Sāmmanasyāni - Spells to secure harmony in a family assembly, village, etc.

iv. Pauṣṭikāni - Charms to secure happiness and prosperity

v. Strīkarmāṇi - Hymns pertaining to women, Love and marriage.

vi. Rājakarmāṇi - Hymns to be used for the welfare of the King.

vii. Ābhicārakāṇi - Charms to curse injurer and to kill the enemy.

viii. Kṛtyāparihāraṇāni - Charms for counteracting the magic employed by the enemy.

ix. Prāyaśeittāni - Spells for expiating sin and defilement.

x. Ādhyātmikāni - Cosmogonic and theosophic hymns.

7.3.3 The arrangement of the Atharvaveda

The *Atharvaveda* is a collection of hymns and spells in twenty books of kāṇḍa. The subdivisions, which are in part modern, are called "lectures" (prapathaka), "recitations" (anuvaka) and 'decads" (dashati). Altogether there are 731 sections and nearly 6,000 verses. The first eighteen books, which form the Atharvaveda proper, are divided into three groups:

I-VII, containing short hymns (less than 20 verses) on various subjects. The books are arranged in ascending order of length, except VII, and each consists of hymns of the same length: thus Book I has hymns of 4 verses, Book II of 5, Book VII consists of the hymns of 1 verse and some have regarded it as a sort of appendix.

VIII-XII contain long hymns on various subjects. The books are of about the same size, and the hymns are classified according to length, but not without exceptions.

XIII-XVIII contain hymns classified according to subject, each book dealing with a separate subject. These books, except XVIII, are arranged in descending order of length.

There remains XIX, a supplement the hymns of which, if arrangement had been systematic, would have been divided among Books I-XVIII: and XX, a more recent supplement, which consists almost entirely of extracts from the Ṛgveda, and particularly from the 8th maṇḍala.

The borrowings from the Ṛik are otherwise considerable: one-seventh of the Atharva comes from the Ṛik, with or without variants, especially from Book X. The variants derive in part from the defective state in which the *Atharvaveda*, has been transmitted. But some variants are authentic, and reveal attempts to adapt the ancient formulae to new purposes.

Recensions and the Authors

Two schools have left texts: that of the Śaunaka (the name is also known as that of an author of sūtras) is the commonly accepted one. That of the Paippalada - also called the Kashmirian recension, because the only known manuscript was found in Kashmir – is arranged very differently and contains many variants, some amounting to profound alterations, and many new passages. Often the Śaunaka text contains no parallel. The linguistic utilization of this important recension still remains to be carried out.

According to tradition, many books of the Atharvaveda are attributed to such or such mythical author: some isolated hymns are also attributed to authors, but no exact information can be derived from this.

Sāyaṇa commented on the *Atharvaveda*, but in a mediocre manner and leaving many gaps. The state of the text leaves much to be desired: it is clear that at an early period the Atharvan material lacked authoritative warrant and floated, so to speak, on the margin of the cannon. We know in any case that the Atharva was given the status of the "fourthVeda" only gradually and at a late period, that some schools have never recognized it, and that in every way its dignity is less than that of the other Vedas. Like the Ṛik it possesses a padapatha, but of far inferior quality.

7.3.4 Contents of the Atharvaveda - (Books I-VII)

Forming a unity, they contain mainly magical prayers for specific objects. Solemn hymns of the type of the Ṛgveda are few, and often adapted to magical requirements,"Atharvanised", as it may be said. These compositions can be classified as "popular poetry" (Bloomfield), as opposed to the priestly work of the Ṛgveda and the Atharvaveda, VIII-XVIII. However, this distinction cannot be pressed too far, and a number of these prayers show an elaboration comparable if not superior to that of the hymns: they may perhaps owe their poetic form to a religious cult. They have given their name to the collection, if it is true that the word Atharvan, the designation of a prehistoric priest of the fire cult (the atharvan of the Avesta), individualised into divine entity, acquired the sense of "magical formula" in particular the formula of white magic, as opposed to angiras which designates black magic : whence the composite name Atharvangiras, an ancient name of the Atharvavveda.

These prayers could be divided into several categories, without very rigid boundaries: charms for long life (ayushya), to cure sickness or demonic possession (bhaishajya), curses upon demons, sorcerers, enemies (abhicharika), love charms (strikarman), charms to bring about concord (ammanasya) and prosperity (paushtika), charms relating to royalty (rajakarman) or to the Brahmanical power, and expiatory prayers (prayaschitta). The corresponding rituals are set forth in a more recent text, the Kauśika.

In these works the gods play hardly any part, except as background. The prayers have little connection with the official cult or society. They are a matter between the sorcerer and his client, who are often the chaplain (purohita) and the king. So far as it is a collection of charms, the Atharvaveda is rather a manual for the laity, the Kshatriya, and from certain points of view a manual of State.

The magical system presupposes a complex world of interrelations, and a rudimentary but rigorous causality. From the anthropological point of view the collection has much importance, especially in view of its great antiquity. Among other things, it gives us the first outlines of Indian medicine.

In some hymns, such as the prayer to Varuna regarded as overseeing the human conscience (IV.16), an imposing prelude in solemn phraseology gives way to the most common place sorcery.

Books VIII-XII

These books, which also form a unity, contain magical prayers like the former books. But in some cases they break out of the normal bounds of this style of composition, making use of certain literary developments: thus the hymn to (curative) plants, VIII.7, or the prayer for the house,IX.3.If it were not for the evidence of the ritual, how could we tell that the hymn to the Earth (XII.I), that extraordinary work, in which the telluric forces are represented from a pantheistic standpoint in a most grandiose composition, was used to endow houses with stability, or rather to safeguard them against earth movements ?

Other pieces, resembling certain Ṛgveda hymns on sacred attributes or instruments, are remarkable for verbal extravagance: such as the hymn to the Brahmanic porridge (XI.I). Some are entirely in the style of the sacrificial hymns, such as the hymn to the cow (X.9), the hymn to the remains of the ritual repast (XI.7), and the funerary prayers of Book X. Some are merely collections of puzzles: but these, and some others which are Upanishads before their time, develop in mystical terms cosmogonic themes on a liturgical or mythological foundation. They constitute one of the distinctive elements in the Atharvaveda. Such are the hymn on the creation of the male (puruśa) sacrificed by the gods (X.2), the glorification of the pillar, a solar symbol (X.7 and 8), that of the Brahman novice, also assimilated to the sun (X.15), that of the breath (XI.4), or of the Viraj, the name of a poetical metre

(VIII.9 and 10); all these pieces is deceptive: They are no more and no less than incantations using an esoteric jargon.

Books XIII-XX

As regards both the nature and the form of their hymns, these books resemble VIII-XII more than I-VII. Book XIII, devoted to Rohita, develops apart from its magical digressions, the theme of a cosmic principle in the form of the sun (sec.131). Book XIV contains prayers for marriages,XVIII for funerals. Book XV concerns the Vratya XIV contains obsecure magical or ritual formulae, and XVII some elements of panegyric. We can ignore Book XIX, which as we have seen supplements the ancient Atharva, and in Book XX, we need only refer to the section called Kuṭapa, containing some obscene hymns, and songs accompanying certain episodes of the cult, in particular the payment to the officiants. This whole of Book XX is in fact conceived as a technical treatise for the use of the officiant Brahmanaacchamsin, as Caland has shown.

7.3.5 Form of the Text

The Atharvaveda contains many passages in prose, a prose often cadenced, a style earlier than that of the Brāhmaṇas. But the greater part of the collection is in verse, though the versification is complex and loose, and is not easily brought within the common metrical rules. The language is definitely later than that of the Ṛgveda, but the style, marked by an expressive use of alliteration, repetition and various associations with magical purposes, gives an impression of greater antiquity even than that of the Ṛgveda. The short prayers have a clarity and compactness which may attain a real intensity; the final verse, presenting the wish as realized, at the same time gives the key to the veiled allusions in the body of the prayer.

7.3.6 Cultural value of the Atharvaveda

The *Atharva-Veda* brings in a new note. There we find signs of a gloomier side in man's life. Black magic, injury to one's enemies, and various other aspects of life, which we are wont to call more primitive, are in the forefront in the *Atharva-Veda*. There is considerable scope for dispute regarding the claim of the *Atharva-veda* to be counted as a Veda at all. Even in Indian literature three Vedas and four Vedas are mentioned side by side. The literature connected with sacrifices recognizes only three Vedas. Jaimini in his *Mimāṁsa-Sūtras* defines only the *Ṛg-Veda*, the Yajur-Veda, and the *Sāma-Veda*, ignoring the *Atharva-Veda*, which has no place in the sacrifices. In a sacrifice there are four kinds of priests: the hotr, connected with the *Ṛg-Veda*; the adhvaryu, connected with the *Yajur-Veda*; the udgair; connected with the *Sāma-Veda*; and the brahman, who supervises the whole sacrifice. Brahman is sometimes connected with the *Atharva-Veda*. This relation is not natural; it is only an attempt at an equation. If one may risk an opinion, it may be said that the *Atharva-Veda* represents a current of Indian culture that runs parallel to the current represented by the other Vedas; and that it is the earlier stage of a current that culminated in the Āgama and Tantra literature. Most of the Upaniṣads composed at a later date, which are mostly of a sectarian nature, have been tagged on to the *Atharva-Veda*.

Although the *Atharva-Veda* was not one of the Vedas, if by Veda we mean the sacrificial literature, yet it will ever remain one of our richest heritages representing the secular and pre-eminently intellectual aspect of our ancients. The term 'Atharvan' was from the very beginning associated with intellectualism. The famous hymn composed by Dīrghatamas is highly philosophical, and the two passages 'Truth is one; sages call it by various names' (Ṛgveda, I.164.46) and 'There are two birds, with fair wings, knit with bonds of union... ' (Ṛgveda, I.146.20), which has been the basic text for latter-day Indian philosophy regarding the relation between the supreme Soul and the individual soul, occur in this hymn; and the author Dīrghatamas belongs to the Atharvan family. In the Raghuvaṁṣa (I), where the King Dilīpa goes to his teacher Vasiṣṭha to consult him on very important State matters, Kālidāsa refers to Vasiṣṭha as the repository of Atharva-knowledge. (*Ātharvanidhi*).

There was no conflict between the civilization represented by the three Vedas and that represented by the Atharva-Veda. They represent two aspects of a civilization that is single and unitary. One can safely say that the three Vedas represent mainly the aspect of ancient Indian civilization dealing with the goal of man in a future life, and the *Atharva-Veda* represents chiefly the other aspect, dealing with the life of man in this world. The three Vedas deal with gods and sacrifices; the *Atharva-Veda* deals with man, his protection from enemies, destruction of foes, kings and politics, welfare in this life, and similar things.

There is another aspect, namely, the aspect of high philosophy. The three Vedas are not so intimately related to the problems of the Absolute as is the *Atharva-Veda*. Even if we reckon the number of hymns related to philosophy, we find a larger number of philosophical hymns in the *Atharva-Veda* than in the *Ṛg-Veda*. And nearly all the philosophical verses in the *Ṛg-Veda* are common to the *Atharva-Veda*. Thus from the point of view of the problems relating to the Absolute, the *Atharva-Veda* has a special importance.

References

1. Edited by L.V. Leipzig, 1900-1910, *Index Verborum* by R. Simon, 1912. For the contents of the Kāthaka see A. Weber, *Ind. Stud.* 3,451 ff.; for the text and its interpretation see Keith, *JRAS*, 1910, 517 ff; 1912, 1905 ff; Caland, *ZDMG*, 72, 1918, 12 ff.

2. See L. V. Schroeder, *WZKM*, 12, 362 f.
3. Leipzing 1881-1886. Numerous quotations from this Saṁhitā in German translation are found in L.von Schroeder: *Indians Literature and Kunst.* (Leipzig, 1887) p. 110-162. See also Schroeder, *ZDMG* 33, 1879, 177 ff; Caiand, *ZDMG*, 72, 1918. 6 ff.
4. Ed. by A. Weber in the 11th and 12th volumes of his *Indische Studien,* 1871 and 1872; with Sāyaṇa's commentary in *Bibl. Ind.,* 1860-1899, and in *Ān. SS.* Nr. 42; translated into English by A. B. Keith, *HOS,* vols. 18, 19, 1914.
5. The White *Yajurveda,* Part I, The Vājasaneyi-Saṁhitā ... with the commentary of Mahīdhara, Berlin-London 1852. An English translation of the same is available by R. T. H. Griffith (*The texts of the White Yajurveda,* translated with a popular commentary, Benaras 1899).
6. It is usually presimed that the name "white" *Yajurveda* means "clear, (ordered) arranged" Yajurveda indicates the pure distinction between sacrificial text and ritual commentary in the same, whereas "black" *Yajurveda* signifies "unarranged" *Yajurveda*. This explanation which can be traced back even to Indian commentators, appears to me, to be highly improbable. But even *Śatapatha Brāhmaṇa* XIV, 9, 4, 33 (of IV, 4, 5, 19) are called "the white sacrificial texts" (*Śuklāni yajūṁṣi*) as *Ādityāni*, "revealed by the sun"; and also the *Purāṇas* narrate that Yājnavalkya received new sacrificial texts from the sun (*Viṣṇu Purāṇa,* III, 5) I believe that "white *Yajurveda*" owes its name to this connection with the sun. As against this the older *Yajurveda* was called "black". It is most probable "that the Saṁhitā of the white *Yajurveda* is most closely related to the original form of the Veda of the Adhvaryu," as Pischel thinks, *KG*, 172. Cf. Keith, *HOS*, Vol. 18, pp. lxxxv ff, on the mutual relationship of the *Saṁhitās* of the Yajurveda.
7. The sacrifices of ancient Indians fall into two broad categories: Food-sacrifices (during which chiefly milk, butter, cakes,

stweed fruit and corns are sacrificed) and Soma-sacrifices (whose main constituents are the Soma-libations). The individual sacrifices fall into one or the other of these two categories. The animal sacrifice is connected with sacrifices of the first category as well as with those of the second. Connected with all these kinds of sacrifices is the fire-cult, which is, in a certain way, the pre-requisite for every kind of worship of gods.

8. According to the law books the drinking of brandy is a sin as great as the murder of a Brahmin.

9. So also Oldenberg, *Religion des Veda,* 2nd Ed., pp. 362 f. and Keith, *HOS.,* Vol. 18, pp. cxxxvii, who says : "There can be no doubt that the ritual is mere priestly invention to fill up the apparent gap in the sacrificial system which provided no place for man." Hillebrandt (Ritualliteratur, *Grundirss* III, 2, pp. 153), however, considers the Puruṣamedha to be a ritual human sacrifice. There can be no doubt that human sacrifices occurred in ancient India, though not in the Brahmanical cult-only survivals of it can be traced in the rite of building the brick-altar for the fire, and in the Śunahsepa legend - just a cruel-human sacrifices occurred even in modern times among certian sects. But this does not prove that the Puruṣamedha was such a sacrifice.

10. Only the first 18 Adhyāyas of the *Vājasaneyī Saṁhitā* are completely presented word for word and explained in the *Śatapatha Brāhmaṇa* belonging to the White *Yajurveda.*

11. Also the Brāhmaṇa-like theological discussions which the *Saṁhitās* of the Black *Yajurveda* contain in addition to the prayers and formulas, are here left out of consideration. For, what will be said in the following chapter about the Brāhmaṇas applies to them as well.

12. *Vājasaneyī Saṁhitā* IV, 1; VI, 12; II, 14; I, 1; III, 9; X, 23

13. "The gods love what is hinted at, what is mysterious," is a sentence, again and again repeated in the Brāhmaṇas, for

example in the *Śatapatha Brāhmaṇa* VI, 1, 1, 2; 11; 2, 3, 7, 1, 23; VII, 4, 1, 10 etc. *Bṛhadāraṇyaka Upaniṣad* IV, 2, 2: "The gods love what is secretively hinted at and hate what is directly said."

14. According to the Aitareya-Brāhmaṇa VII, 18 Om means in the language used for the gods the same thing as what is expressed among men by *"tathā"* (so may it be), "yes". Similarly it is said in the *Chāndogya-Upaniṣad* I, 1, 8: "This syllable Om expresses consent for when one consents to something he says: "Om". With the Hebrew "amen" the syllable *om* coincides only purely accidentally somewhat in its meaning and in its pronunciation.

15. *Maitrāyaṇi-Saṁhitā* I, 8, 5.

16 The rule referred to (iv. 3. 102) is, according to the statement of the Calcutta scholiast, not explained in Patañjali's *Bhāśhya*; possibly, therefore, it may not be Pāṇini's at all, but may be later than Patañjali. The name Taittiriya itself, however, is several times mentioned in the *Bhāśhya,* see *I. St.* xiii. 442, which is also acquainted with '*Titiriṇd prāktah ślokah*' not belonging to the Chhandas, see *I.St.,* v. 41; Goldstucker, *Pāṇini* p. 243.

17. The rule is the same as that for Tittiri. The remark in the previous note, therefore, applies here also.

18. Besides the text, we have also a Ṛishyanukramaṇi for it.

19. For further particulars, see *I.St.,* xiii, 104-106.

20. Amongst them, for example, the enumeration of the whole of the lunar asterisms in the Āpastamba-Saṁhitā, where they appear in an order devisting from that of the later series; which, as I have pointed out above (p. 30), must necessarily have been fixed between 1472 and 536 B.C. But all that follows from this, in regard to the passage in question, is that it is not earlier than 1472 B.C., which is a matter of course; it nowise follows that it may not be later than 536 B.C. So we obtain nothing definite here. (This remains correct, though the

position of the case itself is somewhat different; see the notes above, p. 2 and p. 30. In connection with the enumeration of the Nakshatras, compare especially may easy, *Die vedischen Nachrichten von den Nakshtra,* ii. 299, ff.)

21. Of peculiar interest is the mention of Dhṛitarāshṭra Vaichitravīrya, as also of the contests between the Pañchālas and the Kuntis in the Kāthaks; see *I. St.,* iii.469-472.

22. Bhaṭṭa Bhāskara Miśra, on the contrary, gives Yājnavalka instead of paiṅgi; see Burnell's *Catalogue,* p. 14

23. Atreya was the padakāra of his school; Kuṇḍina, on the contrary, the *vṛittikara.* The meaning of *vṛtti* is here obscure, as it is also in Schol. to Pān., iv. 3. 108 (*mādhuri vṛittih*) [see *I.St.,* xiii, 381]

24. We have, besides, a commentary by Sāyaṇa, though it is only fragmentary; another is ascribed to a Bālakṛishṇa. [In Burnell's Collection of MSS., see his *Catalogue,* pp. 12-14, is found the greater portion of Bhaṭṭa Kauśika Bhāskara Miśra's commetary, under the name *Jnānayana;* the author is said to have lived 400 years before Sāyaṇa; he quotes amongst others Bhavasvamin and seems to stand in special connection with the Atreyi school. A *Paiśāchabhāśhya* on the Black Yajus is also mentioned; see *I.St.,* ix. 176- An edition of the Taittiriya-Saṁhitā in the *Bibl. Indica,* with Sāyaṇa's complete commentary, was commenced by Roer (1854), continued by Cowell and Rāma Nārāyaṇa, and is now in the hands of Maheśachandra Nyāyaratna (the last part, No. 28, 1874, reaches to iv. 3. ii); the complete text, in Roman transcript, has been published by myself in *I. St.*, xi, xii, (1871-72). On the Kāṭhaka, see *I.St.,* iii. 451-479].

25. Ṛgveda. X. 90. 9 - तस्माद्यज्ञात्सर्वहुत ऋचः सामानि जज्ञिरे ।
छन्दांसि जज्ञिरे तस्माद् यजुस्तस्मादजायत ॥

26. Manconell ; *History of Sanskrit Literature* (Delhi, 1961): p. 197: "The Atharva is the oldest literary monument of Indian medicine."

27. Cf. Franklin Edgerton, "The philosophic materials of the *Atharvaveda*", *Studies in honour of Maurice Bloomfield* (1920). p. 120
28. These are - Paippalāda, Stauda, Mouda, Śaunakīya, Jājala, Jalada, Brahmavada, Devadarśa and Caranavaidya.
29. M. Winternitz, 'A History of Indian Literature.' pp. 125
30. *Episches inn Vedischen Ritual*, Proceedings of the Royal Academy at Berlin, July 23, 1891.
31. Cf. Gopatha Brāhmaṇa 1. 2. 18
32. Cf. F. Edgerton, Op. cit. p. 117
33. Cf. TS. 3.5. 2.1 GB. 1.2, 18, 3. 22, 1.2 *Vait*. 1.1, 11.2, Kaus. 17.4; 140.4

Chapter - VIII

The Brāhmaṇa Literature

8.1 Introduction

After the Saṁhitās, there grew up the theological treatises called the Brāhmaṇas, which were of a distinctly different literary type. They are in prose, and explain the sacred significance of different rituals to those who are not already familiar with them. "They reflect the spirit of an age in which all intellectual activity is concentrated on the sacrifice, describing its ceremonies, discussing its value, speculating on its origin and significance.[1]

The Brāhmaṇa form a considerable portion of the Veda. Each *Saṁhitā* has one or more Brāhmaṇas with it. Thus, there are two of the *Ṛk-Saṁhitā*, three of the *Yajus-saṁhitā*, eleven of the *Sāma-saṁhitā*, and one of the *Atharva-saṁhitā*. The Brāhmaṇas contain the ritualistic details concerning the texts of Saṁhitā with which they are related.

The term *Śākhā*[2] is generally associated with the Vedic texts. *Śākhā* is an institution of teachers and pupils devoted to a particular Vedic text.[3] A text belonging to a particular *Śākhā*[4] is at slight variation from the text of another *Śākhā*. We have textual evidences to show that there must have existed many more such *Śākhās* for each Veda, than that are available to us now.[5] It appears that certain texts are lost in course of time, e.g., the *Śāṇkhāyana-Brāhmaṇa* has no corresponding *saṁhitā*.

The following are the names of the Brāhmaṇa texts available to us:

1.	*Aitareya Brāhmaṇa*	(*Ṛgveda*)
2.	*Kauṣītakī* or *Śāṇkhāyana Brāhmaṇa*	"
3.	*Taittirīya Brāhmaṇa*	(*Yajurveda*)
4.	*Śatapatha Brāhmaṇa* - *Mādhyandina*	"
	- *Kāṇva*	"
5.	*Pañcaniṁśa* or *Prauḍha* or *Tāṇḍya Mahā Brāhmaṇa*	(*Sāmaveda*)
6.	*Jaiminīya* or *Talavakāra Brāhmaṇa*	"
7.	*Ṣadviṁśa Brāhmaṇa*	"
8.	*Sāmavidhāna Brāhmaṇa*	"
9.	*Ārṣeya Brāhmaṇa*	"
10.	*Daivata Brāhmaṇa* or *Devatādhyāya*	"
11.	*Mantra Brāhmaṇa*	"
12.	*Saṁhitopaniṣad Brāhmaṇa*	
13.	*Viṁśa Brāhmaṇa*	"
14.	*Jaiminīya-Saṁhitopaniṣad Brāhmaṇa*	"
15.	*Jaiminīya-Ārṣeya Brāhmaṇa*	"
16.	*Gopatha Brāhmaṇa*	(*Atharvaveda*)

The concluding portions of the Brāhmaṇas are called Āraṇyakas.[6] Some of the Upaniṣads (particularly, *Taittirīya, Aitareya Bṛhadāraṇyaka* and *Chāndogya*) form the concluding portions of the respective Āraṇyakas. Yet, generally, it is the modern usage to classify the Brāhmaṇas separately as Brāhmaṇas, Āraṇyakas and Upaniṣads.

8.2 Nature and Scope of the Brāhmaṇas

The *Saṁhitās* with their Brāhmaṇas came to be specialised by certain families of *ṛtviks*, the participants in the *yajña* performance. Thus, only a person who has specialised himself in the *Ṛgveda*,[7] can officiate as the *Hotṛ*, he who has specialised himself in the *Yajurveda* can become the *Adhvaryu*, and a specialist in the *Sāmaveda* can be the *Udgātṛ*. The office or *Brahmā* requires proficiency in all the four Vedas.[8]

The Brāhmaṇas are entirely in prose, but for the quoted Mantras and *gāthās*.

As noticed earlier, the Brāhmaṇas give the ritualistic details. They describe the *yajnas,* set forth the manner of performance and direct the Mantras to be recited therein. They substantiate their prescriptions of Mantras and other ritualistic acts with reasons based on symbolism or etymology or experience or science.[9] They often try to find the hidden meaning and they say repeatedly that the Devas are fond of that which is mystic.

Repetitions and identities are common in these texts. "Just as a relationship is believed to exist between all the constituents of the cosmos, so a psychological relationship is established between words of similar sound[10] or other obvious similarities. "The gifted mind of these cultured Vedic Indians was anxious to come to some unity..... Any kind of instrumentality in producing an effect was often considered as pure identity.[11]

The Brāhmaṇas are technical works. So they may not appeal to a general reader. They should not be approached as works of literary art. The Veda is unique and forms a class by itself, for it is a 'library or literature'.[12] It cannot be said to be either merely literary or merely philosophical or ritualistic work. It calls for a special attitude of approach on the part of the student.

8.3 The term 'Brāhmaṇa'

The very name 'Brāhmaṇa' speaks of the nature of these texts. Generally, Brāhmaṇa is that which is related to "Brahma". Different views are, however, expressed regarding the denotation and connotation of the words 'Brāhmaṇa' and 'Brahma'.

The word occurs in the texts themselves used in a technical sense. A consideration of the meanings of some of these passages will throw light on the technicalities of the term. To take a few examples:

We read in Taittirīya Brāhmaṇa, "This Brāhmaṇa is to be considered in the *Paśubandha,* not in other *yajñas*".[13] Here the words 'This Brāhmaṇa' refer to a statement previously made about a particular procedure. In the same sense it is found in : "This is a Brāhmaṇa in Sāvitra and also Nāciketa,"[14] where the prescription of the auxiliaries (*aṅga*) of Cayana is referred to as Brāhmaṇa. It is clear that it does not point to or quote another Brāhmaṇa book.[15] Sometimes, we find the word used in the sense of a whole section, as noticed in: "These *paśus* mentioned in the Brāhmaṇa..."[16] The word used in certain contexts means *arthavāda* or commentary as in these statements: "That which is the Brāhmaṇa of Gāyatrī"[17;] The word used in certain contexts means *arthvāda* or commentary as in these statements: "That which is the Brāhmaṇa of Gāyatrī"[18]; "The Brāhmaṇa of Gaurivīta has been told"[19]; "Thus is this Brāhmaṇa spoken"[20]; "It will be exposited in the Brāhmaṇa of Divākīrtyās"[21]; etc. While introducing a section of Taittirīya Brāhmaṇa Sāyaṇa writes "Mantras were dealt with so far, and now their Brāhmaṇas will be presented"[22] where he uses the word Brāhmaṇa in the sense of commentary.

The Brāhmaṇas are generally considered as 'commentaries of Mantras'. But they should rather be called 'explanatory notes'. For, their purpose is not to explain the Mantras. The explanations are casual. Only a few important words are explained; some

Mantras are not commented at all.[23] In such circumstances we find the expression that the very structure of the Mantra expresses its greatness[24] or that there is nothing hidden in the Mantra.[25] It is beyond doubt that the Brāhmaṇas are expository texts and it is substantiated by the texts themselves.

Julius Eggeling writing[26] about the *Kṛṣṇa-Yajurveda* refers to the etymology of the term 'Brāhmaṇa' -

''They are essentially digests of floating mass of single discourses or *dicta* on various points of the ceremonial of worship, ascribed to, individual teachers and handed down orally in the theological books. Single discourses of this kind were called Brāhmaṇa - probably either becasue they were intended for the instruction and guidance of priests (brahman) generally; or because they were, for the most part, the authoritative utterances of such as were thoroughly versed in Vedic and sacrificial lore and competent to act as Brahmans or superintending priests.''

Weber, Whitney, Westergaard and others derive the term 'Brāhmaṇa' from brahman, 'prayer, worship'. 'Weber opines that the word Brāhmaṇa signifies "that which relates to prayer, *brāhman*" and S. N. Dasgupta endorses that it is the correct one.[27] Max Muller says that the word mean "originally the sayings of Brāhmans whether in a general sense of priests or in the more special sense of Brahman-priests",[28] Haug in the introduction[29] to his edition of AB feels that "etymologically the word is derived from brāhma'n, which properly signifies the brāhma'n priest." Further on[30] he writes : Strictly speaking, only the rule regarding the performance of a particular rite or the authoritative opinion on a particular point of speculative theology went by this name...... Afterwards, the term Brahmanam which meant only a single dictum, was applied to the whole collection.

Simasrami concurs with this view but adds that 'Brāhmaṇam' could be related to Brāhmaṇa, the priest and need not be taken back to brahman.[31]

To sum up : the term Brāhmaṇa, stands for the statement which give the application of a Mantra or which explain a Mantra or which describe the method of performance of a *yajna.*[32] The text or its portion which contains such statements is also called Brāhmaṇa.[33] From the above conclusion we find that though the scholars quoted above do not seem to have taken cognisance of Āpastamba's position, most of them have followed him very closely. In passing we may notice that the term 'Brāhmaṇa' does not occur in SB 13.4.3.1-15 which hints on the arrangement of Vedic texts.[34]

There is a term, 'Anubrāhmaṇa' in one of the sūtras of Pāṇini.[35] Bhaṭṭoji Dikṣita, following the *Kāśikā* observes that it is a book similar to the Brāhmaṇa[36] Bhaṭṭa Bhāskara names some of the sections of *Taittirīya-Brāhmaṇa* as 'Anubrāhmaṇa'.[37] Agravala translates it as 'supplementary Brāhmaṇa'.[38] By the currency of the term with reference to TB, we may take it to mean 'supplementary Brāhmaṇa' as it suppliments the concerned sections of the Saṁhitā.

8.4 Brāhmaṇas and other sections of Vedic Literature

The term 'Veda' frequently occurs in the Brāhmaṇas. In most of the occurrences, the word is to be understood as knowledge. In others it stands for the repositories of knowledge. For instance, we read in Taittirīya Brāhmaṇa "A person who does not know 'Veda' (*vedavit*) cannot think of That Great."[39] Vedas are considered as endless, *ananta.* Even by learning them continuously for three lives, one can learn only three 'handfuls' of Veda.[40] The end of the Veda cannot be reached even though one might study it for a number of lives.

The Vedas are referred to by the expression *trayīvidyā* triple knowledge.[41] Sometimes, they are expressed distinctly as *ṛk, yajus* and *sāma.* In a certain passage, *yajus* and *chandas* are put side by side.[42] The names *Ṛgveda, Yajurveda* and *Sāmaveda* do occur in the Brāhmaṇas. A passage in Aitareya Brāhmaṇa 25.32 and its parallel passage in *JB* 1.357 and Śatapatha Brāhmaṇa 11.5.8.3 speak of them as originated from Agni, Vayu, and Aditya respectively.[43]

Śatapatha Brāhmaṇa 10.3.1.21 mentions that Prajāpati put forth and arranged the Veda. Prajāpati thought of making *saṁskāra* to the *trayī-vidyā*. He arranged the twelve thousand *bṛhati* (a metre) *ṛks* poured out (*sṛṣṭa*) by himself. They arrayed themselves and became ten thousand and eight hundred *panktis* (a metre). He disposed the other two Vedas which were together twelve thousand *bṛhatis*; eight thousand of *yajus* and four thousand of *sāmans*. The text further gives the total number of syllables as eight lakhs and sixtyfour thousand (8,64,000).[44]

The *ṛk yajus* and *sāma* are glorified as the treasure of Bliss.[45] The *ṛk* and *sāma* are regarded as the fountain of Sarasvati.[46] They are called the two worlds.[47] *Ṛk* is related to Vāk, speech and *sāma* to *manas*, mind.[48] They are the two horses of Indra.[49] Śatapata Brāhmaṇa 10.3.6.20 considers the names - *uktha, yajus, sāman* and so on as the names of Supreme.[50] Aitareya Brāhmaṇa and Śatapata Brāhmaṇa seem to strike a note of history when they say that *ṛk* and *sāman* were evolved first and that *yajus* is intertwined with *ṛk* and *sāma*.[51]

It has been observed that the Brāhmaṇas set forth the details of *yajna*. While doing so all the connected ideas are brought in. These matters were sifted and arranged as it were in the Kalpa-sūtras and the Purāṇas. In the Kalpa, the technical materials are brought together in a logical sequence. The Brāhmaṇas are summarised, as it were, in these books. The Purāṇas from the amplifications of the non-technical part.

8.5 Vedic Character (*vedatva*) of Brāhmaṇas

It was seen that the Mantra and the Brāhmaṇa texts are together called the Veda. Some of the modern scholars consider that "the

Brāhmaṇas are not Vedas, they are only so called." It may be worth discussing the issue here. Svami Dayananda Sarasvati concludes that the Brāhmaṇas are not a part of the Veda. He is of the opinion that Āpastamba and others are wrong in including them into the pale of the Veda. Svami Dayananda's arguments may be summarised as follows: The Brāhmaṇas cannot be called Veda because they are termed Purāṇa and Itihāsa (पुराणेतिहासा:); they are the commentaries (व्याख्यानम्) of Veda; *Ṛṣis* have given expression to them unlike the Saṁhitās which have come from the Lord; they are not included under the name of the Veda by *Ṛṣis* other than Kātyāyana.

Traditionally, it is well known that the Veda was analysed by a sage known after his own stupendous work, Veda Vyāsa. So, what we have now before us is the analytico-synthesis of the Veda brought about by Veda Vyāsa. If we take out the common factor, we find that the Veda is nothing but Mantra and Brāhmaṇa, either of which cannot exist by itself independently. Sāyaṇa, as noticed earlier, admits that it is not possible to define exactly a Mantra or a Brāhmaṇa. This only shows that there is no hard and fast line between the Mantra and the Brāhmaṇa. Each glides into the other. As the *Taittirīya-saṁhitā* and its Brāhmaṇa show, there cannot be any gulf between these aspects of the Veda. They are inter-connected and inter-related. This relation is exemplified in the Brāhmaṇas. So, there is no cogency in the argument advanced to keep the Brāhmaṇas out of the Veda; nor has it any traditional support. We can very well consider the Brāhmaṇas as part and parcel of the Veda and accept the statement मन्त्रब्राह्मणयो: वेदनामधेयम् as valid.

8.6 Authorship of Brāhmaṇas

Although the problem of authorship of the Brāhmaṇas or any part of the Veda for that matter, does not arise in the tradition represented by Sāyaṇa, still, the question of authorship is being discussed for the past two thousand years. Even at that early age there were people who deemed that the Veda had an author. This contention was controverted and the revelatory character of the Veda was vindicated by the traditionists.

We come across in the *Nirukta* of Yāska, an argument that the Veda has no meaning; but the question of authorship is not tackled. It is in the *Pūrvamīmāṁsa-sūtra* (1.1.27-32) that we find a definite formulation of the arguments against authorship. The commentators of the *sūtra* and other independent Mīmāṁsa works have expanded the discussion and advanced their own reasonings to meet the situation. Sāyaṇa has summarised in his Ṛgbhāśyabhūmikā the Mīmāṁsa debate on the point. The subject is briefly discussed in the *Brahmasūtra* and the *Mahābhhāśya.*[52]

While discussing the traditional view on the non-human origin of the Veda, the whole 'books' should not be taken together into consideration. The subject of discussion is confined to the 'Vedic passage'.

The discussion in the *Pūrva-mīmāṁsa-sūtra*[53] may be summarised as follows :

Some people argue that the Veda cannot be *anādi* i.e. beginningless, it must be nearer to us, because its parts go after human names like Kāṭhaka, Taittirīya. Besides, there are names of mortal persons in it. This reasoning, it is pointed out, is not valid. The names after which the texts are called, are only of those who announced it, who gave currency to its parts; they do not speak of their authorship.

We might digress here a little to take into account the testimony of the great linguist Ācārya Pāṇini. The Ācārya records that the names of the Vedic texts "were not used as current except with reference to the students or persons learned in them.... the name of a book applied to the whole body of those students and teachers who devoted themselves to its study and attained proficiency therein." In other words, the text studied by the Taittiriya is called *Taittirīya-saṁhitā*. *Vāiasaneyī-saṁhitā* is to be understood as the text studied by the Vājasaneyins. In the same way, we should take other names like Kāṭhaka or Talavakāra and so on, if we are to follow the tradition recorded by the authorities. It may be observed, by the way, that it is in this style that Śrī Śaṅkara quotes the Vedic passages. For instance, we find these expressions: 'The Taittirīyas read', 'The text of the Tāṇḍins', 'Ātharvaṇikas read' and so on.

Answering the other objection it is said : The mortal names are not proper names but common nouns, and as such they do not refer to any particular individual in a particular space and time. We find the Brāhmaṇaṣ and the Āraṇyakas speaking out that Vasiṣṭha and such other names are not names of human beings but they are the symbols or types of certain characteristics.[54]

The Mīmāṁsakas add that there is no author remembered with reference to the Veda just as it is done in the case of the *Rāmāyaṇa* or the *Mahābhārata*. The opponent points out here an objection: Just because no author is remembered it cannot be said that there is no author at all; no work can emerge without an author and the Veda must have had an author who might have been forgotten in course of time. This argument may appear sensible on the face of it. But a slight retrospect as to how the text got transmitted from generation to generation, shows that the opposition put forth is not a valid grounds. The entire text is transmitted through teacher-pupil tradition. Every letter, every accent, etc. is carefully preserved in tact, and an author is not remembered. The promulgators are given due respect. Therefore, it will be unjust to charge those sages that they 'forgot,' the author, if there was one such.[55]

Looking into the Brāhmaṇas themselves, we get some hints on this problem. The *ṛṣi* is called *kavi*. 'Hearing' is mentioned as a chief characteristic of a *kavi*.[56] *Śatapatha Brāhmaṇa* beautifully expresses a psychological phenomenon thus : "The *devas* dug out the Veda from the sea of mind.[57] The passage seems to make us understand that the Veda was in the *manas-samudra* before it became manifest and it is dragged out, as it were, by the *kavi* or the *ṛṣi*. This corresponds to what the psychologists like Jung say: Water is a symbol of the unconscious level of the mind and 'Mythology' comes out of the Unconscious.[58] Thus the *ṛṣi's* part is only in discovering the Veda and not in inventing or creating it a fresh. 'Seeing' is, however, specifically mentioned regarding the *sāmans*.[59] This 'seeing' does not contradict or come in the way of the Mantra or the *stoma* being 'new'.

There is not consensus among scholars regarding the date of the Veda. The different scholars give different dates. The figures vary from 25,000 B.C. to 1,200 B.C.

The first attempt at fixing a date to the Veda was made by F. Max Muller. He distinguished four periods, viz., Chandas period, Mantra period, Brāhmaṇa period and Sūtra period. He took it for granted that the Sūtra period just preceded the Age of the Buddha which is put as 5th century B.C. and that each period lasted for 200 years. So, the Sūtra period was in the 6th century B.C; the Brāhmaṇa period fell in 8th century, the Mantra period in 10th century and the Chandas period in 12th century. Thus roughly 1200 B.C. can be taken as the origin of the Vedic Mantras according to Max Muller.[60] He has two separate periods for the composition of the *Ṛgveda* and collection of hymns and formulae. A. A. Macdonell adopts two periods with reference to Vedic composition viz., the period of the four Vedas and the period of the Brāhmaṇas including the older Araṇyakas and Upaniṣads. This latter period is put between 800 and 500 B.C. A. C. Das goes as far back as 25,000 B.C. as the date of the Veda on geological grounds. In his paper on the 'Age of the Brahmanas'[61] B. V. Kameshvara Iyer concludes that the date of this second stratum of Vedic literature may be approximately fixed between 2,300 B.C. and 2,000 B.C. Prabodha Chandra Sen-Gupta is "inclined to take the age of the Brahmanas as the period between 3102 and 2000 B.C."[2] Bala Gangadhara Tilak and H. Jacobi reach 4500 B.C. on the basis of astronomical statements in the texts. The linguistic ground, viz., the similarity of the language of the Veda with that of the Avesta, brings down the date of the Veda to 1200 B.C. Striking a *via media,* Winternitz opines that 2000-2500 B.C. is the date of the Veda.[62]

Scholars have not been able to come to a decision in this matter. It is because the grounds for the discussion of the subject are not secure. Attempts are made to fix the date without understanding the import of the texts unprejudiced. It has not yet been possible to understand the Veda in its entirety. Unless this primary condition is satisfied, the efforts to fix its date cannot be fruitful.

Traditionally speaking, we are not faced with this problem. Indeed, for a correct understanding of the Vedic texts, we should follow the tradition. The question of chronology among the several Vedic texts comes in the way of interpretation. We tend to forget the meaning and implication of the texts but follow some wild speculation.

8.7 Interpretation of Brāhmaṇas

Even as early as 8th century B.C., the Veda was subjected to serious study. Attempts were made in the direction of precisely and properly understanding the texts. Lists of synonymous and difficult words were compiled. They were called *Nighaṅṭus*. We have only one such Nighaṅṭu. *Nirukta* of Yāska, which is the only old work of its kind extant, purports to be a commentary on the Nighaṅṭu. Here the meaning of each word is determined after taking into consideration the context in which the word occurs. In interpreting the texts, Yāska follows the suggestion offered by the Vedic texts themselves. In fact, many explanations of Yāska are based on the Brāhmaṇas.

There came up, in course of time, several regular commentators who took up individually various texts. All of them follow a particular pattern of explaining the word-meanings; and they rarely throw light on their implication.

Since the last century, the Western scholars have made contributions to the Vedic studies. A lot of work has been turned out by way of editing and translating original texts and by writin critical essays there on. In respect of interpretation, however, their approach in general is linguistic. The tradition is disregarded as useless for interpretation. But such an attitude is not proper. Sri Aurobindo expresses[63] the impropriety thus:

"Western scholars choose to imagine that the successors of the Vedic *ṛṣis* are in error, that, except for some later hymns, they put a false and non-existent meaning into the old verse and they themselves, divided from the *ṛṣis* not only by ages of time but many gulfs and separating seas of an intellectualised mentality, know infinitely better. But mere common sense ought to tell us that those who were so much nearer in both ways to the original poets had a better chance of holding atleast the essential truth of the matter, and suggests atleast the strong probability that the Veda was really what it professes to be."

Comparative mythology and comparative linguistics which are made use of by the scholars do not seem to take them far into the understanding of the Veda; instead, they may lead the student away from the true import of the Veda. Such a mode of interpretation prompts to divide the Veda into several units and to look upon them as each having no bearing on the other so far as interpretation is concerned.

There is another type of approach which may be called mystic approach. This mystic method has received much consideration by our ancient teachers. Manu records that the Veda is to be taught along with Kalpa, practical application, and '*rahasya*', 'secret' thereof.[64] It is not enough to learn merely the letters of the text; one should try to understand its spirit. It appears that the '*rahasya*' part of the exposition remained to be imparted orally. Somehow or other, it was not committed to writing and it is almost lost to us today.

Probably, it was Śri Ānanda Tīrtha who found it necessary to state in categorical terms that there are three meanings to every word in the Veda.[65] One may not agree with him as to what those meanings are. Yet, one cannot pooh-pooh him for his bold and valid assertion that it is not the expressed sense alone that is of consideration in the Veda, but it is necessary to go beyond it as well.

Dayananda Sarasvati reiterated that we should not be carried away by the expressed sense of the words in the Veda. Sri Aurobindo, too, concludes that the Vedic words are pregnant with deep meaning, they are not merely what they may appear to be on their face. He has laid bare by his own experiences that Vedic interpretation should never confine to mere linguistic or ritualistic motives. He writes thus in one of his books[66] :

"The ritual system recognised by Sāyaṇa, may, in its externalities, stand; the naturalistic sense discovered by European scholarship may, in its general conception, be accepted; but behind them there is still hidden secret of the Veda, the secret words, *ninya vacamsi,* which were spoken for the purified soul and awakened in knowledge. To disengage this less obvious but more important sense by fixing the import of the Vedic terms, the sense of Vedic symbols and the psychological functions of the Gods is thus a difficult but necessary task....."

Of all the modern interpretation of the Veda, it seems that Sri Aurobindo's interpretation deserves a little more consideration.

His arguments gain weight because they come from a yogi who put forth efforts to realise the importance of the Veda, through his own yogic experience.

It is clear from the commentary of Śabarasvāmin that the Pūrvamīmāṁsa is not against symbolic interpretation. For instance, Śabarasvāmin explains in three ways the meanings of the words *Prajāpati, vapā, agni* and *aja,* occurring in the *Taittirīrya-saṁhitā,* 2.1.1.4. First, they are taken respectively as air, rain, lightening and food; then, as space, air, gastric fire and seed; thirdly, as sun, rays, fire and plant. Thus, we find, Mīmāṁsa also favours symbolic interpretation of the Veda.[67]

A perusal of the Brāhmaṇas shows that the Veda itself provides hints for the elucidation of its contents. In fact, we can find some definite principles there. The *Śatapatha Brāhmaṇa*, for instance,[68] speaks of three modes of interpretation. They are : *adhi-devata, adhi-yajna* and *adhyātam.* The *adhi-devata* mode is to interpret the texts as applied to deities. The second, *adhiyajna* is ritualistic interpretation and the third, *adhyātma* is understanding the texts in terms of human life. Here-in we see an attitude of looking at foundamental things in nature. This may be called the cosmic view. It is understanding everything with reference to the universe as a whole. Behind this there is the idea that microcosm and macrocosm are similar in structure. The Brāhmaṇas seem to suggest that the Vedic texts are to be understood in all these three modes and thus have a complete and correct view of them. It may be observed here that Yāska followed this method.[69]

Therefore, it follows that the method of studying Veda has to be revised. There ought to be re-orientation in the mode of our approach, in such a way that both the traditional and modern view-points are compromised. "It is not enough if literature had been admired in ancient times. It is also necessary to show that the literature contains facts that will evoke the admiration of the modern man.[70] For this, "the study of ancient lore has to be approached with faith, free from modern materialistic prejudices which have hampered true appreciation and rendered criticism more destructive than constructive.[71] We must also take note of the suggestions presented in the texts themselves and follow them carefully to arrive at their proper import.

The several methods spoken of above lead to partial views of the Veda.[72] Owing to the limited capacities, environment etc., it may not be possible for scholars in general to acquaint themselves with all these ways of approach.[73] But if we increase our vision through *tapas,* we will be able to comprehend the Veda in its totality. To have a perfect understanding of the Veda, we must have recourse to deep insight as the *Nirukta* says : Nothing is clear here (in the Veda) to the one who is not a *ṛṣi* or the one who is not given to intense penance."[74]

8.8 Ṛgveda - Brāhmaṇas

8.8.1 The Aitareya Brāhmaṇa

The Aitareya Brāhmaṇa belongs to the Ṛgveda. It consists of 40 adhyayas or 'lessons' which are divided into eight pancakas or 'fifths'. Tradition has it that Mahīdāsa Aitareya is the author of this work. In reality he was only the compiler or publisher of the same. This Brāhmaṇa deals mainly with the Soma-sacrifice and in addition only the fire-sacrifice (Agni-hotra) and the festival of the King's consecration (Rājasūya). It is presumed that the last ten chapters are of later origin.

8.8.2 The Kauṣitaki Brāhmaṇa

In the closest relationship with this Brāhmaṇa is the Kauṣītaki or Sāṅkhyāyana-Brāhmaṇa, also belonging to the Ṛgveda and consisting of thirty Adhyāyas or "lessons". The first six Adhyāyas deal with the food-sacrifice (fire-laying, fire-sacrifice, new- and full-moon sacrifices and the sacrifices of the seasons), while Adhyāyas VII to XXX deal with Soma-sacrifice which fairly agree with the Aitareya-Brāhmaṇa. The Kauṣītaki-Brāhmaṇa is late than the Aitareya-Brāhmaṇa. However, while the latter is not the work of one hand and of one period, the Kauṣītaki-Brāhmaṇa is a uniform work. Each of thirty adhyāyas of this Brāhmaṇa is again divided into khaṇḍas. The first thirty adhyāyas deal with the method of performance of Agnyādhāna, Agnihota, Darśapurṇamāsa, Cāturmāsya, Somayāga.

Some significant topics described in this Brāhmaṇa are as below :

1) It mentions Sarpadevajana, Rakṣodevajana (II.2), and clarifies that Devajana carries the sense of 'being beast'.
2) It shows its opposition to the opinions of sage called Paiṅgya.
3) The statement 'यजमानस्यार्षेयमाह' (III) indicates that during age of this Brāhmaṇa, the classification of Gotra-pravara was prevalent.
4) Another statement 'ऋतुसन्धिषु व्याधिर्जायते' (IV) implies that those Acharyas had the knowledge of diseases.
5) The statement 'अग्निरवरार्ध्यः विष्णुः परार्ध्यः' (VII) witnesses the notion of the people during that age, that Vinṣu is the Supreme deity and Agni being lowest.
6) The difference of opinion regarding Viṣṇu's Supremacy or Rudra's Supremacy was there among the people. And, this is implied by the statement 'रुद्रो वै ज्येष्ठश्च श्रेष्ठश्च देवानाम् ।' (15.13).
7) The statement 'उच्चैः निरुक्तमनुब्रूयात्' (XI.1) implies that Nirukta was available then, though not of Yāska.
8) There was a sort of unwillingness of the people regarding meat-eating, animal-sacrifice.

With such comprehensive ideas, the Kauṣītaki Brāhmaṇa text is rich and important.

8.9 Yajurveda Brāhmaṇas

8.9.1 The Taittirīya Brāhmaṇa

The Taittirīya-Brāhmaṇa of the Black *Yajurveda* is nothing but a continuation of the Taittirīya-Saṁhitā for the Brāhmaṇas were already included in the Saṁhitās of the Black Yajurveda. The Taittirīya-Brāhmaṇa, therefore, contains only later additions to the Saṁhitā. We find here only a description of the Puruṣamedha, the symbolical "human sacrifice"; and that this sacrifice is missing in the Saṁhitā is one of the many proofs of the fact that the same is only a considerably late product of the science of sacrifice.

8.9.2 The Śatapatha Brāhmaṇa

To the white Yajurveda belongs the Śatapatha Brāhmaṇa, "the Brāhmaṇa of the hundred paths", so called because it consists of a hunred adhyāyas or "lessons". This is the most famous, extensive and doubtless also by virtue of its content most insignificant of all the Brāhmaṇas. As of the Vājasaneyi-Saṁhitā we have also of this Brāhmaṇa two recensions, that of the Kaṇva and that of the Mādhyandinas. In the latter the hundred Adhyāyas are divided into fourteen books (kāṇḍas). The first nine books are exactly a continuous commentary to the first eighteen chapters of the Vājasaneyi-Saṁhitā. They are decidedly older than the five last books. Probably the books I to V are connected with each other more closely. In them Yājnavalkya who is described at the end of the 14th book as the proclaimer of the whole of the Śatapatha Brāhmaṇa is named as the teacher, whose authority is decisive. As against this, in the books VI to IX which deal with the laying of the fire-altar (Agnicayana), Yājnavalkya is not at all mentioned.

Instead, another teacher, Śāṇḍilya, is mentioned as authority; and the same Śāṇḍilya is also considered to be the proclaimer of the Agni-Rahasya, i.e. the "fire-altar-mystery" which constitutes the content of the XX book. The books XI to XIV contain besides supplements to the preceding books also some interesting chapters on objects which are otherwise not treated in the Brāhmaṇas, for example, on the Upanayana, the initiation of the pupil or the introduction of the pupil to the teacher, who shall teach him the sacred texts (XI: 5,4), on the everyday veda-study (Svādhyāya) which is viewed as an offering to God Brahman (XI: 5, 6-8), and on the funeral ceremonies and the erection of a grave-mound (XIII, 8). The horse-sacrifice (Aśvamedha), the "human sacrifice" (Puruṣa-medha) and the total sacrifice" (Sarvamedha) are treated in the XIII and the Pravargya ceremony is treated in XIV book.

8.10 Sāmaveda-Brāhmaṇas

8.10.1 The Tāṇḍya Mahābrāhmaṇa

To the Sāmaveda belongs the Tāṇḍya-Brāhmaṇa also called Pancaviṁśa, i.e. "Brahmana consisting of twenty-five books". This is one of the oldest Brāhmaṇas and contains some important old legends. Of special interest are the Vrātyastomas and the description of sacrificial ceremonies by means of which the Vrātyas were received into the community of the Brāhmaṇas. The Ṣaḍviṁśa-Brāhmaṇa, i.e. the "Twenty-sixth Brāhmaṇa", is only a completion of the Tāṇḍya which consists of twenty-five books. The last part of the Ṣaḍviṁśa is the so called Ṣaḍviṁśa "Adhuta-Brāhmaṇa", a Vedāṅga-text on miracles and omens. The Jaiminiya-Brāhmaṇa of the Sāmaveda is even older than the Tāṇḍya-Mahā-Brāhmaṇa. This work is of special interest for the history both of religion and legend, but unfortunately the manuscript material is so fragmentary that it cannot be edited. Hitherto only portions of it have been made known.

8.10.2 Ṣaḍviṁṣa Brāhmaṇa

The *Śaḍviṁśa-Brāhmaṇa* belonging to the Sāmaveda, is an appendix to the *Pancaviṁśa-Brāhmaṇa*. It consists of five Prapāthakas, each of which is further divided into khaṇḍas. The fifth Prapāthaka is called *Adbhuta-Brāhmaṇa*. In this, the performances of Śāntikarmas to silence the ups and downs caused by earth-quakes, untime manifestation of flowers and fruits in the trees etc. have been spoken of. A significant commentary on the mantras addressed to the god Subrahmaṇya is available in the first Prapāthaka itself. It ordains the performance of Sandhyā-Vandanam during the sundhi-period of day and night. Thus the statement reads तस्मात् ब्राह्मणो अहोरात्रस्य संयोगे सन्ध्यामुपास्ते- (IV.5.4). Thus, this Brāhmaṇa is a collection of injunctive and prohibitive orders on the performance of respective rituals.

8.10.3 The Sāmavidhāna Brāhmaṇa

The Sāmavidhāna-Brāhmaṇa of the Sāmaveda, comprises three Prakaraṇas entitled as Kṛcchra, Atikṛcahra and Kṛcchrāti-kṛcchra. The sources of Vratas explained in the Smṛti and Purāṇa texts, may be found in this Brāhmaṇa. The method of Sāmagana and performance of Shantikramas to remove the evil effects against wealth-acquisition, destruction of the enemies etc. are well explained. In addition, performance of Kāmya-karmas and Prāyaścitta karmas are explained here. The third Prakraṇa describes the method of Sāmagana to acquire long life, abundant wealth. Nūtana Gṛhapraveśa, animal wealth, victory over the enemies in the battle, direct-vision of Gandharvas, Apsarasas etc. In this manner, this Brāhmaṇa imbibes the delineations of varied topics.

8.10.4 The Ārṣeya Brāhmaṇa

The *Arṣeya Brāhmaṇa* is another Brāhmaṇa that belongs to the Sāma Veda. It contains only three prapāthakas, and eighty-two khandas i.e. the *first* prapāthaka has 28 khandas, the *second* one 25 and the *third* 29. The first one is almost in aphoristic style, and the latter portion is in usual style. The author of this Brāhmaṇa is mentioned nowhere. As the title suggests, it consists of the Sāma chants of various seers, like Gotamasharka, Kāshyapa-barhisha, Bharadwaja.

8.10.5 The Daivata Brāhmaṇa

It is smallest of all the Brāhmaṇas belonging to the Sāmaveda. It also contains three khandas; of them, the first has 26 kandikas, the second 11 and the third one has 25. The *first* khanda gives us the description of Sāma-devatas such as Agni, Indra, Prajāpati, Soma, Varuṇa, Tvaṣṭā, Āngirasa, Pūṣan and Sarasvati. The *second* khanda describes the features of chando-devatas. The *third* khanda explains the derivation of various Chandas. This khaṇḍa is important from linguistic point of view.

8.10.6 The Upaniṣad Brāhmaṇa

The Brāhmaṇa has ten prapāṭhakas. Of them, the first two are widely accepted as mantra-brāhmaṇa, while the rest of eight prapāṭhakas form the *Chāndogya Upaniṣad.* Each of first two prapāṭhakas runs into eight khaṇḍas. This Brāhmaṇa is no doubt, a fine collection of the mantras on Gṛhya-saṁskāras.

8.10.7 The Saṁhitopaniṣad Brāhmaṇa

This is also very small Brāhmaṇa consisting of five khaṇḍas, describing the power of influence caused by singing the Sāman. Its wide popularity is referred to as 'विद्या ह वै ब्राह्मणमाजगाम' by Yāska in his *Nirukta* (II.2).

8.10.8 The Vaṁśa Brāhmaṇa

The Sāmaveda has a so-called Brāhmaṇa, the Vaṁśa-Brāhmaṇa of its own, which contains only such a list of 53 teachers, the last of whom, Kaśyapa, is supposed to have received the tradition from Agni. In the Śatapatha-Brāhmaṇa there are four different vaṁśas. The one that is given at the end of the work begins with the words "We have received this from the son of Bharadvāji, the son of Bharadvāja from the son of Vatsimandari" etc. Then follow 40 more teachers, all with their mothers' names. Only as the 45th in the list appears Yājnavalkya, as whose teacher Uddālaka is mentioned who is known to us from the Upaniṣads. The last (55th) human teacher is Kaśyapa Naidhruvi, to whom the Brāhmaṇa is supposed to have been revealed by Vac - (the goddess of speech). This Vac is supposed to have received it from Ambhṛṇi (the thunder voice) and this again from Āditya, the Sun.

It consists of three Khaṇḍās. It presents a beautiful geneological description of the tradition of the Āchāryas of the Sāmaveda. Thus it is a guide book of the history of ancient seers.

8.10.9 The Jaiminīya Brāhmaṇa

Like the Ṣatapatha, this Brāhmaṇa is a voluminous one. It is also available to us not in all its sections. The Jaiminīya-Upaniṣad-Brāhmaṇa being the part of this Brāhmaṇa consists of more Adhyāyās which are again sub-divided into Anuvākās, which are further divided into Khaṇḍās.

Following is the table showing its division and sub-divisions:

	Adhyāyās	Anuvāka	Khaṇḍa
	1	18	60
	2	5	15
	3	7	42
	4	12	28
Total	4	42	145

This Brāhmaṇa like others, runs into wonderful descriptions with repetitions here and there. The Ākhyāyikās described here are in philosophical style. According to the opinions of the critics, this Brāhmaṇa is posterior to Chāndogya Upaniāṣad. Many Akhyānās of the Chāndogya Upaniāṣad are found in this Brāhmaṇa. The name of Śātyāyana, the author of this Brāhmaṇa has been referred to in this Brāhmaṇa.

The Stōbhās like 'हम्', 'ओम्' to be inserted to Sāmans are included with 'ओवा', 'हूम्भा'. Further this Brāhmaṇa symbolically describes seven divisions of 'Uktha', i.e. 'Stōtriya', 'Anurūpa', 'Dhāyya', 'Prabhātha Sūkta', 'Nivida' and 'Paridhānīya'. This Brāhmaṇa makes the mention of 'Naraka' for the first time in contrast with 'Svarga'. So also, this Brāhmaṇa makes the use of names of the numerals like 'Nikhanva', 'Padma', 'Kśiti' and 'Vyōma' in this manner the Jaiminīya Brāhmaṇa is the collection of the various interesting points of vedic theology.

8.11 Atharvaveda Brāhmaṇas

8.11.1 Gopatha Brāhmaṇa

Of the Brāhmaṇas belonging to Atharva Veda, the Gopatha Brāhmaṇa is the singular one available today. It is considered to have belonged to later period of the Brāhmaṇa literature. In its latter part, the Gopatha follows Vaitānasūtra. It quotes from the earlier Brāhmaṇas like the Aitareya, the Kauṣītakī, the Śatapatha, the Ṣaḍviṁśa among others. Hence, this Brāhmaṇa may be placed exterior to 2000 B.C.

The Gopatha Brāhmaṇa is broadly divided into Pūrva-Gopatha and Uttara-Gopatha. the former one consists of 135 kaṇḍikas grouped under five prapāṭhakas, and the latter portion has 123 kaṇḍikas grouped under six prapāṭhakas. The language of this Brāhmaṇa appears to be not antique. The subject-matter often reads imaginary Ākhyānas. Many upaniṣadic quotations have been referred to herein.

The Brāhmaṇa describes the significance of the Atharva Veda. It also states that all other three Vedas, Oṁkāra have originated from the Atharva Veda. This Brāhmaṇa commences with the mantra : ब्रह्म वा इदमग्र आसीद् ..... तदैक्षत ..... महद्वैयक्षम् । It is elucidated here that, Brahman created first the water through this and placed this seed in that water, through which Bhṛgu is originated. He then became Atharvan. This Bhṛgu further produced ten Ātharvaṇa seers who then manifested the Atharva Veda. Thus, it leaves the idea that the Atharva Veda came to light first, then other Vedas.

Regarding the subject-matter of this Brāhmaṇa following enumeration gives the idea of it.

Pūrvārdha :

First Prapāṭhaka	:	Description of Oṁkara and the greatness of goddess Gāyatri.
Second Prapāṭhaka	:	Discipline of Celibacy. Generally one has to undertake the study course of twelve year for each Veda. This duration may be lessened, if the student is quite efficient.
Third Prapāṭhaka	:	Duties of four Ṛtviks and the stories relating to them.
Fourth Prapāṭhaka	:	Initiation of Ṛtviks.
Fifth Prapāṭhaka	:	Description of Prathama-Saṁvatsara-sacrifice, Agnyādheya, Pūrṇāhuti, Agnihotra, Darśapūrṇamāsa, āgrayaṇa-Cāturmāsya-Paśubandha- Agniṣṭoma-Rājasūya-Vājapeya-Aśvamedha-Puruśamedha- Sarvamedha-sacrifices.

Uttarārdha :

First Prapāṭhaka	:	Description of many other sacrifices, Radra's struggle for oblation, meat offering in the sacrifices.

Second and third Prapāṭhaka	: वषट् and हिंकार - description.
Last three Prapāṭhakas	: Duties to be performed at morning, afternoon and evening time during Ekāha, Uktha and Ekāṣmaka.

This Brāhmaṇa mentions Kurupanchala, Angamagadha, Kashi-Kaushala, Salva, Matsya, Vasha-Ushinara. On this basis of such references it may be said that the sage Gopatha, the composer of this Brāhmaṇa belonged to the central part of India. This Brāhmaṇa gives derivative explanations of many Vedic terms like Varuṇa, Angira etc. Hence, it plays an important role to show its contribution to the science of linguistics. In toto, the Gopatha Brāhmaṇa is comprehensive one in many disciplines.

References

1. A. M. Macdonell, History of Sanskrit Literature, p. 31
2. *Śākhā* is generally translated by the word 'recension' which means "a critical revisal of a text or a text established by critical revision." (*Chamber's Twentieth Century Dictionary,* 1936, p. 774). But *Śākhā* does not appear to be one such.
3. V. S. Agrawala. *India as known to Pāṇini,* p. 286
4. चत्वारो वेदाः साङ्गाः सरहस्याः बहुधा विभिन्ना एकशतमध्वर्युशः सहस्रवर्त्मा सामवेदः एकविंशतिधा बाह्वृचं नवधाथर्वणो वेदो......। *Mahābhāśya* 1.9. For a detailed discussion, see Sāmaśramī. *Aitareya-ālocanam* p. 125
5. For example, we find 'fragments' of some Brāhmaṇas no longer available in full. See, B. K. Ghosh, *Fragments of the Lost Brāhmaṇas.* See also Winternitz, HIL., Vol. 1, p. 189
6. The Āraṇyakas are perhaps but a compilation of such texts as are having a mystic note and to be discussed only outside the township, i.e. away from the average people. T. B. 1.7.7.3 (योऽरण्येऽनुवाक्यो गणः) seems clearly to point to it.

7. The term Veda is to be taken as standing for both the Mantra and the Brāhmaṇa.

8. अथो खल्वाहुः । कथं अध्वर्युः बह्वृचः साम गायेत् । p. 5.9.6. तदाहुः। यतृचा होतृत्वं क्रियते यजुषा आध्वर्यवं साम्नोद्गीथो अथ केन ब्रह्मत्वं क्रियत इति । अनया त्रय्या विद्यया इति ब्रूयात् । p. 1.358

9. These are said to be different aspects of the Brāhmaṇa. हेतुनिर्वचनं निन्दा प्रशंसा संशयो विधिः । परक्रिय पुराकल्पो व्यवधारणकल्पना । उपमानं दशैते तु विधयो ब्राह्मणस्य तु ।। शबरस्वामिन्, मीमांसासूत्रभाष्यम्, 2.1.8

10. B. Heimann, *Indian and Western Philosophy*, p. 128

11. S. N. Dasgupta, *HIP.*, vol. 1, p. 36

12. E. Arnold. *Vedic Metre,* Preface, p. i

13. वेदितृतीये यजेत । ..... तदेतत् पशुबन्धे ब्राह्मणं ब्रूयात् । नेतरेषु यज्ञेषु *T.* 8.12.5.10

14. एतदेव सावित्रे ब्राह्मणमथो नाचिकेते । *T.* 3.12.5.12

15. Similarly observes P. D. Gune : "A Brāhmaṇa does not quote another Brāhmaṇa. Words like तस्योक्तम् ब्राह्मणम् .... do not refer to Brāhmaṇa in the sense of a theological work." P. D. Gune. 'Brāhmaṇa quotations in the Nirukta', *Commemorative Essays Presented to R. G. Bhandarkar,* p. 52-53

16. एते ब्राह्मणवन्तः पशव आलभ्यन्ते। *T.* 1.2.5.43 Sāyaṇa : अनन्तरब्राह्मणोक्तान् ।

17. यदेव गायत्रस्य ब्राह्मणम् । p. *11.3.2.3*

18. गौरिवीतब्राह्मणमुक्तम् । p. 13.3.5; refers to p. 13.3.1.2

19. इति न्वा एतत् ब्राह्मणमुद्यते । S. 1.4.8.8

20. दिवाकीर्त्यानां ब्राह्मणे व्याख्यायते । S. 4.1.5.15

21. एकादशे तन्मन्त्रा व्याख्यायन्ते । T. 3.8.11 मन्त्रप्रतिपादिका अनुवाका समाप्ताः । उत्तरेषु ..... ब्राह्मणमभिधीयते । T. 3.10.9 एतावता ..... मन्त्रा उक्ताः । अथ ..... ब्राह्मणमभिधीयते । T. 3.11.7

22. Keith finds this in the Taittirīya Saṁhitā when he says : "The Brāhmaṇa portion does not attempt to deal with every verse of the Saṁhitā". Keith A.B. *The Veda of the Black Yajus School entitled Taittirīya-saṁhitā*, translated, Intd. (HOS. 18) p. 1 xxiv.

23. रूप एव एषां एतन्महिमानं व्याचष्टे । T. 3.3.2.1; etc.

24. नात्र तिरोहितमिवास्ति । S. 14.1.4.11, 14

25. Eggeling, *Śatapatha Brāhmaṇa,* translated, SBE. 12, Intd., p. xxii-xxiii

26. Weber, HIL., p. 11 note; Dasgupta HIP., vol. 1, p. 13

27. Max Muller, SBE. 1, Intd., p. 1xvi "Originally a Brāhmaṇa was a theological tract, and it was called Brahmana .... because it was composed for and by Brahmanas." Max Muller, *History of Ancient Sanskrit Literature* Allahabad 1912, p. 88.

28. Haug (ed). *Aitareya Brāhmaṇa,* vol.1, Intd., p. 4

29. *Ibid.,* p. 6

30. Sāmaśramī, *op. cit.,* p. 2

31. ब्राह्मणं नाम कर्मणः तन्मन्त्राणां च व्याख्यानग्रन्थः । भट्टभास्कर, तैत्तिरीयसंहिताभाष्यम्, 1.5.1. Bhaṭṭa Bhāskara in his Bhāśya on *Taittirīya-saṁhitā* 1.8.1., speaks of two types of the Brāhmaṇa: Karmabrāhmaṇa and Kalpa-brāhmaṇa. The former gives the details of rituals and the use of Mantras. The latter is only the Mantra text.

32. It may be remembered that the subsections of a *prapāṭhaka* in SB are called Brāhmaṇas. In one instance is SB (तस्मादपि ऋचं वा यजुर्वा साम वा गाथां वा कुम्ब्यां वा अभिव्याहरेत् व्रतस्य अविच्छेदाय। S.11.4.1.10) the word '*kumbyā*' is used for a Brāhmaṇa passage something, perhaps, like the *verga* or *anuvāka*. '*Puraścaraṇa*' is another name of the Brāhmaṇa according to SB. 10.2.5.3 (तदेतद्युजुः सपुरश्चरणमधिदेवतम् । Sāyaṇa : ब्राह्मणापरनामधेयस्य पुरश्चरण-शब्दस्य ।)

33. ऋचां सूक्तं यजुषां अनुवाकं, अथर्वणां पर्व अङ्गिरसां पर्व सर्पविद्याया पर्व देवजनविद्याया पर्व कंचिदितिहासं किंचित् पुराणं, साम्ना दशतम् ।। T. 3.12.8.1-2 : ऋचो यजूंषि सामानि । अथर्वाङ्गिरसश्च ये सर्वास्ताः। इतिहासपुराणं च । सर्वदेवजनाश्च ये । सर्वारताः ।

34. अनुब्रह्मणादिनिः । Pāṇini, 4.2.62

35. सिद्धान्तकौमुदी, 2 1272; ब्राह्मणसदृशः । काशिका–ब्राह्मणसदृशोऽयं ग्रन्थः। Yāska,

36. राजसूयानुब्राहत्रमणम्, अश्वमेधानुब्राह्मणम् ।

37. *India as known to Pāṇini,* p. 332

38. नावेदवित् मनुते तं बृहन्तम् । *T.* 3.12.9.7

39. तं ह त्रीन् गिरिरूपान् अविज्ञातानिव दर्शयांचकार । तेषां हैकैकस्मिमन्मुष्टिमाददे। वेदा वा एते । अनन्ता वै वेदाः । एतद्वा एतैः त्रिभिः आयुभिः अन्ववोचथाः अथ त इतरदनलूक्तमेव ।। *T.* 3.10.11.2.5

40. त्रयी विद्या । *T.* 1.2.1.26; *T.* 2.357.358; *S.* 10.3.1.21

41. जामि स्यात् यद्यजुषा आउयं यजुषा अप उत्पुनाति । छन्दसा अप उत्पुनाति अजामित्वाय । *T.* 3.3.4.5,6

42. ऋग्वेद एव अग्रेरजायत, यदुर्वेदो वायोः सामवेद आदित्यात् । *A.* 25.32

43. स ऐक्षत प्रजापतिः । त्रय्यां विद्यायां सर्वाणि भूतानि । हन्त त्रयीमेव विद्यां आत्मनमभिसंस्करवा इति । स ऋचो व्यौहत् । द्वादशबृहतीसहस्त्राणि । एतावत्यो ह्यर्चो याः प्रजापतिसृष्टाः । ताः त्रिंशत्तमे व्यूहे पङ्क्तिषु अतिष्ठन्ति । ता अष्टशतं शतानि पङ्क्त्योऽभवन् । अथेतरौ वेदौ व्यौहत्। द्वादशैव बृहतीसग्स्राणि । अष्टौ यजुषाम् । चत्वारि साम्नाम् । एतावत् हैतयोः वेदयोः यत्प्रजापतिसृष्टम् । ता अष्टशतं शतानि पङ्क्तयोऽभवन् । ते सर्वे त्रयो वेदाः दश च सहस्राणि अष्टौ च शतानि अशीतीनामभवन् । *S.* 10.3.1.22-25. 12,000 (बृहस्यः) x 36 = 432,000

44. अहे बुध्निय मन्त्रं मे गोपाय यं ऋषयः त्रैविदो विदुः । ऋचः सामानि यजूंषि । सा हि श्रीः अमृतां सताम् ।। *T.* 1.2.1.26

45. ऋक्सामे व सारस्वतावुत्सौ । *T.* 1.4.4.9

46. साम वा असौ लोकः ऋग् अयं यदितः । *P.* 4.3.3

47. वाग् वा ऋचः सत्यै मनस्साम्नः । *T.* 1.326

48. इन्द्रस्य हरी । *T.* 1.6.3.9

49. योऽयं दक्षिणे अक्षन् पुरुषः सोऽत्ता । ..... तमेतमग्निरित्यध्वर्यव उपासते यजुरिति ..... साम इति छान्दोगा ..... उक्थमिति बह्वृचाः .... *S.* 10.3.6.19-20

50. ऋक् च वा इदमग्रे साम च आस्ताम् । *A.* 12.23 तदेतत् यजुः ऋक्सामयोः प्रतिष्ठितम्। *S.* 10.2.6.2

51. *Brahma-sūtra,* 1.3.26-33 (Devatādhikaraṇa) *Mahābhāśya,* 4.3.101

52. पू ।। वेदांश्चैके सन्निकर्षे पुरुषाख्याः । अनित्यदर्शनाच्च ।। सि ।। उक्तं तु शब्दपूर्वत्वम् । आख्या प्रवचनात् । परन्तु श्रुतिसामान्यमात्रम् । कृते वा विनियोगः स्यात् कर्मणः सम्बन्धात् ।। पूर्वमीमांसासूत्रम्, 1.1.27-32. See also Sāyaṇa *Ṛgbhāśya-bhūmikā.*

53. Śaṅkara, *Brahmasūtrabhāśya,* III.2.13; 3.3.24, 25 etc.

54. Kumārila. *Sloka-vartika*; Khaṇḍadeva. *Bhāṭṭa-dīpikā*; Lakshmipuram Srinivasacharya. *Mīmāṁsa-bhāśya-bhūṣaṇa.* न च अनादरात् कर्तुः अस्मरणे अक्षरशः विस्मरणाभावाय शिक्षाछलादीन् रचितवतां ऋषीणां तदधीतप्रामाण्यकस्मृति-कर्तृसामान्यमपि विस्मरतां सर्वज्ञानां वेदकर्त्रनादरोक्तेः अतिसाहसत्वम् । Mysore, vol. I

55. शुश्रुवांसो वै कवयः । *T.* 3.2.2.3

56. मनो वै समुद्रः मनसो वै समुद्रात् वाचा अभ्र्या देवाः त्रयीं निरस्नन् । *S.* 7.4.2.52

57. C. G. Jung. *Integration of Personality,* p. 67

58. कर्णश्रवा आङ्गिरसः सामापश्यत् । *P.* 13.11.15 साम आर्षेयेण प्रशस्तम्। *P.* 12.11.14 of दृष्टं साम । Pāṇini. 4.2.7

59. Max Muller, *History of Ancient Sanskrit Literature,* 1859, p. 497; Macdonell. *History of Sanskrit Literature*, p. 29
60. B. V. Kameshvara Iyer, 'Age of the Brāhmaṇas,' *AIOC* 1, Reprinted, *QTms* 12, 1922, p. 171 ff.
61. P. C. Sen-Gupta, 'Age of the Brāhmaṇas', *IHQ* 10, 1934, p. 540
62. "We shall probably have to date the beginning of this development about 2000 or 2500 B.C. and the end of it between 750 and 500 B.C. The more purdent course, however, is to steer clear of any fixed dates and to guard against the extremes of a stupendously ancient period or a ludicrously modern epoch." M. Winternitz, *HIL.*, 1, p. 310
63. Sri Aurobindo, *Foundations of Indian Culture,* pp. 295-96
64. *Manusmṛti* 2.140. उपनीय तु यः शिष्यं वेदं अध्यापयेत् द्विजः । सकल्पं सरहस्यं च तमाचार्यं प्रचक्षते ।। The word '*rahasya*' in this stanza is taken as referring to the chapters of *Śatapatha Brāhmaṇa*, called Agni-rahasya. But the context here does not seem to favour such an interpretation. Cf. रहस्यमूल ऋक्पर्णो यजुःपुष्पप्रवालवान् । यज्ञकर्मफलश्रीमान् विप्रभ्रमरसेवितः ।। छन्दस्कन्धः शासशासे ब्राह्मो वृक्षः साक्षादेषः । *Kāṇḍānukramaṇidā*, 3.32 'चत्वारो वेदाः साङ्गाः सरहस्याः .....' *Mahābhāśya*, 1.9
65. स्यात्तथेत्थमपि सम्भवितार्थः त्र्यर्थतां श्रुतिषु वित्त, दशार्थ । भारतं ननु, शतार्थमपि स्यात्, वैष्णवं पदसहस्त्रमयं हि ।। Nārāyaṇapaṇḍita *Sumadhvavijaya,* 6.4
66. Sri Aurobindo, *On the Veda,* p. 9
67. तथा यः प्रजाकामो वा स्यात् स एनं प्राजापत्यं तूपरमालमेत इति आकाङ्क्षितत्वादस्य विधेः शेषोऽयं - स आत्मनो वपामुदविखदत् इति । कथं पुनरिदे निरालम्बनमन्वाख्यायत इति । उच्यते । नित्यः कश्चिदर्थः प्रजापतिः स्याद् वायु आकाश आदित्यो वा । स आत्मनो वपां उदक्खिददिति- वृष्टि, वायुं, रश्मिं वा । तमग्नौ प्रागृह्णात् वैद्युते आर्बीसे, लौकिके वा।

ततोऽज इति अन्नं, बीजं वीरुध् वा । तमालभ्य-तमुपजीव्य प्रजाः पशून् प्राप्नोति इति गौणाः शब्दाः ।। Śabarasvāmin. *Pūrva-mīmūṁsa-sūtra-bhāśya,* 1.2.10

68. *S.* 10.2.2.16-18

त्रीणि वा इमानि पञ्चिवधानि - संवत्सरः, अग्निः, पुरुषः । तेषां पञ्चविधाः - अन्नम्, पानम्, श्रीः, ज्योतिः, अमृतम् । यदेव संवत्सरे अन्नं सदन्नम् । या आपः तत्पानम् । रात्रिरेव श्रीः । श्रियां हैतद्रात्र्यां सर्वाणि भूतानि संवसन्ति । अहः ज्योतिः । आदित्यः अमृतम् । इत्यधिदेवतम्।। अथाधि यज्ञम् । यदेवाग्नावन्नमुपधीयते, तदन्नम् । याः आपः तत्पानम् । परिश्रित एव श्रीः । तद्धि रात्रौणां रूपम् । यजुष्मत्यो ज्योतिः । तद्धिअह्नां रूपम् । अग्निमृतम् । तद्धि आदित्यस्य रूपम् । इत्यु अधियज्ञम् । अथाध्यात्मम् । यदेव परिश्रितां रूपम् । मज्जनो ज्योतिः । तद्धि यजुष्मतीनां रूपम् । प्राणोमृतम् । द्धि अग्ने रूपम् । प्राणोऽग्निः । प्राणोमृतम् । इत्यु वा आहुः ।

69. S. V. Venkateswara, *Indian Culture through the Ages,* vol. 1, p.59

70. D. Kunhan Raja, *Survey of Sanskrit Literature,* p.viii

71. H. L. Hariyappa, *Ṛgvedic Legends through the Ages,* p. 129

72. *Cf.* "We will not say these theories (Rele, P. Iyer, Muller) are all wholly conjectures.

73. *Cf.* यावानर्थ उदपाने सर्वतः सम्पलोदके ।

    तावान् सर्वेषु वेदेषु ब्राह्मणस्य विजानतः ।।

74. न ह्येषु प्रत्यक्षमस्ति अनृषेः अतपसो वा ।। *Nirukta,* 13.12

Chapter - IX

The Āraṇyakas and Upaniṣads

9.1 Introduction to the Āraṇyakas

As a further development of the Brāhmaṇas, however we get the Āraṇyakas or forest treatises. These works were probably composed for the persons retiring into the forest (Vānaprasthāśramis), after leading the life through performing sacrifices. In precise, the Āraṇyakas promote an aspirant to climb the step of higher altitude on the path of achieving the final goal of life. In these, meditations on certain symbols were supposed to be of great merit, and they gradually began to supplant the sacrifices as being of a superior order. It is here that we find that amongst a certain section of intelligent people the ritualistic ideas began to give way, and philosophic speculations about the nature of truth became gradually substituted in their place. To take an illustration from the beginning of the Bṛhadāraṇyaka, we find that instead of the actual performance of the horse sacrifice (*aśvamedha*), there are directions for meditating upon the dawn (*Uṣas*) as the head of the horse, the sun as the eye of the horse, the air as its life, and so on. This is indeed a distinct advancement of the claims of speculation or meditation over the actual performance of the complicated ceremonials of sacrifice. The growth of the subjective speculation, as being capable of bringing the highest good, gradually resulted in the contraction supersession of Vedic ritualism and the establishment of the claims of philosophic meditation and self-knowledge as the highest goal of life. Thus we find that the *Āraṇyaka* age was a period during which free thinking tried gradually to shake off the shackles of ritualism, which had fettered it for a long time. It was thus that the Āranyakas could pave the way for the Upaniṣads, revive the germs of philosophic speculation in the Vedas, and develop them in a manner which made the Upaniṣads the source of all philosophy that arose in the world of Hindu thought.

The Āraṇyakas ("Forest-texts"), the concluding portions or appendices to, the Brāhmaṇas are so called (it is generally supposed) because their contents are of so secret and uncanny a nature that they would spell danger if taught to the uninitiated, and had therefore to be learnt in the forest and not in the village. They are concerned neither with the performance nor with any explanation of the sacrifice, but with its mysticism and symbolism. They form a natural transition to the Upaniṣads, the oldest of which are either included in or appended to the Āraṇyakas, the line of demarcation being not always easy to draw. The Āraṇyakas, and Upaniṣads by themselves, and not the system of philosophy based on them, were originally called "Vedānta" (literally, the concluding portions of the Veda)- a title applicable to them in more senses than one as follows:-

(1) From the point of view of relative literary chronology, they stand at the end of the Veda. (2) As the most obstruse and mystical of the Śruti works, they were naturally taught to the pupil towards the close of the period of his apprenticeship with his Guru. (3) They formed the end of the daily Vedic-recital.

9.2 The Aitareya Āraṇyaka

As component (and concluding) parts of the Brāhmaṇas. the Āraṇyakas (and some Upaniṣads) are found attached to as many

Śākhās (Vedic schools) as the Brāhmaṇas belong to. The Aitareya Āraṇyaka is appended to the *Aitareya Brāhmaṇa* of the *Ṛg Veda*. It consists of five books, which are looked upon and designated as five separate Āraṇyakas. The first deals with the Soma sacrifice from the ritual point of view. The second is intermixed with theosophical speculations on Prāṇa and Puruṣa, and is Upaniṣadic in character, the last four chapters actually forming the Aitareya Upaniṣad. The third book contains allegorical and mystical meanings of the Saṁhitā, Pada, and Krama texts (Pāṭhas). The last two books contain miscellaneous matter, such as Mahānāmnī verses and details about the Nishkevalya Śāstra, to be recited in the Mahāvrata, and are attributed to Āśvalāyana and Śaunaka-two Sūtra authors.

9.3 The Sānkhyāyana Āraṇyaka

The *Śāṅkhāyana* or *Kauṣītaki* Āranyaka is the concluding portion of the *Kauṣitaki Brāhmaṇa* or the *Ṛg Veda* and agrees very closely with the *Aitareya Āraṇyaka* in its contents. It consists of fifteen chapters of which 3 to 6 constitute the long and important *Kauṣītaki Upaniṣad*.

9.4 The Taittirīya Āraṇyaka

In the Black Yajurveda, the *Taittirīya Āraṇyaka* is only a continuation of the *Taittirīya Brāhmaṇa*. It consists of ten chapters or prapāṭhakas (commonly called Araṇas), 7 to 9 constituting the important *Taittirīya Upaniṣad*. The tenth chapter called *Mahānārāyaṇa Upaniṣad* is a very late addition to the *Āraṇyaka*. In the *White Yajurveda* the fourteenth book of the *Śatapatha Brāhmaṇa* is in name only an Āraṇyaka-the Bṛhadaraṇyaka - the last six chapters of which constitute the celebrated *Upaniṣad* of that name and the major part of the so-called *Āraṇyaka*.

For the *Sāmaveda*, the only Āraṇyakas are the first Āraṇyaka-like section of the *Chhāṅdogya Upanishad*, which belongs probably to the *Tāṅdya-Mahā-Brāhmaṇa* and the *Jaiminīya Upaniṣad Brāhmaṇa* which is nothing but an *Āraṇyaka* of the Jaiminīya or Talavakāra school of the Sāma Veda and comprises the well-known *Kena* (or Talavakāra) *Upaniṣad*.

9.5 Introduction to the Upaniṣads

The Vedas have two principal divisions, the Mantras and Brāhmaṇas. The former tell us about supersensuous things, which we could not know but for them. The latter, however, are explanatory to the former and delineate their application in sacrifices. Though the Brāhmaṇas are thus subsidiary to the Mantras, both are held to be equally authoritative. The Mantras are of three classes. Those that are metrical and are recited in invocation to the gods are called *ṛc*; those that are in prose and are applied to the sacrificial acts are called *yajus*; while *ṛcas* that are meant to be chanted in sacrifices, and not simply recited, are called *sāman*. These three classes of Mantras have been compiled into four books or Saṁhitās, called the *Ṛg-Veda, Yajur-Veda, Sāma-Veda*, and *Atharva-Veda Saṁhitās*. Some part of the Brāhmaṇas used to be taught in the forest to those who observed particular vows. This was called the Āraṇyaka. The Upaniṣads are generally the last portions of the Āraṇyakas. The Vedas, again, fall into two distinct portions according to their theme: one dealing with the performance of rituals (karmakāṇḍa) and the other mainly devoted to knowledge (jnānakāṇḍa). The Upaniṣads come under the second category.

9.6 Meaning of the term 'Upaniṣad'

The word '*upaniṣad*' is derived from the prefixes *upa* (near) and *ni* (perfectly), joined to the verbal root sad (to shatter, attain, or destroy), and. means the knowledge of Reality, expounded in books of that name, Śaṅkara, defining the word, says in his introduction to the *Kaṭha Upaniṣad*: 'Those seekers after liberation who, being averse to things of the senses, whether here or hereafter, take up this knowledge and practise it with steadfast devotion, have their ignorance etc., which are the seeds of their transmigration, shattered or destroyed.... Or it makes those aspirants attain the supreme Brahman' etc. In the introduction to the *Taittirīya Upaniṣad*, he says: "*Upaniṣad*" means knowledge, either because it *slashes* or *shatters* the miseries of passing through the mother's womb, birth, decay, etc., or because the highest good is established in it. Books also are so designated, as they contribute to that knowledge.' So the word primarily means knowledge or philosophy, and secondarily books relating to it. The Upaniṣads are also called Vedānta, literally 'the end of the Vedas', either on account of their position at the end of certain books of the Vedas or on account of their representing the essence or conclusions of the Vedas. They are also called *rahasya*, or secret, as only qualified initiates had access to them under the direct guidance of the teacher.

9.7 Number and character of the Upaniṣads

The Vedic literature was vast, and was divided into a large number of branches, only a portion of which has come down to us, the bulk having been destroyed either during the Buddhistic cataclysm or through the natural extinction of those Brāhmaṇa families which were their custodians. Hence it is impossible to say definitely the number of the Upaniṣads, and which part of the Vedas contained them. Of the extant Upanisads, we find that, of those which are stated to belong to any particular portion of the Vedas, all except one form part of the Brāhmaṇas, and often of their Āraṇyaka section. The exception is the *Īśāvāsya*, which forms the last chapter of the *Śukla Yajur-Veda*.

The Upaniṣads are further classified under different Vedas thus:

1) ***Ṛg-Veda*** (10) - *Aitareya, Kauṣītaki, Nādabindu, Ātmaprabodha, Nirvāṇa, Mudgala, Akṣmālikā, Tripurā, Saubhāgya,* and *Bahvṛca*;

2a) ***Śukla Yajur-Veda*** (19) - *Iśāvāsya, Bṛhadāraṇyaka, Jābāla, Haṁsa, Paramahaṁsa, Subāla, Mantrikā, Nirālamba, Triāṣikhībrāhmaṇa, Maṇḍala-brāhmaṇa, Advayatāraka, Paiṅgala, Bhikṣu, Turīyātīta, Adhyātma, Tārasāra, Yājñavalkya, Śāṭyāyanī,* and *Muktikā;*

2b) ***Kṛṣṇa Yajur-Veda*** (32) - *Kaṭhavallī, Taittirīya, Brahma, Kaivalya, Śvetāśvatara, Garbha, Nārāyaṇa, Amṛtabindu, Amṛtanāda, Kālāgnirudra, Kṣurikā, Sarvasāra, Śukarahasya, Tejobindu, Dhyānabindu, Brahmavidyā, Yogatattva, Dakṣiṇāmūrti, Skanda, Śārīraka, Yogaśikhā, Ekākṣara, Akṣi, Avadhūta, Kaṭharudra, Hṛdaya, Yogakuṇḍalinī, Pañcabrahma, Prāṇāgnihotra, Varāha, Kalisantaraṇa,* and *Sarasvatīrahasya*;

3) ***Sāma-Veda*** (16) - *Kena, Chāndogya, āruṇi, Maitrāyaṇī, Maitreyī, Vajrasūcikā, Yogacūḍāmaīi, Vāsudeva, Mahat, Sannyāsa, Vajra (Avyakta?), Kuṇḍika, Sāvitrī, Rudrākṣ-ajābāla, Darāana,* and *Jābāli;*

4) ***Atharva-Veda*** (31) - *Praśna, Muṇḍaka, Māṇḍūkya, Atharvaśiras, Atharvaśikhā, Bṛhajjābāla, Nṛsiṁhatāpanī, Nāradaparivrājaka, Sītā, Śarabha, Mahānārāyaṇa, Rāmarahasya, Rāmatāpanī, Śāṇḍilya, Paramahaṁsa-parivrājaka, Annapūrṇa, Sūrya, Ātma, Pāśupata, Parabrahma, Tripurātapana, Devi, Bhāvanā, Brahmajābāla, Gaṇapati, Mahāvākya, Gopālatapana, Kṛṣṇa, Hayagrīva, Dattatreya* and *Gāruḍa*.

9.8 Testimony of the Upaniṣads

The Upaniṣads represent the quintessence of the wisdom that is embedded in the Vedas, those marvellous records of the spiritual experience of man. They treat not of secular knowledge, which any science can teach, but of *Brahma-vidyā*, the knowledge of Brahman, the ultimate Reality of the universe. The province of the scriptures is a unique one. They are one of the means of valid knowledge, known as *śabda pramāṇa* (verbal testimony), along with perception, inference, etc., and their special field is the supersensuous-plane. Perception deals with objects that come within the range of our senses, in which field it is paramount. Inference, which is based on perception, is operative regarding things that are not so perceived, but are accessible to the mind. But where perception, inference, etc. fail to give us definite knowledge, scriptures like the Upaniṣads are our only guide. In that domain, they have infinitely greater validity than even perception, upon which we rely so much in our everyday life. Such questions as whether our personality survives death; whether there is a future life and a world called heaven where a man goes after death; whether he ever returns to this world; what is his final goal; what is the nature and goal of the world; what is the nature of God and of soul and what is their relation with each other and with the world; and what is the ultimate truth of existence-obviously come under this description, and the Upaniṣads-give us the last word on all such matters. Through no other means is it possible for us to get convincing answers to our queries regarding them. In fact, God has been declared in the Srutis as 'the Being that is to be known only through the Upaniṣads'. Not being the work of man, they are free from the usual shortcomings of all human endeavour such as error, doubt, and deception. It is open to us all to verify their statements by actual experience along the lines prescribed by them. The truths inculcated in them are not mere theories, but facts, and as such are invulnerable.

9.9 Methodology of the Upaniṣads

The Upaniṣads develop ideas that are in germs of the Saṁhitās, and in so doing refine them and raise them to a higher level. For instance, heaven looms large in the Saṁhitās. People want to go there after death under the belief that they will get everlasting joy uncontaminated by sorrow. And the performance of sacrifices is thought to be the chief means of attaining heaven. The Upaniṣads take into consideration this desire on the part of man for prolonged enjoyment, but they show the fallacy of clinging to heaven as a permanent source of bliss. They tell him that the joys of heaven, like all other joys, are also evanescent; so he must look elsewhere for abiding bliss, and yet it is right within his reach.

9.10 Summary of the Upaniṣads

9.10.1 The Īśāvāsya Upaniṣad

This upaniṣad, also called saṁhitopaniṣad constitutes 40th chapter of the Vājasaneya Saṁhitā. This upanisad in its 18 mantras, is at once exoteric as it attempts a synthetics of the practical values of life, and esoteric as it reveals the highest goal of life in the best possible way.

The *Īśāvāsya Upaniṣad* gives stress to the immanence of God, advocates active life, cautions to avoid wrong knowledge and contains a beautiful prayer to God. The extra-ordinary nature of God is brought out by mentioning the contradictory attributes such as 'He moves and does not move, He is near and He is away, He is within and He is without'. This is one of the methods of Upaniṣads describing God. This has immense philosophical implication.

9.10.2 The Kena (or Talavakāra) Upaniṣad

This Upaniṣad is named after the first word of its first verse "Kena" meaning "why". It is also known as Talavakāropanisad, after the name of the sage Talavakar, an exponent of the Sāmaveda. It is a small book but is divided into four -parts.

The *Kena Upaniṣad* brings out the regulatorship of God. Our mind and senses are directed and regulated by Him. The problem of the comprehension of God who is Infinite, is also beautifully brought out here. To say that He cannot be known at all will make all philosophical effort fruitless. To say that He is comprehended as any other object will reduce him to a finite object. Therefore, the *Kena Upaniṣad* informs us that He can be known but cannot be fully known. This is another method of describing God in *Upaniṣads*. *Īśāvāsya* description of God is metaphysical while *Kena* description is epistemological. *Kena* also informs the subordinate nature of other deities.

9.10.3 The Kāṭhaka Upaniṣad

The *Kāṭhaka Upanisad*, a perspicuous and poetical Upaniṣad, is one of the more widely known Upaniṣads, as it expounds the highest philosophical dictums through an interesting dialogue between young lad Nachiketas and Yama, the god of death. It belongs to the Kāṭhaka branch of the *Kṛṣṇa Yajurveda*. It comprises two adhyāyas, each of which, is divided into three vallis.

This book is full of philosophical dis-courses, - philosophy of life and death, teachings about human conduct and about the aims and objects of our life.

There is a little story at the background of all these thoughts and ideals, and it is interesting to note how a great and deep philosophy has been blended with a strange little story.

It goes on like this :- Āruṇi, the son of Uddālaka once performed a great sacrifice, for gaining virtue, the fruit of the sacrifice. He promised to give away his all in that sacrifice. He had a son called Naciketā. The young boy was watching the ceremony. When the cows were brought in to be given away as presents to the priests, Naciketā was rather sad, because the cows were old and listless. They certainly were riot capable of bearing calves or giving milk. The boy thought that it would not be proper for his father to make a gift of such cows. It would please neither the one who received, nor the one who gave.

Then again it dawned on him, that a son belongs to his father and when his father's promise was to give away his everything, it should also include the son. So he asked his father :- "Unto whom would you give me ?" Again and again he asked the same question. The father got annoyed and said, "I would give you unto Death".

At this Naciketā indeed felt sorry, both for himself and for his father. But he resolved to go to Death, to keep his father's promise.

So he went to the abode of Yama, the king of death.

The *Kāṭhaka Upaniṣad* contrasts the good and pleasant i.e. *śreyas* and *preyas* in a graphic way and sets the tone of Upaniṣadic ethics. Naciketas asks peace for his father's mind by the first boon. He desires to know the sacrifice, later known by his name, by the second boon, and finally desires to know God by the third boon. These represent three well-marked stages in the spiritual progress. Keeping one's mind free from the anger and the like is the first step, performing activity with dedication to God is the second, and seeking true knowledge is the last. The three boons represent these three stages. *Kāṭhaka* also describes God in terms of contradictory attributes. It also describes Him as *Aśabda, Asparśa* etc. This negative description does not mean that He is nirguṇa. He is only *prākṛtaguṇarahita* or not contaminated with material attributes. *Kāṭhaka* mentions the fact of God controlling the souls in the stages of waking, dream etc. *Kāṭhaka* explains yoga methodology. The metaphors of chariot, Aśvattha tree, fire and sparks are beautifully employed to bring home various philosophical points. The importance of God's grace and a proper preceptor is expressly stated in *Kaṭha*.

9.10.4 The Ṣaṭ-Praśna Upaniṣad

The Praśna Upaniṣad ascribed to the Pippalāda śākhā, is one of the classical Upaniṣads, and belongs to the Atharva Veda. Like the Kāṭhaka Upaniṣad, this Upaniṣad too has its discourses in dialogue form. This is called *Sat-Praśna Upaniṣad*, as it consists of the doctrines of six questions put to sage Pippalāda by his six disciples. And Pippalāda's answer to these questions form the substance of this Upaniṣad. The Upaniṣad opens with an account of six disciples approaching the sage Pippalāda. Those disciples approaching the sage Pippalāda. Those disciples are - Sukeśa Bhāradwāja, Saibya-satyakāma, Souryāyaṇi Gargya, Kausalya Āśvalayana, Vaidarbhi Bhārgava and Kabandhi Kātyāyana.

Kabandhi Kātyāyana, the youngest of them enquires into the nature of Brahman, from which all animate and inanimate objects are produced. *Vaidarbhi Bhārgava* continues the thread of the discussing putting the questions: How many gods support the creatures? Who is the Supreme of all? *Kauśalya Āśvalāyana* inquires into the origin, entry and distribution of the chief Prāṇa. *Sauryāyaṇi Gārgya* in the fourth query, asks his preceptor to instruct on the analysis of deep sleep state and of the dream-state. Further, Sage Pippalāda, being asked by Sukeśa Bhāradvaja, explains the nature of Brahman as All-controller and All-supporter. *Śaibya Satyakāma* enquires into the efficacy of meditating on Om.

9.10.5 The Muṇḍaka Upaniṣad

The Muṇḍaka Upaniṣad belongs to the Atharva Veda, and has three chapters, each of which is divided into two sections. This upaniṣad is so called for various reasons: (l) each chapter of it is called Muṇḍaka, (2) The knowledge of this upaniṣad like a muṇḍaka (razor) cuts off one's ignorance; (3) it is perhaps so called after the tenth mantra of the sixth muṇḍaka in which the Śirovrata is enjoined. It distinguishes clearly the parā-vidyā and aparā-vidyā. Yet it is a synthesis of these two kinds of knowledge; in other words a synthesis of ritualism and metaphysics. As the upaniṣad itself states in the mantra VI.11, its philosophy is too secret to be imparted to the unqualified; rather, one who studies this upaniṣad, must possess the required qualifications.

9.10.6 The Māṇḍūkya Upaniṣad

The *Māṇḍūkya Upaniṣad* is one of the three upanisads belonging to the Atharva Veda. This Upaniṣad like the *Īśāvāsya Upaniṣad*, is a profound collection of mystic teachings on Brahman symbolised as Om. This Upaniṣad has gained much popularity as it posits an elevated explication of Om corresponding with four aspects of Brahman, as it contains the assertion of the text: Ayamatma Brahma which reveals an inspiring representation of the nature of Brahman to help genuine seekers to gains correct attitude to the study of the Upaniṣad.

It consists of four Khaṇḍas. It is said therein that the Upaniṣad is handed down by God Varuṇa in the form of a frog (maṇḍuka). Besides, the exact status of the forty-one mantras of this upaniṣad, in the Vedantic field, has been a matter of controversy. Because, according to the Advaita school this Upaniṣad consists of only twelve prose passages and the remaining metrical verses are regarded as karikas of Gaudapada the paramaguru of Śankara. But the fact that these metrical verses have been cited as sruti texts by Śankara, Ānandagiri, Sāyaṇa, of the Advaita school and Rāmānuja and Vedānta Deśika of the Viśiṣṭādvaita school, establishes that they are originally upaniṣ adic verses.

The *Māṇḍūkya Upaniṣad* gives a full exposition of the mystic significance of 'Om'. The stales of waking, dream and deep sleep being regulated by viśva, taijasa, and prājña are explained in detail. The turiya form is contrasted with other forms. *Upaniṣads* utilise the psychological set up during the states of waking, dream and deep sleep to evolve the concept of soul as distinct from mere psychological states. An analysis of these states is utilised to explain the concept of soul and the turiya state is utilised to explain the transcendental nature of God. *Upaniṣads* utilise the experience more frequently than logic to bring home their philosophical tenets. Psychology and epistemology are utilised more than logic and speculation. *Māṇḍūkya* summarises the different views in respect of creation and finally states its own view. These are : 1) Creation is a modification or manifestation of Brahman (Brahma Vibhūti). 2) Creation is merely a projection, an illusion like dream or magic. 3) Time is the ground of all creation 4) Creation is an outcome of God's will. It is the very nature of God to create. The *Upaniṣad* rejects the first three views and affirms the fourth. As regards the purpose of creation also the *Upaniṣad* rejects the two views: i) it is for enjoyment (bhogārtha), ii) it is a sport. The Upaniṣad holds that it is the very nature of the God to create. God wills to create, and He wills because it is His nature to do so.

9.10.7 The Taittirīya Upaniṣad

The Taittirīya Upaniṣad has its origin in the Āraṇyaka of the Taittirīya or Kṛṣṇa Yajurveda. The Taittirīya Āraṇyaka consists of ten prapāṭhakas, of which the first six from the karmakāṇḍa; the next three prapāṭhakas constitute the three vallis or sections of the Taittirīya Upaniṣad. These vallis are named as Śikṣā, Brahmā and the Bhṛgu. The tenth, the last prapāṭhaka of the Taittirīya Āraṇyaka forms a separate Upaniṣad, the Yājniki and the Mahānārāyaṇa Upaniṣad.

The *Taittirīya Upaniṣad* is unique in more than one respect. The two important definitions of Brahman viz "*Satyaṁ jñānam anantaṁ brahma*" and "*yato vā imāni bhūtāni jāyante*" are found here. The five-layer-analysis of personality in terms of Kośas is a unique contribution of *Upaniṣads* to human thought. The physical, the psychic, and the spiritual aspects of personality are delineated here. These are not mere kośas but have a divine counter part. The process of creation is explained in this Upaniṣad twice from two different points of view. '*Ātmanah ākāśah saṁbhūtah*' etc., is one account, and "*Saccha tyaccha abhavat*" is another account.

The *Taittirīya Upaniṣad* in its three chapters explains the Supra-divine nature of the Supreme Truth. The *Upaniṣad* reveals that this Truth in totality, is inexplicable. Therefore it is not possible to speak about the unspeakable the soul of every individual. But the soul is not individual. It is One and indivisible. The words come back not being able to describe It and even mind fails to find it - yet the seer describes it through similies and metaphors.

Amidst this, the seer advises men again and again to behave like men, - to be human in every way; - being a proper human through righteous work, he will be able to succeed in attaining Brahman, in reaching up to immortality. Because it is only in this life, that it is possible to remove the obstacles, the sheaths of matters and realise the spiritual existence of life.

The *Taittirīya Upaniṣad* builds up men with characters, people who would be the foundations of society, through whom the knowledge acquired by the seers and sages with austere labour and meditation would continue and be carried from generation to generation, and would prove the divine heritage of man, that he is the son of immortality and not of death.

9.10.8 The Aitareya Upaniṣad

The *Aitareya Upaniṣad* belongs to the Aitareya Brāhmaṇa of the Ṛg Veda, Aitareya and Sāmkhyāṇa are the two "Brāhmaṇas" of the Ṛg Veda. Aitareya is supposed to be the older of the two. The author of this massive work was Aitareya, the son of Itara, a woman of inferior caste. According to some, Itara was the name of a woman. But the story which goes round his name proves the former version, that his mother was a commoner, not belonging to the high order of any Brāhmana or Kṣatriya family.

The *Aitareya Upaniṣad* commences with an interesting remark that 'the God is the path to lead to God. He is the prime door and prime knower. He is truth and He possesses infinite attributes. This concept of God conveys His metaphysical as well as theistic aspects. No one should make any attempt to transgress the will of God, be away from God. Those who try to transgress His will miserably fail.

Transgressing God is of various kinds viz., to deny His very existence, to think of others as equal or superior to Him, to underestimate His prowess, to argue that His grace is not necessary for spiritual progress, to think of difference in His different forms, to think of defects in Him. to indulge in evil deeds, etc. These are different forms of atheism. Aitareya warns us not to be atheists in one or the other of these forms.

The *Aitareyā* declares that all words convey God. '*Sarvā ṛcah sarve vedāh sarve ghoṣāh ekaiva vyāhṛtih Prāṇe eva prāṇe ṛcaf ityeva vidyāt*'. The entire Veda conveys God. All hymns convey God. Here is a clear reference to the *Sarvaśabda-vācyatva* of God. The passages "*Yato vāco nivartante*" etc. only inform that God cannot be fully described by words. It is not correct to say that God cannot be conveyed by words at all. In that case, the entire sruti will be purposeless, *Āgama prāmāṇya* will loose all its sanctity. On the contrary, all words convey God, Every word conveys some or the other attribute and God possesses infinite number of attributes.

The *Aitareya* brings out the importance of *Bṛhatisahasra*. The process of creation is also described in this *Upaniṣad*. The mystical meaning of the name Viśṇu is explained. The suggestions of dreams and hints of untimely death are explained. This *Upaniṣad* is strongly theistic.

9.10.9 The Chāndogya Upaniṣad

The *Chāndogya Upaniṣad* belonging to the *Chāndogya Brāhmaṇa* of the Tāṇḍins of the *Sāma Veda,*[1] is one of the two most important *Upaniṣads*, the other being the *Bṛhadāraṇyaka Upaniṣad*. "The name of the *Upaniṣad* is derived from the word *Chand* which means metre, and it is so named because it is capable of being recited in metrical style." [2] It embraces the last eight chapters out of the ten of the *Chāndogya Brāhmaṇa*.[3]

This *Upaniṣad* stands second in rank to the *Bṛhadāraṇyaka Upaniṣad*, so far as its volume of material is concerned. This *Upaniṣad* has been the well known *Śruti* text, the culmination of the intellectual achievement of a great epoch, as it contains many important philosophical teachings through interesting narratives (*ākhyānas*), such as- (1) Śilaka Śālāvatya - Caikitāyana Dālbhya - Pravāhaṇa Jaivali narrative (I- i. 8, 9), (2) Uṣasti narrative (I. x-xi), (3) Jānaśruti-Raikva narrative (iv. i. 1), (4) Satyakāma Jābāla-Hāridrumata Gautama narrative (IV. iv. 1), (5) Upakosala narrative (IV. x. 1). (6) Śvetaketu-King Jaivli narrative (V. iii. 1), (7) Pañca-Mahāśālas [viz. Prācīnaśāla Aupamanyava, Satyayajña Pauluṣi, Indradyumna Bhāllaveya, Janah Śārkarākṣya, Buḍila Aśvatarāśvi] - King Aśvapati Kaikeya narrative (V. xi 1), (8) Śvetaketu-Uddālaka narrative (VI. i. 1), (9) Nārada-Sanatkumāra narrative (VII. i. 1), Indra, Virocana-Prajāpati narrative (VIII. vii. 1).

A doubt might arise here about the warrior (kṣatriya) - preceptors' imparting the knowledge of Brahman to the brahmin disciples. Garbe in this connection, argues "that it can be proven that the Brahman's profoundest wisdom, the doctrine of All-one, which has exercised an unmistakable influence on the intellectual life even of our time, did not have its origin in the circle of Brāhmaṇas at all"[4] and that "it took its rise in the ranks of the warrior caste."[5]

Of course, there are a few exceptional narratives wherein the kings of warrior class such as, Pravahana Jaivali, Aśvapati Kaikeya or Ajātaśatru (*Bṛhadāraṇayaka Upaniṣad* II. i. 1) have instructed the brahmin disciples. Verily in all other narratives, brahmins have discussed and imparted the knowledge of Brahman. But, this scanty reason does not suffice to show any relevancy to the rise of the knowledge of Brahman in the ranks of the warrior caste. S. Dasgupta in this connection, rightly contends against the former's argument i.e., "The truth seems to me to be this, that the Kṣatriyas and even some women took interest in the religio-philosophical quest manifested in the *Upaniṣads*. The enquirers were so eager that either in receiving the instruction of Brahman or in imparting it to others, they had no considerations of sex and birth;[6] and there seems to be no definite evidence for thinking that the *Upaniṣad* philosophy originated among the Kṣatriyas or that the germs of its growth could not be traced in the Brahmanas and the Aranyakas which were the productions of the Brahmins."[7]

The dialogue between Śvetaketu and Uddālaka (VI. i). Among the ten principal *Upaniṣads*, the *Chāndogya* is very important. A number of Vidyas and Upāsanas such as *Udgīthopāsanā, Sāmopāsana, Madhuvidyā, Samvargavidya, Prāṇavidyā, Pañcāgnividyā, Vaiśvānaravidyā, Daharavidyā* are explained here. The correlation of *adhividyā, adhyātma, adhidaiva* and *adhibhūta* is found here in great detail. The importance of Mukhya Prāṇa is clearly brought out. The meaning and the significance of Gāyatri is explained. In the *Puruśayajña*, the whole life of a person is considered as a sacrifice and the various stages and duties in life are compared with the sacrificial item. It is interesting to note that the ethical virtues like truthfulness, non-violence, alms-giving, asceticism are considered as the dakṣiṇā to be offered in Puruṣayajnñ, The *Chāndogya* mentions the five great sins *brahmahatyā, surāpāna* etc., and exhorts to avoid these.

The episodes of Satyakāma-Jābāla, Upakosala, Jānaśruti, Indra-Virochana and Nārada-Sanatkumāra occur in the *Chāndogya*.

The methodology of *Ekavijñānena sarvavijñāna* and the famous passage '*Tat tvam asi*' are already discussed. The nine illustrations given in this context clearly bring out the difference between the jiva and Brahman. The *Bhūmavidyā* is another interesting topic in *Chāndogya*. Majority of the adhikaraṇas of *Brahmasūtras* are based on the passages drawn from the *Chāndogya Upaniṣad*.

9.10.10 The Bṛhadāraṇyaka Upaniṣad

The *Bṛhadāraṇyaka Upaniṣad*, the largest among the ten major Upaniṣads, forms a part of the *Śatapatha Brāhmaṇa* of the Śukla Yajurveda. The Śukla Yajurveda has come down to us in two recensions viz. the Kaṇva and the Mādyandina. This Upaniṣad is found in both the branches with slight variations in the arrangement of the material. It contains eight adhyāyas, but first two adhyayas are not commented upon by the Acharyas of the Vedanta schools, as the treatment of the ritual of the horse sacrifice is explained therein.

The *Bṛhadaraṇyaka Upaniṣad* is largest among principal Upaniṣads. It covers all important questions of Upaniṣadic philosophy. The dialogue between Yājnavalkya and other seers at the court of King Janaka highlights the major points of Upaniṣadic philosophy. Sections like *Antaryāmi Brāhmaṇa, Akṣ ara Brāhmaṇa, Maitreyi Brāhmaṇa* go to the fundamental questions, in the earlier sections mystic significances of sacrifice like Aśvamedha is brought out. Caturmukha Brahmā himself performing Aśvamedha sacrifice assuming the form of Aśva, his participation in the process of creation, assuming the form of male and female in each class of created beings etc., are mentioned. Reference to Pañcamahāyajñas i.e. Vaiśva-deva, Baliharaṇa etc, are found. The special role of Mukhya Prāṇa as sūtra, Madhuvidya., Udgithopāsanā, methods of meditation and a number of connected topics are discussed. This Upaniṣad is very rich in philosophical, ethical, psychological and mystical data. The import of the intricate passage like "*aham bhahma*"- is already discussed. The concept of the central principal of the universe developed here, surpasses all other concepts. "*Idam amṛtam idam Brahma*" "*Etasmin akṣare ākāśa otaśca protaśca*" "*sarvānubhūh*" "*ath eṣa paramānandah*" "*yah prāṇaṁ antaro yamayati*" "*yo devānāṁ pratyabudhyata*" "*idam sarvaṁ asṛjata*" "*sarvaṁ vātti*" etc, a host of passage bring out the concept of this central principal fully.

9.10.11 Critical Exposition of the Upaniṣads

Upaniṣads are very simple in one sense, and are very complex in another. *Upaniṣads* give a lucid exposition of the fundamental questions of philosophy in simple dialogues with fascinating illustrations. The problems that are chiefly dealt with in Upaniṣads are. 1. The nature of Ultimate Reality or the Central Principle of the universe; 2. Cosmology or the process of creation; 3. The nature of soul and its psychological states; 4. Importance of knowledge, meditation and other means of spiritual statement; 5. The nature of liberated state. The principal passages that deal with these main issues could be easily identified and their purport could be broadly understood. But, when one proceeds to check up each and every passage on these problems, one will meet with a number of paradoxes. The central principle is sometimes described as devoid of any attribute and sometimes as possessing a number of attributes. The ritualistic activities are sometimes glorified and sometimes censured. The process of creation is described differently in different places. The nature of first cause is described differently in different places. The individual soul and the universal self are described as distinct in some places and are mentioned as identical in another. This baffles a reader. The terminology and illustrations are so flexible that these can be mended either way. This makes the understanding of Upaniṣadic thought difficult.

Further, Upaniṣads are not mere speculative documents. Their analysis of experience is also not confined to empirical level only. Delineation of mystic experience and transcendental facts is as much their field as that of empirical experience and empirical facts. In fact, the term Upaniṣad means the secret knowledge or mystic experience, and the treatises that delineate such experience. Therefore, it is not merely the verbal meaning or the meaning of each word that helps us to understand the Upaniṣadic thought but it is the grasp of the experience that is communicated through the statement and the illustration as a whole. Such experiences are communicated through different illustrations, symbols and metaphors. Each one has to be understood in the light of the others.

Further, *Upaniṣads* have a multiple approach towards their problems. Metaphysically *Upaniṣads* are in search of reality, theistic in search of God, ontologically the first cause, psychologically the subject and his psychic states, epistemologically these search both the subject and the object, mystically the transcendental. These approaches are inter-woven in many passages, dialogues, illustrations and questions. This has made the Upaniṣads very complex documents. However, a careful analysis of these aspects in the respective passages and a proper appraisal of the illustrations given will help one to understand Upaniṣadic thought from each point of view. Metaphysics, psychology and mysticism are the three dimensions of Upaniṣadic thought.

There is one more aspect of the presentation of Upaniṣadic thought. While describing the process of creation and identifying cosmological entities, *Upaniṣads* describe the steps of growth in terms of physical entities such as ether, air, fire, water, earth etc. Physiological entities such as various sense-organs, vital air etc., theological entities such as the Creator God assuming different forms and entering at different stages, the other deities connected with the respective physical and physiological stages of growth. *Upaniṣads* are fond of establishing correlations of *adhibhūta, adhyātma, adhidaiva* entities with the process of cosmological growth. The correlations of cosmological items with ritualistic items, literary items like the four Vedas, the mystic syllable 'om' and its components are also found. This Upaniṣadic cosmology is not confined only to the evolution of physical world. Those who are interested only in metaphysics and philosophical postulates, may find all this a little tedious but as it is stated above, Upaniṣads are not merely the documents of speculative philosophy. They represent a cultural tradition comprising of philosophy, religion, and certain values of life. Therefore, one who is interested in understanding Upaniṣadic thought has to take into account all that is stated in the *Upaniṣads*. Traditional commentators not only have taken into account all these aspects but have supplemented their exposition by quoting from the allied literature of *Āgama, Itihāsa, Purāṇa* etc. Sri Madhvācārya's tradition has particularly utilised this allied literature for the exposition of *Upaniṣads*.

Now, there is a question whether the Upaniṣadic thought developed as a reaction to *Saṁhitā* and *Brāhmaṇa* thought or was it in continuation and an outcome of it. What conclusion could be drawn from the data available in *Saṁhitā, Brāhmaṇa* and *Upaniṣads*, and what is the view of traditional commentators. Firstly, it is not fully justifiable to say that there is no philosophical thought in *Saṁhitā* and *Brāhmaṇa* portions, and *Upaniṣads* not only lack ritualistic thought but actually censure it. On a careful study of *Ṛgveda Saṁhitā* and *Atharvaveda Saṁhitā*, we find that all the major philosophical postulations found in Upaniṣads are found in the hymns of *Ṛgveda* and *Atharvaveda*. We may particularly note the hymns: *Asya Vāmīya Sūkta*, *Nāsadīya Sūkta*, *Hiraṇyagarbha Sūkta*, *Prajāpati Sūkta*, *Viśvakarma Sūkta*, *Vāgaṁbhṛṇī Sūkta, Pavamāna Sūkta and Puruṣa Sūkta*. These Sūktas contain the fundamentals of Upaniṣadic philosophy. In several other hymns also Upaniṣadic thoughts are sprinkled. Correspondingly *Upaniṣads* introduce some of their thoughts as stated in the hymns. They mention the Vedas with great reverence and correlate the same with different stages of cosmological growth.[8] The *Śikṣā Valli* of *Taittiriya* gives an exposition of *varṇa, svara* etc. In the *kośa-section* of *Brahmā valli* the Vedas are mentioned under *Manomayakośa*. *Chāndogya* alludes to Vedas in several places. Other *Upaniṣads* also speak of Veda with great reverence. No antagonism between *Saṁhitā* and *Brāhmaṇa* portions and *Upaniṣads* is felt anywhere in *Upaniṣads*. The *Ātharvaṇa Upaniṣad* clearly states that the entire *Veda is Parā Vidyā* or philosophical when the exposition of the *Akṣara* or the Supreme Reality is taken into account:[9] When one goes only by the ritualistic meaning then only it is *Aparā Vidyā*. The literature that constitute *Parā Vidyā* and *Aparā Vidyā* are not different. But, it is only the view points that are different. The same Vedic literature yields both the ritualistic meaning and philosophical meaning. Thus, not only the philosophical hymns such as *Asya Vāmīya Sūkta, Nāsadīya Sūkta, Puruṣa sūkta* etc., contain the basic ideas of Upaniṣadic thought but the entire Vedic literature yields a philosophical meaning.[10] This is clearly stated in *Ātharvaṇa Upaniṣad*. Sri Madhvācārya's tradition particularly draws our attention to this position.[11] Therefore, the idea of *Upaniṣads* being a reaction and a revolution against *Saṁhitā* and *Brāhmaṇas* is baseless. In this connection it may be noted that not only the basic thoughts of *Upaniṣads* are found in the Ṛgvedic hymns but even the key expressions, symbols, smile and metaphors prominently found in Upaniṣads are found in Ṛgveda. For instance, the simile of rivers flowing into the sea, the birds returning to their tree, the spokes of a chariot-wheel finding their support etc., are found in Ṛgveda.[12] The verse describing the two birds viz., soul and God sitting on the same tree is verbatum quoted in *Upaniāṣad* from the *Ṛgveda*.

The next important point that throws light on the relation between Saṁhitā and Brāhmaṇa thought and the Upaniṣadic thought is, the relation between *Karma* and *jnāna*. The wide-spread belief that *Upaniṣads* oppose *karma* or ritualistic and other religious activities is not well-founded. *Iśāvāsya* clearly declares that *karmas* must be performed.[13] The *Ātharvaṇa* statement that the *karmas* are like leaking boats does not advise the rejection of *karma* but only advocates the performance of *karma* with the right perspective.[14] The *karma* becomes *avara* or inferior only when it is performed with an eye on worldly benefits. It ceases to lead to sreyas or highest good. Through-out *Upaniṣads* we come across the statements that commend *karma* and that censure the *karma*. The first advocate *niṣkāma karma* while the latter censure *sakāmakarma*. Therefore, it is only a question of a proper perspective but not the total rejection of karma. Though the *niṣkāmakarma* concept is more explicitly stated in *Upaniṣads* it is implicit even in *Saṁhitā* and *Brāhmaṇas*. The progeny, wealth and cattle asked for are not the end but the means for a dedicated life. When Yājṅavalkya was asked whether he is undertaking the philosophical debate for the sake of cows and gold offered or for discovering the truth. Yājṅavalkya retorted he is doing it for both. He knew that how one can be utilised for the other. The great philosophical debate at king Janaka's court was held as a sequel to a great sacrifice. Therefore, *Upaniṣads* do not oppose *karma* as such but only advocate the right perspective. It is true that in Śri Śaṅkarācārya's tradition of the interpretation of *Upaniṣads*, *karma* is considered as opposed to *Jṅāna*. But not in the sense in which modern scholars envisage a reaction or clash between the protagonists of *karma* and *Jṅāna*. Because, *niṣkāmakarma* concept is utilised even in Śri Śaṅkara's tradition for *chittaśuddhi*. However, in Śri Madhvācārya's tradition *niṣkāmakarma* concept plays a very important role, which is fully supported by *Upaniāṣads*. Nachiketa's second boon clearly indicates the place of *karma* with the right perspective in the scheme of spiritual progress. If Nāchiketāgni sacrifice was also meant for the golden chain, then, there was no point in Nachiketa rejecting the golden chain when he came to the third boon. The three boons asked by him were not in supersession of the earlier ones. Therefore, there is no antagonism between *Saṁhitā* and *Brāhmaṇas,* and *Upaniṣads* on the ground of *jñāna-karma virodha* also. One may say that there has been a progress or an enlightened view of *karma* but not opposition. Traditional commentators help us to understand this delicate relation between *karma* and *jñāna*.

In fine, the *Upaniṣads* have their own scheme of giving an exposition of their thought. The central theme of *Upaniṣads* viz., giving an exposition of the Central Principle of the universe or the Supreme Reality is handled by all *Upaniṣads*. In addition to this, the *Upaniṣads* state the eligibility for spiritual pursuit, dedication to duty with a higher perspective, the nature of the soul and its states of waking, dream, deep sleep and liberation, creation of the physical world, mind, senses, vital air etc, mystic significance of 'Om', *Vyāhṛti, Gāyatri, Bāṛhatīsahasra* etc. meditation, *yoga methodology* and *nāḍi scheme*, *bhakti* & grace, eschatology of *Devayāna* and *Pitṛyāna*, the path towards liberation i. e., *arcirādimārga*, *laya*, subordination of other deities to the Supreme God, and the nature of final goal. Each *Upaniṣad* does not cover all these topics. They suppliment each other, elaborate each other confirm each other.

Their style of exposition is also unique. Their thoughts are presented in the form of question and answers, dialogue and narration. Similes, metaphors and illustrations are profusely employed. Symbolism is utilised. Three types of symbol are employed : (i) Nature symbols (ii) Ritual symbols, (in) Mystic sound syllables like 'Om'- Many of the similes, metaphors and symbols are inherited from *Saṁhitā* and Brāhmaṇas. Good many philosophical terms and expressions are also inherited from Vedas. Many Upaniṣadic terms acquired an expanded or modified meaning later when the systems of Vedānta developed. One has to be very careful in not reading a later meaning in Upanisadic terms. For instance, the terms *Māyā* and *Avidyā* have acquired altogether different meaning in later Vedānta systems. The words *Upādāna, adhiṣṭhāna* etc., also acquired different meanings as a result of *Vivarta* theory of causation developed later. It is not correct to read these meanings in the Upaniāṣadic usage of these words.

9.10.12 Message of the Upaniṣads

From the above short sketch the reader may have got a glimpse of the treasures that are strewn broadcast in die Upaniṣads. The value of these ancient records for all, seekers after truth can scarcely be over-estimated. Their message of strength, fearlessness, and hope is as necessary for us now as it was for those who lived in the past. Their appeai is universal, for they probe the very depths of the inner being of man. The Upaniṣads call upon every man and woman, in whatever station of life, to stand up and assert their divine heritage. In this they recognize no limits, geographical, racial, or any other. They are the greatest unifying factor in the world for all time. They break all the fetters of mankind and raise men to their true status as 'children of immortality' (*Śve. U.*, 11.5). 'The regeneration of man the brute into man the God' is their ambitious programme. They are not unethical, as, on account of their not preaching sin, they are supposed to be by some, but supra-ethical. They only, of all the religious literatures of the world, give us the *rationale* of morality-why we should do good to others. Because we are all one! In helping others, we help ourselves; and in hurting them, we hurt none but ourselves.

The Upaniṣads help us to grasp the significance of the lives and teachings of the great prophets of all religions. In their light, we understand that Christ's exhortation, 'Love thy neighbour as thyself', was not a mere figure of speech. We must love him, for he, like the rest of the world, is literally our Self.

The Upaniṣads unflinchingly speak out truths, regardless of consequences. They do not even spare themselves. 'After studying the scriptures and realizing the Truth, an intelligent person should discard them entirely, as one who cares for the rice does with the chaff' (*Amṛtabindu U.*, 18). They declare that it is open to any one to become a *ṛṣi*, a perfected saint. The Upaniṣads are the Magna Charta of human rights. They ask us to desist from our mad search for happiness in the outside world; for the muskdeer will never find the source of that fragrance, which drives him hither and thither, outside of himself. 'There is no bliss in finite things, the Infinite alone is bliss' (*Chā.U.*, VII.23). Whatever bliss there is, is borrowed from the Self. 'On a particle of this very bliss other beings live' (*Bṛ.U.*, IV.3.32). No wonder Schopenhauer remarked: 'In the whole world there is no study so beneficial and so elevating as that of the Upaniṣads. It has been the solace of my life - it will be the solace of my death.'

The goal as well as 'the way has been pointed out to us by the Upaniṣads: 'Know that one Ātman alone, and give up all other talk. This is the bridge to immortality' (*Mu. U.*, II.2.5). It is now left to us to move on. Let us not be overwhelmed with the thought that we are powerless. Are we not potentially the infinite Spirit whose glories even the Vedas can at best only indicate negatively by the method of *neti neti* (not this, not this)? In the words of Swami Vivekananda, 'This infinite power of the Spirit brought to bear upon matter evolves material development, made to act upon thought evolves intellectuality, and made to act upon itself makes of man a god.' We must struggle patiently, perseveringly. The well-being of the modern world depends on a proper understanding of the Upaniṣadic teachings and on their sincere application to the practical problems of our daily life. Thus only can materiality, which is the common enemy of the world, be conquered, and love, instead of hate, be our guiding principle. Even age-long darkness, as Sri Ramakrishna used to say, disappears as soon as a light is brought in. It behoves us, like true followers of the Upaniṣads, to assert our birthright and, armed with the strength of realization, make a determined effort to establish the reign of peace and harmony on earth.

References

1. Vide. S. Dasgupta, *A History of Indian Philosophy*, Vol. I. Motilal Banarasidass, Delhi, 1975. p. 30
2. K. U. Morgan, *The Religion of the Hindus,* New York, 1953, p. 308.
3. Cf. "The *Chhandogya Brahmana* of the *Sama Veda* where of this Upaniṣad forms a part, contains ten chapters (*prapāṭhakas*): of these, the first two are called *Chāndogya Mantra Brāhmaṇa,* the rest constitute *Chāndogya Upaniṣad,*" Rajendralal Maitra & R. E. Roer, *The Twelve Principal Upanisads,* Bombay, 1906, p. 469, fn. 2
4. Grabe's article "*Hindu Monism*" Q. S. Dasgupta, *A History of Indian Philosophy,* Vol. 1, p. 33
5. *Ibid.*, p. 78
6. The story of Maitreyi and Yajnavalkya (*Bṛhadāraṇyaka Upaniṣad*, II., 4) and that of Satyakāma son of Jābāla & his teacher (Chāndogya Upaniṣad, IV. 4).
7. *A History of Indian Philosophy,* Vol. I. p. 35
8. वाच: ऋग् रस: । (छा. उ. 1.1.2) ॥ ऋग्वेद एव पुष्पम् (छा. उ. 3. 1.1) ॥ तस्य यजुरेव शिर: । ऋग् दक्षिण: पक्ष: । (तै. उ. 2.8) ॥ वेदा: सर्वाङ्गानि सत्यमायतनम् । (के. उ. 4.4) ॥
9. द्वे विद्ये वेदितव्ये .... परा चैवापरा च । तत्रापरा । ऋग्वेदो यजुर्वेद: सामवेदोऽथर्ववेद: ..... । अत परा । यया तदक्षरमधिगम्यते ॥ (आथ. उ. 1.4-5) ॥
10. विज्ञानेन वा ऋग्वेदं विजानाति । (छा. उ. 7.7.1) ॥

ब्रह्मणा वाव सर्वे वेदा महीयन्ते । (तै. उ. 1.5.3) ॥
सर्वे वेदा यत्पदमामनन्ति । (कठ उ. 1.2.14) ॥

11. ऋगाद्या अपरा विद्या यदा विष्णोर्न वाचषाः । ता एव परमा विद्या यदा विष्णोस्तु वाचका ॥ (आंथ. उ. भणा 1.4) ॥

12. समानमूर्वं नद्यः पृणन्ति । (ऋ. वे. 2.35.3) ॥ वयो न वसतीरुप (ऋ. वे. 1.25.4) ॥ या आपो दिव्या उत वा स्रावन्ति ..... समुद्रार्था याः शुचयः पावका । (ऋ. वे. 7.49.2) ॥ रथानां न येऽराः सनाभयो .... (ऋ. वे. 10.78.4) ॥

13. कुर्वन्नेवेह कर्माणि जिजीविषेत् शतं समाः ॥ (ई. उ. 2) ॥

14. प्लवा ह्येते अदृढा यज्ञरूपा अष्टादशोक्तमवरं येषु कर्म ॥ (आथ. उ. 2.6) ॥

Chapter - X

The Vedāṅga Literature

10.1 Introduction

The Vedāṅgas are a class of literature auxiliary to the proper cultivation and understanding of the Vedic texts and their application in rituals. The close connection between the Veda and its six auxiliaries is beautifully brought out in the following verse:

> छन्दः पादौ तु वेदस्य हस्तौ कल्पोऽथ पथ्यते ।
> ज्योतिषामयनं चक्षुः निरुक्तं श्रोत्रमुच्यते ।।
> शिक्षा घ्राणं तु वेदस्य मुख व्याकरणं स्मृतं
> तस्मात् साङ्गमधीत्यैव ब्रह्मलोके महीयते ।।

i.e "*Chandas* (Metre) is said to be the feet of the Veda, *Kalpa* (ritual) the hands, *Jyotiṣa* (Astronomy) the eye, *Nirukta* (Etymology) the ear, *Śikṣā* (phonetics), the nose and the *Vyākaraṇa* (Grammar) the mouth. Thereby, one is advised the Vedic lore with its six auxiliaries for a place in the Brahmaloka." Although the word '*vedāṅga*' literary means 'limb (*aṅga*) of the Veda', and the Vedāṅgas in the orthodox view, form part of the Veda, which is 'Śruti' or 'divine revelation', the only working definition of which is: 'the sum-total of Mantras and Brāhmaṇas'. The

Vedāṅgas, which originally meant 'subjects of instruction in a Vedic school, subserving and aiding the preservation of the Veda', fall under the category of 'Smṛti', though euphemistically called 'the limbs of the Veda.'

10.1.1. The Genesis of the Vedāṅgas

During the Brāhmaṇa period, the *mantras* of the Vedas were preserved by oral tradition only. When, at the end of this period, the spoken language drifted far away from the language of the Śruti which was felt to be as antique as it was sacred, the necessity naturally arose of preserving intact the inner substances as well as the external form of the Śruti. Even in the Brāhmaṇas, there are statements that violence is done to the meaning of Śruti passages if they are pronounced improperly. It was therefore felt necessary to lay down general rules on the proper pronunciation and accentuation of the *mantras* and their meter, especially when differences in their pronunciation were sanctioned by the traditions of the different seats or schools of Brāhmaṇic learning. Thus were formulated *śikṣā* and *chandas*.

With regard to the inner substance of the *mantras*, the difficulties were far greater - a situation testified to by the fact that there appear different ritual contexts or liturgical settings for the Ṛg-Vedic *mantras* even in the later Vedic Saṁhitās and endless discussions occur in the Brāhmaṇas regarding their meaning and the propriety of their employment in particular contexts. *Vyākaraṇa* and *nirukta* tried to wrestle with the problems of exegesis of the *mantras*, and *kalpa* and *jyotiṣa* tackled the question of the 'how and when' of their liturgical employment in sacrifices. Thus the six Vedāṅgas were formulated and systematized within the curricula and syllabi of the various Vedic schools.

10.1.2 Literary Style of Vedāṅgas

The Vedāṅgas are composed for the most part in the *sūtra* (aphoristic) style; even when some of them (like the works of

Śaunaka) are composed in mixed *Ślokas,* they are quoted as 'Sūtras' and are ascribed to authors who are otherwise well known as Sūtra-authors (*sūtrakāras*). It is noteworthy that the Vedāṅgas inaugurated a new literary epoch, with their unique *Sūtra* style.

The word '*sūtra*' means 'thread, string or clue.' A Sūtra work strings together the salient points of a text or subject, systematically, in short sentences compressed into the most concise form. The many Brāhmaṇa and Brāhmaṇa-like passages in the midst of the Sūtras make it very probable that the *sūtra* style developed from the prose of the Brāhmaṇas, which consists almost exclusively of short sentences and leaves unsaid all that is supposed to be explained in oral presentation and instruction.

The mass of details in various subjects - ritualistic, religious, and philosophical - that accumulated in the later Saṁhitās and Brāhmaṇas and in the floating tradition, had reached such staggering proportions that it must have imposed an unbearable strain on the memory of the Vedic student. The urgent need of compressing and reducing this vast and diffuse material into a reasonably small size and giving it a systematic shape was answered by the formulation of the *sūtra* style.

10.1.3 The Vedāṅgas in early Literature

The earliest reference to the number of the Vedāṅgas as six occurs in the *Ṣaḍviṁśa Brāhmaṇa* (IV.7) of the *Sāma-Veda*, where they are said to constitute the limbs of the goddess Svāhā. The *Āpastamba Kalpa-Sūtra* (II.4.8), in a different order than the usual, the *Mundaka Upanisad* (I.1.5), and the *Caraṇavyūha* enumerate the six Vedāṇgas, in the traditional order, while the *Manu Smṛti* (III.185) mentions only their number as six.[1]

Obviously, the Vedāṅgas, as subjects of study, must have interested the *ṛṣis* of the Brāhmaṇas and the Saṁhitās, not excluding the Ṛg-Veda Saṁhitā from the earliest times. The

Vedāṅga doctrines must, then, be sought for in the Saṁhitās, Brāhmaṇas and the Sūtras, step by step, rather than in the short and barren tracts, traditionally designated as the Vedāṅgas and appended later to the manuscripts of the Vedas. These tracts, mistaken in the beginning by scholars for the real Vedāṅgas, represent but the last attempts, though not with full success, to abridge the simplified earlier developments in their respective fields, under titles sanctioned by antiquity.

In the *Chāndogya Upaniṣad* (VII.1), Nārada, while detailing the extent of his knowledge, refers to (i) *Nakṣatra-vidyā,* (ii) the *veda* of the Vedas, (iii) *deva-vidyā,* and (iv) *brahma-vidyā,* of which the first evidently means *jyotiṣa* or astronomy; the last three have been explained as meaning, respectively, (ii) *vyākaraṇa,* (iii) *nirukta,* and (iv) *śikṣā, chandas* and *kalpa*. According to a commentator on the *Bṛhadāraṇyaka Upaniṣad* (II.4.10), just as 'Itihāsa' and 'Purāṇa' in the sense of 'epic stories' and 'sections on topics like creation and the first cause' form integral parts of the Brāhmaṇas, so are the Vedāṅgas incorporated in the Brāhmaṇas under different and unusual heads such as *Upaniṣads* (mysteries), *ṣlokas* (verses), *sūtras* (rules), *vyākaraṇa* (comment, and *anu-vyākaraṇa* (explanations) which are the titles of particular Brāhmaṇa passages. We shall, therefore, in dealing with each Vedāṅga separately, try to trace, however briefly, the beginning of an interest in it right from the days of the *Ṛg-Veda Saṁhitā* to those of the Sūtras.

10.2 Śikṣā (Phonetics)

10.2.1 Pre-pratiṣākhya Literature

As the Vedas were transmitted in the early days by oral tradition, and not writing, it is but natural that interest in phonetics should be evinced right from the very beginning. Vāc or personified speech is celebrated in one whole hymn in the *Ṛg-Veda* (X.125), where the deity Vāc describes herself, and the major portion of another hymn (*Ṛg-Veda* x.71) is devoted to the same deity. Particularly interesting is the verse (*Ṛg-Veda* I.164.45): 'Speech is measured out in four parts (steps, stages or grades)... The three[2] of them which are set in secret, they do not emit (or circulate); the fourth (part) of speech, men speak.'[3]

Glender[4] thinks that the fourfold division of speech is on the lines of that of the Purussa in *Ṛg-Veda* X.90.3: 'Three parts of it represent the immortal portion in heaven and the fourth part of it is all these creatures.' He refers to a passage in the *Kāṭhaka Saṁhitā* (II.79.9) which says that speech entered into men and the gods, and the surplus went over to the trees and plants. The *Maitrāyaṇi Saṁhitā* (III.70.16) also speaks of the fourfold division of speech.[5]

According to Professor Varma,[6] three stages in the development of language are mentioned in the *Ṛg-Veda*: (i) inarticulate speech (I.164.65); (ii) primitive articulate speech (X.71.1); and (iii) language proper (X.71.2). As regards his criticisms that 'a strict cleavage between inarticulate and articulate speech may be open to question' and that 'the creation of language by men, if strictly intended, may suggest that language was independent of natural development', the writer thinks that the *Ṛg-Veda* does not lay down such a strict cleavage and suggests not the creation but only the manifestation in an articulate form of (thought) language by men.

The *Aitareya Brāhmaṇa* says '*Vāc* is verily an ocean;' it is never exhausted'. It prescribes (XII.73) *madhyamā vāc* (intermediate speech) for the *stotriya* verses, as refining the soul.[7]

The *Aitareya Araṇyaka* tries to throw light on the distinctive and mutually distinguishable aspects of sounds through different comparisons. In II.2.1, it compares first the consonants to nights and the vowels to days; next the consonants are compared to the body, the voice to the soul, and the fricatives to the breath. This and similar other passages (III.2.2 and 5) hinted at the comparative solidity of the plosives as they are compared to the earth or the bones. When, further, the vowels are compared to the marrow and the semi-vowels to flesh and blood, the idea seems to be to indicate the character of the vowel as the basic sound in the theory of syllabification. Another remarkable passage (III.1.5) reveals the advanced stage of phonetic studies, when *Saṁhitā* is described as a pronunciation of two syallables, neither entirely separated nor united - a view acceptable to modern science, namely, that basically syallabic division is a relative one.

The traditional title for phonetics '*Śikṣā* ' appears for the first time in the *Taittirīya Upaniṣad* (I.2), which gives a bare enumeration of the six elements constituting it, namely, *varṇa* (individual sounds), *svara* (*accent*), *mātra* (quantity), *bala* (organs of pronunciation), *sāman* (delivery), and *santāna* (euphonic laws). According to Sāyaṇa, the 'midway' position of the chapter on phonetics (Śikṣānuvāka) between the ceremonial and philosophical portions (since this Upaniṣad forms part of the *Taittirīya Āraṇyaka*) ensures its utility for both of them.

The meagreness of the material on *Śikṣā* in the Brāhmaṇas and Araṇyakas is probably due to its being supereseded and lost by the rise of the Prātiśākhyas later. Its scope was restricted, so far, to the teaching of correct pronunciation involving rudimentary instruction in individual sounds, accent, quantity and the chanting of Vedic verses as seen in the *Taittirīya Upaniṣad* above.

10.2.2 The Prātiśākhya Literature

The Prātiśākhyas were treatises formally embodying the peculiarities of accent, of *saṁhitā* and *krama* (order) readings of *pragṛhya* vowels, and of the separations or words in particular schools. The so-called irregularities and exceptions that were thus preserved were more apparent than real, as they were due not so much to corruptions as to the elasticity and freedom of the old sacred language which was fast becoming obsolete, and were, in certain cases, a record of ancient dialectal differences. The general laws formulated therefrom became later the phonetic basis of a grammar like that of Pāṇini and thus a scientific study of language was begun.

Since a commentator like Viṣṇumitra speaks of the *Ṛk Prātiśākhya* as a *pārṣada,* the distinction between *śākhā, caraṇa* and *pariṣad* must be stated. The word '*Prātiśākhya*' means literally 'belonging to each *śākha*'. *Śākha* does not mean a 'school' or 'a portion of the Veda', though it may be used loosely in this sense, but a particular traditional text or recension of the Veda, held as authoritative in a particular Vedic school. '*Caraṇa*' indicates a body of people who, though pledged to the reading and study of a particular *śākhā*, have a wider curriculum which may include other texts like a law-book, which will go under the name of the *caraṇa,* but cannot be comprised under a *śākhā*. Distinct from both *śākhā* and *caraṇa* is the *pariṣad*, which, according to the law-codes, is an assembly of Brāhmaṇas, the members of which fulfil certain conditions as regards age and qualification. In other words, it is a Brāhmaṇic settlement to the traditional library of whose members may belong not only a Prātiśākhya, but other texts as well. The *Bṛhadāraṇyaka* (VI.2) refers to a *pariṣad* of the *Pañcālas* which was competent to give decisions on all points on which their advice may be sought by the people under their jurisdiction. Members of any *caraṇa* might belong to such a *pariṣad*.

10.2.3 Number of Prātiśākhyas

Professor Varma holds that there is no evidence to suppose that there were once as many Prātiśākhyas as there were *śākhās* of each Veda and that a Prātiśākhya was a treatise on phonetics applicable to a group of *śākhās* of a particular Veda. Although we have now only one Prātiśākhya extant belonging to each Veda, each of them belongs avowedly to one *śākhā* only of each of the four Vedas. The *Pratijñā-pariśiṣṭa* says that for the fifteen *śākhās* of the Vājasaneyins there were as many law-codes and manuals for the regulation of accents; which latter description could only suit text-books like the Prātiśākhyas. Similarly, Kumārila in his *Tantra-vārttika* (V.1.3) says that for each *caraṇa,* there was a special text or recension of the Gṛhya and Dharma law-code, just in the same manner as there was a Prātiśākhya. It seems reasonable therefore to hold that, although everyone of the many *śākhās* may not have possessed a complete Prātiśākhya, one Prātiśākhya for each of the principal *śākhās* at least existed separately. For example, the Prātiśākhya of Śaunaka is so perfect and complete, and quotes the opinions of so many other authorities on grammar and phonetics, that it appears extremely probable that his work superseded the Prātiśākhyas of the other *śākhās* of the *Ṛgveda*, and is therefore held as authoritative for the two *śākhās* of the *Ṛgveda* that have survived, namely the Śākala and the Bāṣkala. It is, besides, very artificial to take the word '*śākhā*' in the title 'Prātiśākhya' in the sense of 'the whole group of *śākhās* of a Veda', instead of in the very natural sense of a ''*śākhā*.

10.2.4 Character of the Prātiśākhyas

The rigorous insistence of the Prātiśākhyas on accurate pronunciation inevitably implied a minite observation of phonetic phenomena in the recitation of Vedic texts. No wonder the title '*śikṣā*' itself came to be applied later to the Prātiśākhyas. We may demarcate between the respective spheres of the Śikṣās and the Prātiśākhyas thus : The sounds of the alphabet enumerated in the Śikṣās (68 or 64 in number) or the rules of pronunciation taught by them are common to secular and Vedic pronunciation and apply to all *śākhās*, but the Prātiśākhyas specify or select only the sounds peculiar to their own *śākhā*. The proper scope of the Prātiśākhyas was the specification for, and adaptation to, their own *śākhā* of the sounds which they do not trouble to enumerate, evidently presupposing such enumeration in earlier Śikṣā treatises of a general character. The traditional object of the Prātiśākhyas is also to explain the mutual relation of the *pada* and *saṁhitā-pāṭhas*.

If phonetics were the sole basis of the Prātiśākhyas, they would have treated the individual sounds in relation to the *saṁhitā-pāṭha* only; but the starting point of their observations is the *pada-pāṭha*, where the *pada* appears in its strictly grammatical form including the suffix and the terminations. So grammar also was partly the basis of these texts. No surprises occasioned therefore by the statement of the *Āthrvaṇa Prātiśākhya* (I.1) that its object is a description of the characteristic features of the four parts of speech, namely, the noun, the verb, the prefix and the particle in the *saṁhitā* and the *pada-pāṭhas*.

10.2.5 Chronology of the Prātiśākhyas

Only a relative chronology of the Prātiśākhyas can be attempted here.[8] Professor Varma discovered that a passage in the *Taittirīya Prātiśākhya* on the definition of high and low accent (XXII.9-10) is explained word by word in the *Mahābhāṣya* of Patanjali commenting on Pāṇini, I.2.29-30. Since elsewhere also Patanjali refers to the Taittirīyas, it is very probable that he knew the *Taittirīya Prātiśākhya*. So 150 B.C., the accepted definite date of Patanjali, becomes its lower limit. Since the *Ṛk Prātiśākhya*, the oldest of the Prātiśākhyasm quotes Yāska, the upper limit is 500 B.C. (if not earlier). The *Ṛk Prātiśākhya* and the *Vājasaneyi Prātiśākhya*, with their crude verbosity in contrast with the concise style of Pāṇini (400 B.C.), are admitted as pre-Pāṇinian.

As regards the *Taittirīya Prātiśākhya*, although a few grammatical terms used by Pāṇini are known to it, its substance must be pre-Pāṇinian, because there is no trace of the influence of Pāṇini in its treatment. The core of the *Āthrvaṇa Prātiśākhya* was probably earlier, and in no case later than the *Vājasaneyi*

Prātiśākhya. The later phases or parts of the *Taittirīya*, *Āthrvaṇa* and *Vājasaneyi Prātiśākhyas* seem to be post-Pāṇini. Last of all comes the Prātiśākhya of the - the *Ṛktantra-vyākaraṇa* - which, nevertheless, seems to have been composed when Sanskrit, to which it refers as a *bhāṣā*, was yet a spoken language.

The extant Prātiśākhya of the *Ṛg-Veda* is the *Śākala Prātiśākhya* of Śaunaka which professes to follow the Śaiśirīya Śākhā, a sub-branch of the Śākala Śākhā. There is no manuscript of the *Ṛg-Veda* in which the rules of this Prātiśākhya are followed, probably because these rules were not intended for any written literature at all.

The *Taittirīya Prātiśākhya* of the *Black Yajur-Veda* quotes several *caraṇas* of this Veda and alludes in its latest parts to the Mīmāṁsakas, not mentioned in any other Prātiśākhya. Chapters II, VIII and XVI of the work seem to be the older ones, constituting the core, as it were, while chapters I and XVII-XIX appear to be later additions.

The extant Prātiśākhya of the *White Yajur-Veda*, though known as the *Vājasaneyi Prātiśākhya* belongs to the Kātyāyanīyas, a subdivision of the Mādhyandina śākhā, which is itself a sub-branch of the Vājasaneyins. Some *sūtras*, of this Prātiśākhya are repeated word by word in Pāṇini.

The Prātiśākhya of the *Atharva-Veda*, called also the *Śaunakīya Caturādhyāyikā*[9], is a treatise in four chapters belonging to the *Śaunakīya* school, a *caraṇa* of the Atharva-Vedins. The special references to the *Ātharvaṇa* sacrifices and rituals preclude the supposition that the Śaunaka of the *Ṛk Prātiśākhya* had anything to do with this Prātiśākhya, and yet there is some evidence of a connection with Śākalya and Śākalas.

The *Ṛktantra-vyākaraṇa,* the Prātiśākhya of the *Sāma-Veda*, is post-Pāṇinian though not as recent as it is supposed. The *Puṣpa-Sūtra*, another Prātiśākhya of the *Sāma-Veda*, contains the text and the melodies of the *sāman* chants and observations on phonetic and linguistic facts.

10.2.6 The Śikṣā Works

1. The *Pāṇinīya Śikṣā* is a *śloka* (verse) compilation ascribed to Piṅgala, the younger brother of Pāṇini, whose opinions it professes to follow, though it mentions his name once only in the beginning and at the end. Its *ślokas*, numbering sixty, are very modern as compared to those in Śauṇaka's *Prātiśākhya*. A smaller version of it, consisting of twenty-two verses, occurs in the *Agni Purāṇa*. It does not mention even the name of Pāṇini. It could not be the prototype of the Prātiśākhyas, because its views on r, ṛ, and ḷ differ radically from those of the Prātiśākhyas. Even its substance does not belong to a very early period, as it is common to several other Śikṣās. Nevertheless, being the most complete of all the Śikṣās, extant in two recensions belonging to the *Ṛg-Veda* and the *Yajur-Veda,* it has wielded great influence over the other Śikṣās which borrow freely from it.

The number of Śikṣās known comes to sixty-five in all. In the *Śikṣā-saṅgraha* (Benaras Edn.) are published thirty-one. Nineteen others, in manuscript, have been examined by Professor Varma. If the common material borrowed by a number of them from the *Pāṇinīya Śikṣā* is ignored, the residuum contains original discussions of certain important phonetic topics, not treated in the Prātiśākhyas, such as the detailed account of *svarabhakti* after the *svarita* accent. Many others, however, are just catalogues of certain sounds in the Vedas. For example, hte *Māṇḍavī-Śikṣā* gives a list of words in the *Yajur-Veda* containing the consonant *b*, and the famour *Bhāradvāja* and *Siddhānta Śikṣā* catalogue certain words containing different sounds in an alphabetical order. The Śikṣās, especially the minor ones, have received accretions of matter from time to time, just like the Prātiśākhyas which they presuppose. A few of them betray the influence of the Prakritis too. Neither the locale nor the age of the Śikṣās can thus be determined with certainty for lack of internal evidence and the corruption of the texts.

Not many Śikṣās of the *Ṛg-Veda* are known. The *Svara-vyanjana Śikṣā*, the only important one, quotes from, and follows the, terminology of the *Ṛk Prātiśākhya* and is post-Pāṇinian. The *Śamāna Śikṣā* is just a catalogue of the elisions of the *visarga* in the *Ṛg-Veda*.

2. The *Yājnavalkya Śikṣā*, most complete among the Śikṣās of the *White Yajur-Veda,* cites *Yājnavalkya* as an authority and was probably composed not by him, but by a more recent authro (5th to 10th Cent. A.D.). Other fairly complete Śikṣās are the *Pārāśarī* and the *Amoghānandinī*. The *Vāsiṣṭhi*, different from its namesake which belongs to the *Black Yajur-Veda,* is but loosely called a Śikṣā being a selection from the *Sarvānukramaṇī*. The *Varṇaratnadīpikā* is evidently a modern work.

Among the Śikṣās of the *Black Yajur-Veda*, that of the Cārāyaṇīya school is a late work, as it treats of classical metres, while those of the Taittiriya school have advanced the study of phonetics considerably with their penetrating observation on quantity and accent, and were presumably composed in South India, the acknowledged home of Vedic studies in the modern period. The *Vaidikābharaṇa* by Gārgya Gopāla Yajvan (14th to 15th Cent. A.D.), is an extremely valuable work on the Śikṣās in general and the Taittirīya Śikṣās in particular, because it not only quotes from many of the latter that are extant, but also others yet to be discovered.

3. The *Nārada Śikṣā* of the *Sāma-Veda* is one of oldest and most profound Śikṣās treating principally of the accents of the *Sāma-Veda* in their relation to musical notes. According to it, there are *grāmas* (musical gamuts), the *ṣadja* and the *madhyama* current on earth and the *gāndhāra* existing only in heaven. The

Nāṭya-śāstra of Bharata (5th Cent. A.D.) employs just those terms for *mūrchanās* (modulations) attributed to Nārada in the *Saṅgīta-ratnākara* (13th Cent. A.D.). The core at least of this Śikṣā, then, may well be earlier than fifth century A.D. The *Lomaśī Śikṣa*, makes general but pithy observations on doubling. The *Gautamī Śikṣa* exhibits a deep insight into doubling and consonant-groups.

4. The *Maṇḍūkī*, the Śikṣā of the *Atharva-Veda,* quotes freely from that Veda, but it treats of accent common to all the Vedas, especially the Sāma-Veda. It is probably contemporary with, or posterior to, the *Yājnavalkya Śikṣā*, as it contains much material common to it and other Śikṣās of the *White Yajur-Veda.*

10.2.7 Phonetic Observations in the Vedāṅga Literature

When the Prātiśākhyas and Pāṇini deal with phonology and Pāṇini treats of morphology, their observations are based on the linguistic phenomena of a living language used by the cultured and educated classes for conversation and literature. The pictures of the pronunciation of the Sanskrit language present in corroborated by its phonetic structure and *sandhi* rules, the evidence of the inscription, parallel phenomena in the living dialects, and the principles of linguistics. The observations of the Indian phoneticians in general are, on the whole, sound and realistic, and the linguistic facts of the primitive Indo-Aryan noted by them provide a surer basis for modern studies of Indo-Aryan linguistics than the transcriptions of ancient scribes on which the philologist usually has to rely.

Contributions by Indian phoneticians to linguistics are : (i) The rules on syllabification which are important, because variation in the affinity of one sound for another is a fundamental predisposing factor in linguistic change. Very striking are the minute details regarding *abhinidhāna* (incomplete articulation), the 'pivot' of the Indian theory of Syllabification, chiefly responsible for profound changes in the consonant-system of primitive Indo-Aryan. (ii) The noting of proninciation of *y* and *v* in different positions. (iii) The nasalization of finals, as noticed by authors from Śākalya downwards, is a striking fact in the living languages. In pre-classical and classical Sanskrit, the consonantal element of the *anusvāra* was more predominant, but later the vocalic element became more prominent. When *anusvāra* arose before a fricative, it was a case of *abhinidhāna*. (iv) Quantity is described in a remarkably accurate manner, and the various views noted on quantity are on the whole sound. (v) The insertion of a plosive in the group-fricative+nasal consonant (prescribed by the *Taittirīya Prātiśākhya)* will explain modern Indian forms like 'Viṭṭhal' for Viṣṇu through Viṣṇu (compare the modern Bengali: Biṣṭu). (vi) The divergent treatment of Sanskrit plosive+nasal consonant is explained by the observation on the *yamas*. That, in some dialects, there existed actually a tendency for strong nasality in illustrated by the Pali *panna* for Sanskrit *prajñā,* which led to the view that the *yamas* belonged to the preceding syllable. Similarly, the partial nasalization of *h* in *brahma* permitted by the *Ātharvaṇa Prātiśākhya* and the prohibition of the nasalization of fricatives in the Śikṣās seem, each of them, to be based on the observation of different contemporary phenomena among the dialects. (vii) The number of vowels as given by the various Indian authorities is as follows : 13 in the *Ṛk* and *Ātharvaṇa Prātiśākhyas*: 16 in the *Taittirīya Prātiśākhya*; 22 in the *Pāṇiniya Śikṣā*; and 23 in the *Vājasaneyi Prātiśākhya* and the *Ṛktantra-vyākaraṇa*. The variations are due to the fact, according to Ghosh, that the and *Ṛk* and *Ātharvaṇa Prātiśākhyas* omit *pluta* vowels and so does the *Taittirīya Prātiśākhya*, in the case of some vowels. (viii) The different organs of pronunciation and the sounds produced by them were carefully noted by Indian authorities. For example: (a) The Prātiśākhyas all state that the place of origin or '*r*', which according to them is alveolar or dental, is the teeth or the teeth-ridge. The *Pāṇiniya Śikṣā* however, holds it to be cerebral.

(b) Candragohim is the one ancient Indian author who describes the prominent part played by the human tongue in the pronunciation of sounds. Particular sounds are even assigned by him to specific parts of the tongue. Thus the tip of the tongue produces the dentals; the blade, the cerebrals; and the middle of the tongue the palatals. This very assignment is given by modern phoneticians. Other ancient Indian authorities only mention the places of pronunciation, called '*sthāna*' by Pāṇini, such as the lips, teeth etc. But these are only passive agents, the active one being the tongue.

A few of the specific contributions of the Śikṣās are : (i) Interesting details regarding the ideal conditions for correct pronunciation are found in the *Yājñavalkya* and *Nārada Śikṣās*, such as sound health, calm temperament, absence of nervousness, and good teeth and lips. (ii) The relationship of the vowel and the consonant is analysed in detail. (iii) They make the first unambiguous statement that the nature of the Vedic accent was musical and that the later seven musical notes, *ṣaḍja* etc., were evolved from the three Vedic accents, *udātta* etc. Their remarks on the relation of accent to quantity are interesting. (iv) The observation by some Śikṣās that *svarabhakti* becomes an independent syllable after the *svarita* accent should stimulate research into those undiscovered dialects in which the phenomenon may have occurred. (v) Although the *Taittirīya Prātiśākhya* (I.34) speaks of the *anusvāra* as being only short, the Śikṣās state that it was long after a short vowel, and short after a long vowel. This will explain why some modern Indian vernaculars like Nepali and Punjabi have a long vowel without the *anusvāra*, e.g. *mās* for *māṁsa,* and have preserved the *anusvāra* after a short vowel, e.g. *vañjh* for *vaṁśa*. (vi) The Śikṣās carried further the investigations into doubling, incomplete articulation (*abhinidhāna*), and consonant-groups. For example, the *Cārāyaṇīya Śikṣā* states that final consonants in *sandhi* are to be doubled. This is correct with reference to pronunciation in Sanskrit which was in a sense academic, but in another sense a living language current among certain educated circles. Certain Prakrit dialects show the doubling of semi-final consonants, i.e. pre-suffixal finals or finals of prefixes. For example, for Sanskrit *utsava,* we have *ucchava* in Māgadhī and Śaurasenī side by side with *ussava* in Ardha-Māgadhī. Similarly, the remarks of the Śikṣās on the doubling of *s* and *h* may have occurred in some contemporary dialects.

10.3 Nirukta (Etymology)

Nirukta is represented, according to tradition, by a single work, the *Nirukta* of Yāska, which itself states, 'Without this (science), there can be no understanding of the (Vedic) *mantras*' (I.15). However, it is a conmentary on an older list of Vedic words, called the *Nighaṅṭu* or the *Nighaṅṭuka*, to each of which one or more illustrative Vedic passages ought to be understood as attached. The lists and the commentary are both, as constituting one work, ascribed loosely to Yāska, either because he preserved them together, or because the word-lists were studied in his particular Vedic school, or because they existed in his family. Skold believes the Yāska was the author, or rather the collector, of the *Nirukta*, in the sense that it is a commentary on the *Nighaṅṭu*.

10.3.1 Pre-Nirukta Etymological Literature

Yāska himself mentions many earlier *niruktakāras* like Śākapūṇi. Earlier still, the Saṁhitās, Brāhmaṇas, Āraṇyakas and Upaniṣads offer as many as about 600 etymologized words, through etymologies proper synonymous expressions, explanation of one Vedic word by another, and brief annotations of whole verses and hymns. This etymologizing is sometimes done by implication as in *tvaṣṭā takāṣat vajram* (Ṛgveda. x.61.6) Yāska's borrowing from this earlier material is quite evident, though he probably was the first to formulate general principles of etymology. A large number of these etymological equations are due to folk etymology and priestly speculation, but some of them turn out to be surprisingly scientific from the modern linguistic point of view. For example, the *Bṛhadāraṇyaka Upaniṣad* (IV.2.2) has : '*Indho ha vai nāmaiṣah.....; etam indhaṁ santam Indra ity-ācakāṣate.*' The identification here of the two words '*indha*' and '*indra*' perhaps unconsciously presumes the knowledge of the linguistic law that the presence of an '*r*' in a consonant-cluster has often resulted in an aspiration.

The desire to glorify the sacrifice often dictated the necessity of explaining through a derivation, somehow brought into relation with a myth or legend, the various names of the sacrifice, the materials employed in it, and the priests, gods and hostile demons associated with it. Curiously some of the myths and legends do give the clue to the right derivation of the words, and must have been specially designed to make the etymological process less dry to the ritual-minded priests for whom they were primarily intended. The Saṁhitās of the *Black* and *White Yajur-Veda* are virtually liturgical Saṁhitās and therefore constitute a still earlier and important source of etymological equations. The *Taittirīya* and *Maitrāyaṇi Saṁhitās* contain a largest number of Ṛg-Vedic words etymologized. Among the Brāhmaṇas the *Śatapatha* and *Aitareya*, and among the Araṇyakas, the *Aitareya* are notable in this respect. Among the Upaniṣads, only the *Bṛhadāraṇyaka* and *Chāndogya* take now and then to etymologizing.

On the basis of the etymological principles formulated by Yāska, and accepted by modern scholars, these etymologies may be classified thus: (1) Etymologies rendered probable both by the phonetic and semantic history of the word. This principle stresses the value of both sound and sense. (2) Those based primarily on the semantic evolution of a word. Some of the etymological equations exhibit a semantic change, often based on similarities and giving rise to metaphor and transference, of which the latter assumes diverse forms or tendencies. For example, the Ṛg-Vedic word '*asura*' (Zend: '*ahura*'), meaning 'a god', exhibits a pejorative tendency in the post-Ṛg-Vedic period, being used in an antithetical sense through metanalysis. This principle gives prime importance to sense only. (3) Those based primarily on phonetic similarity. For example, some exhibit a phonetic change like metathesis and the dropping of letters in various positions. This last type often deteriorates into folk-etymology which originates from a perverted popular reconstruction of the phonetic make-up of a word.

10.3.2 Folk-etymology in the Nirukta and Pre-Nirukta Literature

A definition of 'Nirukta' in the *Śabda-kalpa-druma* states that a Nirukta contains the doctrine of the fivefold phenomena occurring in words, namely, the addition, transposition, modification, and omission of letters, and the use of one particular meaning of a root (*Varṇāgamo varṇaviparyayaśca, dvau cāparau varṇavikāranāśau*; *dhātostadarthātiśayena yogah, taducyate pañcavidhaām niruktam*).

Vēdah, 'knowledge'; and (3) *Pātṛ*, 'protector' and *pātṛ*, 'drinker'. Sometimes, as in the first example cited above, accent helps to distinguish one from the other of a pair of homonyms. Homonyms are, comparatively speaking, few in Sanskrit.

Sometimes there is the transposititon of two sounds or the interchange of two phonemes within a word. Thus *prayāja* = *prajayā* and *yajña* = *yajña* (*Śatapatha Brāhmaṇa,* I.5.3.3; III 9.4.23); *kaśyata* = *paśyaka* (*Taittirīya āraṇyaka,* I.8.7). Yāska refers to this phenomenon in II.2: *athāpi ādyantaviparyayo bhavati*. According to Yāska, forms like *stoka, rajju* and *sikatā* are formed through metathesis from the roots *scut, sṛj,* and *kas* respectively.

10.3.3 The Nighaṇṭu

The *Naighaṇṭuka* consists of five chapters. In the first three, synonymous words are merely grouped together and the common meaning is indicated at the end of each para with a better-known word. The fourth chapter consists of words, each considered by itself. Each of these words has more than one meaning or is obscure. The fifth chapter contains a list of well-known deity-names-the word 'deity' being used in the very wide sense of 'the topic or subject of a hymn' in the *Ṛg-Veda*. The *Nirukta* (VII.1.3) suggests that the Nighaṇṭu was not the only list of its kind. Even the extant *Nighaṇṭu* appears to be the work not of a single author but of generations of scholars.

10.3.4 Yāska's Nirukta

The *Nirukta* consists of twelve chapters[10] divided into two parts, each containing a group of six (Ṣaṭka) chapters. The 'Pūrva-ṣaṭka' (first sextet) is further subdivided into two divisions: (i) 'Naighaṇṭuka-kāṇḍa', which comments on the first three chapters of the *Naighaṇṭu* in three corresponding chapters and (ii) 'Naigama-kāṇḍa', which also consists of three chapters, and comments on the fourth chapter of the *Naighaṇṭu*. The Uttara-ṣaṭka' (second sextet) comments on the fifth or last chapter of the *Naighaṇṭu*, and is called the 'Daivata-kāṇḍa'. Though the two *ṣaṭkas* appear to have been originally two separate works, the blending of the two parts must have taken place very early, even before the *Bṛhad-devatā*, which quotes both the *ṣaṭkas*. Even in its present interpolated condition, the *Nirukta* betrays a unifying hand, and that hand was the hand of Yāska.

The Vedic Saṁhitā quotations are, as a rule, accented in the *Nirukta*. So unaccented citations may be reasonably suspected as later interpolations.

Etymological equations based on the semantic identification of phonetically similar words (e.g. *aṅgāra=aṅgiras*;

puriśaya=puruśa; etc.) illustrate a tendency inherent in folk-etymology, whereby association by sound may affect the meaning, just as association by sense may bring about changes in the form of words. When two words have the same form, the meaning of the unfamiliar one is assimilated to that of the familiar word. If they have not an identical but a similar form, the less known word assimilates itself phonetically to the better known word. The grouping of words according to their phonemes plays a great part in folk-etymology. The mind seeks to establish relations between the external form of words which are sometimes inversions as regards their meaning and contrary to common sense. It is interesting to note that in Europe, too, the learned etymology of medieval writers, whereby they resolved an unfamiliar word into elements that may yield a possible interpretation of its meaning, the playing with etymology in metaphysical fashion on the part of the Greeks and Romans, and the mistaken ideas of the origin of words in the mind of the uneducated, have all resulted in Brāhmaṇa-like etymologies in European languages. Anecdotal etymologies, which form an important part of folk-etymology, are copious in Brāhmaṇa literature. Thus the etymologies of *agni, aśva, udumbara, vidyut, pṛthivī* etc.are connected with the legend of Prajāpati; those of *aṣāḍhā, aparājitā,* etc., with the legend of the *deva-asura* contest; and those of *puṣkara* and *śakvarī* with the Indra-Vṛtra fight in the *Śatapatha, Taittirīya, Aitareya, Kauṣītaki* and other Brāhmaṇas. The aggreably surprising feature of these attempts at etymologizing is that some of them do give a clue to the right derivation, as for example, *pṛthivī* from *prath*; *śakvarī* from *sak*; and *aṣāḍhā,* from *sah*.

Doublets and homonyms play an important part in the etymological equations of Vedic literature. The phenomenon by which the same root appears under a double form and sense is called dismorphism. A few examples are : *aṅgāra-aṅgiras* (*Aitareya Brāhmaṇa* III.34) from *aṅg*; *aśmā-aśru* (*Śatapatha*

Brāhmaṇa VI.1.2.3) from *aś*; and *lakṣma-lakṣmī* (*Śatapatha Brāhmaṇa* VIII.4.4.11), from *laks*. Myths often form the vehicle of some of these doublets. That the Vedic equations imply a real grasp of etymological principles is seen from their tracing of the correct radical element in these doublets.

A word having the same pronunciation as another, but differing from it in origin and meaning, is a homonym. A few examples of Vedic homonyms are: (1) *iṣṭi* (sacrifice) is to be traced to *yaj,* 'to worship', but *iṣṭi* (desire, search) is from *iṣ* 'to seek, to desire, etc; (2) *vēdah*, 'finding' and this serves as a guiding principle in the investigation which yields the following conclusions:

(a) The influence of the *Ṛg-Veda* is the most dominant. Probably, the original aim of the *Nirukta*, is pursuance of *Nighaṁṭu* trends, was to examine certain Ṛg-Vedic *nigamas* only.

(b) There are clear traces of the influence of the old *yajus*, though no particular school of it can be said to have influenced the oldest form of the *Nirukta*. This is probably to be attributed to Yāska and his successors. The influence of the Kaṇva recension of the *Vājasaneyi Saṁhitā* seems to have been brought to bear on the *Nirukta* at a late stage, a supposition that will satisfactorily account for the phonological peculiarity that '*l*' appears instead of '*ḷ* ' of the Ṛg-Vedic *nigama,* when the word is repeated in the text of the *Nirukta* for comment, although '*ḷ* ' is faithfully reproduced in the accented citation proper. It may be said that sometime or other, the Kaṇva school must have substituted '*l*' and '*lh*' in positions where the Ṛg-Veda has '*ḷ*' and '*ḷh*', respectively, and this has been transmitted to the *Nirukta*.

(c) No influence whatever from either the *Sāma-Veda* or the *Atharva-Veda* can be traced in the original (accented) *nigamas*.

10.3.5 Yāska's Etymological Principles

The etymological theories of Yāska as presented at the beginning of the second chapter of the *Nirukta* testify to the deep insight into, and penetrating judgement on, grammatical matters, and also reveal the linguistic mistakes of the old Brāhmaṇical schools. One of the most vital and fundamental problems of etymology is: Are all nouns derived from verbal roots? All the etymologists, excepting Gārgya, answer this question in the affirmative, whereas all the grammarians, excepting Śākaṭāyana, oppose this view. The pros and cons of this questionnaire discusses by Yāska with such sobriety that his presentation or explanation cannot be improved upon even today. We have to admit with him that the derivative character of all nouns is a matter of belief, rather than of proof. While several objects that share in the same predicate should all receive the same name, yet generic words (homonyms) are found based on one predicate rather than another: e.g. anyone who takes to a road-*adhvcnam aśnuvīta*- should be called *aśva*, but it is only a horse that is called so. Similarly, when the same object possesses various predicates-e.g. a pillar (*sthūṇā*) stands upright, rests in a hole, and joins a beam-, it should be called by different names; and yet only one appellative, out of many, becomes fixed as the proper name of an object. The only explanation is, as Yāska says, that it is so by itself (*svabhāvatah*), through the influence of individuals, poets or law-givers. In other words, it is convention that avoids the confusion that would result if all people or objects associated with the same action were to receive the same designation, or if a thing associated with more than one action were to receive several corresponding designations.

The general and particular rules laid down for the derivation of words may now be briefly stated. General rules: (i) All nominal forms are derived from roots. (ii) In deriving words, due attention must be paid to accent grammatical formation, and meaning, the last being the most important aspect.

The particular rules are: (i) A nominal form is to be derived from a root which has the sense of that act which solely belongs to the thing denoted by the noun, in such a way that its accent and formation are based on rules of grammar, e.g. *kāraka* from *kṛ*. (ii) When the current meaning of a word does not agree with the meaning of the root apparent in it, and when its nominal form cannot be developed from the root by ordinary rules of grammar, one should take one's stand on the meaning only and explain the word through its resemblance to the verbal or nominal form of a root that has the meaning of it, e.g., *hasta* (a hand) should be derived not from *has,* 'to laugh', apparent in it, but from *han,* 'to strike' because the hand is quick at striking. (iii) When there is no resemblance between a word and any form of a root that has its meaning, the resemblance or community of even a (single) syllable or letter (vowel or consonant) should be the basis of etymology (as in the case of the Vedic word '*agni*'). (iv) Even inflected case-forms may be adjusted to the meaning (*yathārthaṁ vibhaktīh saṁnamayet.*) (v) Similarly, *taddhita* derivatives and compounds (whether of one or more members) should be analysed into their component elements and the component elements explained.

The hymns of the *Ṛg-Veda* had beocme unintelligible as early as the time of even the later Saṁhitās, owing to a break in the exegetical tradition. Yāska therefore, in explaining an obscure Vedic word, had to rely on imagination more or less to suggest a number of roots, which could afford a clue to the proper understanding of its sense. Meaning or *artha* being thus the principle element to which other elements were subordinate, the importance of the *Nirukta* for semasiology, which represents the psychological aspect of language, cannot be over-estimated. Another aim of the *Nirukta* was to explain Vedic theology to the Brāhmaṇical schools. When Yāska therefore derived a Vedic word from a verbal root by way of explaining it, the thing, person, or animal denoted by the word came (in his eyes) to share in the action of the verb. The word not only represented the thing; it was also the thing itself. The modern word 'etymology' hardly does justice to this notion of '*nirvacana*'. The whole background was theological, because theology in India, more than in any other country, was the mother of all sciences. We should therefore rather be agreeably surprised at the large number of good and true etymologies in the *Nirukta* than be disappointed at the many etymologies which look absurd to us but were self-evident to Yāska.

10.4 Vyākaraṇa (Grammar)

In the case of the Vedanga *vyākaraṇa,* as in the case of the other Vedāṅgas, it is crystal clear that the traditional claim that it is represented by the grammar of Pāṇini is to be understood only in the sense that grammatical studies culminated in, and were certainly not inaugurated by, the almost perfect work of Pāṇini. Nay, Pāṇini himself mentions no fewer than sixty-four predecessors, whose works were superseded, and virtually obliterated, by his own monumental work.

10.4.1 Pre-Pāṇini Literature

Language was an object of wonder and meditation to the Vedic *ṛṣis*. Soma and Visvakarman are described as lords of speech in the *Ṛg-Veda*, which celebrates *Vāc* (personified speech) as a goddess in one hymn (X.125; cf. X.71 also). Some stanzas of the *Ṛg-Veda* are capable of being given a grammatical explanation. Thus, expressions like '*catvāri ṣṛṅgā*' and '*sapta sindhavah*' have been interpreted by Patañjali in terms of the four parts of speech and the seven cases. The *Taittirīya Saṁhitā* mentions Indra as having analysed (and expounded) speech to the gods.

There are many speculations on letters, syllables, and words in the Brāhmaṇas as also numerous terms like *akṣara, varṇa, vṛṣan* (masculine), vacana and *vibhakit,* which Pāṇini uses without definition, marking a definite advance of grammatical knowledge. In the *Śatapatha Brāhmaṇa* (XIII.5.1.18), we meet with names for singular and plural.

The Āraṇyakas and Upaniṣads not only mention technical grammatical terms for certain groups of letters, but contain details about the phonetic treatment of the Vedic texts. In the *Chāndogya Upaniṣad*, for example we find a classification of letters and technical terms such as *svara* (vowels), *sparśa* (consonants), and *uṣman* (sibilants). The names of certain theological *sparśa* (consonants), and *uṣman* (sibilants). The names of certain theological grammarians such Śākalya and Māṇḍūkeya are mentioned for the first time in this period.

10.4.2 Pada-Pāṭha

'*Vyākaraṇa*'(lit. 'analysis') is the most appropriate name for 'grammar' which pursues the study of linguistic phenomena through the method of 'analysis'. From this point of view, the next landmark in the development of grammar may be said to have been reached when the the Saṁhitā texts of the Vedas were reduced to the *pada-pāṭha*, wherein each word is exhibited separately in its individual grammatical form, followed, when necessary, by word-signs like '*iti*' and also by symbols like the *avagraha* etc. to distinguish case-terminations, to analyse compounds, and to mark out a few special cases of accentuation. The *pada-pāṭhas* thus show that their authors had not only made investigations as toe pronunciation and *sandhi* rules, but also knew a good deal about the grammatical analysis of words, as they distinguish the four parts of speech - noun, verb, preposition and particle - and separate the parts of compounds and the prefixes of verbs as well as certain suffixes and case-terminations of nouns. In their substance, the *Taittirīya, Vājasaneyi* and *Atharva*

Prātiśākhyas are older than Pāṇini and the *Ṛg-Veda Prātiśākhya*, the oldest of all, quotes Yāska.

Yāska distinguishes a Northern and an Eastern school of grammarians and mentions nearly twenty predecessors such as Śākaṭāyana, Gārgya and Śākalya. He distinguishes between the two elements of a word: (i) the *semanteme* (popularly called the 'root'), containing its general meaning, and (ii) the *morpheme* (the inflection, or the suffixes and affixes), which gives definite form to the general meaning. The theory of the verbal origin of nouns, so vital to the structure of grammatical science, which finds elaborate and profound discussion in the *Nirukta,* may be said to be the foundation of the whole system of Pāṇini. Yāska states that there are four kinds of parts of speech - *nāman* (noun), *ākhyāta* (verb), *upasarga* (preposition, and *nipāta* (particle) - terms used later by Pāṇini. The verb, he explains, is primarily concerned with '*being*' and nouns with '*beings*'. The difference is established, as in Aristotle, by ascribing a temporal character to the verb and denying it to the noun. The name for a pronoun '*sarva-nāma*' also occurs in the *Nirukta* (VII.2).

10.4.3 Prātiśākhyas and Grammar

The Prātiśākhyas do not refer to grammar, properly so-called, but presuppose a long-continued study of grammatical subjects quoting as they do (e.g. Śaunaka) the differing opinions of earlier grammarians like the Śākalas. They not only give the fourfold classification of the parts of speech like nouns, verbs, prepositions and particles, but also another division of a purely grammatical nature. For instance, *Kātyāyanīya Prātiśākhya* (IV.170) says: 'Language consists of verbs (*ākhyāta*) with their conjugational terminations, nouns (*nāman*) derived from verbs by mean of *kṛt* suffixes, nouns derived from nouns by means of *taddhita* suffixes, and four kinds of compounds.' They tell us that there are twenty prepositions, which have a meaning if joined with nouns or verbs. Words outside of nouns (expressing 'a being'), verbs (which mark 'being'), and prepositions are particles, some of which have a sense, the others being expletives. The name for a case, '*vibhakti*', is found in the Prātiśākhyas, which mention the number of cases also as even. Only the distinction of genders seems to have been passed over in the Prātiśākhyas, and appears first in Pāṇini. The Prātiśākhyas are not called, because *vyākaraṇas* because they provide the basis only for the phonetic system of Pāṇini, but not for his strictly grammatical theories. As such, the extreme veiw of *Vaidhikābharaṇa* that the grammatical element is the basis element and predominates over the phonetic element in the Prātiśākhyas is as unacceptable as the other extreme view of Goldstucker that Prātiśākhyas were divorced from grammar. He wrongly assumed that tradition dissociated grammatical topics completely from the Prātiśākhyas.

10.4.4 Grammarians preceding Pāṇini

Of the sixty-four grammarians, referred to as his predecessors by Pāṇini, the important ones are Āpiśali and Kāśakṛtsna, who are credited with the founding of grammatical schools and from whom a few passages are quoted by Kaiyaṭa, a later writer,[11] and Gārgya, Kāśyapa, Gālava, Bhāradvāja, Śākaṭāyana, Śākalya, Cakravarmaṇa, Senaka and Sphoṭāyana as well as those referred to under the collective appellation of Eastern and Northern grammarians. As regards the Aindra school of grammarians, the claim of its priority to Pāṇini is advanced by a tradition mentioned by the Chinese pilgrim Hiuen-Tsang and the Tibetan Tāranātha. Though the *paribhāṣā* and technique of the Aindra school look more primitive than those of Pāṇini, the name and extant doctrines of the school, at any rate, must be set down as later, since no important work of the Pāṇinian school mentions the name 'Aindra'.

10.4.5 Pāṇini's Technical Terms

From a rule of Pāṇini (I.2.53), which lays down the principle that a matter which has the authority of a *saṁjñā* ('conventional' or 'settled' terms) is not taught or defined by him, and the commentary of Patañjali thereon, we can safely infer that the terms *pratyaya, dhātu, upasarga, vṛddhi, avyaya, samāsa, tatpuruṣa, bahuvrīhi, avyayībhāva, kṛt* and *taddhita* were of current use in his time. The names of the cases from *prathamā* to *saptamī* were used by the Eastern grammarians before Pāṇini. There are other terms which he defines not because he invented them, but because he employs them in a special sense, viz., *dvandva, karmadhāraya, anunāsika, savarṇa, pragṛhya, lopa, hrasva, dīrgha, pluta, udātta, anudātta, svarita, apṛkta,* and *upasarjana.* As regards purely grammatical symbols which are not *saṁjñās,* we cannot say definitely that he invented them, because some of them at least were, according to Patañjali, already known to Pāṇini, e.g. *ti, ghu* and *bha.*

As regards the *Uṇādi-Sūtras*, the tradition valid among grammarians like Patañjali (*Śakaṭasya tokam*) attributes them to Śākaṭāyana, a predecessor of Pāṇini. Pāṇini himself, in his *sutra* '*uṇādayo bahulam*' (III.3.1), seems to recognize them as authoritative for the most part (not everywhere). Max Muller holds that these sūtras, at least in their original collection, if not in their present enlarged form, were presupposed by Pāṇini. Goldstuckar, however, after a long discussion, arrives at the following conclusions: The *Uṇādi-Sūtras,* which use just those terms which are defined by Pāṇini and in exactly the same sense in which he uses them, were, in their existing collection, composed later than Pāṇini. Ujjvaladatta and Bahttoji Dikṣita hold the same view. The *Rūpamālā*, of Vimala ascribes them to Vararuci (a name of Kātyāyana, who completed the work of Pāṇini). As regards the list of affixes, *uṇādihya,* which Pāṇini quotes twice, the explanation is as follows: All the *uṇādi* affixes have *anubanedhas* which are the same and have the same grammatical effect as those used by Pāṇini. These *anubandhas* could not have preceded him, because Patañjali points out that *anubandhas* of former grammarians have no *anubandha* effect in Pāṇini; so Pāṇini himself must be the author of the core of the *uṇādi* list mentioned by him in his work. It may be stated, in support of Goldstucker's theory, that Indian scholars like Mm. Vasudeva Shastri Abhyankar of Poona look upon them as an *adjunct* to Pāṇini's grammar.

As regards the claim of priority for the *Phiṭ-Sūtras* of Śāntana advanced by Muller, Goldstucker rejects it on the following grounds: (i) Where these Sūtras and Pāṇini cover the same ground, the latter's rules are more incomplete in substance. This would be inconceivable if the *Phiṭ-Sūtras* treat of accent only, it may be pointed out that accent was not confined to the Vedic language only. No word could be pronounced without an accent. Besides, the great bulk of words treated of in the *Phiṭ-Sūtras* belong, with equal right, to the classical language. (iv) Finally, Nāgojibhaṭṭa makes the statement that the *Phiṭ-Sūtras*, considered in reference to Pāṇini, are simply modern and recent.

10.5 Chandas (Metrics)

Piṅgala's *Chandaḥ-Sūtra* treats mainly of post-Vedic (classical) prosody, though it has a section on Vedic metres and many others which are obsolete now. Though presumed to be a Vedic text devoted to Vedic metres in general, it deals with Prakrit as well as Sanskrit metres in the manner of Kātyāyana Vararuci, who composed the *vārttikas* on Pāṇini as well as a Prakrit grammar. Piṅgala's treatment of metres is similar to that of the *Agni Purāṇa* (chapters 328-34). It holds the position of a standard work on classical prosody. Its code like *ya-mā-tā-rā-ja-bhā-na-sa-la-gam,* for the eight *gaṇas* of three syllables each and the long and short sound measures, being well known, has survived other similar attempts.

10.5.1 Pre-Piṅgala Chandas Literature

The *Ṛg-Veda* being a metrical composition, the *ṛṣis* were undoubtedly familiar with the rules and art of metrical expression. If the *ṛc* was the *yoni* (womb), out of which originated the *sāman* (tune or melody), this could happen only if the disposition of letters in it yielded sounds conducive to the harmony of the car. The Ṛg-Vedic bards often constructed fresh metrical schemes, comparing, as they do, their originally and skill to those displayed in the construction of a chariot.

In the *Ṛg-Veda* (X.14.16; X.130.4-5), we meet with several terms which later became well known technical designations of metres. *Gāyatrī* is said to be born of Agni, *uṣṇih* of Savitr, *anuṣṭubh* of Soma, *bṛhatī* of Bṛhaspati, and *virāṭ* of Mitrāvaruṇa. Indra-the god praised most often-invented the *triṣṭubh,* the metre employed most often. The Viśvedevas (All-gods) created the *jagatī*. The *śakvarī* is mentioned when we are told that the Vasiṣṭhas strengthened Indra by loudly chanting in that metre.

A hymn in the eighth *kāṇḍa* of the *Atharva Veda* gives the number of syllables in these seven chief metres of Vedic poetry as increasing by four successively, i.e. from 24 in the *Gāyatrī* to 48 in the *jagatī*. These seven metres are often mentioned with names in the other Saṁhitās.[12]

Fascinated by the charming rhythm of the metres, the authors of the Brāhmaṇas ingeniously show that their harmony is in some mystical and mysterious fashion the fundamental cause of the harmony of the world. The *Śatapatha Brāhmaṇa* (VIII.I.1-2) tells us that metres, like other beings, were created by Prajāpati. In III.9.4.10, it mentions Gāyatrī as a mystical name of Agni who carries off the *Soma*. Gāyatrī, in the form of a bird, fetches the *soma* from heaven.

In the Brāhmaṇa and Upaniṣad speculations on the mystical significance of metres, mumbers play a great part. The *Bṛhadāraṇyaka Upaniṣad* (V.15) says: 'The words *bhūmi, antarikṣa* and *dyu* (to be pronouned as *di-u)* make up 8 syllables; a *gāyatrī pāda* (foot) consists of 8 syllables therefore he who knows the *gāyatrī* gains the three worlds.'

In the *Sāṅkhyāyana Śrauta-Sūtra* (VII.27), inquires into the beginning of the science of metrics lead to the formulation of the principles of versification. In the *Vasiṣṭha Dharma-śāstra* (XIII.3 and elsewhere) the metres are defied enough to have sacrifices offered to them. In the *Śākala Prātiśākhya* of Śaunaka, the last three paṭalas (chapters) are on metres.

The *Nidāna-Sūtra* of the *Sāma-Veda* discusses the metrical aspect of the various parts of that musical Veda, such as: the *uktha, stoma* and *gāna*. It explains the nature and different names of all the Vedic metres and gives an index to the metres of hymns employed in the *ekāha, ahīna* and *sattra* sacrifices.

Among the five or six extant Anukramaṇīs (Indices) which are attached to the *Ṛg-Veda*, the *Chandonukramaṇi* (of about 300 stanzas in the *anuṣṭubh* and *triṣṭubh* metres) enumerates the metres of the Ṛg-Vedic hymns and states the number of verses in each metre.

The extensive *Sarvānukramaṇī* (General Index) epitomizes, in *sūtra* style, the data of the Anukramaṇis. It contains some metrical *pādas,* and borrows a number of passages from the *Ārṣānukramaṇī* and the *Bṛhad-devata,* in their metrical wording, with or without additions. To Kātyāyana is also attributed the Anukramaṇi of the *White Yajur-Veda* in the *Mādhyandina* recension, consisting of five sections, the fifth section of which gives a brief account of the metres occurring in the *White Yajur-Veda*.

10.5.2 Versification in Vedic Literature

The unit of a Ṛg-Vedic hymn is the stanza or *ṛc*. The hymn generally consists of not less than three and not more than fifteen such units in the same metre. A conventional variation is a different metre in the last stanza, to mark the close of the hymn. Some hymns consists of a succession of single stanzas or of groups. A group has either three stanzas in the same simple metre (*gāyatrī* generally) or two stanzas in different metres. This latter strophic type called *pragātha* is found chiefly in the eighth *maṇḍala*. The number of syllables in the common type of stanzas vary from 20 (4 x 5) to 48 (4 x 12).

Historically, the Vedic metres, mainly those of the *Ṛg-Veda,*[13] stand mid-way between the Avestan system and that of classical Sanskrit.

The Avesta has 8 syllable or 11 syllable lines which ignore quantity, but are combined into stanzas which resemble those of the *Ṛg-Veda* in all other aspects. In the *Ṛg-Veda*, the quantity of the initial and final syllables is always indifferent, but rhythmic tendencies determine with varying regularity, the last four or five syllables, the very last syllable being a *syllaba anceps*. The fixed rhythm at the end of the Vedic line is called *vṛtra* (lit. 'turn', from the root *vṛt*), which corresponds etymologically to the Latin *verses* (*vert-ere*).

The metrical unit of Vedic prosody, the line or verse called *pāda,* though meaning literally 'a foot', has nothing to do with the 'foot' of the Greek prosody-a breaking up into such small units as the Greek 'feet' being impossible in ancient Indian poetry. The word is used rather in the figurative sense of 'quarter', from the foot of a quadruped, a stanza having usually four lines. A *pāda* ordinarily consists of 8, 11 or 12 and much less commonly 15, syllables. A stanza or *ṛc* is generally formed of three or four lines of the same kind. Rarer types such as the *uṣṇih* and *bṛhati* are composed of *pādas* of 8 or 12 syllables. Short and long syllables alternate in a *pāda* more in its latter part called the 'cadence' than in its earlier part called 'opening'. The rhythm is, in general, an iambic one in nearly all the metres, since they betray a preference for the even syllables being long rather than short. Verses of 11 or 12 syllables are characterized not only by their cadence, but also by a caesura after the fourth or fifth syllable, and consist of three members, the opening, the cadence, and (in between) the break between the caesura and the cadence, while verses of 8 (or 5) syllables have no such metrical pause.

The 8 syllable line usually ends in two iambics, the first four syllables, though not exactly determined, having a tendency to be iambic also. This verse is therefore a very near equivalent of the Greek iambic diameter. The normal scheme of this line is therefore: 00000-00. Three of these lines combine to form the *gāyatrī* metre, and four of them combine to form the *anuṣṭubh* stanza in which the first two and the last two lines are more colsely connected. In the *Ṛg-Veda*, the *anuṣṭubh* stanzas number only one-third of the *gāyatrī* ones. This relation is gradually reversed until we reach the post-Vedic stage where the has *gāyatrī* disappeared and the *anuṣṭubh* has become the dominant metre - the classical *śloka* - the proper metre of epic poetry. Five or six lines of 8 syllables each constitute the very rare metres, *paṅkti* and *mahapaṅkti,* respectively. The gradual evolution of the epic *śloka* can be traced in the *Ṛg-Veda* itself. In the oldest hymns, all the four verses are the same, i.e. iambic rhythm. In the later hymns, the tendency to distinguish the first and third lines from the second and fourth, by making the former non-iambic, begins to be evident. Finally, in the latest hymns of the tenth *maṇḍala*, the iambic rhythm disappears altogether from the odd lines. Here, among all the possible combinations of quantity in the last four syllables, the commonest variation, nearly a frequent as the iambic, is which is the regular ending of the odd lines in the post-Vedic *śloka*.

The *triṣṭubh* stanza consists of four lines of 11 syllables each, which, from the point of view of their metrical scheme, may be called catalectic-*jagatī* lines. Their scheme is according as the caesura comes after the fourth or fifth syllable.

The 12 syllable line (four of such lines constitute the *jagatī* stanza) is probably an extension of the *triṣṭubh* verse by one syllable, which gives the trochaic cadence of the latter an iambic character. The scheme is either

These two *pādas* or verses, the *triṣṭubh* and the *jagatī,* being closely allied and having the same cadence, are often found mixed in the same stanza.

The normal scheme of a line or verse of 5 syllables is four such verses divided into two hemistichs give us the rare stanza *dvipadā-virāj*.

Let us conclude with a few apt general observations on Vedic metres in the *Jayadāman*:[14] These Vedic metres are based on the *svara-saṅgīta* or the music of voice-modulation, where the time-element plays no important role in the production of the metrical music.... The musical difference between a short and long letter was not yet made use of for the sake of music in Vedic metres, a letter, whether short or long, being considered as the metrical unit in the construction of lines. But since short and long letters had to be used in different orders in a line, in actual practice, the consciousness of this musical difference could not be avoided for long.... By the end of the Saṁhitā period, the earlier metrical music, based on the modulation of voice to different pitches and tunes, seems to have been generally given up in preference to the new kind of music based on the alternation of short and long sounds. The older music was taken up for a special treatment and development by the schools of the *Sāma-Veda,* and the growth of the different *rāgas* and *rāgiṇīs* (modes or melodies) in Indian music must surely be traced to their original and early efforts.

But the poets in general adapted their compositions to the new music.

10.6 Jyotiṣa (Astronomy)

10.6.1 Introduction

The *Vedaṅga Jyotiṣa*, propounding the doctrine as taught by Lagadha, has 36 verses in the Rg-Vedic recension and 43 in the Yajur-Vedic one, 30 being common to both. The *Ātharvaṇa-Jyotiṣa* of 162 verses dealing with *muhūrta* (a particular division of time), *karaṇa* (an astrological division of day), yoga (leading star of a lunar asterism; a variable division of time), *tithi* (lunar-day), and *vara* (week-day) falls outside the Vedic period. It is important as it treats also of *jātaka* (astrology), a branch of *jyotiṣa*. It is however, pre-Siddhanta, as it makes no mention of the twelve *rāśis* (zodiac) borrowed from the Greeks.

The *Vedaṅga Jyotiṣa* helps to determine, for purposes of the sacrifices, the positions of the sun and the moon in the circle of the 27 *nakṣatras* or star-groups of the zodiac. It gives simple rules and concise formulae for the calculation of *tithis, parvans* (new and full moon days), *viśuvats* (equinoxial days) etc.

The basis of calculation is the very convenient one of a five-year cycle called a *yuga,* because the solar year is taken to be of 366 days and five of these (1830 days) accommodate 62 full moons and 62 new moons, i.e. 124 complete *parvans,* which, with the addition of two intercalary months (one in the third and the other during the fifth year), turned the cycle from a lunar into a solar one. The cycle commenced with the coming together of the sun, the moon and the *nakṣatra* Dhaniṣṭhā on the first *tithi* of the bright fortnight of Māgha, at the autumnal solstice (the beginning of uttarāyaṇa). The *Vedāṅga Jyotiṣa* with the zodiac divided into 27 *nakṣatras*, became obsolete, when the Siddhānta calendar, with the zodiac divided into 12 *rāṣis*, became popular later.

The statement in this Vedāṅga that 'in the beginning of Śraviṣṭhā, the sun and the moon turn towards the north' a conjunction observed as occurring in the days of Lagadha - yields by astronomical calculation the very early date of 1200 B.C. for the work, a result somehow explained away by scholars who are sceptical, as the work betrays signs of lateness. But C. V. Vaidya,[15] who points out an earlier position of the *uttarāyaṇa* in the middle of the Dhaniṣṭhā division, argues that the statement cannot be brushed aside as it is accurate and fixes the time of Lagadha, although the preset work may be a late one. It is not, however, as late as it is supposed to be for (i) it is not composed in *sūtras*, (ii) It uses older names of *nakṣatras* and words like *gharma* and *rāṣi* in their older meanings, and (iii) even some of the older Upaniṣads are composed in verse. This work refers to the custom of naming persons from the *nakṣatras* of their birth, as the Gṛhya-Sūtras do.

10.6.2 Earlier Jyotiṣa Literature

Several Ṛg-vedic hymns presuppose a considerable development of sacrificial ceremonies, the regulation whereof required an accurate knowledge of months, seasons and the year. The primitive calendar was, in fact, coeval with the sacrificial system. The *sattras,* which lasted for one year, were nothing but an imitation of the sun's yearly course. They were divided into two distinct parts, each consisting of six months of 30 days each; in the midst of both was the *viśuvat,* i.e. equatorial or central day, cutting the whole *sattra* into two halves.[2] The identification of *saṁvatsara* (year) with the sacrifice in many Brāhmaṇa passages and the etymology of the word '*ṛt-vij*'(=*ṛtu*+*yaj*, 'season-sacrificer') point in the same direction. The meaning of *saṁvatsara* (a period where the seasons dwell, from *vas*, 'to dwell') shows that the year was equivalent to a complete cycle of seasons. The year was thus solar and at the same time sidereal, but not tropical.

The month was determined and measured by the moon. The close affinity of the names for month and moon indicates a knowledge of lunar chronology. As the name for the moon has cognates in Sanskrit, Greek and German, and as the root from which it is derived meant originally 'to measure', the moon seems to have been looked upon as the measurer of time even in Indo-European times. The adjustment of the solar year to the lunar year was effected either by adding the intercalary month every two or three years, as *Ṛg-Veda*, I.25.8 shows, or by insertion of twelve (intercalary) nights at the close of the lunar year, as is suggested by *Ṛg-Veda*, IV.33.7, which tells us that the Ṛbhus (the genii of the seasons) slacken their course and rest with the sun for twelve nights at the end of the year. The latter was, probably, the older device, as the twelve days of preparation prescribed before the commencement of the yearly sacrifice shows. The *devayāna* (*Ṛg-Veda*, I.72.7; X.2.7), equated by *Bṛhadāraṇyaka* and *Chāndogya Upaniṣads* to the six months when the sun is towards the north, must have commenced with the vernal equinox. The *Ṛg-Veda*, V.40 refers to an observation by the sage Atri of a total eclipse of the sun and not (as is supposed) an obscuration of the sun by clouds, and in II.3.2, the phases of the moon have not only received proper names, but they are also invoked as deities.

In the later part of the *Atharva-Veda* (XIX), the lunar mansions are enumerated by names, some of which are different from those in the *Taittirīya Saṁhitā*, the others appearing in a late form. The year-beginning seems to have been shifted from the vernal equinox to the winter solstice at least before the *Taittirīya Saṁhitā* in which there is a discussion as to whether the month should begin with the new or full moon. In the *Vājasaneyi Saṁhitā* (VII.30; XXII.31), the deity of the thirteenth month-the Aṁhasaspati- has an oblation offered to it, along with the deities of the twelve months. Again, *nakṣatradarśa* and *gaṇaka* occur as names for an astronomer (XXX.10.20). The five-year time-unit called the '*yuga*', accommodating two intercalary months, is mentioned for the first time in the *Taittirīya Brāhmaṇa,* giving the names of years as *saṁvatsara* etc. with their overlords. The old names of the months derived from the seasons, namely, Madhu, Mādhava, etc., occur in the later Saṁhitās and the *Taittirīya Brāhmaṇa*, but the new names derived from 12 out of the 27 *nakṣatras* are found in the *Śatapatha*, *Kauṣītakī*, and *Pañcaviṁśa Brāhmaṇas*. It seems that along with the *tithi,* the *sāvana* (lit. sacrificial day), i.e. natural or civil day, was simultaneously in use, and the *Taittirīya Saṁhitā* (VII.5.7.1) and *Tāṇḍya Brāhmaṇa* (V.13) show how an adjustment of the *sāvana* and lunar months was effected by omitting a day from the former. The number of the *nakṣatras* is put down as 27 in the *Taittirīya Saṁhitā*, but as 28 in the *Atharva-Veda* and the *Maitrāyaṇī Saṁhitā*. Abhijit, which is far away from the zodiac, was included first as marking the approach of the *viśuvat,* and later dropped, when *viśuvat* ceased to be the central day owing to the falling back of the seasons. The succession of 27 *nakṣatras*, which all lie not far distant from the ecliptic, were combined into a kind lunar zodiac, employed for the purpose of estimating the position of the moon for prescribing the time for a sacrificial act.

According to Tilak and Jacobi, the Kṛttikās (Pleiades) formed the starting point of the *nakṣatra* series which coincided with the vernal equinox in the period of the Brāhmaṇas, because a passage in the *Śatapatha Brāhmaṇa* reads: *Kṛttikā ha vai prācyai diśo na cyavante,* which means, according to them, 'the Kṛttikās rose due east'. In the Vedic texts, there are also traces of an older calendar in which the vernal equinox fell in the Orion (Mṛgaśiras).[16]

In the time of the *Chāndogya Upaniṣad,* astronomy (*nakṣatra-vidyā*) seems to have attained the status of a science worthy of study by the Brāhmaṇas. In the *gaṇa-pāṭha* of Pāṇini, the title *jyotiṣa* occurs; and in III.1.143, *graha* (planet) is mentioned as different from *grāha* (crocodile).

In the Gṛhya-Sūtras, it is recorded that on arrival at their new home, the bridegroom points out to the bride the pole-star (Dhruva, 'the constant one') as a shining symbol of conjugal constancy. They also refer to the full moon night of Mārgaśīrṣa called *āgrahāyaṇi* (lit. 'coming at the beginning of the year'), probably showing a system of reckoning whereby Mārgaśīrṣa was the first month of the year. The *Gobhila Gṛhya-Sūtra* says that there are three ways of determining the time of the full moon, namely: (i) when it rises at the meeting of the day and night; (ii) when it rises after sunset; and (iii) when it stands high in the sky at sunset. It also adds rough astronomical definitions, such as 'Full moon is the greatest distance between the sun and the moon; new moon is their nearest approach'.

Finally, the *Caraṇavyūha* mentions not only a Jyotiṣa, but also an Upa-Jyotiṣa or a supplementary treatise on astronomy, belonging to the class of the Pariśiṣṭas, of the *Atharva-Veda*. These works, however, fall outside the Vedic peiod.

10.7 Kalpa Literature

10.7.1 Composition of the Kalpa

The Kalpasūtras describe the cult ceremonies, and are the basic documents of the rituals. The tendency of the Vedic people towards elaboration of the ritual aspect reached its climax towards the end of the Brāhmaṇa period. The religious sacrifices grew from simple to complex at this time. Thes Brāhmaṇa works described as 'Theological Tracts' were found difficult in comprehending the forms of their arrangement of contents. A need was therefore felt for preparing shorter and easier manuals of these ritualistic works. This attempt at securing ease and brevity might have resulted in the composition of what are now called the Kalpasūtras. This idea is borne out by the commentary of Sāyaṇa on the Bodhāyana-Sūtras.

विध्यर्थवाद-मन्त्रात्मना त्रिधा व्यवस्थितो वेदराशिः । ततश्च चोदितानां कर्मणां सुसवबोधाय भगवान्बौधायनः कल्पमकथयत् । यतो ह ब्राह्मणानामानन्तर्यदुरवबोधयता, अतो न तैः सुखं कर्मावबोधाय इति कल्पसण्त्राणीमानि प्रतिनियतशाखन्तरा अङ्गीचक्रुः पूर्वाचार्याः । कल्पस्य वैशद्य-लाक्षव कात्स्न्र्य-प्रकरण-शुद्ध्यादिभिः प्रकर्षैर्युक्तस्य....

Again Haradatta in his commentary on Aśvalāyana describes that the chief object of the Kalpasūtras is to explain the rites enjoined in the Vedas:

छन्दोः वेदः तत्कल्पयति प्रतिशाखं शाखन्तराधीतेन न्यायप्राप्तोन चांगकलापेनोपेतस्य कर्मणः प्रयोग कल्पनयोपस्कुरुत इति छन्दः कल्पसूत्राणि । (Aśvalāyana Gṛhya-Sūtra, II.8.11)

Thus the formulation of Kalpa tackled the question of 'how' of the liturgical employment in sacrifices, simplifying the riddle-ridden Brāhmaṇas. But the common name of Veda was not applicable to the Kalpa Sūtras, as these were composed by human authors. Thus says Kumārila: वेदत्वं कल्पसण्त्राणां नो वक्तव्यं मनागपि । (Tantravārtikā, I.3)

10.7.2 Distinct Classes of the Kalpa Sūtras

A complete corpus of the Kalpa Sūtras comprises the *Śrauta, Gṛhya* and *Dharmasūtras*. The *Śrautasūtras* based on Sruti treat systematically the Vedic sacrifices like the great Aśvamedha, Rājasūya, Vājapeya and Soma give directions for the laying of the sacrificial fire for the Agnihotra etc. The Gṛhya Sūtras deal in the main with the domestic conduct and life of the Hindu. On the other hand the Dharma Sūtras also known as Smṛtis treat mainly of the social conduct and life of the Hindu. Together, the two, mutually considered prove to be rich sources of information for us with regard to almost every phase of life of the Hindu in the domestic, social, political, economic, moral and religious spheres. Moreover they deal with almost all the phrases of Hindu life as conceived by them. Even the minutest aspects of a Hindu's family life are described and defined by them to a degree that is astounding. Such a wealth of elaborate details is given in these scriptures that there is hardly any phase of human life, day in and day out, as the Hindu conceives it, that is left untouched by them.

Only a few of the Kalpasūtras belonging to the Yajurveda contain all types of Sūtras mentioned above. As the Kalpasūtras are indispensable for the proper understanding of the Vedic Saṁhitās and the Brāhmaṇas, they are a veritable treasure that augment and explain the cultural data present in them. Thus, the following chart will clearly indicate the pedigree of the Kalpa Sūtras and the Gṛhya Sūtras.

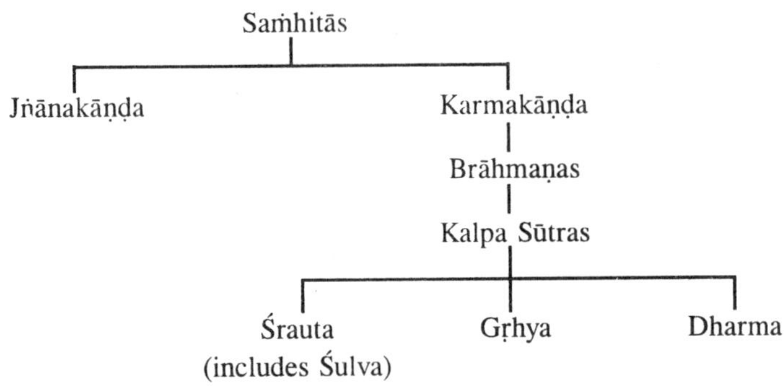

10.7.3 Śrauta Sūtras

Less important speculation on the minute details of ritual, so much in evidence in the Brāhmaṇas, developed in the direction of pure speculation in the *Araṇyakas* and Upaniṣads. It is necessary to remember that it is no less difficult to draw the line between the Brāhmaṇas and the Araṇyakas. Among the Śrauta Sūtras, too, there is at least one text namely the *Baudhāyana Śrautasūtra*, which it is difficult not to regard as a late Brāhmaṇa. Thus a fine line of demarcation between Brāhmaṇa, Araṇyaka and Śrauta Sūtra is out of the question. Yet it would be correct to say that the speculative spirit developed in the Brāhmaṇas in connection with ritual ceremonies tried to burst its irksome fetters in the Araṇyakas, and in some of the Upaniṣads attained the stage of as complete an independence as was ever witnessed by man. The Araṇyakas and Upaniṣads, though nominally connected with the Brāhmaṇas, should rather be regarded as the beginning of purely speculative thinking in India. Much more closely connected with the older Vedic literature (Saṁhitās and Brāhmaṇas) are the Śrauta Sūtras, and to a lesser extent, the Gṛhya Sūtras. Closely connected with this are Sulbasūtras dealing with the measurement and construction of the sacrificial altars.

The Śrauta-sūtras describe the ritual sacrifices in a language that is both vigorous and prophetic in brevity, but is also utterly unintelligible for that they reason. No greater contrast can be imagined than that between the Brāhmaṇas and Śrauta-sūtras, though the subject of treatment is the same in both. Both are obscure, but for different reasons: the Brāhmaṇas, because of loose thinking, and the Śrauta-sūtras, because too much is taken to be understood in them. Moreover the Śrauta-sūtras, isolated the common and special features of the sacrifices and cleverly dealt with them as if they were digits of number, and that by itself must be regarded as an intellectual achievement of no mean order. Truely scientific spirit is unmistakebly reflected in the Śrauta-sūtras, albeit the subject to which this spirit was applied was still magic pure and simple.

The Śrauta-sūtras of Āśvalāyana and Śāṅkhāyana belong to the *Ṛg-Veda*, which means that the ritual duties of the Hotṛi-priests have been presented in them in a systematic form. But some of the verses quoted by Pratīka in the *Śāṅkhyāyana Śrauta-sūtra* cannot be found in the Śākala-recension of the *Ṛik-Saṁhitā*, and so it is summarised that it was affiliated to the Bāshkala-śākhā and not to the Śākala-śākhā of the *Ṛg-Veda*. As regards the

Brāhmaṇas, its affiliation is to the *Kauṣītaki* and not the *Aitareya Brāhmaṇa*. Of its eighteen chapters, the last two, though not necessarily of later origin, were a later addition, dealing with the Mahāvrata, a popular festival that was given a Brāhmaṇical complexion at a later date. The *Āśvalāyana Śrauta-sūtra*, on the other hand, is affiliated to the Śākala-śākhā of the *Ṛik-Saṁhitā*, and the *Aitareya Brāhmaṇa* : Of these two Śrauta-sūtras of the *Ṛgveda*, Śāṅkhāyana should be the older for its language in some places is like that of the Brāhmaṇas. The principal Śrauta-sūtras of the *Sāmaveda* are those of Lāṭyāyaṇa and Drāhyāyana the first affiliated to the Kauthuma-śākhā and the latter to the Rāṇāyanīya-śākhā. A remarkable feature of the *Lāṭyāyaṇa Śrauta-sūtra* is that the Sūdras, Nishāds and Vrātyas have not been treated in it as accursed human beings as is generally the case in other Vedic texts.

The *Āpastamba Śrauta-sūtra* of the Black Yajurveda, belonging to the Khāṇḍikīya school of the *Taittirīyas*, is in many respects the most important work of this genre, for no other single work gives such an ample (though by no means complete) description of the Vedic sacrifices; but the numerous quotations from other ritual texts found in it suggest that it should not be placed too high in date. The *Satyāshāḍha Śrauta-sūtra* is a particular recension of the *Āpastamba Śrauta-sūtra*. The Āpastambians seem to have been prejudiced against the Kaṇvas and Kaśyapas, for their Śrauta-sūtra (XIII.7.5) forbids the giving of presents to them. The oldest and the most archaic of all the known Śrauta-sūtras is certainly the *Boudhāyana Śrauta-sūtra,* also of the Black Yajurveda. In style it still resembles a Brāhmaṇa in most respects, and according to tradition it belongs to the Khāṇḍikīya-school like the *Āpastamba Śrauta-sūtra*. The White Yajurveda is represented in the Śrauta-sūtra literature by the *Kātyāyana Śrauta-sūtra*, of which a striking feature is that three of its Adhyāyas (XXII-XXIV) are devoted to Sāmavedic ritual. Among the teachers cited by name in it are found some of the Black Yajurveda.

Lastly, the Atharvavedins too got their Śrauta-manual in the shape of the *Vaitāna-sūtra*- anomalously enough for the Atharvaveda has, strictly speaking, nothing to do with Śrauta-ritual. But since the Saṁhitā of the Brāhmaṇachchaṁsin, one of the priests participating in Soma-sacrifices, came to the appended to the *Atharvaveda*, the way was apparently opened thereby for the despised Atharvavedins to make inroad into the protected field of Śrauta-ritual. The result of this novel experiment was the *Vaitāna-sūtra*. But as Bloomfield has observed, "it is not the product of practices in Śrauta-ceremonies which have slowly and gradually developed in a certain high priestly school, but a somewhat conscious product made at a time, when the Atharvavedins began to feel the need of a distinctive Śrauta-manual to support their clain that the *Atharvaveda* is a canonical Veda of independent and superior character. Strictly speaking, the *Vaitāna-sūtra* is the Śrauta-sūtra only of the twentieth kāṇḍa of the *Atharvaveda* and not of the whole of it. And since the Kāṇḍa is nothing but the Saṁhitā of the Brāhmaṇāchchhaṁsin, the *Vaitāna-sūtra* may quite appropriately be called the Śrauta-sūtra of the Brāhmaṇāchchhaṁsin. It may be noted that only 18 verses of the twentieth Kāṇḍa of the *Atharvaveda* have not been assigned *viniyoga* in the *Vaitāna-sūtra*.

10.7. 4 Gṛhya Sūtras

The Nature of the Gṛhyasūtras

Though the origin of the Gṛhyasūtras as of other branches, is shrouded in mystery, their origin is based on the customs that originated from popular beliefs and usages before they became codified in the Gṛhya manuals. These Gṛhyasūtras generally refer to the customs of one's own family in the performance of the Saṁskāras. The *Āśvalāyana Gṛhyasūtra* while laying down rules about the Vivāha Saṁskāras says, "the customs and usages of different provinces and villages are high and low, that is variant.

They should be all consulted in marriage. We prescribe what is common." Again with reference to the *Sīmantonnayana* ceremony, the *Āśvalāyana Gṛhyasūtra* recommends that the advise of old Brāhmaṇa women, whose husband and children are alive should be regarded as authoritative. In the same way Āpastaṁba refers to the authority of ladies in the funeral ceremonies. Baudhāyana on Aśauca says, "In the rese, the people should be referred to", for the funeral ceremonies were closely connected with local beliefs and superstitions. The *Pāraskara Gṛhyasūtra* describing the marriage ritual puts forward the view that in matters of marriage and funeral rites, the custom as prevalent in the village concerned is the supreme authority. All these show that there was a mass of floating unwritten customs that could be codified in the Gṛhya rituals. Thus the presence of these floating practices apart from the codofied customs in the Gṛhyasūtras goes back to popular beliefs and customs only.

In the riutal literature proper there is a great elaboration of the simple rites of ancient days. For the development of rituals, the priest was responsible to a great extent. But rites and ceremonies were not his fabrication; rather he mainly drew on common practices and gave them a polish and a rationale. Had these rituals not been popular in their origin, they could not have become so universal and lasting.

At the outset, it is necessary to define the word Gṛhyasūtra. This is a compound consisting of the components Gṛhya and sūtra. *Gṛhya* is expounded as *Gṛhanimitto'gnih*. The rites performed with it are termed elliptically Gṛhyāṇi i.e., *Gṛhyakarmāṇi*. Thus Gṛhyas are the domestic ceremonies performed by means of one domestic fire in opposition to the great sacrifices performed with several hearths called Vaitāna.

These characteristics of a Sūtra apply to the prose passages of the Gṛhyasūtras; but the studied brevity of the grammatical

Sūtras is not widely found in the Gṛhyasūtras. The interweaving of metrical passages inot the texture of the Sūtras is a striking feature of the Gṛhyasūtras. Though the language used in the Gṛhyasūtras is classical Sanskrit, un-Pāṇinīyan expressions do show their presence now and then.

The arrangement of the contents of the extant Gṛhyasūtras is not uniform. We come across different modes of arrangement in them. Some are divided into Prapāṭhakas or Praśṇas or Adhyāyas or Kāṇḍas. Each of them is further sub-divided into kaṇḍikas, khaṇḍas, paṭalas etc. and each of these sub-divisions consists of many sūtras.

10.7.5 Gist of the Gṛhyasūtras

The Gṛhyasūtras of the Ṛgveda

1. *Śāṅkhāyana Gṛhyasūtra* : The reputed author of this Gṛhyasūtra had the proper name Suyajña. This work is divided into six adhyāyas and each adhyāya is sub-divided into khaṇḍas.

   The first adhyāya contains 28 khaṇḍas, the second 18, the third 14, the fourth 19, the fifth 11 and the last 6. The fifth and the sixth adhyāyas of this Gṛhyasūtra are later additions. This Gṛhyasūtra belongs to the Śāṇkhāyana Śākhā of the Ṛgveda and is based on the Bāṣkala recension of this Veda.

2. *Āśvalāyana Gṛhyasūtra* : This Gṛhyasūtra consists of four adhyāyas and each adhyāya is divided into kaṇḍikas. The first adhyāya consists of 24 kaṇḍikas, the second 10, the third and fourth 12 and 8 respectively.

   Āśvalāyana is said to be a disciple of Śauṇaka by Sadguruśiṣya. When Āśvalāyana composed Sūtra, Śaunaka is said to have destroyed his own sūtra and determined that his disciple's Sūtra should be adopted by the students of Āśvalāyana Vedic Śākha. The relation between Āśvalāyana and Śaunaka and the position of Āśvalāyana are discussed in detail by Prof. Oldenburg in his General Introduction to Gṛhyasūtras.

3. *Kauṣītaka Gṛhyasūtra* : This is a composition by Śāmbavya. This consists of five adhyāyas and is closely allied to the Śāṅkhāyana Gṛhyasūtra.

The Gṛhyasūtras of the Sāmaveda

1. *Gobhila Gṛhyasūtra* : The peculiarity of this Gṛhyasūtra is that this presupposes besides the Saṁhitā of the Sāmaveda, another collection of Mantras under the title 'Mantra Brāhmaṇa' which evidently was composed expressly with the purpose of being used at Gṛhya ceremonies. The credit for an accurate edition and translation of this Gṛhyasūtra goes to Prof. Knauer of Kiew.

   This Gṛhyasūtra consists of four Prapāṭhakas and each of the Prapāṭhaka is sub-divided into kaṇḍikās. The first consists of 9 kaṇḍikās, the second, third and fourth consists of 10 kaṇḍikās each.

2. *Khādira Gṛhyasūtra* : This Gṛhyasūtra belongs to the Drāhyāyana school of the Sāmaveda and this is based on the Gobhila Gṛhyasūtra. This Gṛhyasūtra serves as a very clear example how a Sūtrakāra of a later time would remodel the work of a more ancient author, trying to surpass him by a more correct arrangement and especially by what become more and more appreciated as the chief accomplishment of Sūtra composition, the greatest possible succintness and economising of words.

   This consists of 3 paṭalas and each paṭala is further sub-divided into khaṇḍas. The first three paṭalas consist of 5 khaṇḍas and the fourth consists of 4 khaṇḍas.

3. *Jaimini Gṛhyasūtra* : This has been published in the Punjab Sanskrit Series. This Gṛhyasūtra belongs to the Jaiminīya Śākhā of the Sāmaveda. This consists of two halves, the first containing 24 khaṇḍas and the other consisting of 9

khaṇḍas. In point of language, this Gṛhyasūtra harmonizes with the tradition of the Jaiminīyas.

The Gṛhyasūtras of the Śukla Yajurveda

1. The Pāraskara Gṛhyasūtra : This Gṛhyasūtra forms an appendix to Kātyāyana's Śrautasūtra and all the credit for the edition and a German translation of this Gṛhyasūtra goes to Prof. Stenzler.

This consists of three kāṇḍas and each kāṇḍa is further subdivided into kaṇḍikās. The first kāṇḍa consists of 19 kaṇḍikās, the second 17 and the third 16 kaṇḍikās. The saying and verses which are quoted in the Pāraskara Gṛhyasūtra by initial words belong to the Mādhyaṁdina Śākhā of the Śukla Yajurveda. The commentator Jayarāma uses the expression 'Kātīya Gṛhyasūtra' for the Pāraskara Gṛhyasūtra and the Vājasaneyi Gṛhyasūtra is said to be still another name of the same Gṛhya. Pāraskara is regarded as the author of this Gṛhya.

A Bhaijavāpa Gṛhyasūtra is said to belong to this *Śukla Yajurveda*.

Gṛhyasūtras of the Kṛṣṇa Yajurveda

1. *Baudhāyana Gṛhyasūtra* : This forms part of the Baudhāyana kalpa authorised by Baudhāyana. This is regarded as the oldest of the extant kalpas affiliated to the Taittirīya Śākhā. This consists of four Praśnas.
2. *Bhāradvāja Gṛhyasūtra* : This forms a part of the Bhāradvāja kalpa belonging to a sub-division of the Taittirīyas. This consists of three Praśnas.
3. Agniveśya Gṛhyasūtra : This is ascribed to one Agniveśya. Some of the topics, Nārāyaṇa-Bali, Saṇnyāsa vidhi, Vānaprastha vidhi etc., treated of in this Gṛhya are absolutely foreign to the tenor of the other Gṛhyasūtras and this Gṛhya bears the stamp of recent origin.

4. *Āpastambīya Gṛhyasūtra* : This forms one Praśna of the great corpus of the Āpastambīya kalpasūtra and stands among the Gṛhya texts, in closest connection with the Hiraṇyakeśi Gṛhyasūtra.

   This Gṛhyasūtra, like the Gobhila gives only the rules for the performance of the Gṛhya rites without the Mantras which are contained in a special collection, the Mantrapāṭha, standing by the side of the Sūtras.

   This consists of 8 Paṭalas and there are twenty-three sections in these eight Paṭalas. The first three Paṭalas consist of three sections each, the fourth and the fifth consist of two sections each, the sixth consists of three sections, the seventh four and the eighth three sections.

5. *Hiraṇyakeśi Gṛhyasūtra* : This consists of two Praśnas and each Praśna is divided into Paṭalas and each Paṭala has sections in it. The first Praśna consists of 8 Paṭalas with 29 sections. The second also contains 8 Paṭalas and there are twenty sections in all. In this Gṛhya work, the Mantras to be recited at the performance of th Gṛhya ceremonies are given in full. The style of this Sūtra is diffuse and in some cases this Gṛhya does not follow the rules of Pāṇinīan Grammar.

6. Kāṭhaka Gṛhyasūtra : This is known as the Laugākṣi Gṛhyasūtra and this belongs to the Kāṭhaka Śākhā of Kṛṣṇa Yajurveda. This presupposes a collection of Mantras to be used at the domestic ritual.

7. Mānava Gṛhyasūtra : This is known as Maitrāyaṇīya Mānava Gṛhyasūtra and this is designated as a Praśna by its commentator Aṣṭāvakra. This is said to have been composed by Mānavācārya. This Gṛhyasūtra is divided into two Puruṣas and each Puruṣa is subdivided into a number of khaṇḍas. The worship of four Vināyakas and Ṣaṣṭi Kalpa are peculiar to this Gṛhya work. According to Prof. Lele's observation, this Sūtra is a product of different schools.

8. *Vaikhānasa Gṛhyasūtra* : This Gṛhya like the Gobhila presupposes a collection of Mantras known as Mantra Saṁhitā Vaikhānasīya.
9. *Varāha Gṛhyasūtra* : This Gṛhyasūtra belongs to the Varāha subdivision of Maitrāyaṇīya, a division of the Caraka Śākhā of this Yajurveda and this does not contain any worthwhile information.

Mutual relationship between some of the Gṛhya Sūtras

As the Gṛhyasūtras deal with a common theme, a sort of loose and general agreement amongst them is to be expected; but the differences between them are far more numerous than would appear to us at first sight.

The Gṛhyasūtras belonging to the same Veda and to the same Śākhā are generally found to be closely allied to each other. There is exception also to this rule in that the Āśvalāyana Gṛhyasūtra and the Śāṅkhāyana Gṛhyasūtra though belonging to the same Ṛgveda do not form this alliance.

The Śāṅkhāyana and the Kauṣītaka are very closley related. In fact the first four adhyāyas of both have verbal agreements. In the same way, there is verbatim agreement between the Śāṅkhāyana and the Pāraskara Gṛhya. The Khādira Gṛhyasūtra is more or less an abridged edition of the Gobhila Gṛhyasūtra. The Jaiminīya Gṛhyasūtra shows a great amount of similarity with the Sūtras of the Kṛṣṇa Yajurveda. The Mānava Gṛhyasūtra, the Kāṭhaka Gṛhyasūtra and the Varāha Gṛhyasūtra have close relationship. But the relation of the Varāha Gṛhyasūtra with the Mānava Gṛhyasūtra is more close than that with the Kāṭhaka Gṛhyasūtra.

The differences between the Gṛhyasūtras are mainly due to the differences of traditions prevalent in the Vedic Śākhās, based on variations in local customs.

The Kauśika Sūtra of the Atharvaveda

Introduction

The most important accessory text of the Atharvaveda is the Sūtra of Kauśika. It comprises along with a good deal of medicinal and abhicāra practices, the themes ordinarily treated in the Gṛhyasūtras. Consequently much of the material found in the Kauśika is unknown to the other Gṛhyas.

The Kauśika Gṛhyasūtra belongs to the Śaunakīya Śākhā of the Atharvaveda. Among the Pañca-kalpas or the five Sūtra works belonging to the Śaunakīya school of the Atharvaveda, Kauśika Sūtra is probably the earliest and foremost, since all the other four Vaitāna, Nakṣatrakalpa, Āṅgirasakalpa, Śāntikalpa depend on it. This is corroborated by the statement of Sāyaṇa in the introduction to his commentary on the Atharvaveda Saṁhitā :

संहितामंत्राणां शान्तिकपौष्टिकादिसु कर्मसु विनियोगविधानात् संहिताविधिर्नाम कौशिकसण्त्रम् । तदेवेतरैः सूत्रैरुपजीव्यत्वम् प्रधानं च ॥

In addition to the commentary of Dārila, the Paddhati of Keśava, and other minor paddhatis, the Kauśikasūtra seems also to have been commented upon by Bhadra and Rudra.

The Atharvan has also a Śrautasūtra Vaitāna by name and the Vaitāna treats the Kauśikasūtra as though it were a Saṁhitā.

In his introduction to the Kauśikasūtra Prof. Bloomfield opines that the Sūtra ascribed to Kauśika is a work dating from the later Sūtra period. But the work seems to be one of the earliest Sūtras on the Gṛhya ritual.

Pāṇini refers to Kalpa works (IV.3.105) promulgated by ancient authors of which the Paiṅgi Kalpa and the Aruṇaparāji Kalpa are cited as examples. Pāṇini (IV.3.103) refers to works of two other *ṛṣis* named Kāśyapa and Kauṣika which Kātyāyana takes to be Kalpa works. These were studied in Vedic Caraṇas by students called after them Kāśyapinah and Kauṣikinah. It is also pointed out that the literary activity of these two old schools was confined to their Kalpa Sūtras only round which centred a group of their students and teachers. काश्यपकौशिकग्रहणं च कल्पनियमार्थम् - (II.286). Perhaps this mention of Pāṇini refers to our work, Kauṣika. These references point to the conclusion that the Kausika Sūtra is earlier than Pāṇini. Thus Kauṣika may be regarded as one belonging to the earliest Sūtra period.

Kauṣika Sūtra is arranged in fourteen adhyayas. Each adhyaya is sub-divided into kaṇḍikās. The kaṇḍikās are numbered continuously through all the adhyāyas and their total is one hundred and forty one.

Fusion of Atharva Sūtras and Gṛhya Sūtras

This Sūtra contains various strata prominent among them being Gṛhya and Atharvan practices, not properly assimilated to hide their individual character, due to separate authorship or their varying period of composition.

Prof. Bloomfield holds that the Kauṣika Sūtra is a mixture of two distinct kinds of Sūtras viz., Atharva Sūtras and Gṛhya Sūtras. The same scholar further states that the distinction between Atharva Sūtras and Gṛhya Sūtras is justified by their difference in subject-matter, style and Sūtra technique. This opinion of Bloomfield will appear true on a thorough study of the Kauṣika.

A strong current of Atharvan life flows through from kaṇḍikā 7 to kaṇḍikā 53 (except for kaṇḍikā 42.15 to end of kaṇḍikā 45). The practices connected with Atharva sūtras seem to be the nucleus of this work around which the later Gṛhya chapters upto the end of adhyāya 12 are hanged. Condensed Sūtra style marks the Atharvan-Sūtras and these contain the most original practices like the Bhaiṣajya and Abhicāra. The language of these Sūtras is striking for its lexical materials and their value towards the exegesis of the Atharva Saṁhitā is of a very great order. Another speciality of these Sūtras is that they quote very few mantras which are not found in the Atharva Saṁhitā.

The style of the Gṛhya Sūtras on the other hand is verifiably broader than the Atharva Sūtras; visible through their mode of quoting pratīkas. The conspicuous edge which distinguishes the Gṛhya Sūtras are the Mantra material not derived from the Atharva Saṁhitā and therefore given in Sakalapāṭha.

Many technical points too differentiate the two divisions. Thus the impression left upon the persual of the redaction represents the fusion of Atharvan Sūtras with an ordinary Gṛhya Sūtra.

The strange position of the first six kaṇḍikās of the first adhyāya treating of the darśapūrṇamāsa ceremonies and their situation not in harmony with the following chapters is beautifully analysed by Bloomfield in his learned introduction to the Kauṣika (pp.xxvii-xxviii). He feels that the first six kaṇḍikās originally did not stand where they are now found and that they were placed there in deference to the ordinary habit of the Yajussaṁhitā or still more primarily the Śrautasūtras opening with this performance. The writer goes on to show some technical evidence also in support of his view (Ibid.p.xxviii). Without urging any conclusion on his opinion Bloomfield opines that he does not venture to decide, whether they once stood in some other part of the work, or merely represent a different stratum, worked over by some special hand, or dating from a later period (Ibid). He feels that they might have stood fittingly between kaṇḍikās 52 and 53, immediately after the Atharva Sūtra proper and the beginning of the Gṛhya chapters (Ibid).

Regarding the scope of the special set of Paribhāṣās (9-21) in the first kaṇḍikā dealing with differences between the worship of gods and manes, Bloomfield is of the opinion that these Paribhāṣās allude to a later part of the work.

10.8 The Bṛhaddevatā

10.8.1 Date and Authorship

What evidence does the relationship of the Bṛhaddevatā to other texts furnish towards determining the question of its date? It may however be said here that the Bṛhaddevatā, while posterior to the Nirukta, is anterior to the Sarvānukramaṇī. This conclusion at the same time takes us a considerable way towards an approximate estimate of the actual date of our text. It must thus be later than 500 B.C., but earlier than the time of Kātyāyana. Owing to the concise character of their style, both the Sarvānukramaṇī and the Śrauta Sūtra of the White Yajur-veda probably belong to the later Sūtra period. Both works were composed by Kātyāyana. The Vājasaneyī Anukramaṇī, which has nearly the whole of its introduction in common with that of the Sarvānukramaṇī, is also the work of a Kātyāyana. All this points to the author of these works being the same Kātyāyana, who, because the diction of the Sarvānukramaṇī shows several Vedic peculiarities and forms not sanctioned by Pāṇini's Grammar, could hardly be identical with Pāṇini's commentator of that name. Hence it seems likely that the Sarvānukramaṇī, as a later but still probably pre-Pāṇinian Sūtra, dates from not later than the middle of the fourth century B.C. The Bṛhaddevatā, its chief source, could, therefore, hardly be placed later than 400 B.C. Though ślokas have undoubtedly been added here and there and some modifications of diction have probably crept in, the authenticity of the text as a whole is better guaranteed than that of perhaps any other ancillary Vedic work, by the fragments of it which are found embedded, from beginning to end, in the Sarvānukramaṇī, itself a text which has been handed down with peculiar care. The early character of the Bṛhaddevatā is further indicated by its mythological standpoint, which is that of the Vedic triad Agni, Indra and Sūrya; Indra, moreover, is the predominant deity. The comparatively large proportion (one-fourth) of narrative which it contains, in illustration of the hymns of the Ṛg-Veda, is thus the earliest collection of epic matter which we possess, dating as it does from a period when the Mahābhārata could only have been in an embryonic state. The fact of its containing this additional epic matter, points to its being somewhat later in date than the Devatānukramṇī, which though not extant is known from ten quotations in Sadguruśiṣya and was doubtless an index of deities only. There seems no reason to doubt the tradition which attributes this and the other short Anukramaṇīs to Śaunaka.

But is the ascription to him of the Bṛhaddevatā also probable? There can be little doubt that the Devatānukramaṇī, as the simpler of the two, was also the earlier. It is in itself unlikely that the same author should have reproduced this work in another form with exactly the same object, viz., to give a serial account of the deities of the Ṛg-veda. This assumption is borne out by the internal evidence of the Bṛhaddevatā itself. The writer several times speaks of himself in the first person. On the other hand, Śaunaka is mentioned fifteen times by name, generally with other authorities, especially Yāska, when different views are stated. Indeed, the impression is once or twice conveyed, that Śaunaka's view was not shared by the writer. In any case, the author could not possibly have meant himself when speaking of the 'ācārya Śaunaka' (ii.136; vi.9), or of 'Śaunaka and other ācāryas' (v.39), or the 'ācāryas Śaunaka, Yāska, Gālava (vii.38). The conclusion, therefore, is that the writer was not Śaunaka himself, but a teacher of his school, who was not separated from him by any great length of time.

10.8.2 Summary of the Contents

The contents of the eight Adhyāyas of the Bṛhaddevatā do not correspond in any way to the eight Aṣṭakas of the Rg-veda. Thus the enumeration of the deities of the hymns does not begin till near the end of the second Adhyāya (ii.126). Each Adhyāya contains about thirty vargas of generally five ślokas. The division into Adhyāyas and vargas is quite mechanical, as it often cuts into the middle of a discussion or a story (e.g. the end of vi, or the seventh varga of viii).

The Bṛhaddevatā begins with a long introduction embracing the whole of the first Adhyāya, and twenty-five vargas of the second. This introduction consists mainly of a classification and enumeration of the Vedic deities, in connection with Prajāpati as representing them collectively, and with the Vedic triad of Fire, Indra or Vāyu, and Sun, as representing respectively the gods of the three worlds. Seven vargas at the end of the introduction contain an interesting grammatical discussion, closley related to the Nirukta, and dealing with particles, prepositions, nouns, pronouns, compounds and the analysis of words, together with a criticism of Yāska's errors in dividing words.

The main body of the work, commencing with the twenty-sixth varga of the second Adhyāya, is, for the most part, concerned with stating the deities, in their successive order, for the hymns and stanzas of the Ṛg-veda. It is, however, by no means a mere index of deities, such as the Devatānukramaṇī doubtless was. On the contrary, it contains a considerable amount of other matter, notably about forty legends, meant to explain the circumstances under which the hymns they are connected with, were composed. About 300 ślokas, or approximately one-fourth of the whole work, are devoted to these legends. This is the most important as well as the most interesting portion of the book, for it comprises the oldest systematic collection of legends which we possess in Sanskrit. Narrated in an epic style, they are historically connected with a number of stories told in the Mahābhārata. This historical connection deserves to be carefully examined. Dr. Sieg, in the first part of his meritorious work, 'Die Sagenstoffe des Ṛg-veda und die indische Itihāsatradition', has done this is the case of some legends. It cannot, however, in the present state of our knowledge, be agreed with him in supposing that the Bṛhaddevatā has borrowed from the Mahābhārata. He thinks that the story of Devāpi Ārṣṭiṣeṇa is a clear example of such borrowing. In my opinion, the evidence is all the other way. The single fact that Devāpi's patronymic, Ārṣṭiṣeṇa, has, in the Mahābhārata, become an independent name designating another person, but mentioned along with Devāpi, is a clear indication of the posteriority of the Mahābhārata form of the story; a differentiation of this kind being a not infrequent phenomenon in mythological development. In the Mahābhārata, moreover, a third brother appears, and the name Śantanu has become Śāntanu. It is, besides, impossible on general grounds that a Vedic work which is undoubtedly earlier than the Sarvānukramaṇī, and not much later than Yāska, should have borrowed from the Mahābhārata, which must have assumed the form known to us so many centuries later. The possibility even of interpolation appears to be entirely precluded by the internal evidence of the Bṛhaddevatā.

Our text further contains other matters connected with the deities of the Ṛg-veda, such as an enumeration of *ṛṣis*, of female seers, of the steeds of the various gods, a detailed account of the Āprī hymns, and a full discussion of the character of the Vaiśvadeva hymns. The concluding nine vargas state the gods presiding over various kinds of ritual verses and over the different tones, with some remarks about knowing the deities of the Veda. Important and interesting is the statement, occurring in the Anuvākānukramaṇī also, as to a different sequence of the groups of hymns in the first Maṇḍala. The statements of the Bṛhaddevatā about the khilas, or supplementary hymns, are curious. Both of these subjects have been ably discussed by Prof. Oldenberg in his Prolegomena with reference to the evidence then available.

10.8.3 The Khilas of the Ṛg-veda in the Bṛhaddevatā

With regard to the khilas, a more trustworthy text than Mitra's and the discovery of new evidence, enable us now to speak with greater precision on many points. Thus we can now say with certainty that the Bṛhaddevatā knows nothing of four khilas which Meyer, in his preface to the Ṛgvidhana (p. xxvi), supposes to be referred to in the corrupt MS. (b) of the Bṛhaddevatā which he used.

The relation of our text to the khilas is peculiar in two ways. In the first place, the Sarvānukramaṇī, which is so largely based on the Bṛhaddevatā, makes no mention of the thirty-seven khilas to which the Bṛhaddevatā refers. It only notices the group of khilas in the eighth Maṇḍala, besides referring to the existence, after Ṛg-veda i.99, of a group of hymns by Kaśyapa.

In the second place, of the twenty-five khilas printed in Aufrecht's and of the thirty-two in Max Muller's edition of the Ṛg-veda, the Bṛhaddevatā refers to only seven, while, on the other hand, it mentions thirty other khilas not in Aufrecht.

Of the total of thirty-seven khilas, eleven occur after Ṛg-veda i.73, seven are found at the end of the fifth Maṇḍala, one after vi.44 (B), the remaining eighteen being scattered through the latter half of the tenth Maṇḍala. Of the thirty not in Aufrecht, about twenty have been known to exist from the mention of their pratīkas or some general reference in other Vedic works, but of the rest not a trace has been found till now.

The khilas are here arranged in five Adhyāyas, which are subdivided into vargas. Each Adhyāya has prefixed to it a regular Anukramaṇī giving the pratīka, the Rishi, the deity and the metre of the following group of hymns. The position of the khila is indicated by the appended pratīka of the hymn of the Ṛg-veda which immediately follows. The first Adhyāya contains twelve khilas, the first corresponding to Aufrecht's no.i, from which it differs in the initial pāda only. Then there are eleven Sauparṇa hymns, of which, as they have been the subject of a good deal of speculation; here are the beginnings, along with the number of stanzas contained in each: 1. *śaśvan nāsatyā* (14); 2. *pra dhārayantu madhunah* (7); 4. *jyotiṣman taṁ ketumantaṁ tricakram* (10); 4. *kṛśas tvaṁ bhuvanasya te* (II); 5. imāni vāṁ *bhāgadheyāni sisratah* (7); 6. *ayaṁ somas suṣomo adribudhnah* (6); 7. *yadā yuñjāthe maghavānam āśum* (3); 8. *yaṁ gachathas sutapā devavantam* (6); 9. *ayaṁ somo devayāvān sumedhāh* (4); 10. *idaṁ devā bhāgadheyaṁ* (8); 11. *āśvinā vahataṁ pīvarīh* (8). This makes an aggregate of eighty-four stanzas.

The second Adhyāya contains seventeen hymns, eleven of which are printed in Aufrecht's edition (ii-xii). The six others which follow the Śrisūkta are described in the notes on Bṛhaddevatā v.91, 92. The thirteenth (*cakṣuh*) and the fifteenth (*svapnah*) each consist of a single stanza only, while the corresponding khilas in Aufrecth (viii and x) have two and eight additional stanzas respectively.

The third Adhyāya contains twenty-two hymns, the last being that of Nakula (*brahma jajñānam*). Of these only five appear in Aufrecht, and one besides in Max Muller. Two of the latter are much shorter than in Aufrecht or Max Muller. The tenth, beginning *pāvamānīh,* in which there is a lacuna after the middle of the third stanza, has six stanzas according to the Anukramaṇī; while in Aufrecht this khila has no fewer than twenty. The seventeeth (*dhruvā*), which consists of a single stanza, forms the conclusion of a khila of six stanzas in Aufrecht. Aufrecht's xvi, consisting of one stanza, is not to be found in the collection.

The fourth Adhyāya consists of fourteen khilas, most of which are quoted by the Bṛhaddevatā and all of which are described in the notes. Six of them are found in Aufrecht, one of these, however (*ā rātri*), having only four stanzas to Aufrecht's fourteen.

The fifth Adhyāya comprises at least twenty-three khilas, of which, however, only the first four are noticed in the Bṛhhadevatā. The fifth, of eleven stanzas, beginning *agnir deveddhah* and characterized in the Anukramaṇī as *yajūṁṣi,* is mentioned in the Aitareya Brāhmaṇa. The eighteenth, with eighteen stanzas, beginning *etā aśvāh* (= Atharva Veda. xx. 129.I), is in the Anukramaṇī ascribed to Aitaśa. The nineteenth, of six stanzas, beginning *vitatau kiraṇau* (Atharva Veda.xx.133. 1-6), is referred to in the Bṛhaddevatā (i. 57) as an example of 'enigma'. It is quite possible that several of the stanzas which seem to be quoted in the Bṛhaddevatā from other Vedas, may really be meant to refer to khilas of the Ṛg-Veda.

10.9 The Anukramaṇī

Although they form no part of the Vedaṅga, the Anukramaṇī, "index", are inseparable from the auxiliary texts of the Vedas. The only ones which are directly known (similar works must have existed for all the Vedas) are those of the Ṛik. These brief verse-texts give lists of the authors of the hymns, the metres, the divinities presiding over the hymns, and the sections of the Veda. They are ascribed to Shaunaka, except the Sarvānukramaṅī, "general index", a more systematic work in prose, and probably more recent, which is by Kātyāyana. Anukramaṇī has been compiled in later times, as by Madhava (10th century), who wrote two in a mnemonic verse.

References

1. The commentary on the *Śākala Prātiśākhya* (XIV), which enumerates *śikṣā* as the fourth instead of as the first, has *chandovicito* for *chandas* and *jyotiṣam-ayanam* for *jyotiṣa*.
2. The three grades of speech, deposited in secret, which move not, are explained in the *Śatapatha Brāhmaṇa* (IV.1.3.16) as being inarticulate (*anirukta*) and as the three progressively higher stages represented by (i) the hissing of serpents or te humming of insects ; (ii) the notes of birds; and (iii) the inarticulate speech of brutes.
3. This description probably gave the cue to the later mystic division of speech into *parā, paśyantī,* and *madhyamā,* originating from the navel, the lungs, and the throat,

respectively, i.e. the three unvoiced stages, and the fourth, the *vaikahrī,* expressed through the tongue.

4. *Der Ṛgveda,* p. 213
5. Compare also the association of Indra with speech in the *Taittirīya Saṁhitā* (VII.4.7).
6. *Critical Studies in the Phonetic Observations of Indian Grammarians* (=*CSPOIG*)
7. If the traditional data (*CSPOIG,* p.2) of the *āśvalāyana Śrauta-Sūtra* (VII.11) are based on the actual occurrence in the time of the *Aitareya Brāhmaṇa* of the *nyūṅkha* pronunciation which is prescribed generally during the recitation of certain verses on the fourth day of the *navarātra* ceremony, then, this would indicate a considerably advanced stage of phonetic studies even during this period. (*c. 1000-800 B.C.*).
8. The *Atharva-Veda Prātiśākhya,* edited by Vishva Bandhu (Punjab University, Lahore, 1923), is different from *Śaunakīya Caturādhyāyikā,* which has been edited and translated as an *Atharva-Veda Prātiśākhya* by W. D. Whitney (New Haven, 1862)) - Winternitz, *History of Indian Literature* (Calcutta University, 1927), I, p. 284, f. n. 4)
9. The edition published by the Nirnayasagar Press, Bombay (1930), contains a thirteenth chapter consisting of 13 sections as *pariśiṣṭa* (appendix). The Bhandarkar Oriental Research, Institute edition (1942) has sections 14-50 in addition, which are either treated as part of the thirteenth chapter or as a separate fourteenth chapter.
10. Belvalkar in his *Systems of Sanskrit Grammar* mentions that extracts from the works of these authors appear in the writings of later grammarians.
11. *Vājasaneyiī Saṁhitā*, V. 2: cf. *Śatapatha Brāhmaṇa*, III.4.1; VIII.5.2
12. The stanzas of the *Ṛg-Veda* are composed in some fifteen metres, only seven of which are really frequent. Three of the,

the *triṣṭubh,* the *gāyatrī* and the *jagatī* are by far the commonest metres, claiming between them about four-fifths of the stanzas in the *Ṛg-Veda* and individually accounting for about two-fifths, one-fourth, and three-twentieths, respectively.

13. Compare the word '*chandas*' with '*zend*'.
14. H. D. Velankar, *Jayadāman* (Bombay, 1949), pp. 9-11
15. *History of Sanskrit Literature,* I. p. 92
16. Dr. Haug quoted by Tilak in his *Orion*.
17. Incidentally, this fixes the time of the *Śatapatha Brāhmaṇa* at 2500 B.C. and of the older Orion calendar at 4500 B.C. Winternitz, however, is sceptical about this theory.

Chapter - XI

The Dharmaśāstra Literature

11.1 A. Introduction to the Dharmaśāstra

For the first time, we find mention of the eighteen kinds of sciences (*Śāstras*) in the *Viśṇupurāṇa* (3.6.28) and the *Yājnavalkyasmṛti* (1.3). Of these two, the *Viśṇupurāṇa* designates those sciences as vidyā whereas Yājnavalkya terms those as *vidyāsthāna* or *dharmasthāna*. Both the sources include Dharmaśāstra in the list of the eighteen sciences. It is an accepted view that all the orthodox sciences have their own sources in the Vedas. In this regard, the Vedas are treated as *ṣaḍaṅgas*. They are : Śikṣa, Kalpa, Vyākaraṇa, Nirukta, Chandas and Jyotiṣa. Of these six, Kalpa is viewed as the hands of the Vedapuruṣa. It has four divisions : *Śrauta, Gṛhya, Dharma,* and *Śulba*. All are written in aphorisms being termed as Śrautasūtra, Gṛhyasūtra, and Dharmasūtra and Śulbasūtra. The Śrauṭasūtras deal with sacrificial manuals whereas Gṛhyasūtras describe domestic rituals. The technological materials are put in the Śulabasūtras. The Dharmasūtras are different from those three literature. They deal with social codes. Having been originated from the Vedas, the Dharmasūtra are compiled both in aphorisms and meters. The metrical texts are termed as Smṛtis. By this way Dharmaśāstras comprise the Dharmasūtra and the Smṛti. The important contents of the Dharmaśāstra are : the sources of Dharma, the Vedas, the Smṛtis, and time -honored practices of the great people; the duties of the four *varṇas aśrams*; various moral *saṁskārs* of man, like *upanayana* and marriage according to the different castes, the avocation of four *varṇas* in life; the duties and responsibilities of the King, rules of taxation, ownership, guardianship, witness, money-lending, payment of debts and different kinds of *śrāddhas*, rules about food, duties of women and their property, *niyoga* (levirate) and its conditions; sins and their expiations and penances along with conditions. The Smṛtis deal with those topics in a more analytical and systematized form under three main heads: *ācāra* (rites), *vyavahāra* (dealing) and *prāyaścitta* (expiation).

11.2 Beginning of the Dharmaśāstra

At the outset, the time of the composition of the texts on Dharmaśāstra is a pertinent question to be answered. But it is nor possible to give a definite answer to this question. The *Nirukta* (3.4-5) shows that long before Yāska heated controversies had raged on various questions of inheritance, such as the exclusion of daughters by sons and the rights of the appointed daughter : *putrikā*. The *Nirukta* was composed by Yāska during 600-300 B.C. Therefore, it is ascertained that the composition of the Dharmaśāstra works was started prior to this period. However, the chronology of the Dharmasūtras works was started prior to this period. However, the chronology of the Dharmasūtras and the Smṛtis is still an unsettled question. It is held by a few western scholars that the Dharmaśāstras are earlier than the sources of the metrical Smṛtis. But since Manu and his extant Smṛti and a few others are found cited by many Dharmasūtras, it is very difficult to maintain that all the metrical Smṛtis are evolved from the Dharmasūtras. On the other hand, it can be asserted that both kinds of texts in the form of Sūtras and verses, which were equally popular during that period have developed side by side, with the result that many Dharmasūtra texts have also incorporated the verses in anustubh and sometimes in other metals also.

Mentions may be made here that there are certain points which distinguish the Dharmasūtras from the Smṛtis:

(a) Many Dharmasūtras are either parts of the Kalpa belonging to each *sūtrācaraṇa* or are intimately connected with the Gṛhyasūtras.

(b) The Dharmasūtras sometimes are not unique in showing their Vedic quotations for the texts of the corresponding Veda to which they belong or in the *caraṇas* of which they are studied.

(c) The authors of the older Dharmasūtras do not claim to be the inspired seers or super human beings, while the other Smṛtis such as those of Manu and Yājñavalkya are ascribed to gods like Brahmā.

(d) The Dharmasūtras are in prose or in mixed prose and verse; while the other Smṛtis are in verse.

(e) The language of Dharmasūtras is generally more archaic than that of the other Smṛtis.

(f) The Dharmasūtras do not proceed upon any orderly arrangement of topics while the other Smṛits arrange their contents and treat of the subjects under three principal heads viz. *ācāra, vyavahāra*, and *prāyaścitta*.

(g) Most of the Dharmasūtras are older than most of the other Smṛtis. Importance is given both the *Gautamadharmasūtra* and the *Manusmṛti* as Dharmasūtra and Smṛti respectively. Those are the oldest of all in those two lines.

In the Kalpa tradition the Dharmasūtras, as a rule, follow the Gṛhyasūtras. At present only for Gṛhyasūtras namely the *Baudhāyanagṛhyasūtra*, the *āpastamba-gṛhyasūtra*, the *Hiraṇyakeśi-gṛhyasūtra*, and the *Vaikhānasa-gṛhyasūtra* are found to be follwed by the Dharmasūtras of their respective schools. The other Gṛhyasutras have no Dharmasūtras to follow them. It is a moot point whether each Gṛhyasūtra possessed Dharmasūtras belonging to the same school or the however, undeniable fact that in distinction from the Gṛhyasutras the Dharmasūtras cover a wider range of subjects which are by no means confined to the school of the Sūtras itself. On the other hand, the Dharmasūtras lay down rules and regulations for the guidance of social as well as spiritual life of the community in its wider perspective. They deal with the rights and duties of different classes of society and prescribe the duties which an individual should discharge during different periods of his life. Matters relating to civil and criminal laws have also been dwelt upon in the Dharmasūtras. A few of the subjects, such as the duties of a student and those of *snātaka*, which have already been touched upon in the Gṛhyasūtras, are treated in detail by the Dharmasūtras. The Gṛhyasūtras deal with the rites and customs which are concerned with the domestic life of an Ārya, whereas the Dharmasūtras devote more attention to the social life of an Ārya. The essential difference, therefore, between the outlook of the Gṛhyasutras and the Dharmasūtras lies in the fact that the outlook of the Gṛhyasūtras is mainly limited to the customs and conventions of their respective schools, whereas the Dharmasūtras take a broader view of the whole society comprising various schools and communities.

B. Dharmaśāstra I : Sūtra Texts

11.3 Gautama-dharmasūtra

The *Gautama-dharmasūtra* is believed to be the earliest among the Dharmasūtras available. Since it is specially studied by the *chāndogas*, it is conjectured that it belongs to the Sāmaveda. It has twenty-eight chapters and deals with almost every topic exhaustively. Its treatment of marriage of eight kinds and of sub castes by *anuloma* and *pratiloma* marriage in which the wife is respectively of superior or inferior caste in chapter IV is noteworthy. It allows niyoga under certain conditions as stated in chapter XVIII. Like Manu, Gautama recognizes twelve sons in chapter XXVIII. Baudhāyana, Āpastamba, Vasiṣṭha, and Yājnavalkya presuppose Manu. His earliest limit is decided by his Sūtras in chapter XXVI, which is based on the *Sāmvidhāna Brāhmaṇa* and by the *Sūtra* II. 28; which is probably a reminiscence of the *Nirukta*, II. 3. Hence, this Sūtra is approximately placed between 600 B.C. and 300 B.C. Ācārya Maskarin was the first author who has commented upon the *Gautama-dharmasūtra* in a period between A.D. 900 -1100. Next to him is Haradatta who wrote the *Mitākṣara*. He was a grammarian. Most probably he has borrowed the ideas from the *Bhāṣya* of Bhartṛyajña. According to Dr. Kane, it is believed that both Asahāya and Bhartṛyajña have written separate *Bhāśyas* in different times. In the year 1989 Pandit Kulamani Mishra has written a Vṛtti named *Sūkṣmā*. It was published in 1991.

11.4 Āpastamba-dharmasūtra

The Āpastambadharmasūtra belongs to the Taittirīya recension of the Black Yajurveda. It forms the supplementary section of the *Āpastambaśrautasūtra* and the *Gṛhyasūtra*. It is a fullfledged Kalpa comprising Śrautasūtra, Gṛhyasūtra, Śulabasūtra and Dharmasūtra. The age of Āpastamba is settled within only approximate limits. It is later than the *Gautamadharmasūtra* and the *Baudhāyanadharmasūtra* and before A.D. 400. It is an authoritative Smṛti work according to Śabarasvāmin. Āpastamba is enumerated by Yājñavalkya (1.5) as a writer on *dharma*. Haradatta has written a commentary called *Ujjavalā* upon it. This has been edited several times. Professor G. Bhuler has translated it with an introduction which has been included in the *Sacred Books of East*, Vol. II. This Dharmasūtra is written in a more concise and compact style than that of Baudhāyana and has more archaic and non -Pāṇinian forms than any other extant Dharmasūtra. Each of the two prasnas of the *Āpastamba-*

dharmasūtra is divided into eleven paṭalas, there being 32 and 29 *kaṇḍikas* in the two paṭalas respectively. This Dharmasūtra stands in a peculiar relation to the Pūrvamīmāṁsā. It is the only extant Dharmasūtra that contains many of the technical terms and doctrines of the Mīmāṁsā.

11.5 Baudhāyana-dharmasūtra

The Baudhāyana-dharmasūtra belongs to the Black Yajurveda. This Dharmasūtra which now comprises four praśnas, is regarded as part of the *Baudhāyana-kalpa* ascribed to Baudhāyana. The spirit, style and language of the fourth *praśna* distinguish it from the preceding three *praśnas*. The fourth *praśna* mainly consists of verses, and some of its rules are incongruous with those contained in the preceding *praśnas*, the *Baudhāyana-dharmasūtra* is considered to be the supplementary portion of the *Baudhāyanaśrauta* and *Gṛhyasūtras*. The author of the *Baudhāyanagṛhya* and *Dharmasūtra* is known as Baudhāyana and, as such, might be a descent of this Kaṇva Baudhāyana. Govindasvāmin is known to be only commentator of this *Dharmasūtra*. He explains Baudhāyana in it (I. 3. 13) as *Kaṇvāyana*. The important chapter of the *Baudhāyana-dharmasūtra* is the *Tarpaṇa* (II. 5.21). In the *Tarpaṇa*, Baudhāyana mentions several appellations of Gaṇeśa, viz. Viṣṇu, Vināyaka, Sthūla, Varada, Hastimukha, Vakratuṇḍa, Ekadanta, Lambodara, etc. In the Tarpaṇa (II. 5. 23) we have the seven planets mentioned in the order of the days of the week and also Rāhu and Ketu. Dr. Kane places the Baudhāyana-dharmasūtra between 600 B. C. to 300 B. C. English translation of it is included in the *Sacred Books of the East*, Vol. XIV.

11.6 Hiraṇyakeśi-dharmasūtra

The Hiraṇyakeśi-dharmasūtra (HKD) belongs to Taittirīya recession of the Yajurveda. It forms the 26th and 27th *Praśnas* of the *Hiraṇyakeśikalpa*. However, it is an independent work. It has been written long before A. D. 200 - 400. Its chapters are named as *Praśnas*. The number of *paṭalas* in the first and second *Praśna* of HKD is 31 and 20 respectively. As a matter of fact, HKD forms the 26th and 27th *Praśnas* of the *Hiraṇyakeśikalpasūtra* which has no independent existence. The contents of it are practically the same as those of the *Āpastambadharmasūtra*. It forms a *sūtracaraṇa* of the Khāṇḍikeya section of Taittirīya school.

11.7 Vasiṣṭha-dharmasūtra

The *Vasiṣṭha-dharmasūtra* (VDS) belongs to the Ṛgveda. It has 32 chapters. Vasiṣṭha allows *niyoga* (levirate) and the re-marriage of child-widows. He mentions only six forms of marriage: *brāhma, daiva, ārśa, gāndharva, kṣatra* and *mānuśa*. In many places his views are different from those of Gautama, Baudhāyana, etc. the *Vidvanmodinī* is known to be the oldest commentary of the *Vasiṣ ṭha-dharmasūtra*. The relation between the *Vasiṣṭha-dharmasūtra* and the *Manusmṛti* is most important. The *Vasiṣṭha-dharmasūtra* expressly mentions the quotations as *mānavaṁ* or *mānavaṁ ślokaṁ udāharantī*. It is assigned to a period between 300 B. C. and 100 B. C. English translation of *Vasiṣṭha-dharmasūtra* is included in *Scared Books of the East*, Vol. XIV.

11.8 Viśṇu-dharmasūtra

The *Viśṇu-dharmasūtra* belongs to the Kaṭha school of the Yajurveda. Nandapaṇḍita Vināyakadharmādhikari has written a commentary named *Keśavavaijayantī* upon it. *Viśṇu-dharmasūtra* contains one hundred chapters. Though the number of chapters is so large, the Sūtra is not very extensive. The first chapter is so large, the Sūtra is not very extensive. The first chapter and last two chapters are entirely in verse. The remaining chapters are in mixed prose and verse. This work has a few chapters on *rājadharma* and punishment which are comparatively old and stand on a level with the Sūtras of Gautama and Āpastamba. It allows a Brāhmaṇa to marry from the four castes and does not envisage *niyoga* as Manu and others do. It advocate specially the worship of Vāsudeva. Indication of *suttee* is found in it. The date of its composition is fixed between 300 B. C. Dr. Julios Jolly's English translation of it is included in the *Sacred Books of the East*, Vol. XXXIII.

11.9 Vaikhānasā-dharmasūtra

The *Vaikhānasa-dharmasūtra* by Vaikhānasa is an authority on the duties during *vānaprasthas*. Manu, Gautama, Baudhāyana and Vasiṣṭha mention Vaikhānasa. It has four *Praśnas*. It gives four kinds of Brahmacārins, four kinds of householders, *vārtā · vṛtti, śālīna, yāyāvara* and *ghoracārika*, two kinds of *Vānaprasthas*; *sāpātrika* and *apātrika* with their further subdivisions and four kinds of Sannyāsins. From its style it appears to be a later production by a devotee of Nārāyaṇa. Historians speak of a *Vaikhānasagṛhyasūtra* in seven *Praśnas*.

11.10 Auśanasa-dharmasūtra

The *Auśansa-dharmasūtra* in seven chapter deals mainly with the duties of the four castes. It is both in prose and verse, some of the verses being found in the *Manusmṛti*. It refers to Vasiṣṭha, Hārīta, Śaunaka, and Gautama. From the later *Nibandha* works like the *Smārticandrkia* and Haradatta's commentary on the *Gautama-dharmasūtra*, the *Aśanasa-dharmasūtra* is supposed to have dealt with all topics: *ācāra*, *vyavahāra* and *prāyaścitta*. Kauṭilya quotes it several times. He speaks of the Auśanasa method of partition in allowing one tenth as an additional share to the eldest son. The *Mahābhārata* also refers to a work on politics by Uśanas. Later works like *Nītiprakāśikā*, *Mudrārākṣasa* and the commentaries on the Smṛtis of Manu and Yājñavalkya mention the Auśanasa system of politics, which is yet to be unearthed.

11.11 Hārīta Dharmasūtra

Baudhāyana, Āpastamba and Vasiṣṭha quote harita as an authority. It is related to the *Maitrāyaṇīya-saṁhitā*. It mentions the Kaśmīrian word *Kaphella*. It has two fold classification of the Sūtra and its explanations. Quotations in commentaries and digests show that Hārīta dealt exhaustively with the same topics that are found in other Dharmaśāstras. Kumārila mentions Hārīta as Dharmaśāstrakāra but does not assign him to any assign him to any particular *caraṇa* as he does to Āpastaṁba and others. In notable doctrines Hārīta mentions worship of Gaṇeśa. Hārīta's verses of *vyavahāra* quoted in the *Nibabdhas* are later than the Sūtra quoted by Aparārka, the *Kalpatarubrahacāri-kāṇḍa* and the *Smṛticandrikā*. The works of Laghu Hārīta and *Vṛddha Hārīta -Smṛtis* are also found which are later than the work of Yājñavalkya, Nārada and Kātyāyana.

11.12 Śankhalikhita Dharmasūtra

From the *Tantravārtika* it appears that Dharmasūtras of Śaṅkhalikhita was studied by the Vājasaneyins. The *Mahābhārata* (*Śāntiparva*. 23) contains the story of brothers Śaṅkha and Likhita. The Pāli story in the *Digghanikāya* seems to be based on the story in the *Mahābhārata*. Various compilations ascribed to Śaṅkha alone or Likhita alone or to both are made. The verse *Śaṅkhasmṛti* is stricter than the prose of Śaṅkhalikhita which is used in the commentaries. It speaks of twelve secondary sons, allows *niyoga*, speaks of several ordeals and defines the *Āryāvarta* as between Sindhu Sauvāīra and Kampilya. The probable age of the Śaṅkhalikhitadharmasūtra is fixed between 300 B.C. - A. D. 100.

Besides the writers of Dharmasūtras mentioned above, there were many more, such as Atri, Kaṇva, Kaśyapa, Devala, Paiṭhīnasi, Gārgya, Cyavana, Jātukarṇya, Bharadvāja. Śātātapa, and Sumantu whose dealt with all topics of *dharma*.

C. Dharmaśāstra II : Smṛti Texts

The term Dharmaśāstra is generally applicable to both the Dharmasūtras and the metrical codes, otherwise known as the Smṛtis. The term *smṛti* indicates that these codes are authorities on the basis of *śruti*, which is considered a revelation: *pratyakṣa* from which smṛti (remembrance) arose.

Side by side with the comparatively late Dharmasūtras, metrical Dharmasastras of varied lengths came to be composed with the growing demand of society for new provisions in matters of *dharma*, religious and secular. Out of these works, which were very numerous, only those of Manu and Yājñavalkya and a few others deserve special notice here.

11.13 Manusmṛti

Manu is mentioned as the father mankind in the *Ṛgveda* and in the other Vedas. Manu is indicated in the *Śatapathabrāhmaṇa*. He is quoted in the *Nirukta* and also quoted as law-giver in *Gautama, Āpastaṁba*, and the *Mahābhārata*. In introduction to the *Nāradasmṛti*, the *Manusmṛti* is narrated. Here four versions of Svāyaṁbhuva Śāstra according to the *Bhaviṣyapurāṇa* are also mentioned. It is almost impossible to say who composed the extant *Manusmṛti*. The *Mānavagṛhya* differs from the *Manusmṛti* in several particulars. The *Vināyakaśānti* of *Manavagṛhya* and tests for selecting a bride are not contained in our Manu. The *Mahābhārata* distinguishes between Svāyaṁbhuva Manu and Prācetasa Manu, former promulgating the Dharmaśāstra. These two works are combined in the present Manu. Extant Manu has 12 chapters and 2694 verses. The author of the *Manusmṛti* is not the first legislator. He is recognized as an ancient writer on the Dharmaśāstra in the Dharmasūstra. They mention number and names of the Manus. Confusion is caused by the ancient texts referring to Svāyaṁbhuva Manu, Prācetasa Manu and Manu.

Views of Svāyaṁbhuva are mentioned in the *Manusmṛti* VI.54, VIII.124, IX.158, the Manu Prajāpati is mentioned in I.34-36, X.78, XII.123. Among ten Prajāpatis primeval Manu is mentioned. The *Manusmṛti* says about the creation of the world by Paramātman. The fact that the *Manusmṛti* mentions human authors like Atri, Bhṛgu, etc. and refers to *dasyus* who speak *mleccha* and *Ārya* languages, etc. indicates that the extant *Manusmṛti* is not older than 200 B. C. Medhātithi is the first extant commentator on the *Manusmṛti*. Visvarupa quotes 200 verses from the *Manusmṛti*. Śaṁkara, Kumārila and Śabara refer to the *Manu*. Bṛhaspati had the present text of Manu before him. Aśvaghoṣa in his *Vajrasūcī* quotes several verses from the *Mānvadharma* some of which are found in our *Manusmṛti*. The *Rāmāyaṇa* (*Kiṣkindhā* 18.30 -32) contains the same ideology that we see in the *Manusmṛti* VIII. 318 and 316. Manu had attained present form long before 2nd century A. D. There are earlier and later strata in the *Manusmṛti*. Contradictory statements as to Brāhmaṇa marrying a Śudra woman, about appropriate forms of marriage, about *niyoga*, about flesh-eating, etc. are found in it. The *Manusmṛti* has not suffered several recasts. Quotations cited as Vṛddha Manu and Brahn Manu are later than the *Manusmṛti*. Extant Manu is older than Yājṅavalkya. Manu mentions Yavanas, Kambojas, Śakas, Pahlavas and Chinese. Extant *Manusmṛti* was composed between century 2nd B. C. and 2nd century A. D. Relationship of *Mahābhārata* and Manu is noteworthy. There was a mass of floating verses ascribed to mythical Manu on which both *Manusmṛti* and the *Mahābhārata* drew attention. Manu mentions stories and names that occur in the *Mahābhārata*, but these names go into Vedic antiquities. Manu never names the *Mahābhārata*, while the latter often refers to *rājadharmas* or *śāstra* of Manu or to what Manu said. The *Anuśāsanaparvan* and *Śāntiparvan* knew a *Manusmṛti*, but earlier books, whenever they speak of Manu, refer to floating mass of popular verses. Long before 4th century B.C. there was a Dharmaśāstra in verse attributed to Svāyaṁbhuva Manu. There was another work on *rājadharma* attributed to Prācetasa Manu, that probably was one work between 200 B.C. and A.D. 200. The *Manusmṛti* was a recast. Extant *Mahābhārata* was later than extant *Manusmṛti*. Vṛddha -Manu, if a separate work, must thave been composed before 7th century A. D. Influence of Manu has been spread to Cambodia and other countries beyond India. Manu has several commentators like Medhātithi, Govindarāja, Kullūka, Nārāyaṇa, Rāghavananda, Nandana and Rāmacandra. Asahāya has commented on the *Manusmṛti*. Udayakara was another commentator and so was Dharaṇīdhara. Nārāyaṇa flourished between A. D. 1100 -1300. Rāghavananda was later than A.D. 1400.

Contents of the Manusmṛti

It would be useful first to have an idea of the range of subjects dealt with by Manu. The opening chapter sets forth the origin of the world, creation on beings, the origin of the text as Manu taught it through Bhṛgu, the epochs of time: *yugas* and the difference in *dharmas* according to them, the four classes of men, and the differences in their respective dharmas. It gives also a list of the topics to be subsequently dealt with in the work.

The second chapter, with which, the main subjects matter begins, speaks of the four sources and grounds or proofs of *dharma*, the person for whom this *dharma* holds good, and the area where it prevails. After dealing with these general questions, the text proceeds to describe the *dharma* as applicable to each of the four castes: Brāhmaṇa, Kṣatriya, Vaiśya and Śūdra. Of these first three, the twice -born : *dvijas*, are considered first; and the sacraments: *saṁskāras* are described for them in relation to the four stages of life : the *aśramas*. These are dealt with primarily with reference to the Brāhmaṇa. This chapter takes us through the *saṁskāras* beginning with birth and going up to study in the establishment of the teacher, that is up to the end of the first stage called *brahmacarya* (studentship).

In chapter III, the householder's life, which is the second stage, is taken up. Marriage and its eight different forms, married life, daily and periodical observances of a householder, the vital character and the importance and the important social role of the householder, his five daily *yajñas* or sacrifices, viz. study and teaching of scripture, propitiation of the manes, adoration of the gods by oblations in the fire, reception of guests, gratification of other living beings and the periodic *śrāddhas* are described.

Chapter IV continues the description of the householder's life with many details, such as some are related to *dharmas* already mentioned and some are enjoining further *dharmas*, other relating to the ways of earning one's livelihood, and yet others relating to a number of personal habits and details of daily routine and principles of character and conduct.

Chapter V opens with the subjects of proper food; two other topics dealt with here are the death together with obsequies and pollution and purificatory ceremonies. The last section of this chapter speaks of woman (wives and widow) and their special *dharmas*.

Chapter VI is devoted to a description of the further stages of man, the *vānaprastha* and *saṅnyāsa*, denoting life of retirement in forests and complete renunciation respectively, both having spiritual aim and resignation by one who continues to be in the household life is also dealt with at the end of the chapter.

Chapter VII and VIII together form a section about rules and their duties : *rājadharma*, which include not only their qualities and equipments, but also the art of statecraft in peace and war. Ministers and counsel, diplomacy, messengers, army, fort, wars, conquest, treatment of the conquered, administration of villagers, communities, merchants, collections of revenue, punishment and clearance of anti-social elements: these are spoken of in Chapter VII.

Chapter VIII deals with administration of justice and describes legal procedure in respect of the eighteen titles of civil and criminal disputes, judges, evidence, offences and punishments.

Chapter IX states the detail about women, particularly from the standpoint of law, their *dharmas*, duties, expected of and towards them, their importance regarding progeny and the family, property, inheritance and partition which arise in the wake of the family. The latter part of the chapter speaks of other matters coming under the administration of justice, like debts, gambling, contracts between the employer and the employed and theft. After touching upon some of the other *rājadharmas* left over, the chapter concludes with a brief description of the *dharmas* of the Vaiśyas and Śūdras.

In Chapter X, the people outside the pale of this system of *dharma* and those born by promiscuous mingling of the four classes and a system by which they could be fitted into the scheme are set forth. In the case of the four classes and their ordained duties, confusion may occur owning to extraordinary developments of private or public nature; *dharmas* permissible under such emergencies: *āpaddharmas* are, therefore, dealt with.

The main subject of chapter XI is different kinds of sins, major and minor and their expiations: the *prāyaścittas*.

The last chapter XII falls into two sections: The former section speaks of the theory of *karman*, the fruits and kinds of birth, high and low, which result from different acts, good and bad and through which the soul has to pass. The latter speaks of those *dharmas* which help of spiritual goal -the seeking of self-knowledge. The *ātmajnāna* and the attainment of the everlasting good: the *nihśreyasa*. Identically, the matter of doubts on questions of *dharma* and the constitutions of *pariṣad* (assemblies of the learned) for deciding such questions is also dealt with in the latter sections of the last chapter.

11.14 Ātreyasmṛti

Atri is named in the *Manusmṛti* (VII. 16). The *Ātreyadharmasūtra* is found in nine *adhyāyas*. The form of *Atridharmasūtra* is very systematic. Several works are styled as the *Atrismṛti*. Summary of the *Atrisaṁhitā* was printed by *Jīvānanda*. Atri is quoted as an authority on adoption. The *Laghu* and *Vṛddhatreyasmṛti* are also found. The *Mahābhārata* (*Anuśāsanaparvan* 65.1) quotes a verse of Atri. Aparārka quotes about a hundred verse of Atri on various topics. The *Ātreyasmṛti* was edited by K. V. R. Aiyangar.

11.15 Bṛhaspati - Smṛti

Bṛhaspati as an ancient teacher of the Arthaśāstra is mentioned in Kauṭilya. The *Mahābhārata* (*Śāntiparvan*. 59.80-85) credits him with compression of vast work of Brahmā on *trivarga* and mentions several of his views. The *Kāmasūtra* speaks of Bṛhaspati as a writer on *artha*; peculiar views of Bṛhaspati according to Kauṭilya are also mentioned. Bṛhaspati also wrote a prose work on *vyavahāra* and *prāyaścitta*. Probably the authors of the two works may be different. Seven hundred verses on *vyavahāra* ascribed to Bṛhaspati are quoted in the *Mitākṣarā*. This is an independent work composed between A.D. 300 -500. Smaller compilations in verse ascribed to Bṛhaspati are also made. The *Bṛhaspatya Arthaśāstra* edited by Dr. Thomas is a later work.

11.16 Bharadvāja - Smṛti

A *Śrautasūtra* and a *Gṛhya* of Bharadvāja exist at present. Viśvarūpa's work establishes existence of a Sūtra work on *dharma* of Bharadvāja. There was a Smṛti in verse also attributed to Bharadvāja. Kauṭilya shows that Bharadvāja was an ancient author on Politics. Some views of Bharadvāja are found in the *Mahābhārata*. He may be the sage of the sixth Maṇḍala of the *Ṛgveda*. He is mentioned by Pāṇini as a predecessor. The *Mahābhāśya* mentions Bhāradvājīyas, a school of grammarians. Kauṭilya probably lumps Bharadvāja, Vyāsa and Manu and refers to them collectively as *ācāryāh*. Verses on *vyavahāra* attributed to Bharadvāja are found. This may probably the different from the work on politics.

11.17 Śātātapa - Smṛti

A Sūtra work of Śātātapa on *dharma* dealing with *prāyaścitta, śraddha* and *ācāra* must have existed. Verses of Śātātapa are quoted in the *Mitākṣarā* work. Several verse compilations ascribed to *Śātātapa*, the *Vṛddha Śātātapa* and *Bṛhat Śātātapa* are also made.

11.18 Sumantu - Smṛti

A Sūtra work on *ācāra* and *prāyaścitta* is ascribed to Sumantu. Paiṭhīnasi includes Sumantu among thirty -six expounders of the Dharmaśāstra. Sumantu is quoted by Viśvarūpa and Aparārka. It is also quoted in the *Kalpataru*. Yājṅavalkya and Parāśara do not enumerate Sumantu among expounders of *dharma*. Sumantu is mentioned in the *Mahābhārata* and the *Bhāgavata*. Verses from Sumantu on *dharma* are citied by Aparārka. It characteristically differs from the other Dharmaśāstra works with its distinct identity. There are numerous verses on *vyavahāra* quoted from Sumantu in the *Sarasvatīvilāsa*. Professor T. R. Chintamani has reconstructed the ideas of Sumantu on the basis of the *Sarasvatīvilāsa*, with a view to emphasizing the *vyavahāra* concept.

11.19 Yājnavalkyasmṛti

Yājṅavalkya as a most illustrious name among the Vedic sages is noteworthy. Stories about strained relations between Vaiśampāyana and Yājñavalkya are mentioned. Yājñavalkya and Janaka are referred in the *Śatapathabrāhmaṇa*. Yājñavalkya is specially named as a great philosopher in the *Bṛhadāraṇayaka*. The *Yājñavalkyasmṛti* claims that the *Araṇyaka* and *Yogaśāstra* were composed by the author of the *Smṛti*. Slight variation in the number of verses is found in the *Yājñavalkyasmṛti* according to Viśvarupa and Aparārka. Arrangement of different verses in Viśvarūpa's, *Bālakrīdā* and the *Mitākṣara*, particularly in the *Prāyaścittakāṇḍa*, is remarkable. Readings of the two commentators are also different. The *Agnipurāṇa* affords excellent check for consideration of text of Yājñavalkya. While comparing the readings of the *Agnipurāṇa* with those of *Viśvarūpa* and the *Mitākṣara* show that the *Agnipurāṇa* represents a text midway between Viśvarūpa's work and that of the *Mitākṣarā*. So the *Agnipurāṇa* represents a text of Yājñavalkya current about A. D. 900. Total number of verses on *vyavahāra* in the *Agnipurāṇa* is 315, out of which the first thirty-one are not taken from the *Yājñavalkyasmṛti*. Almost all of these thirty -one are taken from the *Nāradasmṛti*. The *Garuḍapurāṇa* (ch. 93) expresses that the *dharma* promulgated by Yājñavlakya was imparted therein. It (ch. 93 -106) contains the Dharmaśāstra material taken from *ācāra* and *prāyaścitta* sections of Yājñavalkya. It also deals with *ācāra* and (ch. 93 -106) *prāyaścitta*. The *Garuḍapurāṇa* omits *rājadharma* section of Yājñavalkya. Only a few verses of the Yājñavalkyasmṛti are repeated word for word, while a summary only is given of several verses. Comparison of the text of the *Garuḍapurāṇa* with Viśvarupa's text and that of the *Mitākṣarā* is required. Comparison of the*Yājñavalkyasmṛti* with the *Mnausmṛti* idicates a close agreement in phraseology between the two. Yājñvalkya usually tries to compress Manu's dicta. Yājñavalkya adds the *Vināyakaśānti* and *Grahaśānti* and ordeals, while Manu omits first two and cursorily refers to two ordeals. Yājñavalkya is silent on the origin of world which we have in Manu. The style of Yājñavalkya, contents of Smṛti literature known of the *Yājnavalakyasmṛti* and nineteen authors on *dharma* are historically developed in the *Yājñavalkyasmārti*. The *Yoga-yājñavalkya* is different. It is a small work on Yoga and has little to do with the Dharmaśāstra. There is a close agreement between VIS. D. S. and Yājñavalkya and between Kauṭilya and Yājñavalkya, Manu and Yājñavalkya and difference on several points. Yājñavalkya represents a more advanced state of thought than Manu. Manu allows Brāhmaṇa to marry Śūdra girl, but Yājñavalkya does not. But Manu condemns *niyoga* but Yājñavalkya does not. Same case is with gambling also. Yājñavalkya takes the *Vināyakaśānti* from the *Mānavagṛhya*. The *Yājñavalkyasmṛti* has an intimate relation to White Yajurveda. The probable date of Yājñavalkya is between 100 B. C. and A. D. 300. The *Laṅkāvatārasūtra* (*Gāthās* 814 -816) refers to the *Yājñavalkyasmṛti*. Yājñavalkya shows acquaintance with Greek astrology. Dr. Jacobi's theory that naming of week days after planets was first introduced by Greeks and borrowed by Indians is untenable. Yājñavalkya does not mention week days, but only the nine planets (I. 296.). Yājñavalkya does not mention the zodiacal signs. He arranges the Nakṣatras from Kṛttika to Bharaṇī (I. 268) as the Taittirīyabrāhmaṇa. does. Yājñavakya is explained by Viśvarūpa without reference to zodiacal sings from Vedic times. *Nakāṣatras* are divided into auspicious and inauspicious. Yājñavalkya refers to *nāṇakas*. Yājñavalkya, regards the sight of yellow and robed people as an evil omen. There is a Vṛddha-Yājñavalkya, a Yoga-Yājñavalkya and a Bṛhad-Yājñavalkya and Vṛddha-Yājñavalkya. All are quoted by Mādhava and Aparārka. Bṛhad-Yājñavlkya is quoted by Jitendra and the author of the *Mitākāṣara* and as such must be earlier than A. D. 1000. Bāṛhadyogī-Yājñavalkya is a large work in twelve chapters and has about 930 verses. It quotes dozens of verses from the *Manusmṛti*, the *Bhagavadgīta* and several Upaniṣadic passage without acknowledgement. We find several commentaries on the work of Yājṅavalkya, by Viśvarūpa, Vijnāneśvera, Aparārka, Śūlapāṇi and Mitramiśra.

11.20 Pārāśarasmṛti

Yājnavalkya mentions Parāśara, but the extant *Parāśarasmṛti* is probably a recast of an older Smṛti. The *Garuḍapurāṇa* (chapter 107) gives a summary of thirty -nine verses of the *Parāśarasmṛti*. From Kauṭilya it appears that there was a work of Parāśara on politics in which *vyavahāra* was also dealt with. Extant Parāśara in twelve chapters and 592 verses deals with *ācāra* and *prāyaścitta* alone. Parāśara mentions ninteen Smṛti writers. Parāśara has some peculiar views on the contents of the Smrtis. In the *Parāśarasmṛti* view of Manu is frequently cited. Several identical verses in *Manusmṛti* and *Parāśarasmṛti* are found. Age of the Parāśarasmṛti is fixed between A.D. 100-500. A *Bṛhat-parāśarasaṁhitā* in twelve chapters and 3000 verses is available. It is a later work. The *Vṛddha-parāśara* is quoted by Aparārka. The *Jyotih-parāśara* is quoted by Hemādri, Bhattoji and in the *Smṛticandrikā*.

11.21 Nāradasmṛti

Two versions of the *Nāradasmṛti* on *vyavahāra*, a smaller and a larger one are available. Commentary of Asahāya on the *Nāradasmrti* and revised by Kalyāṇabhaṭṭa is contained in Dr. Jolly's edition. Nārada is not mentioned by Yājṅavalkya or Parāśara in the list of expounders of *dharma*. He is mentioned by Manu (I.35) as one of the ten Prajāpatis. Sage Nārada is frequently figured in the *Mahābhārata*. Three introductory chapters on judicial procedure and on *sabhā*, then eighteen on *vyavahārapadas*, then an appendix on theft are included in the *Nāradasmṛti*. Some difference in the names of titles between the *Nāradasmṛti* and *Manusmṛti* is found. Printed versions of the *Nāradasmṛti* contains 1028 verses. About 700 verses of the *Nāradasmṛti* are quoted in digests. Viśvarāūpa's and Medhātithi's quotations from the

Nāradasmṛti agree with the printed *Nāradasmṛti*. The Agnipurāṇa (chapter 253) contains thirty verses of the *Nāradasmṛti* defining the eighteen titles from *ṛṇādāna* to *prakīrṇaka* in the same order. Nārada's verses on *ācāra*, *śraddha* and *prāyaścitta* are quoted in *Smārticandrikā* and Hemādri. Probably this is a different Nārada. Form, style and metre of the *Nāradasmṛti* are systematic. About fifty verses are identical in Manu. Many more verses of the *Nāradasmṛti* closely correspond to Manu's. The *Nāradasmṛti* is based upon the *Manusmṛti*. Some verses of the *Mahābhārata* are same as in the *Nāradasmṛti*. Some verses of Kauṭilya and Nārada agree. In many points Manu and Nārada differ. Some topics are found peculiar to Nārada, viz. fourteen kinds of important persons, three *punarbhūs* and four *svairiṇīs*, etc. Nārada was some what later than Yājnavalkya. Nārada propounds several juristic and political principles, fixes the period of minority at sixteen. Nārada was earlier than 8th century at the latest. Nārada wrote a work on politics also. *Dināra* occurs in the *Nāradasmṛti Dināras* may have been introduced into India about beginning of Christians era. Nārada flourished between A.D. 100 -300.There was another *Nāradīya -manusaṁhitā*. The longer and shorter versions of the *Nāradasmṛti* were published by Jolly. Bhavasvamin, the Bhāṣyakāra of Nārada, was Brāhmaṇa from Kerala. His date is not free from doubt. He may be placed conjecturally between A.D. 700 -1000. Home of Nārada cannot be ascertained. There are many texts ascribed to Nārada viz. The *Jyotir-nārada*, the *Bṛhan-nārada* and *Laghu-nārada*. The Mahābhārata quotes Nārada's views of flesh-eating and *utpātas* also.

11.22 Kātyāyanasmṛti

The Vyavahāra section of the *Kātyāyanasmṛti* has been reconstructed by P. V. Kane. It follows closely the works of Manu, Bṛhaspati, Nārada and Kauṭilya. It specially deals with *strīdhana* (dowry). Like Nārada, Yājṅavaklya and Kauṭilya and some

Dharmasūtrakāras like Baudhāyana and Gautama, Katyāyana allows *niyoga* under certain conditions.

Among others mention may be made of the Smṛtis of Āṅgiras, Dakṣa, Piṭamaha, Prajāpati, Marīci, Yama, Viśvāmitra, Vyāsa, Saṅgrahakāra and Saṁvarta, who are known from citations in the later *Nibandhas* as writers on *dharma*; a few of their works, some being abridgements only, are found in the Jivananda and Ānandāśrama collections.

11.23 Other Smṛti-Texts

Besides these sūtra and Smṛti texts on Dharmaṣāstra, other text too have been found to exist either in complete or fragmentary form. Some texts are found to have referred to by latter Dharmaśāstra exponents, commentators like Vijnānabhikṣu, Medhātithi, among others. Such sūtra texts are like Atri-Dharmasūtra, Kaṇva Dharmasūtra, Kaśyapa-Dharmasūtra, Gārgya Dharmasūtra, Cyavana Dharmasūtra, Jātūkaraṇya Dharmasūtra, Devala Dharmasūtra, Budha Dharmasūtra, Bṛhaspati Dharmasūtra, Bharadwāja Dharmasūtra, Śatātapa Dharmasūtra, Sumantu Dharmasūtra, etc. And, the Smṛti texts are like Bṛhaspati Smṛti, Āṅgīrasa Smṛti, Ṛṣyaśṛṅga Smṛti, Kārśṇājini Smṛti, Caturviṁśatimata Smṛti, Dakṣa Smṛti, Pitāmaha Smṛti, Pulastya Smṛti, Prācetas Smṛti, Prajāpati Smṛti, Marici Smṛti, Yama Smṛti, Laugākṣi Smṛti, Viśvāmitra Smṛti, Vyāsa Smṛti, Hārīta Smṛti among others.

Chapter - XII

A Retrospect

A general survey of the Vedic literature reveals that the Vedas, the Vedaṅgas, the Upaniṣads and the Dharmaśāstra texts, have left to us a great deal of wisdom of various disciplines. The four Vedas - Ṛg, Yajus, Sāman and Atharva, are the earliest record of ancient Indian literature. The Ṛgveda is the book chants in praise of various gods. The Yajurveda speaks of the employment of many religious sacrifices. The mantras of the Sāma Veda are solely with references to their place and use in Soma sacrifice. The Atharva Veda is a collection of hymns from the Ṛgveda and they contain mainly magical prayers for specific objects, viz. charms for long life, curses upon demons, sorcerers, enemies, love charms. charms to gain prosperity, charms relating to royalty, expiatory prayers, charms of medicine etc.

The mantra portion may be identified as the religion of Nature of the Vedic poets; the Brāhmaṇas ritualism, the region of Law, of the priests; the upaniṣadic portion, the religion of spirit of the philosophers. The Brāhmaṇas in prose style explain the sacred significance of the different rituals. They reflect the spirit of an age in which all intellectual activity is concentrated on the sacrifice, describing its ceremonies, discussing its value, speculating on its origin and significance.

The Āraṇyakas pave the way for the upaniṣads, revive the germs of philosophic speculations in the Vedas, and develop them in a manner which made the Upaniṣads the source of all philosophy that arose in the world of Indian thought. Thus, the seeds of the important philosophical trends can be traced in the literature of pre -upaniṣadic period. There has been gradual development of the philosophical thought from the Vedic mantras and the Brāhmaṇas through the Araṇykas to the Upaniṣads.

The passage of Indian mind from the Brāhmaṇic to the Upaniṣadic thought is probably the most remarkable event in the history of philosophic thought. The upaniṣads are also known as the Vedānta, for they are considered to be the concluding portions of the Vedas. The ideals preached therein show that they are the culmination of the intellectual achievement of a great epoch. These upaniṣads are a repository of diverse currents of concepts like, the quest after Brahman, doctrine of Ātman, the World, causation, transmigration, emancipation etc.

Aurobindo Ghosh, the great Indian scholar-mystic, is of the opinion that the Vedas are the replete with suggestions of secret doctrines and mystic philosophies. He looks upon the gods of the hymns as the symbols of the psychological functions. Sūrya signifies intelligence, Agni will, and Soma feeling. The leading principle of the mystic nature of the Vedic gods, was the sacredness and secrecy of the divine knowledge. This wisdom, if revealed to an incompetent of ordinary human mind, is liable to perversion and misuse and the loss of virtue. Therefore, the ancient seers favored inner disciplines to be cultivated by a person, inquisitive of acquiring spiritual wealth through the study of the Vedas.

The Vedāṅgas, Ṣikṣa Kalpa, Nirukta, Vyākaraṇa, Chandas and Jyotiṣa, help to understand the Vedic texts and perform rituals in the right sense. Further, the texts on Dharmasastra have given a fresh impetus to the personality and perform rituals in the right sense. Further the texts on Dharmaśāstra have given a fresh impetus to the personality development, with the help of which, the person can lead a successful life, and can rejuvenate the upliftment of the society which he belongs to. The precepts laid down in the Vedic texts, the Upaniṣads, the Smṛti texts and so on, lay forceful impact on the values of social, political, economical psychological, ethical and metaphysical spheres. The path of life shown, and the ideals upheld by the ancient seers, apply to entries mankind. Factually the performance of the rituals enjoined in the Vedic texts, command to follow the ethical way of life, and thereby to visualise the metaphysical truth. To be precise, the statements like -

सत्यं वद । धर्मं चर । स्वाध्यायान्मा प्रमदः ।
अचार्याय प्रियं धनमाहृत्य प्रजातन्तुं मा व्यवच्छेत्सीः ।
सत्यान्न प्रमदितव्यम् धर्मान्न प्रमदितव्यम् ।
कुशलान्न प्रमदितव्यम् । भूत्यै न प्रमदितव्यम् ।
स्वाध्यायप्रवचनाभ्यां न प्रमदितव्यम् ।
देवपितृकार्याभ्यां न प्रमदितव्यम् ।
मातृदेवो भव । पितृदेवो भव ।
आचार्यदेवो भव । अतिथिदेवो भव ।
यान्यनवद्यानि कर्माणि। तानि सेवितव्यानि। नो इतराणि।।

etc. declared in the Taittirīya Upaniṣad, (I.11.1-2), emphasize the essentiality of disciplines of human character to build up one's bright career. Thus, the Indian culture, civilization and the concept of life have the basis of these enlivening truths. It is therefore, that the Indian culture inherits irresistable power of influencing any individual even of abroad country.

Bibliography

Agrawala V.S., *India as known to Pāṇini,* Lucknow University, Lucknow, 1953.

Aitareya Brāhmaṇa (with Sayana's Bhāṣya), Ananda Ashram, Pune, 1930.

Aitareya Brāhmaṇa (with Sayana's Bhāṣya), Ananda Ashram, Pune, 1943.

Aitareya Brāhmṇa, Chawkhambka Sanskrit Series Office, Varanasi,1978.

Aithal K.P. (Ed.), *Āśvalāyana Gṛhyasūtra*, Adyar Library, Madras, 1980.

Anandcandra Vedantavagish, *Tāṇḍya Mahabrāhmaṇa* (with Sāyaṇa's Bhāṣya) Calcutta, 1870.

Ananta Sharn Tiwari, *Vedic Myth, Ritual and Philosophy,* Pratibha Prakashan Delhi, 2001.

Arnold E., *Vedic Metre,* Motilal Banarasidass, New Delhi, 1980.

Aurobindo, *Vedic Glossary*, Pondicherry, 1960.

Bhattacharya N.N., *History of Indian Cosmological Ideas*, New Delhi, 1971.

Bloomfield Maurice, *The Religion of the Veda*, G.P. Putnam's Sons, New York, 1908.

Bloomfield M., *Sacred Books of the East*, Vol.42, Motilal Banarasidass, Delhi, 1984.

Braj Bihari Chaubey, *Treatment of Nature in the Ṛgveda*, Vedic Sahitya Sadan, Hoshiarpur, 1970.

Caland W., *The Śatapatha Brāhmaṇa (in the Kāṇviya Recension)*, Punjab Sanskrit Series, Motilal Banarasidass, Delhi, 1926.

Chakraborti H.P., *Vedic India,* Calcutta, 1981.

Chaudhari K.P.S., *Vedic Mysticism,* Vishva Bharati, Vol, XXXI, Calcutta, 1965-66.

Dandekar R.N., *Rudra in the Veda,* Journal of the University of Poona, Pune, 1953.

Dandekar R.N., *Visnu in the Veda,* Poona, 1941.

Das A.C., *Ṛigvedic Culture,* Delhi, 1979.

Dasgupta, S.N. *History of Indian Philosophy,* Vols, I-V, Motilal Banarasidass, Delhi.

Dayananda Saraswati, *Yajurvedabhāṣā-bhāṣya,* Aryapratinidhi Sabha, Delhi, 1954.

Eggaling Julins, *The Satapatha Brāhmaṇa* (5 parts), The Sacred Books of the East, Vols 12, 26,41,43, 44, Motilal Banarasidass, Delhi, 1963.

Ghate, *Ghate's, Lectures on Ṛgveda,* Oriental Book Agency, Poona, 1959.

Gilbert K., *The Wisdom of the Veda,* Pondicherry, 1973.

Gonda Van, *Change and Continuity in Indian Religion,* Vol. 9, Mouton and Co., The Hugue, 1965.

Gopalacharya M.R., *The Heart of the Ṛgveda,* Somaiya Publication, Bombay, 1971.

Gopatha Brāhmaṇa, Chowkhamba Sanskrit Series Office Varanasi, 1969.

Griffith R.J.H., *Hymns of the Ṛgveda,* Vol. 1, Chowkhamba Sanskrit Series Varanasi, 1963.

Griswold H.D., *The Religion of the Rigveda,* (The Religions Quest of India), Oxford University Press, London, 1923.

Haug Martin, *Aitareya Brahmana of the Ṛgveda,* Bombay, 1863.

Hanns Oertel, *Jaiminīya or Talavakāra Upanisad Brāhmaṇa,* Journal of American Oriental Society, 16 (1896) : 79 (260)

Haragovinda Shastri, *Manusmrti,* Chowkhamba Sanskrit Series Office, Varanasi, 1970.

Hariyappa H. L., *Ṛgvedic Legends through the Ages.* Deccan College Research Institute, Poona, 1950.

Herman W. Tull, *The Vedic Origins of Karma Cosmos as Man in Ancient Indian Myth and Ritual,* Sri Satguru Publications, Delhi, 1990.

Jnāni Shivadatta, *Vedakālina Samāja,* Chawkhamba Vidya Bhavan, Varanasi, 1967.

Keith A.B., *The Religion and Philosophy of the Veda and Upamsads,* Vols. I & II, Motilal Banarsidass, Delhi, 1970.

Keith A.B., *Rigveda Brāhmaṇas,* (The Aitareya and Kauṣitaki Brahmanas of the Rigveda), Harvard University Press, Cambridge, 1920.

Keith A.B., *The Veda of the Black Yajus School,* 2 Vols. Motilal Banarasidass, Delhi, 1967.

Krishnamurthy K., *Sayana's Subhaṣita—* Sudhānidhi, Karnatak University Dharwad, 1968.

Kunchan Raja C. (Ed.), *Rgveda—Vyākhyā of Mādhava Bhatta,* Adyar Library, 1937.

Laxman Sarup (Ed.), *Yaska's Nirukta,* Motilal Banarasidass, Delhi, 1967.

Laxman Sarup, *Ṛgartha Dipikā,* Motilal Banarasidass, Delhi, 1955.

Macdonell A.A., *Vedic Mythology,* Oxford University Press, *A Vedic Reader for Students,* Madras, 1917.

A History of Samskrit Literature, Delhi, 1965.

Bṛhaddevatā of Śaunaka, (Vols I & II), Motilal Banarasidass, Delhi, 1965.

Mahabharata, Vols. I -VI, Gita Press, Gorakhpur.

Mainkar TG., *Mysticism in the Ṛgveda,* Bharatiya Vidya Bhavan, Bombay, 1961.

Mankad D.R., *Date of the Ṛgveda,* Anand, Baroda, 1951.

A. Mahadeva Shastry (Ed.), *Madhaviya Dhatuvṛtti,* Oriental Library, Madras, 1971.

Max Muller, *Vedic Literature: Samhitas and Brāhmaṇas,* A History of Indian Literature Vol 1, Otto Harrosowitz Weisbaden, 1977.

Max Muller, *Ṛgveda Saṁhitā :* (The Sacred Hymns of Brahmans), I -VI. Vols., Trubner, London, 1849-74.

Max Muller, *History of Ancient Sanskrit Literature,* Allahabad, 1912.

Max Muller, *The Vedas,* Calcutta, 1956.

Mishra R.L., *Ārsānukramani* (with Bṛhaddevatā), Bibliotheca India, 1892.

Mishra V.B., From *the Vedas to Manu—Samhitā—A Cultural Study,* Delhi, 1982.

Morgan KU, *The Religion of the Hindus,* New York, 1953.

Oldenbery O Max Muller F. (Ed), V*edic Hymns,* Part II, Sacred Books of the East Motilal Banarasidass, New Delhi, 1964.

Prasad Mantrini, *Language of the Nirukta,* Delhi, 1975.

Pandurangi K.T., *Visnutattva—vinirṇaya of Madhva,* Dvaita Vedanta Studies and Research Foundation, Bangalore, 1992.

Radhakrishna S. *Principal Upanisads,* George Allen and Unwin Ltd. London, 1953.

Raghuvira and Lokesh Candra, *Jaiminiya Brāhmaṇa of the Sāmaveda,* Sarasvati Vihar Series Vol. 31, International Academy of Indian Culture, 1954.

Ṛgveda with Sayana's Commentary, Vaidika Samshodhana Mandala, Pune, 1976.

Rahurkar V.G., *The Seer of Ṛgveda,* University of Pune, Pune, 1964.

Raj Bali Pandey, *Historical and Literary Inscriptions,* Chowkhamba Sanskrit Series Varanasi, 1962.

Rajendralal Maitra and Roer RE., *Twelve Principal Upanisads,* Bombay, 1906.

Ramgopal, *India of the Kalpasūtras,* Delhi, 1959.

The History and Principles of the Vedic Interpretation, Concept Publishing Company, New Delhi, 1983.

Ranade R.D., *A Constructive Survey of Upanisadic Philosophy,* Bharatiya Vidya Bhavan, Bombay, 1968.

Rangaswamy Iyenger H.R., *Āpastamba Śrauta Sūtra,* Mysore, 1944.

Renou L., *The Civilization of Ancient India,* Delhi, 1959.

Renou Louis, *The Religions of Ancient India,* Munshiram Manoharlal, New Delhi, 1972.

Rudolph Von Roth and W. D. Whitney, *Atharva Veda,* III Edn, Bonn, Ferd, Dummlers Verlag, 1966.

Sāṅkhyāna Śrauta Sutra, Vaidik Samshodhana Mandal Pune, 1980.

Śatapatha Brāhmaṇa, Vols I-III, The Research Institute of Ancient Scientific Studies, Delhi, 1969.

Satwalekar S.D., *Sāmaveda kāsubodha bhāsya,* Swadhyaya Mandal Poradi, 1967.

Satyavrita Samashrami, *Śatapatha—brāhmaṇa,* (with Sāyaṇa's Bhāṣya), Vols 7, Calcutta, 1903-11.

Sharma U.C., *Ṛgveda Sarvanukramani,* Aligarh, 1977.

Sharma Ramasvarupa Gauda, *Sāmaveda Saṁhitā,* (with Sāyana's bhāṣya), Varanasi, 1989.

Sharma U.C., *The Viśvāmitras and the Vaśiṣṭhas,* Viveka Publications Aligarh, 1975.

Shashi Tiwari, *Vedic Studies,* New Bharatiya Book Corporation, Delhi, 2004.

Shastri G. *Ās'avalāyana Śrauta—sūtra,* Pune, 1917.

Shastri Mangaladeva, *Vaidika Samskriti ke tattva,* Varanasi, 1969.

Shastri Ramakrisha, *Atharva Veda Saṁhita,* Chawkhamba Vishvabharati, Varanasi, 1977.

Shende N.G., *The Religion and Philosophy of the Atharva Veda,* Pune, 1952.

Sreekrishna Sharma E.R., *Kauśitakī Brāhmaṇa,* Wiesbaden: Franzstecner Verlag, 1968.

Shripada Sharma, *Maitrayanī Saṁhitā,* Svādhyāya Mandala, Paradi, 1998.

Sudhama Misra, *Janapada State in Ancient India,* Motilal Banarasidass, Delhi.

Sukla—Yajurveda—Kāṇva-Saṁhitā, (with Sayana's bhaṣya), Sampumananda Vishwavidyalaya Varanasi, 1978.

Suryakanta, *Vaidik Kośa,* Benaras Hindu University, Varanasi, 1963.

Suryakanta, *Vaidik Devashastra,* Delhi, 1962.

Swami Madhavananda (Ed.), *Vedānta Paribhāṣa of Dharmaraja Adhvarindra,* Advaita Ashrama, Calcutta, 1989.

Taittiriya Araṇyaka, (with Sāyanabhaṣya), Ananda Ashram, Pune, 1897.

Taittiriya Araṇyaka, (with Sāyanabhaṣya), Ananda Ashram, Pune, 1838.

Taittiriya Araṇyaka, (with Sāyanabhaṣya), Ananda Ashram, Pune, 1901.

Tiwari Shashi, *Rigvedic Adhyayana,* Delhi, 1999.

Tiwari Shashi, *Sūrya-devatā,* Meharchand Lachmandas, Delhi, 1994.

Thaneswar Sarmah, *New Trends in Interpretation of Vedas,* Sundeep Prakashan, New Delhi, 2006.

Trivedi Ramagovinda, *Vaidka Sahitya,* Bharatiya Jnana Peetha Prakashan, 1968.

Vishva Bandhu, *Atharva Veda, (Śaunaka Śākha),* 4 Vols, with Sayana Bhaṣya, Hoshiarpur, 1960.

Vishva Bandhu (Ed.), *Atharva Veda Pratis'ākhya,* Punjab University, Lahore, 1923.

Weber Albrecht, *Vājasaneyī Saṁhitā* (the white Yajur veda), Berlin, 1853.

Weber Albrecht, *Śatapatha Brāhmaṇa,* Berlin, 1855.

Weber A., *History Indian Literature,* Motilal Banarasidass, Delhi, 1981.

Winternitz M. *History of Indian Literature,* Vol I, Motilal Banarasidass, Delhi, 1982.

Whitney W.D., *The Atharva Veda,* Harvard Oriental Series Vols 7-8, Harvard University Press, 1905.

Yajurveda—mādyandina-saṁhita, with Vedarthaparijāta-bhāṣya), Radhakrishna Dhanuka Prakashana, Calcutta,

Yaska, *Nirukta,* (with Durgāchārya's Commentary) Venkateshwara Mudraṇalaya, Mumbai, 1982.

Index